THE
WILDERNESS

THE WILDERNESS

Deep Inside the Republican Party's Combative, Contentious, Chaotic Quest to Take Back the White House

McKay Coppins

LITTLE, BROWN AND COMPANY
New York Boston London

Little, Brown and Company
Hachette Book Group
1290 Avenue of the Americas, New York, NY 10104
littlebrown.com

First Edition: December 2015

Little, Brown and Company is a division of Hachette Book Group, Inc.
The Little, Brown name and logo are trademarks of Hachette Book Group, Inc.

The publisher is not responsible for websites (or their content) that are not owned by the publisher.

The Hachette Speakers Bureau provides a wide range of authors for speaking events. To find out more, go to hachettespeakersbureau.com or call (866) 376-6591.

ISBN 978-0-316-32741-1
Library of Congress Control Number: 2015950324

10 9 8 7 6 5 4 3 2 1

RRD-C

Printed in the United States of America

For Annie

Contents

PART III: WANDERING

PART IV: PROMISED LAND

A Note on Sourcing

This book is based on more than three hundred interviews, conducted between November 2012 and September 2015, with elected office-holders, Republican Party officials, conservative movement leaders, media figures, top political operatives, consultants, activists, donors, and a wide range of family members, friends, and other confidants who have known the story's principal subjects at various stages of their lives. My conversations with these people occasionally stretched on for hours, and certain key sources graciously spoke with me dozens of times over the course of this project. The majority of these interviews took place on the record, but some were granted on the strict condition of anonymity so that sources could candidly recount private conversations, provide behind-the-scenes details, and pass along other potentially sensitive information and insights. Wherever possible, their accounts were independently confirmed with notes, recordings, or interviews with other people who had knowledge of the given situations. In cases where substantive discrepancies existed between accounts, I worked to reconcile them through additional reporting and ultimately used my best judgment to provide the most accurate and complete version of events. (In a few instances, I have noted where a specific assertion is in dispute.)

Where dialogue is quoted, it is based on the recollection of the speaker, or someone else who was present for the conversation. If sources could not remember or agree on the specific wording, I reconstructed the dialogue without using quotation marks. Similarly, the considerable sections of this book that portray the various subjects' internal thoughts and feelings are based on descriptions from the subjects themselves, or from people in whom they confided; though my characterizations don't comprise direct quotes, they represent a sincere effort to accurately and empathetically capture the subjects' thinking.

Finally, portions of this book are drawn from my reporting and published stories at BuzzFeed News, as well as from the work of many talented authors and journalists at other outlets. I have relied occasionally on the official memoirs of my subjects in order to collect biographical information and sort out narrative timelines, but in general I have treated these books like campaign documents, with all the journalistic skepticism such a category calls for. I certainly don't claim to know these men and women better than they know themselves, but the pursuit of political power requires even the most straightforward strivers to sterilize their personal narratives—a process that too often conceals the untidy chapters, unsightly secrets, and off-message anxieties that make them interesting human beings. Among its other objectives, this book intends to tell those stories.

THE
WILDERNESS

Introduction

The houselights in the campus auditorium fall. The audience grows quiet. A producer initiates the countdown — "... four ... three ... two ..." — and at precisely 9 p.m. eastern time the cameras go hot.

All at once, seventy million Americans are seeing the same tension-packed scene unfold in real time: Two commanding figures, both national celebrities loved and hated by millions, stride confidently toward each other from opposite ends of a vast, elaborately retrofitted stage. A white-hot glare beats down from the klieg lights above. A clamorous applause rises from the seats below. Thousands of reporters in a nearby gymnasium sit with their eyes glued to closed-circuit TVs, their twitchy fingers hovering over keyboards, preparing to chronicle every micromoment. The two figures meet in the middle of the stage and shake hands with the menacing intensity of cage fighters entering a match.

It is October 2016. The presidential race is in its final, frenetic weeks. And the Republican nominee is about to go head-to-head with the Democratic candidate in the critical first debate of the general election.

The stakes are high. Whoever wins the election will take office at a moment of uncommon uncertainty and upheaval in American life — tasked with setting the national agenda for the most contentious issues of the era, from racial injustice to religious freedom, from police accountability to privacy rights, from immigration to income inequality. The average age of the Supreme Court justices has now passed seventy, and the next president could plausibly make as many as four new appointments to the bench, on top of thousands of other appointments across the judiciary and executive branches — an almost unprecedented opportunity to shape American jurisprudence for decades to come. Abroad, the growing terrorist threat of the Islamic State and the geopolitical bullying of countries like Russia will present the new commander in chief with a host of life-and-death, war-and-peace decisions that could have lasting global repercussions. And back home, the outcome of the election will almost certainly make the difference between an Oval Office occupant who celebrates, solidifies, and builds upon President Obama's liberal domestic policies and one who spends the next four years actively working to unspool his legacy.

The choice facing the country is stark, its consequences far-reaching—and it could all hinge on what happens onstage over the next ninety minutes. Tonight, the eyes of the nation are fixed on those two figures planted behind their podiums.

Who does the audience see?

When that pivotal moment arrives on an early October night in 2016, the candidate who shakes hands with the Democratic nominee in front of seventy million people will have traveled an unprecedented path to get there. He will have fought off the largest field of Republican contenders in a century, vanquishing at least sixteen serious rivals in all. He will have raised enough money to dominate the most expensive presidential race in American history, with an expected price tag of $5 billion. He will have logged enough miles in flight on the campaign trail to circle the globe a dozen times.

And he will have done it all amid the high-drama, high-octane clashes of ego and ideology that have raged inside the GOP—in cinematic public spectacles and clandestine cutthroat maneuvering—since the Republicans' dizzying defeat on the night of the 2012 election.

What follows is a chronicle of that once-in-a-generation battle over the future of the Republican Party, told through its most influential, provocative, and fascinating combatants—virtually all of whom hope to make it to that debate stage, and ultimately, the White House.

PART I

EXILE

Chapter One

The Exodus

If ever there was a moment when Senator Rand Paul needed to make use of his God-given poker face — the small mouth that rested in a gently sloped, unreadable frown; the impassive, pale-blue eyes that betrayed no hint at his innermost thoughts — it was right now. This instant. This night. In this dimly lit, log-framed, antler-adorned restaurant function room in Bowling Green, Kentucky, with these crestfallen conservatives standing all around him.

The national Republican Party was imploding on live television; dispatches from the calamity were being beamed in from Fox News headquarters and blasting out of TVs mounted on the walls of Montana Grille in Rand's small hometown. Colorado going blue. North Carolina too close to call. Todd Akin getting pummeled in Missouri; Scott Brown down in New Hampshire. And then the contingent of local Republicans who had gathered to watch the returns fell silent as the candy-colored chyron delivered the doomsday headline:

BARACK OBAMA REELECTED PRESIDENT

Rand was the most senior Republican official in the room, and he knew all eyes were on him. The appropriate, senatorial thing to do here was to quietly broadcast his sober disappointment in a country gone astray; to nod in solidarity at the "Tough night"s and "What a shame"s; to express solemn regret that Americans were going to miss out on such a fine, righteous president as Willard Mitt Romney. It was not a pose that came naturally to Rand, but he had picked up a few things since his scrappy, successful Senate bid in 2010—enough that he knew how to play the part of the grown-up statesman, at least for an evening.

And so the gentleman from Kentucky tightened his lips, clenched his jaw, and mustered every last ounce of self-discipline he had stored up over the course of his brief but educational time in Washington—and he managed to swallow any sign of the visceral glee that was secretly consuming him.

It wasn't that Rand took any pleasure in knowing that the socialist in the Oval Office would get another four years to ransack America's liberties with his congressional comrades. That was, indeed, a shame. But the fact that Romney's humiliating defeat might finally expose the GOP's moneyed, Waspy, corporatist breed of country-club patricians for the frauds that they were—well, that was cause for celebration in the Paul household.

For Rand, this was personal. As far back as he could remember, his family and friends had been getting their lunch money stolen by political bullies in the GOP who looked and behaved like Romney. Rand had been just thirteen years old when his family piled into a camper and drove north to the 1976 Republican National Convention in Kansas City—the site of a bitter, emotionally charged floor fight between President Gerald Ford's well-heeled establishment princes and Ronald Reagan's rowdy right-wing insurgents. As a newly elected libertarian congressman and head of the Texas delegation, Rand's father, Ron, entered the weeklong fray as a frontline soldier in the Reagan revolution, and young Randy had watched, wide-eyed and appalled, as the GOP party bosses ruthlessly beat back—sometimes literally—the populists at the gate. He could still vividly remember, three and a half decades later, the image of Vice President Nelson Rockefeller snatching up a floor sign during a heated exchange and taking a swing at one of the Texas delegates. Ron and his fellow Reaganites fought back by relentlessly heckling the Ford family, who were perched in a private box above the Texas delegation. On the last night of the convention, after Ford had prevailed and won his party's nomination, one of the president's sons dumped garbage on the rabble-rousers below.

As far as Rand was concerned, not much had changed since those polyester-clad combatants were fighting for the soul of the party inside Kemper Arena. Even as Ron Paul had emerged in the ensuing years as the philosopher-king of American libertarianism—marshaling a rambunctious grassroots movement as a serial protest candidate for the presidency—Rand observed a procession of entitled establishment Republicans seizing every opportunity to mock, deride, marginalize, and sneer at his father's life's work.

A fastidious scorekeeper in a family that passed down grudges like prized heirlooms, Rand had taken note that many of the prominent Ford delegates back in '76 grew up to be Kentucky good ol' boys who fiercely opposed him in the 2010 Senate primary. His surprise tables-turning victory over those snoots had been among the greatest pleasures of his adult life.

As for Romney himself, Rand had nothing personal against him—not really. The candidate had largely stayed out of his dad's way during the 2012 presidential primaries, having apparently crunched the data and realized that he had little to gain by alienating a passionate bloc of libertarian voters like the Paulites. But Mitt's opportunistic politeness did little to dampen the sheer, tribal satisfaction Rand felt as he watched the Massachusetts millionaire deliver a sad, hurried concession speech on TV. This was bigger than any one man. Over the past decade, establishment Republicans of Romney's sort had helped run up a multitrillion-dollar federal deficit; sent American troops into a series of disastrous, unwinnable foreign wars; and allowed the government to expand—practically unchecked—to unprecedented size and power.

Along the way, they had weakened a once-great party by shrinking the proverbial Republican tent to such a ludicrously small size that just about the only people who could fit under it were the five Romney sons and the job creators who sold them their skis. Over the past year Rand had stumped for both his dad, in the primaries, and Mitt, in the general, and he had been repeatedly struck by the differences between the crowds the two men drew. Unlike the veritable *Glee* cast of supporters who showed up at Ron Paul rallies—sporting tattoos and nose rings and gay pride buttons—Mitt's campaign events had been populated by a tribe of aging, white, aggrieved conservatives who would never again get to elect a president on their own. If this hadn't been clear before tonight, it was painfully obvious now. The

9

only shot the party would have at rebuilding a winning national coalition was to shed its hawkish orthodoxies, shred its intolerant dogmas, and embrace a new libertarian future.

Yes, the reckoning had finally arrived for the establishment bullies — and the picked-on Pauls, at long last, would be ascendant.

Washington Republicans could scoff all they wanted at the kooky cast of misfits who plastered "Ron Paul Revolution" stickers across their pickup truck bumpers: they were going to have to deal with Rand now. And unlike his father, the Kentucky senator had no interest in running hopeless, quixotic campaigns in the name of principle, or in preaching to a choir of noisy activists who were playacting revolution. Rand was out for an *actual* revolution — a new party, an upended order. And he wouldn't have to storm the gates to get there. He was going to walk in through the front door.

West Miami, Florida

Marco Rubio tried to make the best of his peaceful election night at home, but it was no use. He was bouncing and bobbing and brimming with enough pent-up energy to power Sun Life Stadium for an entire Dolphins season.

In the last weeks of the race, few Republicans had worked harder, hustled faster, or put in longer hours to help Mitt Romney win the presidency. The young Florida senator had taken on such a full schedule of stumping that the Romney campaign had actually chartered a small plane to shepherd him around the country. Some days, Rubio worked longer hours than the pilots themselves, and he would end up waiting on a swing state runway as they brought in a new shift.

But a couple of days before the election, his daughter had gotten injured in a minor golf cart accident and he left the campaign trail to attend to his family. Rubio had visions of spending the night playing Madden and intermittently checking his iPhone to keep tabs on the election, but of course it was a fantasy. He was now monitoring the news obsessively on multiple screens — jumping from channel to channel on the TV, refreshing his Twitter app, and furiously clicking through websites on his computer to see how the news was playing.

And, as it turned out, the news was playing very well for Marco Rubio.

The most immediate takeaway among the reporters and pundits skimming through exit-polling data was that Romney's crushing defeat was in large part due to his abysmal showing among Latino voters. And as several Republican talking heads were now eagerly pointing out, it just so happened that their party had a youthful, dynamic, Spanish-speaking superstar just waiting to take center stage and begin rectifying Romney's failures. In a succinct summary of the fast-gathering consensus in the conservative commentariat, George Will declared on ABC News, "If there's a winner tonight, it's the senator from Florida, Marco Rubio." (The president had, apparently, slipped Will's mind for the moment.)

As he took in the coverage, Rubio was a bundle of competing impulses and conflicted emotions. On the one hand, the punditry was exhilarating—all these people were on television talking about *him* as the next president of the United States. Him! He couldn't precisely remember the first time he pictured himself in the Oval Office, but it was a safe bet that it had happened prior to the first time he drove a car. Now he was actually poised to get there.

On the other hand, he was genuinely dismayed by how the election was ending. Four years earlier, Rubio had watched Barack Obama's Grant Park victory speech from the studio of the local Miami Univision affiliate, where he worked as an on-air Republican analyst. He was no Obama supporter, of course, but as Rubio listened to him speak that night, he became so overwhelmed by the weight of the moment—and its meaning for the country—that he found himself fighting back tears. In the years since that hallucinatory evening, however, Rubio had lost all confidence in the president's ability to unite Americans or, frankly, do anything that would seriously help his constituents. And though Rubio's hard work on behalf of Romney that year had started out as an act of personal ambition, he had come to sincerely admire the nominee, believing he had the potential to be one of the country's great presidents. That the majority of voters had rejected a man of such caliber in favor of Obama's divisive politics and deceptive emotional appeals was deeply disappointing, even disturbing.

But Rubio didn't have it in him to mourn just now; it was time to look forward. He felt as though he needed to do something. *But what?* He couldn't very well rush out of his house in search of a TV camera at this hour; he would look tactless, and overly ambitious. Yet he couldn't stand the thought of just sitting here, cooped up at the end of a quiet cul-de-sac while the entire political world was talking about him.

He fired off emails to his advisers, clamoring for a plan of action. He drafted and discarded statement after statement, press release after press release, in his head. He called up his longtime friend and aide Alberto Martinez, who had worked on Latino outreach for the Romney campaign and was now in Boston with his despairing colleagues. The two spent a few minutes on the phone glumly diagnosing the various reasons for the Republicans' 2012 defeat. They vented about the Romney campaign's operational failures and grumbled about the dishonesty of Obama's winning message. But both men also agreed that their party faced a larger systemic weakness — and unless it was fixed, this country would never see another Republican elected president.

Before Rubio went to bed, he typed up a short note on his Facebook page in which he promised to roll out an ambitious agenda in the coming session of Congress that would aim to reach the same voters who had overwhelmingly rejected his party tonight.

"The conservative movement should have particular appeal to people in minority and immigrant communities who are trying to make it," he wrote, "and Republicans need to work harder than ever to communicate our beliefs to them."

Rubio hit publish.

It was just a small step, but it was enough to satisfy his anxious, jittery, restless need for forward motion, at least for tonight. Starting tomorrow, he would set off on a full sprint — and he wouldn't let anything or anyone slow him down.

Coral Gables, Florida

A couple of miles away, Jeb Bush leisurely took in the election coverage at his stylish, million-dollar townhome, afflicted with no such eagerness for motion. He was good and comfortable right where he was: rich, rested, and reaping the rewards of a genetic lottery ticket that would pay out its installments of wealth and privilege until he was in the dirt. He genuinely felt he had done some good with the advantages he'd inherited. And now, six years after retiring as one of Florida's most beloved and successful governors in decades, he was settling in nicely to the role of elder statesman. He felt no particular urge to disturb it.

Of course, the same could not be said of his wide orbit of allies, advisers, and admirers. As soon as it seemed safe to acknowledge that Romney was finished, the Bush dynasty's national network—and especially those in Jeb's own Florida fiefdom—began buzzing with the prospect of a "Bush 45" presidency. Emails, texts, and phone calls zipped up and down the Sunshine State and across time zones, as donors, operators, and hangers-on trawled for inside info and clamored to know how they could help.

What is he thinking? How can we convince him? What does he need from us?

A few of these messages landed in Jeb's own inbox, but he had little interest in entertaining the notion at the moment. This same crowd of "family friends" had pleaded with him to run in 2012, and he had denied them. When interviewers had then spent the year asking Jeb whether he would consider a future presidential run, he'd made no effort to keep his supporters' hopes alive. In one particularly conclusive-sounding interview earlier that year, Jeb solemnly suggested to Charlie Rose that he had missed his last chance for the White House when he decided to forgo the 2012 race.

"This was probably my time," Jeb said. And his time had passed.

In fact, watching this election unfold had convinced Jeb of just how miserable the whole campaign process had gotten even since the last time his brother ran. He didn't say this part in interviews, of course, but he had been struck in 2012 by just how much coarser and crasser and crazier the political circus now seemed. The point was driven home for him when pizza magnate Herman Cain had spent a not-inconsiderable period of time at the top of the Republican primary polls. *Herman Cain!* Part of him found the whole thing amusing—but then he pictured actually running for president and somehow trailing a comic-relief candidate like that, and the thought just depressed him.

He frequently complained to friends about how immature and unstatesmanlike it was that these aspiring leaders of the free world were duking it out on Twitter with sarcastic hashtags and so-called memes. He had always prided himself on being on the cutting edge of technology and media. His early adoption of email and his penchant for responding to electronic missives from constituents at all hours had become part of the popular mythology surrounding Jeb—so much so that his BlackBerry was included in his official gubernatorial portrait. But if running for president now meant doing...*this*...he had no interest in it. He was happy to let Rubio, clearly ambitious and eager to enter the fray, take on all that nonsense.

That said, Jeb's vast following of party insiders and establishment elites was obviously undeterred by the signals he'd been sending that he was done with national politics. He felt no rush to start rallying the troops tonight—but if he eventually decided he needed them, he had little doubt they would quickly fall in line.

Baton Rouge, Louisiana

As Bobby Jindal paced the floors of the palatial plantation-style governor's mansion in Baton Rouge, he searched his memory for missed warning signs.

The forty-one-year-old governor of Louisiana had spent the final, frenzied days of the election inside the Romney campaign bubble, stumping for his party's nominee in front of crowds so big and so hysterically passionate that he had been hypnotized by their conviction. He wasn't privy to any of the campaign's internal numbers or the secret strategy memos coming out of Boston headquarters. But everywhere he went, he found the candidate's operatives coolly predicting victory, armed with some promising new scrap of polling data out of Pennsylvania or some vague notion about how things in Ohio were looking very, *very* good, or just generally acting as though they knew something he didn't.

Jindal considered himself a rational guy—a smart guy—and so he had never quite bought into the theory, fervently clung to by many on the right, that the polls showing President Obama with a persistent lead throughout 2012 were systemically biased because they were undersampling Republicans. This idea had gripped conservative political junkies across the country, and one obscure blogger had even gained national notoriety with a website, unskewedpolls.com, that reengineered the raw polling data to predict a Romney landslide. Jindal knew that such efforts exhibited a dubious grasp of reality, let alone mathematics, and he had winced as prominent Republicans, including his friend Texas Governor Rick Perry, enthusiastically touted the website. Yet in that final stretch of the race, as Romney's staffers radiated confidence, Jindal, too, became convinced that Republicans were on the cusp of triumph, Gallup be damned.

Now, as the election returns filtered in from swing states and he could see the bubble bursting, it was clear that there was never any evidence to support such certainty except for the certainty of other Republicans; it was gut feelings and tainted instincts and unskewed polls all the way down—and Jindal, however fleetingly, had been taken in by the con.

But while he faulted himself for this temporary lapse into gullibility, he wasted little time on self-censure. Another realization was beginning to take hold as he watched the electoral votes pile up in the president's corner on Fox News—one that he knew he could use to his advantage.

Mitt Romney, he thought, *ran a fantastically stupid campaign.*

Jindal did not know Romney well, and from a distance the man seemed sharp enough, but he was shocked by the frequency with which Romney had undermined his campaign's message by saying some moronic thing or another. And the few times Jindal had actually interacted with the candidate, he was left baffled by the political ineptitude on display.

This impression was cemented the day after the Republican National Convention, when Romney flew to Louisiana to tour a flood-ravaged fishing village on the bayou with Jindal. The trip was a political no-brainer—an easy photo op that would make any third-rate politician look presidential. But soon after the two men climbed into the SUV that was to shepherd them to the flood zone, Romney began complaining to Jindal that the Hurricane Isaac victims they were on their way to meet really shouldn't be living in areas outside the reach of the state's flood protection levee system. After all, Romney reasoned, wasn't it reckless of them to make their homes in places they knew could be flooded every hurricane season?

Jindal politely responded that he saw Romney's point, but that it was probably best to keep such observations to himself when he was talking to the victims. Yet, unbelievably, Romney went on to spend the bulk of their forty-five-minute drive pressing the point so adamantly that Jindal began to worry that the newly minted Republican nominee was actually about to turn a feel-your-pain photo op into a lecture on personal responsibility. As they neared the site of the flood damage, he urged Romney to drop the subject before they got out of the car.

"I get it," Jindal said. "But, Mitt, you *can't* say that to them. These people have just lost their homes."

Romney appeared to mull over the advice before exiting the vehicle and greeting some first responders and victims who had gathered to meet him. The visit went off without incident, and Jindal was so relieved that his exhortation had gotten through that he minded only a little when the candidate spent the forty-five-minute drive back to the campaign plane reciting his arguments all over again. The episode had left Jindal with the distinct sense that the GOP's standard-bearer, while certainly "smart," was not exactly brimming with social intelligence.

More troubling to Jindal, though, was the Romney campaign's defensiveness and lack of substantive ideas. The Republican strategy in 2012 reminded him of basketball players before the shot clock was introduced, idly dribbling at half-court for minutes at a time, nursing a narrow lead in hopes that they could just run out the clock without making any mistakes. The Romney campaign's message, Jindal thought, hadn't been anti-intellectual so much as intellectually petrified — devoid of ambitious thinking, stripped of substance, chained to meaningless maxims, and scared of using big words.

He knew that by morning, the political world would be consumed with a blizzard of post-campaign analysis that blamed the Republican Party's losses on everything from tactical failures to a fundamental disconnect with the American electorate. But Jindal, the Rhodes scholar and lifelong smartest-kid-in-class, couldn't help but view the party's meltdown tonight in terms of intelligence. The GOP had suffered a national embarrassment because a clueless candidate had run a vacuous campaign filled with dumbed down bumper sticker slogans aimed at what the operatives running the show must have believed was a nation of imbeciles.

Yes... Jindal liked the sound of that. Not only was it true, but it would also perfectly set the stage for the political comeback he was plotting. What the party needed now was an intellectually ambitious messenger with a detailed, forward-thinking agenda. Someone who would stop reducing every complicated issue to mindless taglines and trust the intelligence of the American people. Someone who was smart—and not afraid to show it.

Someone, he thought, like Bobby Jindal.

Houston, Texas

It took a little less than forty-five minutes for Ted Cruz to tell his first noble lie to the Tea Party as senator-elect. Standing triumphant on a stage at the head of the Hilton Houston Post Oak ballroom, Cruz was flanked by his wife, Heidi, and his two young daughters—all three dressed for the occasion in Red State red dresses—and set against the backdrop of an indoor billboard emblazoned with his all-caps campaign tagline, "TED CRUZ: PROVEN CONSERVATIVE."

Cruz, a rare winner in a night of Republican losses, had already cheerfully run through most of the standard box-checking platitudes for a victory speech of this kind—the recap of the "gracious" concession call from his opponent, the gentle told-you-so to the nameless naysayers who claimed it "couldn't be done"—and now he wanted to get serious. Lowering his voice and angling his head downward a few degrees to signal gravity, Cruz laid out the big picture.

"Every few decades we have a particularly consequential election. Nineteen thirty-two was a consequential election. Nineteen eighty was a consequential election." He paused. "And 2012 is a consequential election."

Cruz looked down at the podium and bit his lower lip before raising his eyes and proclaiming sternly, "At issue is, what sort of nation will we be?"

By now it was a little after 9 p.m. Houston time — 10 in the east, where the data jockeys in the TV network boiler rooms were meticulously sorting through swing state precinct returns and tallying electoral votes. Officially, they wouldn't call the election for Obama for about another hour, but the writing was on the wall: Mitt was cooked. Cruz knew it; the networks knew it; the operatives and the donors and the Twitter political junkies and every sentient human being who worked on either campaign knew it. Everybody in the know knew it.

But the grassroots patriots who had filled this ballroom were not all "in the know" types. Most of them were stalwart believers who would cling to their faith until the bitter end — and there was no sense in Cruz squandering his agenda-setting victory speech to kill the mood and shatter their illusions. It was important that they stay excited. He needed them to pay attention. So he fibbed.

"At this point, we don't know for sure what's going to happen nationally," he said. "I continue to hope and believe that Mitt Romney's gonna be elected our next president.

"However," he continued, "if President Obama is reelected..."

At this, the ballroom erupted in a loud chorus of *"Booo"*s and shouts of *"No!,"* and Cruz had to raise a reassuring hand to steady the crowd.

Firmly, he reiterated, "And I don't believe he will be..."

There was some scattered applause, and the room quieted. In the pantheon of great political liars, this minor deception would barely earn Cruz a small engraved placard. Plenty of Republican politicians had spent the past year telling far greater whoppers in the service of pretending to like the presidential nominee Cruz would later refer to as "screamingly awful." It was just good partisan manners.

Besides, tonight this small, noble lie had a greater purpose, as it set up Cruz to unambiguously lay out the mission of the conservative movement for the remainder of the Obama years — and the audacious role he planned to play in it.

"Let me say this," Cruz told the patriots. "If President Obama means what he says on the campaign trail—if he is interested in working to bring people together and reduce the deficit and get people working—then I will work with him."

A solitary "Whoo!" echoed across the otherwise cemetery-silent ballroom.

"But," Cruz continued, jabbing an index finger into the air, "if he is reelected and intends to continue down this same path, then I will spend every waking moment working to lead the fight to stop it."

The ballroom patriots rewarded this declaration of war with an ebullient round of applause, and Cruz allowed himself a satisfied grin. There was plenty more to cover from the notes on the podium in front of him, and he would get through all of it. He would promise to go after spending cuts and tax reform in the Senate. He would thank the cast of right-wing icons—Sarah Palin, Sean Hannity, Glenn Beck, Mark Levin, and more—who had helped him defeat the entrenched establishmentarian in his primary race. And he would give a warm shout-out to his campaign team, the "ragtag bag of warriors who stood against all assails."

But even as he celebrated tonight, he was already positioning himself for the *next* victory—the one he was destined for. When Cruz had said 2012 would go down in the history books as a "consequential election," he was telling God's honest truth. But it certainly wouldn't be because of footnote-bound Mitt, or even the hapless left-wing lame duck he planned to spend the next four years thwarting. No, 2012 would be remembered as the year the conservative movement finally found its champion—the man who had the gifts and guts to burn down Washington, and rebuild it in their image. Yes, he was quite sure that 2012 would mark the beginning of the consequential rise of Ted Cruz.

Boston, Massachusetts

Paul Ryan was slumped like a banged-up crash test dummy—silent, motionless, damaged—on one of the cream-colored sofas in the Westin hotel's presidential suite. The curtains were pulled shut, blocking the room's expensive waterfront views of Boston Harbor, and a dour circle of campaign advisers and Romney family members sat silently staring at their laps or feebly studying their smartphones—anything to distract from the bitter scene around them. Fox News was calling Ohio for President Obama. Mitt was about to get on the phone with the president to concede the election. The race was over, and they had lost—badly.

Now here was Ryan, forced to endure the first true flameout of his career in front of the nominee he had let down, the campaign he had failed, and the country—sixty million TV viewers and counting!—he had failed to convince. And as if all that weren't miserable enough, he had to do it while putting on a brave face for the family he had dragged along on this whole misadventure.

Ten weeks ago, when he and his wife, Janna, had informed their three young kids that Daddy was going to run for vice president, the prospect of having to leave their friends in Janesville, Wisconsin, set off a mini-tantrum. But since then, the kids had grown to appreciate the perks of the campaign trail: the decimated bedtimes, the traffic-stopping motorcade rides, the special plane that shepherded them all over the country, their favorite snacks always stocked. By election night, the kids wanted to soak up every last minute of this big, fun family adventure they were on, and after the Ryans tucked their seven-year-old son, Sam, into bed and prepared to depart for the Romneys' suite, Liza and Charlie begged their parents to let them tag along. Ryan looked at his two oldest children now, in this sad, crowded hotel room full of grown-ups with the sternest of don't-bother-me scowls on their faces—Mom crying softly to herself, and Dad a useless, quasi-catatonic hunk of charcoal-gray wool and disappointment. Liza had tears streaming down her face, and quiet, shy Charlie was visibly retreating inward. Ryan wished he had left them in bed.

Soon the gears of the campaign machine began churning around him—preparing to crank out one last public performance—and it became glaringly obvious once again that Ryan was the only cog in the apparatus without a meaningful function. Stuart Stevens was in charge of hammering out a hastily prepared concession speech. Mitt, of course, would have the task of delivering it. And sometime tomorrow morning, the operatives in this room would begin the laborious process of collapsing the whole Believe-in-America operation into a pile of cardboard boxes and shredded files. Even Mitt's twenty-four-year-old body man, Garrett Jackson, had a job to do: setting up the concession call with Obama.

Ryan's only job, meanwhile, was to square his considerable shoulders, jut out his photogenic jaw, and clap dutifully for the captain of their sunken ship. Not exactly heady work for the guy who had very recently been dubbed "the intellectual leader of the Republican Party."

But Ryan tried to shoo away the encroaching feelings of resentment and self-pity. No, he was *happy* to do whatever the campaign asked. Thrilled. Honored. Stoked.

Pumped!

From the moment he joined the ticket, Ryan had made a conscious choice that he would be a team player on this campaign, that he wouldn't emit so much as a whiff of the ego and self-indulgence that Sarah Palin had used to derail John McCain's 2008 presidential bid. No showboating, glory-hogging, grandstanding, game-changing, or rogue-going. He would execute the plays that Boston headquarters called for him with workmanlike efficiency and diligence. Though he could never publicly admit it, for fear of offending the stilettoed polemicist's rabid fan base, Ryan's guiding decision-making template throughout the campaign amounted to WWPD: What Wouldn't Palin Do?

When consultants suggested early on that Ryan trade in his baggy Brooks Brothers suits and oversize dress shirts for a less Beltway-inspired wardrobe, his first thought was of Sarah from Alaska's infamous $150,000 shopping spree with the McCain campaign's charge card. "I saw what happened to Palin and I was like, no way I'm letting the campaign buy me clothes," he later recalled. "Besides, my clothes are fine!" (After a series of media reports mocked the excessive reams of gingham he was prone to wrapping himself in, Ryan eventually conceded that last point and invested in a few bicep-hugging polo shirts for the stump.)

When he was given a set of talking points by the bosses in Boston, he recited them virtually word for word. When he was asked to head down to a Florida retirement community and paper over his signature entitlement reform proposals, he put on his best pair of khakis and brought along his mom as a stage prop. He had been the very definition of a line-toeing, low-maintenance running mate. Kept his head down, followed his orders.

But tonight, the good soldier could no longer deny that he had some...*let's call them "frustrations"*...with the way this campaign had been run. His thoughts weren't fully formed yet, and certainly weren't coherent enough for public consumption, but they were there all the same—gnawing at him.

For instance, he was frustrated that Mitt had jealously guarded so much of himself from the voters that he allowed the Left to turn him into a *Scooby-Doo* cartoon villain. The Mitt Romney he had gotten to know personally during the campaign was an authentically decent, humble, service-minded man. Even funny, and a little weird in an endearing way. He watched *Game of Thrones* (though he didn't care for all the nudity) and adopted a Southern twang to quote from his favorite movie, *O Brother, Where Art Thou?* But Mitt seemed so unwilling to reveal even the tiniest glimpse of his inner life that his trim, starched, clean-cut, gee-golly persona came off like cynical shtick—"the guy on top of the wedding cake," as Ryan would later tell me. Just for display. Void of substance.

Ryan was also frustrated by the Romney family's baffling queasiness when it came to talking about their Mormon faith. When Ryan first began the vice presidential vetting process, he took his House colleague Utah representative Jason Chaffetz out for a long dinner and peppered the LDS convert with questions. Given how reticent the Romneys had been to engage the topic of their religion in the election so far, Ryan half expected that his chat with Chaffetz would reveal some sort of bizarre, Scientology-like belief system, but as far as he could tell it was fairly benign. More to the point, many of Mitt's most humanizing stories occurred in the service of his church. Between the accounts of Brother Romney gently crafting wills for dying children at their bedside and his seemingly endless service as a volunteer bishop in the Boston area, there were enough good deeds to fill a veritable sequel to the Book of Acts. And yet Mitt was constantly skittish whenever the subject came up. Ryan eventually concluded that the nominee was nervous about becoming the public face of his global faith. "He sees it as his responsibility, and my guess is that it's a responsibility he didn't want," Ryan later hypothesized to me. "You know, his campaign was going to come and go, but the impression of the church on the minds of Americans could be set for a generation if he screws up."

Still, would it have killed him to break out some of these deathbed ministry stories *before* the Obama campaign carpet bombed the swing states with ads making Mitt look like a plutocratic monster?

More than anything, though, Ryan was deeply frustrated with how the campaign's strategists had insisted on framing the 2012 election as a referendum on Obama, and not as a choice between two competing visions. Long before he was tapped as Mitt's running mate, Ryan had written a series of idealistic memos to the candidate urging him to articulate an ambitious conservative agenda and take his case to voters who didn't traditionally vote Republican. When Ryan eventually joined the ticket, many in the political world predicted that his presence would turn the election into a grand ideological battle. Ryan thought so, too. Inside the campaign, he argued vigorously to make the election about more than just listing the president's myriad screw-ups. In one case, he lobbied the campaign to put out its own agenda for financial reform, and he had his staff working on a speech to introduce it. "They're out there killing us, saying we just want to let Wall Street run wild," Ryan argued to the campaign's strategists.

But his arguments fell on deaf ears: the game plan was all but chiseled in stone, and advocating for specific conservative policies was considered "off message."

"The strategy set, I focused on the job I had to do as a running mate," he would later write. "I needed a good rollout, a good convention speech, and a good debate. Those were my duties."

But duty, Ryan was beginning to decide, was overrated.

Shortly after midnight, Ryan followed Mitt and his entourage down to the ballroom, where disgruntled, half-drunk supporters were awaiting the concession speech. Romney's remarks were brief, clocking in at four minutes and forty-eight seconds, but they included a shout-out to his running mate: "Besides my wife, Ann," Mitt said to applause, "Paul is the best choice I've ever made."

But as Ryan shuffled onstage at the end of the speech to hug Mitt, clap, wave, hug his wife, clap, and wave some more—like a loyal labradoodle reflexively following commands—that potent cocktail of grievance, regret, and frustration continued to simmer just beneath the surface of his dutiful exterior. Paul Ryan was finished being brought to heel.

Boston, Massachusetts

Donald Trump didn't stick around for the concession speech at the Westin. The instant he realized the election-night victory party to which he had been invited would instead be a hotel ballroom full of sad sacks wallowing in failure, the billionaire bolted the scene in a black SUV—fleeing Mitt Romney's fast-approaching admission of defeat with the life-or-death urgency of an island villager trying to escape a tsunami. Publicly palling around with losers was bad for the brand. And for Trump, the brand was everything.

Indeed, among the vast array of garishly expensive toys and trophies the real estate mogul had accumulated over the years—all glittering, and gold-plated, and conspicuously monogrammed—it was his phenomenally lucrative billionaire-for-the-blue-collar-masses *brand* that stood alone as the one possession Trump treated as truly priceless. He labored over it. Luxuriated in it. Prized it, polished it, and protected it from even the smallest blemishes. If there had ever been a time when Trump's public persona was merely a shtick he performed to amuse the New York City tabloids, the caricature had long since come to consume him and define his business empire. It radiated off of the line of fat silk neckties and machine-washable French cuff shirts that filled his collection's designated aisle at Macy's. It sparkled in the giant gold lettering stamped across his eponymous hotels and skyscrapers. It permeated his illustrious and ever-growing list of self-awarded superlatives: *Star of the NUMBER ONE show on TV! Author of the bestselling business book of ALL TIME! The most recognized man in the WHOLE world!* ("It used to be Muhammad Ali, and now it's me," Trump once bragged to me, hastening to add that the legendary boxer was "a friend of mine, and all that stuff.")

That few of these boasts were, strictly speaking, true only added to Trump's deliberately honed image as a brash, outspoken, rule-breaking billionaire—each rhetorical embellishment brightening the sheen of his flamboyant, diamond-encrusted brand.

For most of the 2012 election cycle, Trump had channeled his talent for self-marketing toward politics—first as a right-wing noise-maker championing conspiracy theories about Obama, then as a potential presidential candidate, and finally as an unignorable campaign sideshow. He'd endorsed Romney because the guy seemed like the least pathetic candidate in the parade of primary contenders who'd trekked to Trump Tower in 2011 to kiss his ring. Mitt had at least built up a respectable little fortune for himself, even if he *was* just a small-time hedge fund guy, and even if Trump's own net worth was—as he never tired of pointing out—many, *many, MANY* times greater. (As he would later take to bragging, "I have a Gucci store that's worth more than Romney!")

But as the election wore on, Trump began to suspect that the Republican nominee's campaign was filled with losers, weaklings, and idiots who had no idea how valuable The Donald's support was to them. For example, when the billionaire had magnanimously offered to bestow his highly coveted endorsement at a flashy ceremony in his Las Vegas hotel—*Number one in all of Nevada!*—the national media flocked to the event. Trump could tell just by looking at the gaggle of assembled reporters that the turnout was unprecedented. Historic. *HUGE.* And yet, the Romney campaign didn't have the first clue how to put on a show in front of all those cameras. Mitt only spent five minutes on stage, looking uncomfortable and squirrelish as he shook hands with Trump, and then scurried away to his campaign's charter plane. ("Romney had a really shitty plane," a chuckling Trump would later tell me. "Total piece of shit. Not presidential at all.")

This pattern had then repeated itself in the run-up to the 2012 Republican convention. As the event approached, *everybody* was demanding that Trump give a keynote speech in primetime. "People were writing me thousands of letters and emails, all going crazy!" he remembered. To satisfy these rabid, letter-writing multitudes he brought in a film crew—*Really talented! Top award-winners!*—to produce a convention video that revolved around Trump deploying his famous TV catchphrase against President Obama: "You're fired!" When Trump saw the final product, he knew right away it was a guaranteed hit—maybe even a game-changer for the whole election. But what did Romney's gutless campaign operatives do when he handed them pure primetime gold? They scrapped the whole thing, claiming it was "too controversial" to show at the convention. *What a joke.*

Eventually, Trump arrived at the only logical explanation for these snubs: Romney was obviously worried he would look puny and small by comparison if he spent too much time next to The Donald. "He was afraid of me," the billionaire would later conclude with a shrug. "His people didn't even want him going in the same room with me because they thought he'd look secondary, and not like a presidential contender."

Now, as he raced toward Boston's Logan Airport with his entourage, Trump wished he had never made the mistake of tarnishing his treasured brand with an unsightly smear of loserdom like Mitt Romney. "Trump doesn't like to be associated with failure," one of his aides would tell me the next day. "Trump's a winner."

Still, electoral outcomes aside, Trump considered his 2012 foray into presidential politics a success. Not only had he repeatedly hijacked national news cycles with an increasingly incendiary succession of publicity stunts—an achievement of showmanship that he relished—he had also, along the way, built up a devoted following of die-hard fans on the conservative fringes of the Republican Party.

This had come as a pleasant surprise to Trump. In business, his trademark aesthetic had long been tailored to appeal to a certain type of consumer. "If you have no education, and you work with your hands, you like him," one of his aides explained to me. "It's like, 'Wow, if I was rich, that's how I would live!' The girls, the cars, the fancy suits. His ostentatiousness is appealing to them." But it wasn't until Trump (who had enthusiastically praised Obama just a few years earlier) reinvented himself as a right-wing populist that he realized his blunt, macho, shouty style was perfectly attuned to the mood in the conservative movement circa 2012. He found he was able to effortlessly channel the id of a certain subset of the GOP's right-wing base—aggrieved nativists, fevered conspiracy theorists—simply by applying his regular routine to the art of Obama-bashing.

Whereas the political class had increasingly turned up their noses at his antics over the course of the election, Trump's new cheering section showered him with validation, and egged him on. They rooted for him when he pledged to uncover Obama's true African birthplace and expose the president for the fraudulent foreigner that he was. And they reveled in his unrepentantly rude stream of insults directed at Obama and his lefty supporters.

To Trump's political booster club, he was more than just a reality TV star or an entertaining loudmouth or the owner of the world's classiest hotels: he was a gutsy truth-teller. A model leader. *Presidential* material. Throughout the election, these fans had been a source of immense satisfaction—and consolation—for Trump. So what if the sniveling haters on Romney's staff wanted to blow him off? *These* folks, he told himself, were his true target demo.

And tonight he was going to give them a show.

Trump arrived at the airport at around 11:00 p.m., and soon he was on board his private helicopter, barking out tweets for one of his yes-men to post under his name. Someone had informed him (wrongly) that Romney was going to win the popular vote while still losing the election, and in this Trump saw a perfect opportunity for outrage-mongering.

The first tweet by @realDonaldTrump went out at 11:30 p.m.: "Let's fight like hell and stop this great and disgusting injustice! The world is laughing at us."

Then, three minutes later: "This election is a total sham and a travesty. We are not a democracy!"

And then: "More votes equals a loss...revolution!"

Trump continued in this vein with several more tweets, each one whipping his followers into a frothier state of frenzy. His yes-man kept him briefed minute to minute on the reaction the rant was generating—*Five thousand retweets on this one! Fifteen thousand on that one!*—and the online hysteria pleased the billionaire. His fans were rallying; his haters were going nuts; and Trump was soaking up his last stolen spotlight of the 2012 presidential election.

Amid all the vehement criticism, however, there was *one* comment that got under his skin. During a short segment that night about Trump's attempts to foment revolution on Twitter, NBC News anchor Brian Williams briefly broke character from his usual on-air role as the affable, objective newsman to proclaim that Trump had "driven well past the last exit to relevance, and veered into something closer to irresponsible."

The put-down made Trump fume. His long-running reality show, *The Apprentice,* had brought in *hundreds of millions of dollars* to the same network that cut Williams's paychecks—and this was how he got treated in return? He fired back with a barrage of tweets ripping Williams's "totally boring" nightly newscast, taunting him over the lackluster ratings for his newsmagazine show, and snarling, "I hope NBC isn't paying you too much." But even after unloading on the anchor, he still found himself seething over the remark. "Irresponsible" Trump could live with—but *irrelevant?* He couldn't let that go. And he wouldn't let it stand.

As Donald Trump ascended into the sky, raining down thunderous calls for mass political mutiny, the Republicans back on earth were forced to grapple with a disorienting new reality taking hold across the country that night. For the past four years, many in the GOP had dismissed Obama's 2008 election—and the historic surge of young, progressive, and minority voters he had inspired—as a one-time fluke made possible by an uncommonly charismatic candidate who'd hypnotized the country with savvy sloganeering. This theory had only been strengthened by the Tea Party wave of 2010 that flooded Congress with new conservative lawmakers. Now, however, the comforting illusion was crashing down around them. Republicans had just faced a weak Democratic incumbent, a disenchanted liberal base, and a national electorate restless over the languid economy—and still they had been pummelled. Their presidential nominee had lost every swing state but one, in some cases by historic margins. And though many would try to pin blame for the party's defeat on Romney alone, the truth was that the Republican Senate candidates in almost every state had performed even worse than he had.

Meanwhile, a flurry of election-night dispatches from culture war battlegrounds were bringing news of unexpected progressive victories.

In Maine and Maryland, same-sex marriage won at the ballot box for the first time in the nation's history. In Wisconsin, Tammy Baldwin became the first lesbian ever to get elected to the United States Senate. In Colorado and Washington, voters passed initiatives legalizing recreational pot use. This was no longer the same center-right country in which national elections were dominated by tough-on-crime, just-say-no, family-values conservatives. Cultural attitudes had evolved, demographics had changed, the electoral map had been redrawn—and the Grand Old Party was now indisputably in exile.

As Republicans were thrust into the wilderness that night in November, consigned to a period of indefinite wandering, they found themselves without a Moses to point the way to the promised land. For the first time in more than forty years, the GOP had no consensus heir-apparent, no next-in-line standard-bearer, no revered party eminence around whom the nation's Republicans would naturally coalesce. Indeed, with their party fracturing into a chaotic cluster of warring tribes, they were forced to confront the fact that there would be no foreordained figure coming down from the mountaintop to deliver them from disarray. Instead, a large and unruly cast of self-styled, tablet-toting prophets would emerge from the mayhem to vie fiercely for that mantle—each peddling his own vision for the party's future; each preaching redemption for American conservatism; and each promising a path back to the presidency.

It was now early in the morning on November 7th. Ballots were still being counted in city halls and county courthouses. Concession speeches were still being delivered in function halls and hotel ballrooms. Reporters were still reporting their final campaign stories, and talking heads were still talking 2012 on TV. But for the rising class of Republican strivers and presidential aspirants, the race toward 2016 was already under way.

Chapter Two

The Biltmore Caucus

The tony enclave of Coral Gables rests quietly amid Miami's noisier, flashier, more famous attractions: to its north, Calle Ocho's Cuban cafés and musty cigar shops, Hialeah's casitas and concrete driveways; to its east, South Beach's neon-lit tourist traps, topless seashores, and speedy cigarette boats slicing through the turquoise bay; to its south, the palm-lined campus of the University of Miami (technically within its boundaries, but culturally walled off); and to its west, twenty miles of suburbia that stretches out, block after block, until running up against the Everglades. The town sprang forth from the imagination of a wealthy heir named George Merrick, who in 1911 inherited thousands of acres of citrus groves and envisioned erecting on the land an "American Venice," replete with flowing canals, wide boulevards, and picturesque houses clustered in neighborhood villages with distinct architectural themes. His grand plans were ultimately thwarted by the Great Depression and a pair of havoc-wreaking hurricanes, but he left behind a monument to his vision in the form of Miami's Biltmore Hotel.

The soaring Spanish-Mediterranean structure—built in 1926 and exquisitely crafted with terra-cotta tiles, groin-vaulted ceilings, and elegant archways—stands at the center of town, towering importantly over the golf courses, banyan trees, and pricey Spanish-revival homes that surround it. It once played host to a diverse array of early-twentieth-century society fixtures—from Judy Garland and Bing Crosby to the

Duke of Windsor and Al Capone—but when Gene Prescott, a wealthy Democratic fund-raiser, bought it in the nineties, he was intent on transforming it into a playground for America's political elite.

After a $40 million renovation, he persuaded President Bill Clinton to hold a summit of Latin American leaders on its grounds. The First Family ended up taking to the place—returning often for vacations and fund-raisers—and the Clintons' ongoing patronage turned the hotel into a political destination. Candidates, congressmen, and presidents of all partisan stripes made sure to book suites during their swings through South Florida, where they would spend their nights mingling and drinking with Miami's influencers by the Biltmore's pool. George W. Bush became a regular guest when he was president, though he was annoyed by the photo of Bill and Hillary that hung by the front desk. "What am I, chopped liver?" he once complained. On another occasion, Bush and his sworn enemy in the Senate, Democratic leader Harry Reid, ended up at the hotel on the same night for separate events, setting off a panic among Biltmore brass as they worked to keep the peace between the two camps. In 2012, both Barack Obama and Mitt Romney held glitzy fund-raisers at the hotel.

The frequent visits from dignitaries bestowed an aura of outsize influence upon the local crowd of Biltmore regulars—a swirling, chattering circle of political donors, power brokers, activists, and other prominent Florida politicos. The hotel became a place where Miami-Dade's important people went to exercise and amplify their importance; to revel in their status; to bask in the belief that their idle, cocktail-buzzed gossip had the power to shape laws, move markets, start wars—and pick the next president of the United States. And in the wake of the 2012 election, no one was more eager for their approval than Florida's freshman senator.

Everybody wanted a piece of Marco Rubio. *Todo el mundo* was clamoring for him (yes, *him!*)—his endorsement, his opinion, his attention, his name on this bill, his signature on that pledge, his presence at any number of Capitol Hill galas, leadership dinners, party fund-raisers, and policy roundtables. His Senate office had a list of media requests that seemed longer than the football fields he used to run down in high school—not "fast," his old athletic director had told the author who wrote the biography of Rubio (yes, *him!*), but "quick," which meant, "You get to the right spot on the field at precisely the right time."

And it wasn't just the political rags begging for access to him either. The *New York Times* was sending its star magazine writer down to Miami to write his second long-form profile of Rubio in as many years. *Time* was talking about putting him on the cover. Every English- and Spanish-language cable channel in the country wanted him on their air. Even filmmaker Robert Rodriguez had tried to get him to make a cameo in the upcoming *Machete* sequel. He felt like a rock star. Even better, he was hanging out with *actual* rock stars!

When Bono had come to the Hill in 2011 to lobby Congress for aid to Africa, Rubio had impressed the iconic U2 front man with his uncommonly informed musings about hip-hop.

"Wow, I don't think I've ever in my life heard a senator talk about Eminem versus Tupac," Bono had confessed to Rubio, which opened the door for the senator to offer his theory about how U2's music had been "the beginning of modern Christian rock."

What do you mean? Bono had asked him. (Yes, *him!*)

"Well, your songs were about social justice, and had these bigger messages with a Christian bent, but without cramming it down anyone's throat," Rubio had explained. "You guys inspired a lot of Christian bands that came later on."

And then Bono had actually *agreed* with his analysis! I never thought about it that way, he said, but it's true. They traded phone numbers and now kept in touch via text message.

Yes, these were heady times for Marco Antonio Rubio. Mitt Romney had lost. The GOP was in disarray. The consensus among the Beltway opinion makers, the greenroom mainstays, and the blue check mark Twitterati was that Republicans needed to find a "fresh face" to rebrand their party. And at the moment there wasn't a face in American politics that looked fresher than the boyishly handsome visage of the junior senator from Florida—with his soft features, his brown eyes, his wrinkle-free forehead framed by that neat coif of dark hair that was...*yes, that item in* Esquire *had noted it, and it was true...*

thinning a little on the top, but it was barely noticeable as long as he kept it combed just so. And was it any wonder that his party had just tapped him to deliver the official Republican response to President Obama's State of the Union address in February? *GQ* magazine was calling his speech at the Republican National Convention earlier that year "the best of its kind since Obama's." Karl Rove was calling him "the best communicator since Ronald Reagan." In the early assessments of the 2016 Republican presidential field, every oddsmaker in the political universe had him (yes, *him!*) at the front of the pack.

Just as his high school athletic director once forecasted, Rubio had gotten himself to the right place on the field at precisely the right time, and he felt now as if he was sprinting down the sideline, a static-like roar emanating from the stands—unbeatable, untouchable, unstoppable...

Right up until the moment he stepped foot in the Biltmore.

The hotel was a couple of miles from Rubio's house in West Miami, and whenever he was home he made a point of working out at the Biltmore's gym—partly because the facility was first-rate and he liked its spin classes, but also because it was a political necessity for a Miami officeholder such as himself to put in face time there. The small talk with the local donors during water breaks, the chance encounter with the state representatives in the lobby, the offhand compliment extended to the Cuban exile power brokers on his way out—all of it was crucial to keeping his South Florida political network well fertilized.

But these days running the gauntlet of the hotel lobby lobbyists had a way of draining Rubio of the high-flying hustle that powered him when he was in Washington. Up there, he was a superstar, a media sensation, a standard-bearer for a new generation of Republicans. But here at the Biltmore, he was the kid who used to sneak onto the golf course late at night with his buddies to get drunk on beer; the young lawyer who received a free upgrade on his wedding night so that he and his bride, Jeanette, could stay in a suite; the baby-faced freshman senator who had lots of potential, but so far seemed unwilling to live up to it.

Here, he was just Marquito.

Oh sure, the Biltmore crowd was rooting for him—The local kid making good! Their little *chiquito* all grown up!—but it was agonizingly obvious to Rubio that they weren't yet sold on his presidential timbre. Part of the reason was the omnipresent comparison he had to face whenever he was here. Jeb Bush, the godfather of Florida Republicanism himself, lived nearby and worked out of the hotel's office suite. The heroic tale of Jeb's governorship had been reverently retold over the years at a hundred Lincoln Day Dinners from Palm Beach to Pensacola, and it was the stuff of legend among the Republicans who hung out at the Biltmore. The story went like this: Once upon a time, Prince Jeb rode into Tallahassee on a white steed and gallantly wrested the capitol from the hands of the fire-breathing Democrats, becoming Florida's first Republican governor since Reconstruction to enjoy a GOP-controlled state legislature while in office. He ruled for two glorious terms, presiding over an economic boom, enacting a slew of conservative reforms to education and gun laws, and helping turn the Republican Party of Florida into an unstoppable force. By the time he left office in 2007, he had consolidated GOP gains in the state and spawned an entire generation of new conservative leaders—Rubio included—all of whom had Prince Jeb's righteous reign to thank for their success.

These days, Jeb could often be seen eating lunch at one of the Biltmore's restaurants, or holding court at a poolside table surrounded by admirers, or chatting warmly with service staff in Spanish. This was the man that Florida Republicans had wanted to see in the White House ever since...well, since Jeb's dull-witted older brother had unjustly landed himself in the Oval Office instead.

And compared to Jeb, with his quiet confidence, commanding presence, and DNA-encoded gravitas, Rubio looked—and sometimes felt—like a scrawny kid drowning in his dad's oversize sport coat, struggling to fit in at the grown-ups' table.

None of Miami's Republican elite would risk saying such things outside their little Biltmore circle, of course. These were early days, and they didn't yet know how 2016 would shake out—no use in publicly declaring allegiances before they even knew if there would be a civil war. Instead, it had become a matter of social survival to develop a pithy, sometimes playful nonanswer when asked who they would support in the event that both men decided to run for president.

"If they both run? I think it would be a great ticket!" South Florida congressman Mario Diaz-Balart liked to exclaim. (If pressed, he'd insist, "That's my quote, and that's as much as I'm gonna say.")

"All of their mutual friends are hoping and praying this thing sorts itself out, including myself," Al Cardenas, the chairman of the American Conservative Union, offered.

And Ana Navarro, the grande dame of the Biltmore herself, encapsulated the approved message by declaring a hypothetical Rubio-Bush face-off "the nightmare scenario for everyone here." As the longtime girlfriend of the hotel's owner, Navarro had a built-in perch at the center of Miami's political world that she had leveraged over the years to gain proximity to both Rubio and Bush—as well as a regular gig on CNN, where she weighed in on the day's political news as a "Republican strategist." Navarro, a zaftig brunette with a taste for designer labels and bright colors, generally responded to questions about the potential intra-Biltmore rivalry by jabbering theatrically— to the delight and amusement of all within earshot—about the unthinkable inhumanity of such a Sophie's choice.

"I'd get into the fetal position and lock myself in a room for nine months!" she exclaimed to me. "If we have to all lock ourselves in the Biltmore until white smoke comes out and we pick one, that's what we will do!"

But even as members of Miami's political class busied themselves asserting friendly neutrality, Rubio knew where their loyalties lay at the end of the day—and it wasn't with him. This reality was laid bare in a *Tampa Bay Times* survey of Florida's most "plugged-in political players" in December; it found that an overwhelming majority—81 percent—believed Jeb would be a stronger candidate than Rubio. And despite all the national media coverage and 2016 hype he was enjoying, most of the Florida insiders didn't even believe Marquito would get a chance to enter the presidential race.

As one of the paper's anonymous respondents put it, "Rubio will make 2016 noises and preparations to increase his profile and lay the stage for himself in case Jeb doesn't run. But if Jeb does decide to run, he will step aside...Jeb Bush is heads and shoulders above Rubio, literally."

For the Biltmore crowd, the contrast between Jeb and Rubio had been thrown into particularly sharp relief in recent weeks, as postelection Washington was arriving at a rare moment when it actually seemed politically feasible to pass a bipartisan overhaul to America's broken immigration system. With Republicans smarting from their electoral rout in 2012—a year in which their presidential nominee had the worst showing among Latino voters of any election in decades—even right-wing mouthpieces like Sean Hannity were suddenly trumpeting the need for the GOP to embrace a pathway to citizenship for the country's eleven million illegal immigrants.

The conservatives in Miami-Dade didn't need any convincing. Their county was probably the only cluster of zip codes in the country where immigration reform had long been a top priority for Republican voters. Sixty-five percent of the county's nearly three million residents were Hispanic, and the local conservative movement was dominated by Cuban Americans. While exiles from Castro's regime had special privileges carved out for themselves in U.S. immigration law, they still overwhelmingly supported overhauling the system to make room for their Latino brothers and sisters. Now, for once, it looked as though the Republicans in Washington were ready to get on board. And where was their bright young senator—so brimming with promise, so hungry for the spotlight—at this exciting moment in national politics?

Paralyzed by indecision.

Rubio hemmed and hawed and hedged and hesitated every time one of the local Republican players raised the issue with him. He had waded into the festering cesspool of national immigration politics before, and as far as Rubio was concerned, it had been a disaster. During his Senate race in 2010, the Arizona legislature had passed a bill that allowed law enforcement officers to demand proof of residence from anyone in their custody who they suspected of being an illegal immigrant—and if they didn't have it, the officers handed them over to Homeland Security. Rubio found the legislation appalling, and thought it would quite clearly lead to racial profiling. But when he said so, he faced an immediate backlash from the Tea Party voters he was trying to court. He then backpedaled, saying that while he didn't think states should be crafting their own immigration laws, he understood why Arizonans—facing gunrunners, human traffickers, and drug cartel violence on their southern border—supported such a crackdown. That little show of deference, in turn, got the pro-immigrant activists up in arms. "I had managed to unite both sides against me," Rubio later wrote.

Rubio dipped his toe back into the immigration policy waters in 2012, proposing a bill that would have granted residency to some undocumented immigrants who had been brought to the country by their parents when they were young. But then the Obama administration took his legs out with an election year executive order unilaterally giving legal status to the same group—and Rubio spent the rest of the year stumping for a presidential nominee whose primary immigration proposal was to incentivize "self-deportation."

I can't win with this issue, Rubio tried to explain to the Biltmore arm twisters. The game is rigged.

But they simply urged him to man up, take heart, and bravely convert his convictions into action.

Ten valor, Marquito! came the refrain from the Biltmore chorus. Have courage!

"What's the point of having political capital if you're never going to use it?" an exasperated Navarro demanded during a conversation with Rubio.

Navarro was one of the most persistent lobbyists agitating for Rubio to start leading on immigration. Born in Nicaragua to a father who fought against the leftist Sandinistas, she had come to Miami at age eight to escape the political violence in her country. At the time, Ronald Reagan's fierce anticommunism had placed the Republican Party firmly on the side of Nicaragua's "freedom fighters," and she remembered as a little girl hearing the president declare, "They are the moral equal of our Founding Fathers." She decided right then and there that she was a Republican. Back then, the GOP understood the plight of the immigrants and wanted to assimilate them into

American society. "But somehow, somewhere, it turned into this," she lamented. "The inmates have taken over the asylum." Rubio, she believed, could finally steer the party back to its Reaganite roots, and bring the message of conservatism to a whole new generation of Latinos like her.

But even though he clearly agreed with her on the immigration issue, he couldn't bring himself to commit to anything concrete. He went back and forth, talking through an endless loop of pros and cons, agonizing over every potential pitfall. It was classic Marquito.

"He just lets these little things get to him, and he worries too much," one Miami Republican complained to me after spending close to an hour sitting next to Rubio on a flight as he fretted over a mildly critical process story about him in a small DC political magazine. "I'm just like, 'Marco, calm down.'"

As the year drew to a close, with the outlook of a major bipartisan congressional push on immigration looking better than ever, everyone in the Biltmore scene was grousing about Marquito's wishy-washiness, and some were even doing so on the record.

In one particularly whispered-about bit of Marco bashing, Jeb Bush's son Jeb Jr.—a Coral Gables resident and Biltmore stalwart—granted me an on-the-record interview in which he heaped praise on several Republican senators for their eagerness to solve the country's immigration problem, but then grumbled of Rubio, "He's got to actually execute and get something done, rather than just talking." Jeb Jr. went on to add, with a veneer of sympathy, "Marco's gotta be careful. My dad can kind of say anything he wants because he's not running for anything."

In truth, it was precisely Bush's politics-be-damned attitude that so endeared him to the Biltmore set—and so thoroughly distinguished him from the anxiety-ridden Rubio. Jeb had spent his years since leaving office vocally championing causes he cared about—from immigration reform to tougher federal education standards—as well as lobbing bombs at his own party whenever he thought they were on the wrong side of an issue.

"These last few years, we've had Jeb Bush unplugged, and it's so fun," Navarro gushed.

Unlike Rubio, who was prone to geeking out over his newfound political celebrity, Jeb responded to media speculation about his presidential aspirations with a too-cool-for-school shrug. One Miami Republican noted the contrast by describing a pair of recent visits paid by *New York Times* reporters to the Biltmore: "When Jim Rutenberg came down here to do a profile, Jeb blew him off. When Mark Leibovich came down, Marco took him to a Dolphins game." Jeb had never been the type to thrill at the sight of his mug on a magazine cover, and as governor he had been legendary for ignoring, demeaning, deriding, or toying with the press—depending on what his mood called for that day. Once, when a local television reporter asked him a question about abortion that he deemed unfair, Jeb proceeded to put her down in front of her colleagues with such ruthlessness that some thought she might cry. On another occasion, as journalists were filing out of the crowded Capitol basement after a gubernatorial press conference, a male reporter felt a pinch on his rear. When he turned around, he found the governor smirking at him like a towel-snapping frat boy. Jeb gave the reporter a little wink, and then strode away without a word.

Now, as Rubio was fussing and fretting over how to position himself in the immigration debate, Jeb was putting the finishing touches on a book he believed would reshape the national discussion on the subject. He spent the final weeks before Christmas shuffling in and out of his office at the hotel, making tweaks to the manuscript and trading emails with his coauthor, the conservative lawyer and activist Clint Bolick. Most in Jeb's Biltmore booster club hadn't read a word of it yet, but they had no doubt that his book would be a force for good.

As for Marquito's influence, the jury was still out. But his dithering over immigration only reaffirmed to many that Rubio should step aside in 2016 and make room for Jeb to run.

"I have always seen Rubio as a very respectful person," said former West Miami mayor Rebeca Sosa. "I have no question in my mind that if one day he needs to sit down with a friend and discuss issues of importance for the nation...he and Jeb will do it." Navarro was similarly hopeful that the two men would huddle and hash out some sort of agreement well before the election. "We're not going to have to pick between Jeb and Marco," she told me at the time. "They'd never do that to each other, or to those of us who love them both."

"But," she added, "time is a factor. Marco has plenty of time. Jeb doesn't." From Navarro's perspective, there was no guarantee that Rubio would be ready for the presidency by 2016. Jeb, on the other hand, "is ready now. He's been ready for years, and we've been ready and waiting."

One day in 1968, John Ellis Bush—a long-limbed, long-voweled tenth grader with a permanent look of discontent tugging at his features—placed a record on the turntable in his dorm room and dropped the needle. As the peppy guitar riff to Steppenwolf's psychedelic-rock hit "Magic Carpet Ride" popped out of his speakers, Jeb introduced Peter Tibbetts, a classmate and toking buddy, to the wonders of hashish. Outside, students across the pastoral campus of Phillips Academy in Andover, Massachusetts, were cramming for tests and cranking on term papers; scions from the nation's wealthiest families were plotting Ivy League applications, and politically inclined liberals were plotting revolution. But here in Jeb's corner of the red-brick Pemberton Cottage dormitory, both ambition and activism were in short supply. He just wanted to light up and escape, and tonight he had a travel companion. "The first time I really got stoned," Tibbetts would later recall, "was in Jeb's room."

At the time, the popular political portrait of Jeb—the thoughtful policy wonk with a heart of gold; the compassionate conservative attuned to matters of social justice; the smarter, better, more *worthy* Bush brother—had not yet been painted. In its place was a considerably less appealing sketch: the unpleasant, cocksure prince who reeked of privilege and seemed bitterly beset by the problems of the aristocracy. As the great-grandson of wealthy industrialist Samuel Prescott Bush, the grandson of U.S. senator Prescott Sheldon Bush, and the son of newly elected congressman George Herbert Walker Bush, Jeb had arrived at the prestigious prep school with a legacy to preserve and expectations to meet—and he hated everything about it. The winters were too cold. The customs of the East Coast, all-boy student body were unfamiliar. And the classes were far more difficult than what was offered at the Texas public schools he was used to.

"There was a high expectation that you were to be part of the Andover community, and you were supposed to do your work," Jeb would later recall. "If you didn't, they'd just leave you at the side of the road... This was wartime conditions, dog eat dog."

But rather than rise to the occasion, Jeb seemed content to coast, knowing that even as he unhappily sulked over the unjust demands his last name placed upon him, his family's money and influence would shield him from any real repercussions for his behavior.

"The thing that really struck me about Jeb more than anyone I ever met, is he understood that he was from the world that really counted, and the rest of us weren't," Phil Sylvester, Jeb's Phillips Andover room-mate, would later tell the *Boston Globe*. "It really was quite a waste of his time to engage us. This was kind of his family high school. There wasn't anything he could do to be kicked out, so he was relaxed about rules, doing the work. This was just his family's place."

The combination of brooding and rudderless entitlement left a less-than-favorable impression on many of his classmates. One would later remember "a kind of arrogance to him," while another would describe him as "slightly snarly and spoiled." Even Jeb himself would look back decades later on his Andover days and confess, "I was a cynical little turd at a cynical school."

But at the time, Jeb wasn't quite so self-aware. He saw himself as someone trapped in a gilded prison—a martyr at the hands of his overbearing parents and these oppressive New England snobs, but without any real cause to give meaning to his suffering. As the son of an ascendant statesman, he had stubbornly refused to take an interest in politics: when his family had moved to Washington upon George Sr.'s election to Congress, Jeb had been the only one to stay put in Houston, moving in with friends so he could finish the school year. Later, at Andover, with the Vietnam-era culture wars reaching a fever pitch, he remained aloof and uninterested in idealistic crusades— even as antiwar students in black armbands marched across campus, and activist groups campaigned aggressively against the school's administration.

Instead, Jeb found low-stakes, rich-kid ways to rebel. He smoked a lot of pot and hung out with Andover's self-styled "freaks." At one point, classmates would recall, he might have been involved in some sort of clandestine liquor-selling scheme. And in a rare act of teenage defiance that would actually bring him a measure of pride years later, he went out of his way to befriend the small group of African American students at the school. Through it all, his only discernible ideology was a determination to break rules he didn't care for, shirk responsibilities he didn't want, and violate expectations he didn't invite.

He also showed glimpses of a trait that would become more pronounced later in life: a proclivity for using blunt force to get his way and exert dominance. At six foot four, he towered over most of the boys on campus, and his size—combined with his cavalier confidence—made him an intimidating figure to some. He picked fights with classmates he felt had crossed him, and hulked over students who were smaller and less self-assured than he was. Andover alum Gregg Hamilton, who weighed just ninety-eight pounds as a senior, would later liken the school to "a *Lord of the Flies* situation," in which Jeb was at the top of the food chain and he was at the bottom. "Jeb was large, physically imposing, and traveled in a crowd that was, I guess, somewhat threatening to an outsider like myself." Jeb's friend Tibbetts, meanwhile, would remember with some regret following Jeb's lead as they taunted and tormented a smaller classmate, once sewing his pajama pants together so he couldn't put them on. (As an adult, when a reporter asked him about classmates' perceptions that he was a bully, Jeb claimed to have no recollection of such incidents.)

The first outlines of the more attractive Jeb portrait—the one that would come to define his political persona—weren't rendered until he spent a winter abroad in central Mexico during his senior year. Despite his lackluster grades, he had always been smart, and Jeb picked up the language more quickly than his fellow exchange students. He used his Spanish to score tequila for the group and flirt with local muchachas—until, one Sunday afternoon, he met the muchacha who would finally pry him out of his stupor of mediocrity.

The story of how Jeb met Columba Garnica Gallo would take on many romantic incarnations over the years, but the Bushes' favorite version begins many centuries earlier in Spain. There was a popular courtship ritual in those days in which, after Catholic Mass, young bachelors and bachelorettes would form concentric circles around a town's plaza and stroll in opposite directions, stealing glances at one another. "My version of that story that's been told thousands of times over the last six or seven centuries is that my wife was driving a car around the town square and I was in the town square," Jeb would recall. "She looked out the back of her car. She was in the backseat and I saw her." Columba was half a torso shorter than Jeb, with dark eyes and a mesmerizing voice, and he was immediately lovestruck. "She was very alluring, very mysterious . . . I was captivated."

Columba was in love, too — but she had reservations. She detected in Jeb the laziness of a young man for whom life is all one leisurely downhill drift, and sensed the recklessness that comes with the training wheels affixed by elite social status. Where other girlfriends might have found such qualities fun and alluring and contented themselves with a fling, Columba made clear to Jeb that he would have to shape up if he wanted to truly win her over. And so he returned to Andover that spring with a new sense of purpose, earning straight As for his final trimester as he sought to impress the *novia* he'd left behind. "She kept me wrapped around her little finger," he said later. "I just couldn't keep her out of my thoughts. It was all consuming. I wrote her almost every day."

Upon graduating, Jeb forsook Yale, the Ivy of choice for three generations of Bushes, and enrolled instead at the University of Texas at Austin in order to be closer to Columba. Having survived Andover's academic boot camp, he cruised through his course work in Latin American studies, easily making Phi Beta Kappa between regular jaunts across the border. Jeb's mother, Barbara, was delighted with her son's sudden turnaround and called him at college one day to congratulate him. "He told me he had done it for Columba because he wanted to prove he was serious," she would later write. "She thought he was a rich man's son and a playboy."

Jeb returned home for Christmas break soon after that and told his family about his intentions to marry the Mexican girlfriend that none of them had met (and who still didn't speak much English). At first, it seemed to some in the family like just the sort of impetuous, immature decision Jeb would make in the interest of provocation or subversion. Barbara recorded her concern in a fretful diary entry: "How I worry about Jeb and Columba. Does she love him? I know when I meet her I'll stop worrying..."

Jeb proposed during the same Christmas break at a restaurant in Mexico City. He gave Columba a ring that his mother had helped him pick out; she gave him a ring with a peace symbol on it. On February 23, 1974, they married in a modest ceremony at a University of Texas chapel to which Jeb had invited none of his friends. Whatever concerns the Bush family might have harbored about the marriage at the outset, none of them could deny Columba's positive influence on Jeb. "I was struck by lightning by my now wife," he would recall. "I got smarter."

He also began to look at his family's connections and influence in a new light. By now his father had become one of the most prominent Republicans in Washington, doing stints as President Nixon's envoy to the United Nations, and as chairman of the Republican National Committee, where he was beginning to draw chatter about a presidential run. Jeb still told himself that he wanted to be his own man, rise on his own merits. But surely there was no harm in using his name as a launching pad.

If Jeb had once fancied himself the nobly conflicted heir to royalty — reluctant to take his place in the monarchy, and longing for a simpler life — he was now developing a sense of destiny. He was ready to claim his birthright.

Marco Rubio did not grow up with a birthright waiting to be claimed at his leisure. In 1979, he was eight years old and living with his family of six in a compact one-story house on a working-class block a few miles off the Las Vegas Strip. Space was tight, and everybody could hear everything. Often, in the middle of the night, Rubio would awake to the familiar jingle of keys in the front door as his dad returned from another sixteen-hour workday.

His parents had fled their native Cuba before he was born, and they now worked themselves ragged in a relentless effort to carve out advantages for their kids. Rubio's mother, Oriales, worked as a maid at a nearby casino. His father, Mario, had done odd jobs and grunt work, toiled at an assembly plant, and dragged a vendor's cart through the streets. He fantasized about owning his own business, but every one of his attempts — the dry cleaner, the vegetable stand, the grocery store — failed or fell through. Instead, he took a full-time job as a bartender at a Vegas hotel, mixing drinks into the wee hours and sleeping while the sun was out.

Years later, as an adult with children of his own, Rubio would look back on his parents' daily sacrifices with a profound sense of gratitude — punctuated by occasional pangs of guilt — and conclude of his childhood, "I come from extraordinary privilege."

From an early age, Rubio displayed a gift for gab and a penchant for performance. At ten years old, he recruited his cousin and sister to form a singing group with him; their repertoire consisted of a single song by the Osmond Brothers to which they subjected their families over and over again. In high school, he enthusiastically entered the all-boys King Cobra talent show, where he gained a reputation as a ham. One year, he adopted a pompous, swaggering stage character as he belted out a Lionel Richie ballad, and then stormed off the stage in faux-*divo* mode, spiking the microphone on the ground as he left. Another year, he stripped down to perform a Chippendales-style dance routine with his buddies, showing off washboard abs that would be immortalized in the school yearbook. On the football field, Rubio was an undersized defensive back who relied on his confidence and hustle to succeed, lithely swerving around the much bigger bodies in his way, and peacocking in such a manner that often convinced observers he was one of the best players on the field, even when he wasn't.

But despite his outgoing nature, Rubio was consumed with a sort of social wanderlust and a constant suspicion that he was surrounded by people who didn't like him. Once, while in junior high, he pleaded with his parents to send him to a nearby private Catholic school. They couldn't really afford it, but they knew that education was important, so they scraped together the tuition money and sent him off. He didn't last a week with the stuffy uniforms and competitive academics before he began begging to transfer back to the public school just across the street. Every day, as he watched his old classmates file into the modest, boxy building, Rubio would wrestle with the restless feeling that he didn't belong anywhere—the first pangs of a nagging status anxiety that would follow him all the way to the heights of American political power.

In 1985, Rubio's family moved to Miami at the height of the so-called Cuban miracle—a massive influx of exiles that was infusing the city's DNA with a distinct entrepreneurial drive. In heavily Cuban neighborhoods like Little Havana, Hialeah, and West Miami, it was common for the vehicles that lined the streets to be plastered up and down with commercial decals, proudly announcing to one and all that these *camiones* and *furgones* were driven by business owners. Rubio soon became acutely aware that his parents did not belong to the celebrated league of the self-employed.

Meanwhile, at his new high school, Rubio was mocked for his crisp polo shirts and "American" accent. The other students called him a gringo. The next year he transferred to South Miami High, where he found he got along best with his black classmates. Still, he never quite felt that he fit in with them either. At the end of each day, his friends would return to the predominantly black South Miami, and he would trudge home to Cuban West Miami. He spent most of his evenings alone.

By senior year, his varsity football credentials were his only ticket out of a high school where just 14 percent of the last graduating class had gone on to college. His shot at a scholarship made him one of the luckiest kids in his school, but his small frame and mediocre 2.1 grade point average meant he was not headed for a powerhouse state university. He ended up at a tiny 550-student religious college in Missouri that was on the verge of losing accreditation. Here, too, he struggled academically, and he loathed the static nature of small-town life. He left after a year, and following a short-lived stint at a community college, he finally landed at the University of Florida. The high tuition and absence of a scholarship meant that he constantly struggled with money, sharing a tiny one-bedroom apartment and turning down invitations to join fraternities because he couldn't afford to pay the dues. At one point, he was so hard up for cash that he nearly had to drop out.

But even as he barely managed to eke out a degree in political science, Rubio refused to settle, or to stay put. He wasn't yet sure where he was going, but he knew he needed to keep moving his feet to get there.

A few days before Christmas in 2012, Rubio glanced at his iPhone and noticed a voice mail from his mom. He tapped play.

"Tony," she said, speaking in Spanish and calling him by the nickname—short for Antonio—he had gone by as a kid. "Some loving advice from the person who cares for you most in the world: don't mess with the immigrants, my son. Please, don't mess with them... They're human beings just like us, and they came for the same reason we came. To work. To improve their lives. So please, don't mess with them."

Of course, Rubio thought. It was only appropriate that it had come to this.

Once contained to a small contingent of pesky politicos in Coral Gables, the lobbying campaign to get him on board with the Senate's big immigration overhaul had become inescapable. When Rubio was in Washington, Senate colleagues like Dick Durbin were cornering him at the Capitol gym during early-morning workouts and bathing him in flattery as they talked about how *honored* and *overjoyed* they would be to have him join the gang of lawmakers drafting the legislation. Meanwhile, that hundred-yard call sheet maintained by his aides was filled with queries from reporters who wanted to know what he was going to do about immigration. And now his own mother was twisting his arm.

Rubio knew he had no choice but to join the fray. It might end up being a political loser for him—in fact, he thought it probably would be—but if he sat out this fight, he worried that he wouldn't be able to look his mom in the eye (or himself in the mirror, for that matter). He really did care about the immigrants suffering in America's shadows— *los pobrecitos,* his mom called them—and he figured this was as good a hill as any to risk dying on. The next month, he announced his desire to tackle immigration in a splashy interview with the *Wall Street Journal.*

Navarro and her Biltmore compatriots were elated. "Marco's very smart and very astute, and he has a deliberative process that he goes through, but he has a strong internal compass that tells him where north is," she gushed after learning the news. The reaction from the national news media was even more laudatory.

One day in February, Rubio got his hands on a copy of the new issue of *Time* magazine and tried to contain his euphoria as he studied its cover. There was the familiar red border around the edges, the tall lettering of the title across the top, and—right smack-dab in the middle—a beautifully lit, masterfully choreographed portrait of him (yes, *him!*) striking a square-shouldered pose that exuded power and authority.

He adored the photo, but even better was the imposing, bright-yellow headline stamped across his torso with the force of a gavel-pounding verdict:

THE REPUBLICAN SAVIOR:
HOW MARCO RUBIO BECAME THE NEW VOICE OF THE GOP.

Chapter Three

Battle Hymn of the Bleeding Heart Conservatives

While the news cycle gods were busy anointing a new Republican savior, Paul Ryan returned to Washington in a punishing fall from grace.

It had been weeks since the end of the 2012 election, but the stink of defeat still clung to him. The typically genial congressman was churlish and irritable—gloomily stalking the Capitol with headphones in his ears to avoid unwanted conversation, and sarcastically snapping at colleagues without warning. Before Mitt Romney had tapped him as his running mate, Ryan existed in the collective Washington mind as the bright, conservative budget wonk with a reputation for seriousness. Now? He was the plucky little sidekick who had ridden shotgun on a campaign that came to define all that was wrong with the modern Republican Party.

Worst of all, Ryan seemed eternally doomed to relive one of the most gut-wrenching experiences of his life, because everywhere he went people kept asking him the same question about the campaign: what did you learn?

Any honest answer to that question would necessarily take him back to perhaps the worst moment of the race.

It was late one afternoon in September 2012, and Ryan's DC-9 campaign jetliner was about to take off when the links began landing in his aides' inboxes. "SECRET VIDEO," the headline shouted from the screens on their smartphones. "Romney Tells Millionaire Donors What He REALLY Thinks of Obama Voters." As the plane's engines revved, campaign staffers began frantically forwarding the MotherJones.com article to one another and hunching over their colleagues' shoulders, squinting to get a better look. By the time the video loaded, the plane was ascending into the sky and a sense of panic was settling in among the Republican vice presidential nominee and his team.

The clandestinely recorded video, taken at a Boca Raton fundraiser, showed an impatient-sounding Mitt Romney, his voice taking on a metallic quality as he laid out what appeared to be his unfiltered view of the electorate to a room full of donors.

"There are forty-seven percent of the people who will vote for the president no matter what," Romney hissed. "All right, there are forty-seven percent who are with him, who are dependent on government, who believe that they are victims, who believe the government has a responsibility to care for them, who believe they are entitled to health care, to food, to housing, to you name it. That that's an entitlement. And the government should give it to them. And they will vote for this president no matter what..."

The video cut off before its conclusion as smartphones and portable Internet air cards on board lost service in the sky; Ryan and his team would have to wait until the in-flight wireless kicked in above ten thousand feet before they could fully assess the damage done to their campaign. But everyone could already tell it would be devastating: the video had gone viral on Paul Ryan's own airplane within minutes of its appearance on the Internet. There was no telling how fast it was traveling down on the ground

"Paul was fucking livid," one Ryan aide who was on the plane later told me. "He was apoplectic. He couldn't believe it. Obviously, it was a dumb thing to say and obviously it was bad politically." But there was another reason for the good-natured Wisconsinite's rage.

Since joining the presidential ticket in August, Ryan had been working on a major campaign address about poverty in the tradition of Jack Kemp, his onetime political idol and a self-proclaimed "bleeding heart conservative." For inspiration, his staff had asked the Jack

Kemp Foundation to send them every speech the former congressman and vice presidential nominee had ever given on the subject, and
Ryan had one of his speechwriters, Stephen Spruiell, working on a
draft. Ryan's vision was to make the poverty address the grand finale
of a gutsy campaign swing through poor, urban neighborhoods that
the GOP hadn't reached since the Depression-era shantytowns that
lined the Hudson River were named after Herbert Hoover. He
thought it would send a message that a Romney administration would
not forget about the poor once it reached the White House.

But as the election wore on, and Ryan found himself ping-ponging
from one identical Midwest swing state stop to the next, it became
increasingly obvious that the campaign commandos had no interest
in letting him stray from the poll-tested, focus-grouped, statistics-
soaked schedule they had him on. The number crunchers in Boston
believed that every hour spent on inner-city photo ops would be a lost
opportunity to rally middle-class suburbanites who might actually
vote for them. And whenever Ryan tried to get Romney's consultants
to sign off on his idea for a big poverty speech, they treated him like
an irritating six-year-old who kept asking for a unicorn for his
birthday.

Now, with this "47 percent" video threatening to define their entire
campaign, Ryan knew that any chance he had of getting out his
desired message in a genuine, pathbreaking way had evaporated. Even
if the campaign did green-light the speech, it would seem like a cynical stunt performed as an act of repentance for Romney's rhetoric.

"It's going to look totally reactive now," Ryan seethed to his staff.
"It's going to look totally insincere."

And there was nothing Ryan hated more than looking insincere.

There was a part of Ryan that wanted to ream out the Boston operatives with a big fat "I told you so," to tell Mitt that this was amateur
hour, and to insist that he get a seat at the strategy table going forward. But then the running mate received his damage control instructions for the next day. He was to don a blazer, perch himself in front
of an appropriately patriotic-looking backdrop in Reno, Nevada, and
do a series of local news interviews in which he would repeat the talking points he was given: Mitt's comments may have been inarticulate,

but his broader point was that "under the Obama economy, government dependency is up and economic stagnation is up."

Ryan bit his tongue and dutifully agreed. He was *happy* to do it.

In the days following the "47 percent" leak, Ryan felt lost—adrift in his own campaign. The void of vision in Romney's operation had always bothered him, but now it was proving to be poisonous to their prospects. They were so busy attacking President Obama all the time that they had failed to articulate a positive message of their own— and now they were being defined by off-the-cuff comments made behind closed doors.

Frustrated and restless, Ryan sent a note to Peter Wehner, a prominent Republican speechwriter and an old friend. When Ryan had first joined the ticket Wehner had emailed him with some friendly advice: "You may only get one bite at the apple. Make it count." Now, the disgruntled veep candidate vented to his friend that he feared he was squandering his time on the national stage by parroting political platitudes. Ryan expressed particular exasperation with his repeated, failed attempts to get buy-in from campaign headquarters for a big poverty speech.

Wehner responded with a suggestion: "Just do the speech, and make them stop you."

So Ryan did. He informed Mitt's band of consultants that he was moving forward with his plan, and would be giving a speech in October centered on poverty. If they had any thoughts on the event, they were welcome to share them. It was a relatively mild act of rebellion compared to Sarah Palin's 2008 antics, but it was as close to "going rogue" as Ryan would get during the campaign.

As it turned out, though, Ryan didn't need to do much convincing. As he had bitterly predicted when he first saw the video, the campaign was much more enthusiastic about the idea of a poverty speech in the aftermath of "47 percent," and they were now eager to work something out. A big inner-city campaign swing was out of the question, but they proposed a compromise to Ryan: he could give the speech in Cleveland, and hold an off-the-record roundtable with community leaders who worked with the poor—but the campaign would have to vet all of it.

To put together the event, Ryan enlisted the help of Bob Woodson, a seventy-five-year-old civil rights leader and community organizer whom he had met when he first moved to Washington. Woodson went to work compiling a list of black ministers, homeless shelter volunteers, and halfway-house owners that he thought Ryan should meet. It was a motley lot, and most of them, Woodson later acknowledged with some pride, were "ex-something: ex–drug addicts, ex-alcoholics, ex-convicts."

When the list was turned over to the Romney campaign and the Secret Service for approval, "it was like the machines exploded," a Ryan aide later told me. "There were so many red flags—guys that had multiple felonies in their background. And they kept coming back and picking out names, saying, 'Absolutely not, we cannot have this person.'"

Woodson, who was no fan of Romney's and felt he was doing an unappreciated favor to the campaign, quickly grew tired of the meddling. At one point, when an operative was inquiring about one of his friends' criminal record, Woodson exploded.

"Do you guys know *anything* about poverty?" he demanded. "This is where these guys come from! They are working with the poor because they had hit rock bottom."

The substance of the speech itself was also caught in a tug-of-war between Romney's campaign strategists, who wanted to turn it into a sharp indictment of President Obama's failure to help the poor, and Woodson, who thought the speech should be forward-looking and nonpartisan.

"They were sending me copies of Paul's speech, and it was standard campaign stump, bashing Obama…And I said, 'I'm not going to bring my people there to sit and listen to them trash Obama, because they may have voted for him!'" Woodson told me. After several frustrating drafts, he considered pulling the plug on the whole thing. "I said, 'Man, forget it.'"

Finally, Ryan called him up and begged for patience. "Look, work with me here," he pleaded. Woodson relented, and in the end the final draft of the speech contained just one polite jab at the president by name.

"There was always tension between Romney and Ryan," Woodson later told me. "Paul won't say it, but I know firsthand there was tension there. Paul wanted to do more events going to lower-income communities, but according to Romney's campaign, that would have taken them 'off message.' The whole message of the Romney campaign was to demonize Obama. That's why they lost—thank God."

On October 24, the day of the speech, Ryan slipped into a high-ceilinged backstage room at Waetjen Auditorium, on the campus of Cleveland State University, with a small group of aides and Secret Service agents. No reporters. About a dozen of Woodson's grassroots poverty fighters were waiting for him. They took turns telling stories from the front lines of the losing war on poverty, recounting their own struggles with addiction and homelessness, and testifying of redemption. As the meeting wrapped up and Ryan prepared to depart to deliver his speech, Paul Grodell, a tattooed minister who had arrived at the meeting on his Harley, asked the candidate if he could lay hands on him and pray.

Ryan looked momentarily panicked, but then he shrugged. "I'm Catholic," he responded, smiling nervously. "But I'm cool with that."

Secret Service agents tensed up as the group surrounded Ryan, and Grodell placed his hands on his shoulders—inches away from the candidate's neck. Ryan made the sign of the cross, and the minister called on the power of God to give the candidate strength, to help him fulfill his divine mission. He prayed specifically for God to help Ryan serve those who were languishing in poverty. When the group said "Amen," they opened their eyes to find Ryan struggling to hold back tears.

In those first, miserable weeks after the 2012 election, Ryan found his thoughts returning often to that private prayer in Cleveland. It was one of the rare memories from the campaign that evoked a clarity of purpose, rather than a sense of helpless frustration. "To me, that moment is how the things we believe in, and what we're trying to do, can really revitalize our country," he would later tell me.

As people continued to ask him the same irritating campaign-related question—"What did you learn?"—Ryan soon realized that this was his answer. For a man who had spent his congressional career focused primarily on budget deficits, the idea of using his position to directly defend the cause of the poor and needy felt like a revelation. The prospect began to pull him out of his funk.

One day, while speaking with a close aide over the phone, Ryan recounted the meeting in Cleveland and called it the most powerful experience he had had on the campaign trail. He also said he felt strongly that he needed to act on it.

"This is my next 'Roadmap,'" Ryan told the aide, referring to the name of his career-making budget proposals. "I want to figure out a way for conservatives to come up with solutions to poverty. I have to do this."

Paul Ryan's life came into focus late one morning in Janesville, Wisconsin, in the summer of 1986. He was awoken at his family's suburban home by a frantic phone call from his father's secretary. "Do you know where your dad is?" she asked. "He's got clients here."

His mother was out of town and his brother had already left for work, so Ryan drowsily made his way to his parents' bedroom. When he pushed open the door, he found his dad's lifeless body on the bed.

The loss of his father would become the defining experience of Ryan's young life, melting and remolding his psyche in myriad ways. It shattered his faith in God, pushed him to grapple with his own mortality, and shaped his views of civil society and the social safety net. But one result of the tragedy came to define him more than anything else: it sharpened and enhanced Ryan's sense of personal ambition.

A few days after his dad died, Ryan went for a long, late-night run and ended up on his back in the middle of a field, staring up at the stars. "I decided right then and there that I needed to step up," he wrote in his 2014 book, *The Way Forward*. "The way I thought about it was 'sink or swim,' and I decided I was going to swim like hell. I wouldn't wallow. I wouldn't let the sadness and self-pity pull me down."

As a perception-conscious politician, Ryan was savvy enough to recognize that overly ambitious officeholders risk summoning images of Machiavelli or Brutus. And so he took pains in his book to cast himself as a just-like-you everydude who fell into a political career only because of his nerdy interest in economics. But many who were close to Ryan as he bounded from adolescence into early adulthood told me that he had a laser-like focus on résumé building and ladder climbing. The year after his dad died, he ran for class president and won. He began closely following the conservative heroics of the Reagan era in the news, and he started taking his workouts more seriously.

Looking back on that time, Father Randy Timmerman, the Ryan family's longtime priest, recalled Paul as a young man in a hurry after his dad's death. "It may have increased his drive, but it may also have inspired urgency," Father Timmerman said. "To act, to take the chance, to step out." The priest also noted that Ryan was "pretty—what's the right word?—*religious* about exercise. You know what I mean? And that certainly comes from an awareness of the family genetics that he received." Later, when Ryan was a famous politician, his obsessive iron pumping and devotion to P90X would become one of the goofier aspects of his public image, especially after he posed for a widely mocked workout-themed photo shoot in *Time,* sporting a backwards cap and grinning as he flexed his biceps. But for Ryan it wasn't really about vanity, it was about staying alive as long as he could. His father, grandfather, and great-grandfather had all died before they were sixty, and he didn't know how much time he would have to make his mark.

The phenomenon of "eminent orphans"—children for whom the loss of a parent becomes a propellant toward greatness—has been studied by psychologists. In his book *David and Goliath,* author Malcolm Gladwell highlights studies that show that one-third of U.S. presidents throughout history and a staggering 67 percent of British prime ministers in the nineteenth and early twentieth centuries lost at least one parent when they were young. What's more, a survey of encyclopedias found that of the 573 people who merited an entry longer than one column, nearly half had to bury a parent before they reached twenty years old. When I told Ryan about these figures one morning during an interview twenty-eight years after his father's death, he grew quiet at first. "Really?" he asked. "I never heard that."

After thinking for a moment, he said, "It's true. It makes you scrappy and tough. Makes you a self-starter. You don't really have a choice. You just kind of got to go." He paused. It was as though the numbers confirmed something he had long known about himself. "That's interesting—it makes you resilient, too."

What was unique about Ryan's youthful thirst for world conquering was that it manifested itself with peculiar politeness. His was not a sweaty, macho ambition; even as he plotted a big future for himself, he was well-mannered, patient, and even acquiescent to those around him. In a bit of trivia that would become a mainstay in the many profiles written about Ryan, his high school classmates voted him "biggest brownnoser." The superlative was a friendly act of razzing from his peers, but it wasn't an anomaly. Friends, acquaintances, colleagues, and competitors at virtually every stage of his life and career would describe Ryan in terms that suggest that the Joseph A. Craig High School class of 1988 had him pegged. He was a "Boy Scout," a "team player," a "real diligent kid," a "respectful young man," a "suck-up."

This strain of Ryan's personality could also be traced back to his father's death. At a get-together after the funeral, one of his dad's best friends pulled him aside and told him that it would fall on him to become the man of the house. Ryan had grown protective of his mom in recent years as his dad's struggle with alcoholism cast a shadow over their family, and so he took this charge seriously. From that moment on, there was little time for the careless high jinks and petty rebellions that were typical of most kids his age. "I kind of had to grow up faster than most," Ryan told me.

This set up the defining tension of Ryan's rise: by the time he left for college at Miami University in Ohio, he had become an eager-to-please model of nice-guyness who was also driven to make a dent in history. On the surface, those two reflexes might have seemed incompatible; few revolutionary figures, after all, have been known for their good-natured temperaments. (See: Steve Jobs, Napoleon.) But Ryan channeled these competing impulses to great effect.

In college, he made a project of befriending Richard Hart, the sole conservative economics professor on campus. "He would come to the office quite a bit, and very rarely to ask any questions about the course material," Hart recalled. Instead, the student peppered the professor with earnest queries about Austrian economics, then politics, and eventually philosophy—hanging on Hart's every word as though the man were a mountaintop guru in possession of the secrets to the universe. Along the way, the professor wrote a few glowing letters of recommendation for Ryan, and helped set him up with his first Capitol Hill internship after graduating, in the office of Senator Bob Kasten.

Ryan, who seemed most in his element when he was under someone's wing, had a knack for making friends with important and connected people wherever he was, and Hart was the first in a long line of men who would count him as their protégé. But Ryan didn't turn to just anyone for advice; he distinguished himself as a connoisseur of well-chosen role models, a savvy collector of strategic father figures. From conservative luminaries like Bill Bennett and Kemp to veteran colleagues in Congress and eventually the Republican Party's presidential nominee, Ryan's mentors tended to be people who could get him places.

Meanwhile, Ryan conducted his life in college as though for the benefit of future campaign vetters. He joined Delta Tau Delta and took part in some mild frat boy antics—once accidentally shooting a firework into a rival fraternity's house, starting a fire—but he mostly kept the partying PG-rated, and he was never so hungover on Sunday mornings that he couldn't get up early and watch the political talk shows.

Ryan graduated from college and moved to Washington in 1991, but after a short entry-level stint on a congressional committee ended with his boss losing reelection, he found himself juggling part-time jobs as a fitness instructor and a waiter at a Capitol Hill Mexican restaurant called Tortilla Coast. He would later write in his book that he considered chucking it all and following through on his original postcollegiate fantasy of moving to Colorado and becoming a ski bum. But those who knew him at the time said this was never really in the cards.

Joe Mcalear, a fellow waiter at Tortilla Coast, told me that Ryan always seemed acutely aware of how his actions might influence a future career in politics. After their shifts ended at night, the restaurant's staff would take their tips to a nearby pub called Irish Times, where they drank beer and listened to an amateur folksinger who perched himself on top of the bar and cycled through a narrow repertoire of songs. Their favorite drinking game required each person to assume the identity of one of the musician's go-to artists—James Taylor, Simon and Garfunkel, the Beatles—and chug his drink once his song came up. The would-be troubadour's usual rotation was predictable enough to get most of them drunk most nights, but Ryan was always careful not to get too far beyond buzzed. "He was, like, the Boy Scout," Mcalear realled.

The extent of Ryan's ambitions became clear one day while they were discussing their taxes. Mcalear had moved from Virginia to the District in the middle of the year and was thinking about fudging on his returns so that he wouldn't have to file to two different states. Ryan was aghast.

"Oh, no, no!" Ryan protested. "That's how they get you! They get you on the taxes! You gotta make sure you got your taxes in order because they'll look that up."

Mcalear was confused. "What the—who finds me? What are you talking about?"

"Yo, politics!" Ryan, twenty-three, responded. "That's always how they get you. You've always got to get your tax records in order if you're going to run for office."

Bob Woodson was skeptical when he first got the phone call from Ryan a few weeks after the 2012 election. Fresh off the worst loss of his political career, the congressman had apparently decided that for his next act, he would recast himself as a champion of the poor, and he was asking Woodson to act as his Sherpa—guiding him through the rough terrain of America's poverty-stricken, drug-ravaged inner cities, and introducing him to the ministers, volunteers, and activists who were making progress at the grassroots level.

A spry, swaggering veteran of the civil rights movement who parted with black leaders in the seventies over the issue of forced busing, Woodson had spent the past several decades in Washington, lobbying on behalf of the needy as head of a nonprofit called the Center for

Neighborhood Enterprise. But doing God's work in America's petty, dysfunctional, status-obsessed capital had left him less than idealistic when it came to politicians' motives.

Early on in his DC career, Woodson discovered that his communitarian, up-by-the-bootstraps approach to combating social ills appealed to Republicans. And while he was no right-winger—he described himself as a "radical pragmatist" when it came to politics—he was eager to do what he could to focus the attention of the powerful on the plight of the poor, regardless of party affiliation. He would often tell friends that he saw himself as a matchmaker for modern-day Josephs and Pharaohs—connecting the righteous but obscure with the rich and powerful, in hopes that together they would bring about miracles. If the only Pharaohs who were interested happened to be conservatives, so be it.

But Woodson wasn't in Washington long before he noticed an odious pattern: some Republican looking to gain cheap outreach points by allying himself with a black elder statesman of the civil rights era would seek out his "counsel" in antipoverty policy making; Woodson would oblige by setting up a couple of visits to poor urban neighborhoods; and, after a photo op or two, the politician would promptly lose interest, having checked his "noblesse oblige" box for the year. Average number of poor people helped during these episodes: zero.

In one emblematic example, Newt Gingrich recruited Woodson to help him sell the Republicans' welfare reform proposals ahead of the 1994 elections. Woodson organized a diverse cast of former welfare recipients and advocates for the poor to appear in commercials for the party on the promise that they would get a seat at the policy making table once Republicans took control of the House. "Next thing I know, Newt hires a white liberal from Atlanta to come and do minority outreach for him...and instead of helping us raise money, he sets up a separate nonprofit to raise millions of dollars, hires the friends of his colleagues—all white—and he reaches out to liberals and abandons us," Woodson told me.

He said the cycle repeated itself so many times that he took to morbidly boasting, "I've been screwed by the most famous and most influential people here in Washington."

Woodson wanted to believe that Ryan was different. He had first met the congressman when he was a young aide to Jack Kemp in the early nineties, and he respected what Ryan had tried to do in the Romney campaign. He had been especially impressed when word got back to him that after the election Ryan personally wrote thank-you notes to every one of the people who had attended the roundtable in Cleveland. But Woodson had long ago stopped trusting every wide-eyed Republican who came to him with a spiel about looking out for "the least among us." So he devised a plan to test Ryan's motives.

"Why don't you come with me to Pastor Holloway's ministry?" Woodson offered.

Nestled deep in DC's southeast quadrant—far away from the brightly colored row houses and trendy eateries frequented by the political class—Holloway's homeless shelter functioned as a combination hotel and self-improvement seminar for the down-and-out. At Graceview, vagrant addicts and ex-felons were given apartments, enrolled in counseling and drug treatment, and provided with assistance in finding gainful employment—but they were expected to pull their weight. They had to stay sober, pass drug tests, keep their rooms clean, and show up for work; as long as they followed the rules, they were allowed to stay for as much time as they needed to get back on their feet. Since its founding in the early nineties, Graceview had become an oft-cited model of the teach-a-man-to-fish approach to social welfare, contrasting sharply—conservatives liked to point out—with state-funded shelters where residents were allowed to drink on the premises and the facilities often became magnets for drug dealers.

For Woodson's purposes, the visit to Graceview would give him a chance to see what the shelter's residents—consistently keen judges of character in his experience—thought of Ryan's sincerity.

"The criminal lifestyle makes you very discerning," Woodson later told me. "You can't lip-synch authenticity around people like that."

The day of their scheduled visit arrived, and as the two men toured the shelter with Pastor Holloway, Woodson had to admit that Ryan made a good first impression. The congressman had come without a camera-wielding aide in tow, and he spent the bulk of the tour asking detailed, insightful questions about how the program worked, in the manner of an earnest pupil striving for extra credit. The stilted conversations he tried to drum up with the residents made it clear that he was outside his comfort zone—but at least he lacked the ego and smarm that seemed to ooze out of so many of his congressional colleagues like a festering pus. He actually seemed as though he was really trying to connect with the people here.

This guy might actually be for real, Woodson thought.

A few weeks after the tour, they went to dinner at Charlie Palmer's, an upscale steak house on Capitol Hill. As they dined on fussily plated protein, Woodson enacted phase two of his sincerity test for Ryan: an aggressive, in-your-face grilling intended to fluster the congressman and expose any ulterior motives he was harboring.

"Why the hell do you care about poor people?" Woodson demanded during the dinner.

When Ryan met the question with a confused beat of silence, Woodson pressed harder.

"Really! I want to know why you care. You're a political celebrity. Everywhere you go, people want to talk to you. You don't need this. The campaign is over. So, why do *you* care?"

Ryan was taken aback by the sudden hostility, but he responded calmly with his trademark earnestness: "I'm concerned about this country."

He explained that he was worried the identity politics and class warfare that President Obama had so effectively deployed during his reelection bid were threatening to permanently impede the country's ability to tackle big problems, like poverty an issue where he believed that good-faith members of both parties could work together constructively.

"We're splintering," Ryan said. "We're being divided. I'm worried about that, and I want to do something about it. But I've got some gaps in my knowledge, and I'm hoping you can help me out with that."

This was part of the story, but it was really only the job interview truth.

In reality, Ryan's personal motives for this new antipoverty push were marked by a combination of genuine idealism and calculated self-interest. "Paul's really sincere," one former Ryan aide told me, echoing others who had worked with the congressman. "But I mean, he's still a politician."

True, he was wrestling with a spiritual unrest that had lingered since that backstage prayer during the campaign, and he felt called to commit his influence and energies to helping the poor. But if he was being honest with himself, Ryan had to admit that he was concerned about his political profile as well.

Much like the GOP itself, Ryan was suffering a political identity crisis. He sensed that the winds in Washington were shifting away from the austerity politics he had spent years championing. Back in 2009, when he authored his first deficit-hacking budget, it earned him rave reviews from figures on both sides of the aisle, where Washington rules dictated that statesmen must pay lip service to sound fiscal policy. Ryan's plan was "gutsy" and "courageous" and "visionary" and "serious-minded." Three years later, though, the Left had just won an election in part by subjecting his proposals to a populist pummeling, while many on the right complained that his budgets didn't go far enough in shrinking the federal government. (Ryan was particularly vexed by the criticism from his own side, lamenting privately to friends, "I used to be a bomb thrower; I was the Tea Party before there *was* a Tea Party. Now I'm just part of the establishment.")

In the Darwinian evolution that American politics was now undergoing, Ryan was choosing to adapt rather than die—and he wanted to bring his party along with him. In this new political era, Republicans would have to work harder than ever to prove they were interested in the problems of the so-called 47 percent. What better way to save the soul of his party—and his own career—than by embarking on a listening tour in America's forgotten ghettos and barrios?

Ryan didn't say any of this at Charlie Palmer's, of course. But his earnest monologue wasn't what won Woodson over anyway.

What did it for Woodson was Ryan's reaction to the steady stream of schmoozers that approached their table throughout the evening to say hello to the newly famous congressman. Ryan was polite to the interrupting glad-handers, but he kept his focus trained consistently on Woodson and his other dining companions. By the end of the dinner, Woodson was *almost* convinced of Ryan's sincerity, but he had one more test: he demanded that the congressman pay a tithe of his time.

I can show you what's working on the ground, and introduce you to some people who are making a real difference in these communities, Woodson said. But you need to give me at least one day a month, where you leave the budget committee meetings and postpone the fund-raising phone calls, and spend some actual time visiting poor neighborhoods, meeting poor people.

Given the carefully guarded schedule of an in-demand member of Congress who also had a young family at home, Woodson knew this was no small ask. But Ryan readily agreed.

As the men shook hands, Woodson thought, *You better not screw me, too.*

On the evening of December 5, 2012, Ryan took the stage at the Mayflower Hotel in Washington to deliver his first speech since the election. He was the keynote speaker at the Kemp Leadership Award Dinner, named for the mentor who loomed over his life, and he had chosen this venue—a crowded ballroom full of Republican dignitaries and political reporters—to begin his atonement for the sins of the Romney campaign, and reintroduce himself to Washington as a champion of the poor.

"Both parties tend to divide Americans into 'our voters' and 'their voters,'" Ryan said that night. "Republicans must steer far clear of that trap. We must speak to the aspirations and anxieties of every American…We have a compassionate vision based on ideas that work, but sometimes we don't do a good job of laying out that vision. We need to do better."

Ryan offered little doubt about his new direction, using the word "poverty" fifteen times in the space of a twenty-minute speech—once every eighty seconds, on average—and declaring, "When Lyndon Johnson launched the war on poverty in 1964, he predicted we would eliminate poverty in thirty-five to fifty years. Here we are, forty-eight years later, and poverty is winning."

Marco Rubio also spoke at the dinner, sounding similar themes in his remarks, and together their speeches generated a flurry of headlines about the coming fight over the GOP's soul—and how these two most high-profile combatants were positioning themselves for 2016. Several commentators noted that Ryan's rhetoric about inclusiveness and compassion seemed like a less-than-subtle attempt at distancing himself from Mitt "47 percent" Romney.

The contrast, of course, was exactly what Ryan had been hoping for. But he also knew that throwing his party's ticket topper under the bus over a stupid gaffe wasn't going to reshape the Republican Party, reinvigorate his career, or shift the momentum in America's war on poverty. To accomplish that, he would have to do something that virtually nobody in Washington's gilded political class had done with any regularity in decades: start spending unchoreographed, unbuffered, unpublicized time with actual poor people.

Chapter Four

The Coroners

Paul Ryan wasn't the only Republican doing a postmortem. Shortly after the 2012 election, Reince Priebus, the chairman of the Republican National Committee, assembled five well-regarded party functionaries and charged them with diagnosing what had gone wrong for the GOP in the last election. Officially, the initiative was given the cheerful title "The Growth and Opportunity Project." Internally—and eventually in the press—it was referred to as "the autopsy."

The designated party coroners were all loyal partisans, with ties to the establishment and reputations in GOP circles for seriousness and competence. There was Ari Fleischer, the former Bush White House press secretary and now head of the Republican Jewish Coalition; Sally Bradshaw, a top Florida strategist and longtime adviser to Jeb Bush; Henry Barbour, nephew of Mississippi's beloved former governor and now a committeeman in the state party; Glenn McCall, an official in the South Carolina GOP; and Zori Fonalledas, a Republican committeewoman in Puerto Rico. Their assignment was to prepare a report that identified systemic weaknesses in the party and proposed solutions.

In another era, establishment fixtures like these would have been among the cigar-chomping cloakroom dwellers who hashed out the Grand Old Party's presidential nominations over stiff drinks and dirty jokes. But the influence of this political priesthood had been on the wane in both parties for decades. In the GOP especially, the power of establishment leaders had been decimated by the Supreme Court's 2009 *Citizens United* ruling and the subsequent rise of the Tea Party in 2010. With political spending now virtually unlimited and unregulated, the official party committees—which once held immense sway over fund-raising—were forced to compete for attention and influence with billionaire megadonors like the Koch brothers, conservative kingmakers on talk radio and cable, and well-funded Tea Party pressure groups like FreedomWorks. Some from the old guard had figured out how to stay in the game in this new era, most notably Karl Rove—the former Dubya strategist who had gone on to build a lavishly funded political organization, American Crossroads, and a multimedia pundit platform that made sure his voice mattered. But by and large, the party insiders had become something more like outsiders, left to compile their opinions in a PDF report and post it online in hopes that someone with real influence might read it and agree with them.

Fleischer was emblematic of the type the RNC had tapped for the autopsy. Once, he had been among the most high-profile Republicans in the country, delivering daily press briefings at the White House, where he rigorously defended the Iraq War and routinely denounced the press corps' coverage of the president. After leaving his post in 2003, he was a hot commodity on the political speaking circuit for a while, pulling in a reported $36,000 per speech. He penned a buzzy memoir and remained an ardent Bush defender on Sunday morning political talk shows.

Now he worked in a small office building shared with a local realty company in the quaint Westchester town of Bedford, New York. His desk overlooked a main road leading to the elementary school he had attended as a child. The walls of his office were adorned with tiny monuments to his past proximity to power: photos of Fleischer with the president on 9/11; a rendering of Fleischer in an old political cartoon; a framed cover of Fleischer's 2005 memoir, *Taking Heat*. He still went on CNN occasionally to talk politics, but he dreaded the commutes to Manhattan, so he performed his appearances from a makeshift studio the network had rigged in his house. These days, he made most of his money as a behind-the-scenes PR consultant in the professional sports industry.

Fleischer's self-imposed exile from Washington and distance from the new Wild West of conservative politics had left him richer and more rested—allowing him to sport a year-round tan and a wardrobe full of pricey designer suits—but considerably less influential within his party. And for a while, he didn't mind. "I was out," he told me. "I didn't want to do much TV. I would just look at [the political landscape] and shake my head at so much of the stuff. And then the longer I was out, the more I thought, 'You know what? I want to play, I want to go back, I want to see what I can do.'" After the 2012 election, he called Priebus and asked how he could help.

Fleischer undertook his assignment from the RNC with vigor. For months, he and the other coroners fanned out across the country to hold focus groups and listening sessions and pore over exit polls and survey data—and then they would reconvene every week on a conference call to discuss their findings.

What they found was depressing. In one focus group after another, they heard their party described as "out of touch" and full of "stuffy old men." Fleischer soon concluded that unless the GOP found a way to change this reputation, its future would be even bleaker than anyone realized. "You cannot come out of the 2008 and 2012 elections and think that Republicans have a strong future in presidential [races] unless we deal with the demographic changes," he said.

He became consumed with the question of how to alter the party's demographic destiny. After talking to pro-gay Republicans like Ana Navarro and Margaret Hoover both of whom served alongside him as CNN's in-house conservative voices, much to the consternation of many on the right—he became convinced that the party needed to cast off its image as uniformly opposed to same-sex marriage. For millions of younger voters, Fleischer believed, marriage was a "gateway" issue that would prevent them from even thinking about voting Republican.

During his weekly conference calls, Fleischer began adamantly arguing that their little commission should propose adopting a more inclusive stance on the marriage issue. Some of his fellow coroners were extremely resistant at first, worrying about how such a proposal would go over with conservatives, but eventually they arrived at a compromise. The final report contained no policy recommendation on the subject, but signaled that there should be room within the party for disagreement.

"For the GOP to appeal to younger voters, we do not have to agree on every issue, but we do need to make sure young people do not see the party as totally intolerant of alternative points of view," the final report would read. "Already, there is a generational difference within the conservative movement about issues involving the treatment and the rights of gays—and for many younger voters, these issues are a gateway into whether the party is a place they want to be."

As the months wore on, the coroners continued to probe their corpse for causes of death, conducting interviews with everyone from right-leaning suburban voters in Ohio to more unlikely sources of wisdom, like Howard Dean, the left-wing former governor of Vermont. By the end, the one thing they all agreed on—and the only explicit policy prescription that would make it into the report—was that Republicans had to get behind a legislative effort to produce a compassionate overhaul of U.S. immigration policy.

"As the five of us got into it, we realized that with so many of the things we were writing about—demographic changes in America, Republicans being more inclusive—immigration was the elephant in the room," Fleischer later recalled. "We couldn't talk about inclusiveness…and then ignore immigration. Otherwise, it would've rung hollow, I think."

They knew that their report wouldn't single-handedly infuse the entire population of conservative voters with newfound empathy for undocumented immigrants, but they hoped to create a "safe zone" for the GOP's secretly immigrant-friendly officeholders—those who had become too afraid to voice their support for reform, too intimidated by the Laura Ingrahams and Rush Limbaughs of the world. The coroners chose their words carefully, urging the party to "embrace and champion comprehensive immigration reform" and adding few other specifics. Altogether, they were proud of the work they had done and excited to present their findings. The autopsy was published in

March 2013, to much fanfare, with Priebus hyping the findings in a series of high-profile interviews and declaring a new era for the GOP. "Instead of driving around in circles on an ideological cul-de-sac," the coroners wrote in the tone-setting introduction, "we need a party whose brand of conservatism invites and inspires new people to visit us."

Large portions of the party revolted immediately.

Conservative activists viewed the report as an assault on the burgeoning power of the grass roots. Not only had the coroners called for surrender in the fights over immigration and gay rights, they had also proposed revamping the party's presidential nominating system with fewer debates and a condensed primary calendar. The goal was to spare the eventual 2016 nominee from the prolonged barrage of friendly fire that Romney had suffered in 2012. But these changes would make it harder for an insurgent candidate on a shoestring budget to break out.

The forces behind such conservative figures as Rand Paul and Rick Santorum dug in their heels. One anonymous Paul aide was quoted in the press warning that the procedural changes amounted to a "nuclear war with the grass roots." Santorum adviser John Brabender said the report was designed to boost "the wealthiest candidates."

Meanwhile, the religious Right was appalled at how the report called for increased tolerance of gays while making virtually zero reference to the conservative Christian movement that had been the backbone of the Republican Party for decades. The report contained no mention of so-called values voters, and the words "Christian," "marriage," and "abortion" were entirely absent from its text. Social conservative leaders considered the snub deeply troubling.

"The report didn't mention religion much, if at all," huffed Tim Wildmon, president of the American Family Association. "You cannot grow your party by distancing yourself from your base, and this report doesn't reinforce the values that attracted me and many other people into the Republican Party in the first place. It just talks about reaching out to other groups."

Among hard-core conservatives, there wasn't just disagreement with one or two points in the report—they objected to its fundamental premise. Limbaugh summed up the sentiment on the right during an on-air diatribe against the RNC's conclusions. "They think they've gotta rebrand, and it's all predictable. They gotta reach out to minorities. They gotta moderate their tone here and moderate their tone there. And that's not *at all* what they've gotta do," he bellowed. "The Republican Party lost because it's not conservative. It didn't get its base out in the 2012 election."

Fleischer and the other coroners were dismayed by the visceral backlash. They had anticipated some pushback but didn't expect their recommendations to be interpreted as a knife-in-back betrayal of their party's base or its founding principles. "We knew we'd hear from some conservatives," said Fleischer. "What was disheartening was that some people interpreted being more opening and welcoming and inclusive as changing our ideology."

Meanwhile, Priebus embarked on a nationwide tour touting the GOP's new direction. He waved around the autopsy in front of black and brown and nose-pierced young people, pledging that his penitent party had turned over a new leaf.

During one early stop at a black megachurch in the Brooklyn neighborhood of East New York, Priebus stood side by side with a prominent African American pastor—and in front of more journalists than black voters—as he preached outreach and inclusion, touting the RNC's plan to spend millions on a permanent political infrastructure that would employ Republican field staffers in minority-heavy communities. Still, he stressed that the RNC didn't have it all figured out yet.

"Today is about listening, and today is a start," he told reporters as he headed into the church for a private meeting with black Republican activists. As the doors closed, he could be heard asking the group, "The question we really want to hone in on is...what are the things you believe the Democrats are doing really well?"

Much of the motivation undergirding the GOP's hearts-and-minds campaign in America's black and Latino communities was genuinely idealistic. But there was also simple electoral arithmetic at play. "If you can steal enough votes from the other team's base you will win," Fleischer explained to me. As a model, he pointed to the gains Republicans had made recently with American Jewish voters, traditionally a reliable Democratic constituency. Back in 1992, George H. W. Bush had won just 11 percent of Jewish votes. By 2012, Romney won 30 percent. The expectation wasn't to turn these constituencies into permanent cornerstones of the new Republican coalition: it was simply to deprive the other side of the votes they needed. "If we can do this in the black community, and have similar success in the Hispanic community, we will doom the Democrats to defeat."

But as Fleischer observed the conservative backlash in the weeks that followed the release of the coroners' autopsy, he became increasingly convinced that no well-intentioned RNC commission would, on its own, be able to save the Republican Party from careering toward disaster. No rigorously prepared reports, or little-known RNC officials with unpronounceable names, or small-ball pilot programs conceived of in Washington were going to reverse the demographic tide crashing down on the party. What Republicans truly needed was a high-profile, singularly gifted leader capable of uniting the conservative movement with the young voters and people of color who made up the coalition of the ascendant.

Of course, every White House hopeful with a pulse and a plane ticket to New Hampshire would spend plenty of time in the sprint toward 2016 flapping their lips about "minority engagement" and "big-tent conservatism" and "returning to the party of Lincoln." But only one Republican in the winter of 2013 appeared willing to bet his own presidential prospects on the idea: Marco Rubio. And he would soon find that the stakes were even higher than he realized.

Chapter Five

Outreach

On the afternoon of January 28, 2013, so many reporters and photographers had crammed into the Senate TV gallery that when the C-SPAN camera zoomed out, the shot of the press conference was framed by rumpled journalists leaning enthusiastically forward, as though they were about to rush the lawmakers lined up behind the podium and hoist them into the air in celebration. After four years of covering a Congress gripped by an almost nihilistic dysfunction, the Capitol Hill press corps had before them something rather exotic: a bipartisan band of senators who wanted to actually *do something.* They were dubbed the Gang of Eight, and they were here to solve the nation's immigration crisis.

The star of the show was Marco Rubio—the Spanish-speaking Tea Party senator who was at least two decades younger than most of the comrades he had joined today. For the majority of the press conference, Rubio stood in silence, his hands clasped neatly in front of him as the geezers droned on. When his turn finally arrived, he stepped up to the podium to a frantic click-clack chorus of cameras that would persist throughout the entirety of his comments.

"I am clearly new to this issue in terms of the Senate," he said. "I'm not new to it in terms of my life. I live surrounded by immigrants. My neighbors are immigrants. My family is immigrants. I married into a family of immigrants. I see immigration every single day."

His cadence was measured and firm, his pace quick but coherent, his rhetoric compelling and lucid. He spoke of the need to adopt tougher security measures at the Mexican border, and to reform the process of legal immigration with an eye toward bolstering free enterprise—hitting each conservative note with just enough force before then striking a compassionate chord.

"We are dealing," Rubio said, "with eleven million *human beings* who are here undocumented—the vast and enormous majority of whom have come here in pursuit of what all of us would recognize as the American dream."

What deftness! What agility! What poise! Ah yes, this was their star, all right—the darling of the national media, in his element. The cameras click-clacked furiously as Rubio wrapped up his remarks and then retook his spot in the line of senators, confident and unfazed.

He was just getting started.

When Rubio's colleagues had persuaded him to join the Gang of Eight, they envisioned his role as ambassadorial in nature—venturing out into the wilds of the right-wing blogosphere and talk radio to pitch their immigration plan to the Tea Party. Rubio didn't quite see it that way himself: he viewed his primary function as representing conservative interests in the legislative process. Still, he had never been one to turn down an interview request from a friendly media outlet, and he felt quite confident in his ability to charm even the most ardent dissenter on the right. After all, these people *loved* him.

Rubio got started in earnest the day after the press conference, calling in to Rush Limbaugh's show to make his case for immigration reform. It wouldn't be an easy sell. Like most on the right, Limbaugh was dead set against any immigration plan that granted "illegals" a pathway to U.S. citizenship—something the Gang of Eight had already made clear would be part of any legislation they came up with. By and large, conservatives believed that allowing illegal immigrants to stay in the country amounted to granting "amnesty" to a bunch of criminals—and by signing on to the Senate's effort, Rubio had already violated this core tenet. But in doing so, he had extracted a major concession from the Democrats working on the Senate bill: the legislation would require that not a single green card would be dispensed until substantial improvements were made to the nation's border security and immigration enforcement.

Rubio wielded that accomplishment like a weapon as he entered Limbaugh's lion's den, forcefully arguing that it was better for conservatives like himself to be involved in the legislative process, rather than simply boycotting it on principle. "I'm just trying to do the best I can with what's already a tough situation," he told Limbaugh. "I pray it works out. I can't guarantee that it will, but we're gonna do our best." Rubio also displayed his characteristic optimism—and unrelenting confidence in his own persuasive abilities—by arguing that fixing the immigration system would eliminate one of the Democrats' favorite wedge issues, and allow Republicans to start converting these eleven million new Americans to the cause of conservatism.

"I am confident, I really am...that given a fair chance, I can convince most Americans, including Americans of Hispanic descent, that limited government and free enterprise is better for them...than big government is," Rubio said earnestly.

Limbaugh spent the fifteen-minute interview alternating between uncharacteristically polite pushback and effusive praise for the senator. While the host expressed skepticism that Democrats would actually negotiate in good faith, he told Rubio, "What you are doing is admirable and noteworthy." When the senator hung up, Limbaugh lavished praise on him for taking his pitch to the right-wing airwaves: "Is that guy good or what? Here's a guy who doesn't fear talk radio. He embraces it!" Rubio found a similarly warm reception in interviews that week with Sean Hannity and Mark Levin, the Right's other two biggest talk radio stars. He was getting the treatment of a beloved quarterback who had called a risky audible; some of the fans may have disagreed with the play, but they were still rooting for him. All of them were wearing the same colors.

But while Rubio was a vocal champion of the Senate's effort in the conservative media, he was relatively quiet inside the room where the lawmaking was getting done. In his two years in the Senate, he hadn't yet spent much time engaging in the mechanics of crafting legislation—and he was astounded by just how thoroughly the process was governed by personality quirks and petty ego trips. Often, as he looked around the table at his colleagues, he found himself wondering how these babbling blowhards had managed to win so many elections. *No wonder they can't get anything done here,* he thought.

In one session early on, Illinois Democrat Dick Durbin raised a legislative issue by relating the experience of "a constituent of mine" (he was always delivering anecdotes about one "constituent of mine" or another). He talked about a Mexican woman who had lived in the United States illegally for many years with her husband and kids, and whose papers were in order. After her mother died, she went back home to Mexico to attend the funeral, and when she tried to return to the United States she was caught at the border and deported, separating her indefinitely from her family.

"What about people like her?" Durbin wanted to know. Would their bill allow any relief for the recently deported who would have qualified for residency under the new law, and who had left family members living in the States?

The story tugged at Rubio's heartstrings, but he also knew how complicated it would get to begin allowing such people to cut the line of visa seekers. He considered the issue in silence for a moment, trying to formulate an opinion, but before he could say anything, John McCain piped up.

"You know what?" the Arizona Republican said. "That's a tough story, but she knew goddamn well that if she went back over that border she could get caught."

Rubio was startled by the senator's harshness. McCain had long presented himself as a model of compassion in the immigration debate. *So much for Mr. Touchy-Feely...*

Durbin was visibly irritated by the eruption, but Senator Chuck Schumer quickly stepped in to mediate. He acknowledged how difficult the woman's situation was, but then added, "John has a point. We can't legislate by anecdote."

Rubio would come to appreciate Schumer, a long-serving New York Democrat, for his pragmatism and love of deal making. Whereas McCain seemed constantly preoccupied with controlling as much of the process as possible inside the room and hoarding credit outside the room, Schumer seemed genuinely motivated by a desire to get something done. Rubio had bonded with the New Yorker over their shared disdain for the perpetually dissatisfied immigration activists who kept showing up at both senators' public events to wave signs and shout things at them because they had not perfectly conformed to their agenda. In private, Schumer would often boast mischievously about how he used the term "illegal immigrants"—over the strong objections of progressives, who preferred softer adjectives like "undocumented"—just because he knew it made the activists upset.

After Schumer resolved the dispute between McCain and Durbin, the issue was dropped and everyone agreed to move on—until Bob Menendez arrived. The New Jersey Democrat often missed these sessions, or showed up late to them, and his colleagues knew why. Conservative news sites had been antagonizing Menendez for months with vaguely sourced reports that he had cavorted with underage prostitutes during trips to the Dominican Republic—and he was often frazzled and preoccupied with efforts to debunk the claims, which he firmly denied. (Evidence would later emerge that the Cuban government was spreading the rumors in an effort to smear one of the most vocally anti-Castro members of the Senate.) When Menendez learned of Durbin's constituent, he was outraged that his colleagues were unwilling to make room for her situation in the bill, and he threatened, dramatically, to blow up the negotiations over it. This, too, would become a habit of his—something Rubio found endlessly frustrating (though occasionally amusing).

Though Rubio tended to stay quiet during these meetings, he often made a point of reiterating to his colleagues in the room that whatever reluctant restraint the conservative movement was exercising at the moment when it came to immigration, their surrender shouldn't be taken for granted.

"If you guys think they're going to go along with a bad bill just because they're scared of losing the Latino vote, you're crazy," he told the senators at one point.

Rubio said this mostly as a way of keeping the Democrats' political bravado in check—but he didn't entirely buy it himself. As he scanned the political landscape of 2013, he saw a Republican Party that was downright desperate to win back Hispanic voters, and getting a deal done on immigration was crucial. After all, there was a reason, Rubio thought, that he had been given such substantial leeway in the conservative press at the outset of this effort. Even if they weren't willing to say it out loud, the Limbaughs of the world could recognize reality... *Couldn't they?*

Rubio got his answer in April, when the Gang of Eight finally introduced their 844-page bill—and all hell broke loose. Now several months removed from their stinging 2012 defeat, Republicans had rediscovered their passion for blocking Obama's agenda and no longer felt the need to acquiesce to Democrats' demands. The right-wing noise machine cranked up the volume with combative conservative websites like Breitbart waging a full-blown campaign of misinformation against the bill. The site immediately began publishing shocked-and-appalled stories about a provision in the legislation that would supply rural, border-dwelling Americans with cell phones so that they could more easily report illegal crossings to law enforcement. Breitbart dubbed them "Marcophones" and suggested that the bill was actually angling to give free cell phones to undocumented immigrants. The claim was patently false, but the story spread rapidly throughout certain nativist quarters of the online Right.

Feeling cornered for the first time since he'd arrived in Washington, Rubio instructed his Senate office to push back aggressively against the false information. His aides spent the following days and weeks releasing detailed statements that vigorously debunked "myths" about the bill and called out certain conservative reporters by name for perpetuating them.

Suddenly, Rubio no longer seemed like a team player to the Tea Party, but rather an enemy—someone to be reflexively distrusted. When, during a Spanish-language interview with Univision, Rubio misspoke in a way that made it sound as though the security measures of the bill were softer than they appeared, the conservative talk radio crowd exploded with outrage. Glenn Beck called Rubio a "dirtbag" and accused him of adopting the tactics of Hezbollah. "They say one thing in Arabic and then another in English!" he exclaimed, urging listeners to get off the "Marco Rubio bandwagon" once and for all. Meanwhile, conservatives were flooding the senator's office with angry phone calls, emails, and letters accusing him of betraying the movement.

Rubio was distraught by the intensity of the reaction. He continued trying to defend the immigration bill to the Right, but he became testy during radio interviews and obsessed with correcting the record at the expense of all else. On June 26, the day before the legislation was set for a vote, Rubio stood on the Senate floor and went through several of the ill-informed criticisms coming from conservatives, and begged them to fully educate themselves about the bill before making up their minds.

"To hear the worry, anxiety, and growing anger in the voices of so many people who helped me get elected to the Senate, who I agree with on virtually every other issue, has been a real trial for me," he admitted.

The next day, the bill soared through the Senate on a sixty-eight to thirty-two vote. It was a tremendous legislative feat: the most significant overhaul of U.S. immigration policy in a generation had just earned the support of a huge bipartisan majority of lawmakers. But for Rubio, the victory was hollow. The right-wing backlash had created a climate that ensured the Republican-controlled House would never pass the bill—and the process had led to an epic collapse of support for Rubio on the right. That same week, a Rasmussen poll had landed with a thud in the senator's inbox, reporting that his favorability rating among Republicans had dropped from 73 percent in January to 58 percent now—a fifteen-point swing that could only be attributed to his high-profile advocacy for the immigration bill. The poll numbers fed a new narrative in the national news media about conservative disenchantment with Rubio, and the same reporters who had only months earlier been writing about his rising star were now writing him off.

As his advisers watched him grapple with the fallout, Rubio seemed to cycle through the stages of grief with the destinationless speed of a spin class instructor. Denial, then anger, then bargaining, then depression—and then right back to denial again. He felt like he was mourning the death of his career (or at least his White House dreams).

In the coming months, as it became increasingly clear that the Senate's bill had no chance of becoming law, a resigned Rubio began distancing himself from the legislation. He returned to his earlier support for a "piecemeal approach" to immigration reform that would enact small policy changes over time (something everyone knew Democrats would never go along with). And by October, he had fully withdrawn his support for his own bill, instructing his staff to put word out that he no longer believed the House should even vote on it.

They broke the news of Rubio's one-eighty by giving the "exclusive" to Breitbart.

Jeb Bush's entry into the national immigration debate that spring was a whole different kind of disaster. His book, *Immigration Wars,* was released in March and trumpeted as a bold manifesto by a man who had long been a leading voice for immigration reform in his party. But the timing turned out to be terrible. He and his coauthor had written the book during the 2012 presidential race, as Mitt Romney was stomping around swing states spewing hard-line rhetoric about "self-deportation" that drew approving cheers from conservative audiences everywhere he went. In that context, Jeb had made the calculated decision to scale back his vision, and use the book to call for only a pathway to temporary residency—not full citizenship—for undocumented immigrants. He had figured that going any further would make his proposals dead on arrival, immediately dismissed by most of his party as "amnesty."

But by the time the book actually came out, the Senate was in the midst of drafting a dramatically more ambitious bill that would, among other things, move to transition eleven million immigrants toward full citizenship. What's more, these suddenly emboldened senators had somehow gotten Marco Rubio hand wringing, fence sitting, anxiety-ridden *Marquito!*—to become the fresh, bold face of the effort. In an unwelcome role reversal, Rubio was suddenly the courageous man of principle leading with his chin—while Jeb looked like the overly ambitious politician making weasely concessions to the Right for the sake of his future presidential bid.

This was not supposed to happen. As a husband who had fled Texas decades ago in part to spare his wife the indignities of casual racism, and as a father whose blood had boiled when hecklers called his son a "spic" on the baseball diamond, Jeb *despised* the nativist wing of his party, and couldn't stand the thought of being seen as someone who pandered to them.

But here he was, now forced to promote a book that positioned him to the right of Sean Hannity on immigration. Caught flat-footed, Jeb stutter-stepped his way through an awkward, unimpressive book tour during which he seemed to reverse his position on citizenship multiple times, before finally offering, "I'm not smart enough to figure out every aspect of a really complex law."

Except, of course, that a central feature of Jeb's appeal had always been that he *was* smart enough. He was the guy who thought hard, figured it out, tinkered with it until it worked. Everybody knew this. The Biltmore politicos, and the RNC coroners, and the Bush family loyalists, and the entire Republican establishment knew this. Throwing up his hands in resignation on an issue about which he cared deeply was antithetical to the Legend of Jeb—and rather un-Bush-like to boot.

By the time he completed his miserable promotional tour—which, to top it all off, only managed to move about five thousand copies of his book—Jeb was ready to return to Coral Gables and lie low for a while. He was still leaving the door open to a 2016 bid, but he saw no sense in inserting himself into every intraparty squabble and national shoutfest over the next two years. That game was for the prospective candidates who *didn't* have a stalwart, two-term record of conservative governing and a political family network that would spring into action with a snap of the fingers. It was for the lean and hungry.

Both Jeb and Rubio had come to the cause of immigration reform from years spent striving and thriving in Miami's fiercely competitive, one-of-a-kind, polyglot political scene. But their experiences couldn't have been more different—and the lessons they took away would shape their distinct approaches to politics for decades to come.

It was January 1, 1981, when Jeb and his young family first touched down on the tarmac at Miami International Airport, emerged from a commercial jetliner, and squinted out over the muggy, sun-drenched terrain they were now to call home.

Columba viewed the new scenery through the eyes of a refugee.

She had spent the past few years in Houston being subjected to a humiliating parade of prejudices at the hands of the Bushes' wealthy, conservative cohorts, many of whom were suspicious of this Mexican girl who had managed to wriggle her way into the Texas aristocracy. There were racist jokes slurred by liquored-up oilmen, and judgmental remarks whispered among primped ladies in pearls, and disapproving glares stretched across the all-white faces that always surrounded her, and finally one day she'd had enough.

She gave her husband a choice: they could move to Mexico, or they could relocate to Miami, where her mother and sister had recently settled. Whatever they did, she would *not* raise their brown-skinned, bilingual children in that miserable place called Texas.

Jeb, for his part, had greeted the ultimatum as an opportunity, and as he surveyed their new surroundings, he did so with the zeal of a conquering commander consumed by manifest destiny. In nineteen days, his father would be sworn in as vice president of the United States, and Jeb, now twenty-seven years old, no longer harbored any ambivalence about the family dynasty: he wanted in.

Jeb knew that in order to prove his mettle, he would have to leave Texas. "There was an uncertainty about living in Houston, with my dad being from there and being vice president," he would later explain. "I felt comfortable being someplace else and starting out on my own." And in Miami — with its booming economy; its brash, vibrant multiculturalism; its noisy, Cuban-infused politics — Jeb had found the perfect place to establish his own distinct fiefdom in the Bush kingdom: he couldn't have conjured a city more fully removed from his father's genteel world of Texas blue bloods. "Miami is wide-open," he marveled. "It's a frontier town ... It doesn't have a lot of people with roman numerals behind their names."

Jeb and his family settled in a place called Pinewood Estates, a gated suburban subdivision covered in manicured lawns and swimming pools, and then he got to work. His first order of business was to make himself into a millionaire. He had always been taught that Bushes don't run for political office until after they've made their fortunes, so as to avoid any suggestion that they might be bought or bribed. Jeb was blunt about his financial ambitions from the outset. "I'd like to be very wealthy," he told the *Miami News* in 1983. "And I'll be glad to let you know when I think I've reached my goal."

He didn't have to fill out many job applications, though, before he received the sort of offer generally reserved for people whose fathers have job titles that appear in the Constitution. Armando Codina, a prominent Florida real estate developer and longtime supporter of the newly elected vice president, invited Jeb to join his firm as a partner, invest no money, and collect 40 percent of the profits—all in exchange for allowing Codina to add "Bush" to the company's name. That sounded equitable enough to Jeb, and so they shook on it.

Now well on his way to independent wealth, Jeb turned his attention to politics, deciding in 1984 that he would run for chairman of the Dade County Republican Party. He was only thirty-one years old and still relatively new to Florida, and some allies advised him against plunging into Miami's notoriously fractious local politics, where city council meetings were known to descend into fistfights, and political debates were frequently won or lost in cantankerous shouting matches on Spanish-language radio. The Dade County party, in particular, was sharply divided at the time, primarily between moderate Anglo suburbanites and the fast-growing community of rowdy right-wing Cuban exiles.

Things worked out for Jeb, though, as things usually did. He easily won the race on the strength of his family's fame, and proved to have a knack for navigating Miami's fraught political landscape. As a well-heeled son of the establishment who also happened to have a Latina wife and a brood of Spanish-speaking *chiquitos* at home, Jeb was well suited to bridge the divide between the GOP's two local tribes, and soon he had the party machine humming, registering nearly sixty thousand new Republicans in the county during a period when the Democrats lost around twenty thousand.

He also became a local celebrity, especially beloved by the Cubans, who delighted in seeing this giant lumbering man prop his oversize frame at a table in one Little Havana café or another, downing *tazitos* of Cuban coffee as he breezily chatted in his gringo-accented Spanish.

Often, they would approach him to ask for help with a relative's immigration status, or lobby him to lean on his contacts in Washington on behalf of an exile cause.

"Si, si, voy a tratar," he would promise.

Yes, yes, he would try.

"It's difficult sometimes to live up to the expectations of other people," Jeb lamented to a reporter one afternoon amid the fawning and favor begging at a crowded Cuban restaurant. "They think I can call up President Reagan and solve anything. They think I live the life of Prince Charles rather than my middle-class life."

Of course, even if Reagan didn't take his calls, his father certainly did—and Jeb called often, laying the foundation for a career in Florida politics with a series of strings pulled and favors called in to the White House. In 1988, Jeb energetically lobbied his father's staff to appoint a key Miami political ally, Dexter Lehtinen, as U.S. attorney, and when he sensed that they were dragging their feet, he fired off an impatient note to White House counsel C. Boyden Gray: "Boyden, it's time to act." He made appeals on behalf of other loyal supporters as well, recommending them for jobs that ranged from IRS commissioner to Supreme Court justice. Once, he even helped facilitate an introduction between an official at the Department of Agriculture and a Florida entrepreneur (and political donor) who was trying to warm the American palate to the taste of cooked rabbit. "The enclosed letter is a bit unusual," Jeb wrote to one of his father's top White House aides on behalf of the budding bunny meat magnate, "but it is serious."

Not all of Jeb's requests were granted, but by drawing on his father's political capital and investing it in scores of microloans sprinkled across Florida's GOP power brokers, he was able to accrue enough goodwill to assure himself an inside track to the governorship. It was the beginning of an ascent that would be remembered—with the nostalgic, golden-hued quality of a beloved home video—by a generation of Sunshine State conservatives for years to come. As longtime Tallahassee lobbyist Rich Heffley would later effuse, "What Ronald Reagan meant to many Republicans nationally, Jeb means to Republicans in Florida."

*   *   *

Marco Rubio's political rise in Miami was considerably scrappier than that of his Florida forebear. He had none of the cash, connections, or clout that came preassembled and gift-wrapped to every newborn baby with a birth certificate that read "Bush." The glaring contrast was clear from Rubio's very first political internship, in the office of Representative Ileana Ros-Lehtinen. Whereas Jeb had curried favor with the South Florida congresswoman by using his White House pull to get her husband, Dexter, appointed interim U.S. attorney, Rubio's only connection to the couple was that Dexter had once put his brother-in-law in prison for drug dealing.

But what Rubio lacked in a privileged pedigree, he made up for with a distinctly Cuban, can't-sit-still drive to succeed. In 1996, while working toward a law degree at the University of Miami, Rubio scored a gig as a floor manager at the GOP presidential convention, and from there he sweet-talked his way into the role of Bob Dole's campaign chairman in Miami-Dade and Monroe counties. In this capacity, he regularly went to bat for Dole on local Spanish talk radio, serving up sharp and often funny sound bites in defense of the Republican nominee. He showed a prodigy's talent for crafting quotable one-liners.

"If this election was an audition for host of a talk show, Dole wouldn't stand a chance," Rubio told *Maclean's* magazine at the time. "This is a campaign that will truly test whether we're a nation of style or substance." The nation chose style that year, but Rubio was hooked on politics nonetheless.

In 1998 he took his first step toward public office by walking across the front lawn of his tiny town's mayor, Rebeca Sosa, and extending a hand. She paused from tending to the flowers in her garden and listened as this little boy—polite, conscientious, and all of twenty-six years old—told her about his plan to run for a seat on the West Miami City Commission.

Sosa, who was forty-two, looked him up and down and replied, "You're too young. Why would you run?"

But Rubio won her over—as he would millions of others in the coming years—by stirringly reciting his family's story, and expressing reverence for the cause of the Cuban exiles. He ended up winning the city commission race, and along the way he banked a twenty-five-dollar donation check from one Jeb Bush, who had heard good things.

But Rubio wouldn't stay put for long. He was jittery with ambition, positively caffeinated by it. And when a seat in the Florida House of Representatives opened up unexpectedly, he practically leapt to his feet and high-kneed his way into the special election. He had no political network to lean on or record to speak of: his greatest accomplishment had been establishing West Miami's first bike cop, which he hailed as the "cornerstone" of his campaign. But he relied once again on his silver tongue to snag a coveted endorsement from the *Miami Herald,* whose editors marveled, "He can turn an anecdote about planting trees in one sun-parched neighborhood into a reverie about the power of public service." In January 2000, Rubio achieved his second landslide electoral victory in as many years.

By now he had married his girlfriend—a striking blonde-haired Colombian named Jeanette who had recently worked as a Miami Dolphins cheerleader—and money was tight for the couple. They had only recently moved out of his parents' house, and so when he reported for duty in Tallahassee at the start of his first legislative session, he spent nights crashing on the couch of a buddy named Danny Diaz. The newly elected lawmaker shared his inauspicious living quarters with his friend's pet parrot, which greeted each day's sunrise with a noisy chorus of squawking. One morning, Diaz awoke to the sound of a loud crash in his living room, and when he went to investigate he discovered that a bleary-eyed Rubio had hurled his shoe at the birdcage in frustration.

Soon after arriving at the capitol, Rubio volunteered to join the redistricting committee, and he threw himself into the tedious, tit-for-tat grind of reshaping state congressional districts—a job that meant spending long days cooped up in a conference room while lawmakers and their aides meticulously combed through a giant map of Florida, block by block, border by border, hashing out the boundaries one at a time. The work was eye-deadeningly dense and deeply unglamorous, but being inside the room gave Rubio access to inside information—namely, which of his colleagues were at risk of getting drawn out of their districts—and he knew he could quietly parcel it out in exchange for political IOUs. By 2003, he was actively gathering support for a future bid for the speakership, and by 2006, he was sworn in as Florida's first-ever Cuban American Speaker. At just thirty-five years old, he had hustled his way in to one of the top perches in Florida's state government on the strength of nothing but his own ingenuity.

The suddenness of Rubio's ascent—combined with his piles of law school debt and continually tight personal finances—led him to indulge joyously in the perks available to a person in his position. He watched his beloved Miami Dolphins from box seats belonging to professional influence peddlers. He made liberal use of the Florida Republican Party's credit card. And as a new Speaker, he was astonished by how easily someone in his role could cash in.

"It's amazing," Rubio marveled to a friend at the time. "I can call up a lobbyist at four in the morning, and he'll meet me anywhere with a bag of forty thousand dollars in cash."

As Rubio neared the end of his final legislative term in 2008, he started to feel that familiar itch of the achievement junkie again— the restless shoe shuffling, the nervous knee jiggling, the eyes darting this way and that in search of his next fix. But unlike the straightforward course of Rubio's path up to now, the next step was not immediately obvious. He would claim, years later, that he "couldn't wait to be liberated from public office—from its crowded, rigid schedule; from its news clips, phone calls, and emails; from the too many nights spent away from my wife and kids." But his closest political allies in Miami would remember it differently.

During an intimate breakfast meeting at the Biltmore shortly after his final legislative session ended, Rubio huddled with a coterie of friendly donors, activists, and friendly local media figures to weigh his options. The consensus at the table was that he should wait for the right statewide race to open up—attorney general, maybe, or even governor. But Rubio wasn't having it. He was practically panicked at the thought of spending any time out of office and away from the spotlight.

What if my donors are poached when I'm away? he fretted. What if my supporters abandon me? I could be finished in politics!

As his voice betrayed a growing agitation, some at the table began exchanging sideways glances, perplexed by the spectacle and slightly embarrassed for Rubio. "He was just missing that sense of maturity you want," one of the breakfast attendees would later tell me.

Finally, Ninoska Pérez Castellón, a popular local radio personality who frequently interviewed Rubio on air, felt it necessary to interject with some tough love.

"Marco!" she snapped. "You could be governor, or even in Congress! You don't want to burn yourself as mayor of Dade County." Slow down and stop worrying so much, she told him. "People aren't going to forget you."

But Rubio couldn't help himself. Within months, he would shock the Florida political world by launching a long shot Senate bid against the state's popular Republican governor, Charlie Crist. Entering the race was by any objective measure a terrible idea. Hasty. Ill considered. Imprudent. Dumb. And then, of course, the young underdog won.

In the rise of Marco Rubio, success always rewarded audacity—until his 2013 immigration flameout. He limped away from the arena at the end of that summer bruised, bloodied, bludgeoned, but not changed. He was still restless, still anxious, still possessed of a world-beating charisma. And with 2016 on the horizon, Rubio's most audacious gambit yet was still ahead of him.

While Rubio and Bush spent 2013 picking a big, visible, high stakes fight to widen the Republican tent—and then losing—Paul Ryan quietly embarked on his own personal, pared down outreach mission to the same end.

At the outset of his expeditions into the world of urban poverty, Ryan approached the project with the general demeanor of a fanny-pack-wrapped tourist gawking through binoculars at all the exciting new scenery. The objective of the trips was straightforward: his tour guide, Bob Woodson, would introduce him to ministers, volunteers, and grassroots leaders who were successfully combating the effects of poverty on the ground, and Ryan would try to figure out how the federal government could better empower them.

Ever since the New Deal, conservatives had argued that the ever-expanding welfare state threatened to crowd private charities and ministries out of the public square—creating widespread dependence on ineffective one-size-fits-all federal programs at the expense of America's diverse and creative civil society. The problem was that while Republicans had spent a lot of time over the years figuring out how to make their vision sound pretty—George H. W. Bush memorably likened local charities to "a brilliant diversity spread like stars, like a thousand points of light in a broad and peaceful sky"—they often had too little real-life evidence to point to. Ryan's 2013 poverty tour would be about arming himself with the anecdotal ammunition he knew he'd need to make his case. In the meantime, the congressman insisted that they keep the trips off the media's radar for a while. He worried that letting reporters tag along would get in the way of his fact-finding—or, even worse, make the trips look cynical and calculated.

They started in early February with a visit to Milwaukee, where they toured a Christian ministry that fought urban blight by collecting unused building materials from local construction companies and selling them to needy customers for pennies on the dollar. A month later, they stopped by Pastor Holloway's shelter for women and children in Maryland, which had helped hundreds of homeless families—many of them escaping abusive men—put their lives back together. Over the next fourteen months, Ryan followed Woodson to an innovative halfway house in Cleveland; a black church in New Jersey that schooled congregants in how to escape predatory lenders and personal debt; and a "boot camp" in Indianapolis that sought to whip the underachieving men in one disadvantaged neighborhood into shape with tough-love counseling and a forward-thinking work placement program.

The more Ryan saw, the more disorienting it all was. His tourist-like enthusiasm quickly wore off, replaced by a somber recognition of just how much he didn't know. Up until now in his career as a policy maker, Ryan had interacted with communities like these from a distance, primarily in the form of canned talking points and budget debates about funding NGOs (Beltway-speak for nongovernmental organizations). Now he was being exposed to the complexities of low-income life that didn't fit in the thirty-second spot, the outlay spreadsheet, or the stump speech applause line. It was gritty and uncomfortable—and it was even starting to change his mind on some political issues.

One particularly eye-opening experience came on a rainy night in San Antonio while Ryan toured a ministry for heroin addicts called Outcry in the Barrio. The pastor in charge, Jubal Garcia, escorted Ryan, Woodson, and a couple of other visitors to a makeshift intake facility, where about a half dozen men lay shivering in bunk beds as they suffered through the first throes of gut-wrenching detox. A couple of volunteers—recovering addicts themselves—ministered to the men, while Garcia made introductions. A few of the detoxers, Ryan learned, had spent the previous night passed out under a bridge, and had been driven to the rehab center that day by some holy combination of rock-bottom resolve, divine intervention, and high- and low-pressure fronts. A longtime addict named Tony, who had tattoos running up and down his arms to cover the track marks, told Ryan it was his fourth time at Outcry. "I believe in God, and I believe that he keeps bringing me back, trying to tell me that it's time to change," he said. "Either that or I am going to die in the street."

For all the phony photo ops that Beltway bubble dwellers employed to prove they were in touch with real America, few officeholders had ever been put in a position to chat with heroin addicts hours after they shot up—and the experience jarred Ryan. He followed Garcia around in a sort of daze at first, trying to process it all without accidently doing something insensitive. When one of the detoxers began convulsing, Garcia invited Ryan to join him in praying for the man. Tentatively, the congressman knelt at the addict's bedside, and together he and the pastor laid hands on him and asked God to give him strength in his battle with addiction. When they finished, Garcia suggested that they offer prayers to the rest of the men in the intake room, and Ryan agreed. One by one, they blessed each man, and by the time they finished, Ryan felt spiritually invigorated. As Garcia was preparing to leave the room, the congressman spotted one more addict in the corner and called out, "We have another one over here."

The intensity of the night was seared into Ryan's mind, and in the weeks that followed he thought often of the addicts and volunteers he had met at Outcry. The ministry was inspiring, but its task seemed utterly Sisyphean: no matter how many people it successfully treated, a new group of desperate, strung out addicts would ramble in through the doors the next day. As he struggled with how he could do anything in Washington that might possibly make a tangible difference to the men in that room, he kept coming back to the issues of prison reform and drug sentencing laws. By default, Ryan had been a standard-issue tough-on-crime Republican throughout his career, but his conversations with the men in San Antonio — many of whom had spent huge chunks of their lives in a destructive cycle of addiction, imprisonment, relapse, and recidivism — led him to believe there had to be a better way to help drug addicts find redemption than locking them up.

While talking to Woodson one day about their visit to the rehab ministry, Ryan remarked, "You know, I wasn't always an advocate for prison reform, but after having gone to San Antonio, I changed my mind."

Woodson was elated. "Paul actually said that — he said, 'I changed my mind'!" Woodson later recalled. "I don't think I've ever heard a politician say, 'I've changed my mind' before. I'm serious."

Ryan was experiencing a change of heart as well. When he had first embarked on this project, his good intentions were founded on a carefully considered political calculus designed to rehabilitate his career and his party. But as he continued his monthly excursions into the forgotten cracks and crevices of American society, Ryan became less preoccupied with how bad it *looked* that his party was so disengaged on issues that mattered to the poor, and increasingly convinced of how bad it actually *was:* Republicans had failed America's most vulnerable citizens.

He regretted that the Romney campaign had written off this suffering swath of the electorate in 2012, but he also recognized that the party's negligence began well before the last election. "I think that by the time it got around to 2012, it was a little too late," Ryan told me one day while he was in a particularly reflective mood. "It wasn't, 'Oh gosh, four months to go, let's get this right now!' It's not a box checker at the end of a campaign. It's a consistent and continual thing...It just atrophied in our party. And I was part of that atrophy. I focused on budgets and economics, macroeconomic policy, because that was sort of the crisis in front of us. I think we all, as a party, just fell away from that."

The Republicans' post-2012 soul-searching had yielded many epiphanies of this general variety, and lately earnest proclamations of repentance had become as common in the party's establishment as the chirping chorus of summertime cicadas in Washington. Among the mainstream fixtures of the GOP—from Bush and Rubio to Ryan and the RNC coroners—the consensus was that the path to the promised land required moderation, compromise, and a renewed commitment to serious-minded governance.

But the guerrilla freedom fighters of the conservative movement had a different idea—and they were about to make their move.

PART II

PROPHETS

Chapter Six

The Stand

R and Paul had a question for President Obama. An oddly specific, plainly incendiary, deeply weird hypothetical question that probably would have been laughed off by most reasonable adults as silly and paranoid if not for the chilling fact that, so far, no one in the White House was giving him a straight answer.

The question went like this: does the president believe he has the authority to unilaterally send a military drone to kill an American citizen sitting in a café in San Francisco?

Rand had first posed a version of this question — along with several other queries about the legality of the U.S. drone program — in a letter to Obama's nominee for CIA director, John Brennan. Since taking office, the president had dramatically expanded the use of military drones in the Middle East as a ruthlessly efficient weapon to seek out and destroy enemy combatants, while posing minimal risk to the U.S. soldiers who piloted the aircrafts from the safety of stateside military bases. The program had been called into question, however, when it was revealed that the administration had used a drone to assassinate Anwar al-Awlaki, a United States citizen believed to be working as a recruiter for Al-Qaeda in Yemen. While Rand knew his café drone strike hypothetical was provocative, he believed the clandestine al-Awlaki operation raised serious and alarming questions. If the president felt he had the authority to order a military hit job on an American citizen abroad without even the pretense of due process, what was to stop him from doing the same to a target who resided in San Francisco, or Houston—or his own Kentucky hometown of Bowling Green, for that matter?

Twelve days after sending his letter to Brennan, Rand received a blithe, dismissive note from Attorney General Eric Holder that confirmed all of Rand's worst suspicions about this arrogant administration and its reckless disregard for civil liberties. "The U.S. government has not carried out drone strikes in the United States and has no intention of doing so," Holder wrote, before cavalierly dropping in a mushroom cloud–size caveat. "It is possible, I suppose, to imagine an extraordinary circumstance in which it would be necessary and appropriate...for the president to authorize the military to use lethal force within the territory of the United States." But if something like that ever happened, Holder assured Rand, "I would examine the particular facts and circumstances before advising the president on the scope of his authority."

He knew what Holder *really* meant to say: Sit down, shut up, and let the grown-ups handle national security, kid.

Rand found the response outrageous in its ambiguity: Holder was suggesting that the executive branch had the right to summarily assassinate American citizens on U.S. soil without a jury trial or even an arrest warrant. And yet, the scandalized senator had a hunch that few would take note of this creeping tyranny. After all, he had been interrogating the legality of the drone program for months already—writing little-noticed op-eds, and ranting to half-interested colleagues in Congress—and for the most part, the reaction from official Washington had been radio silence.

So at 11:47 a.m. on March 6, 2013, the junior senator from Kentucky stood up at his desk on the Senate floor and started to make some noise.

"I rise today to begin to filibuster John Brennan's nomination to the CIA," Rand declared from the well of the Senate, prompting puzzled looks from a few of the lawmakers and reporters in attendance. "I will speak as long as it takes, until the alarm is sounded from coast to coast that our Constitution is important, that your rights to trial by jury are precious...I don't rise to oppose John Brennan's nomination simply for the person. I rise today for the principle."

And he was off.

For all the grandiose trappings of the performance, the filibuster had been a spur-of-the-moment thing. A mischievous *What if?* tossed out to an aide during his drive to the Capitol just that morning; a stroke of luck that Senate Majority Leader Harry Reid had left a window open by not ending debate earlier in the day; a last-second impulse to actually go through with it and seize the floor.

Now, here was Rand—with no plan, no snacks, few notes, and a pair of terribly uncomfortable shoes on his feet—declaring to all the world that he would not sit down until he had made his point.

But in the ensuing hours, as the filibuster proceeded to draw manic national media coverage—spawning a Twitter hashtag, #Standwith-Rand, that would become the tagline for the senator's political rise—it was soon obvious that Rand was doing much more than demanding clarity on a single pet issue. With every sentence he uttered, he was redrawing the battle lines in America's decadelong, Bush-era debate over national security and civil liberties. Here was a conservative Republican accusing a liberal Democratic president of recklessly abandoning constitutional principle in the name of fighting terrorism—an astounding role reversal from the politics of the recent past.

The irony wasn't lost on Rand, who noted early on in the filibuster, "Obama of 2007 would be down here with me."

While the script flipping made for great TV, Rand's high-profile crusade set off a chaotic, off-camera scramble inside his own party. In well-appointed offices across Capitol Hill and in governor's mansions across America, Republican politicians eyeing 2016 were huddling with advisers, poring over polling data, and obsessively monitoring coverage of the filibuster—struggling to gain their footing in this suddenly shifting landscape. Time was of the essence, and they needed now to make a bet on the new politics of national security: Should they get in on the ground floor of this risky ideological start-up and hope to strike it rich, or pay their dues at the conglomerate of hawkish neoconservatism and patiently climb the ladder?

Utah senator Mike Lee was the first to make a move. A political outsider who had ridden into Congress on the Tea Party wave of 2010, he felt little obligation to toe the party line, or defend the GOP's win-at-all-costs approach to the War on Terror. As a constitutional lawyer with a libertarian bent, he was well versed in the issues at hand and knew he could bring some firepower to Rand's fight against executive overreach. (And as long as the executive in question was a Democrat, Lee felt certain his red-state constituents wouldn't object.) Plus, as one of his aides would later tell me, Lee had long harbored a romantic, little-boy-like fantasy of standing up in the Senate and heroically lending his voice to a righteous filibuster. Watching the spectacle unfold from his office, he felt a pang of urgency. When else would he get this chance?

At the top of the filibuster's fourth hour, the Utahn walked onto the Senate floor and asked his colleague from Kentucky to yield for a "question." Rand consented, and Lee proceeded to deliver a five-thousand-word lecture on the rule of law and the Fourteenth Amendment—a childhood dream come true.

Ted Cruz was another early ally. The Texan had been sworn in only six weeks earlier, and he had yet to make a speech on the Senate floor. But he knew a Tea Party rainmaker when he saw one, and he had no doubt that this little show would be a hit on the right; he only wished he'd thought of it first. In preparation for his cameo, Cruz asked an aide to print out a list of #StandwithRand tweets that he could read on the floor—nothing too angry or crazy, just general rah-rah stuff. This was Rand's big night; if Cruz had to hold the pom-poms for a few minutes, he could live with that. But as he reviewed the effusive messages from legions of conservative activists on Twitter, Cruz was struck by just how much appetite there was in the movement for big, gutsy, high-stakes, hashtag-able moments like this one. *Something to keep in mind.*

With coverage of the spectacle reaching a fever pitch by hour nine, a parade of conservative House members marched into the gallery to show their silent support, while a number of Rand's Republican Senate colleagues began joining him on the floor.

Some of the senators were less fluent in this newly elevated issue than others, and at times the filibuster took on a theater of the absurd quality. Senator Ron Johnson of Wisconsin spent several minutes rambling about Senate dysfunction and the national debt before feebly attempting to get back to the point—a comically bad attempt at improv that drew comparisons on Twitter to Steve Carell's dunce-like character in *Anchorman*. ("Senator Johnson has just voted 'I love lamp,'" tweeted journalist Jeremy Scahill.) Marco Rubio, meanwhile, detailed how Democrats had changed their tune on drones ever since Obama got into the White House, bending some Jay-Z lyrics almost to the point of breaking in the process. "It's funny what seven days can change," Rubio said, quoting the rapper. "It was all good just a week ago."

At one point, when Rand got hungry, he sent an aide to raid the communal candy drawer that had been kept in the back row of the Senate since the 1960s, and as he spoke, he struggled to keep the sticky gobs of chewed caramel from spilling out of his mouth.

But the off-kilter moments of weirdness only made the event a bigger media sensation, which in turn increased pressure on other Republicans to join in. Even Mitch McConnell — the Senate Minority Leader who had worked feverishly during the 2010 Kentucky primary to defeat Rand — materialized on the floor before it was over.

By the time Rand's bladder forced him to call it quits, just shy of the thirteen-hour mark, there was no question that he had won. His stunt forced the Obama administration to clarify its position on U.S. drone policy. Within hours of the filibuster's finale, Holder would send a snippy follow-up letter answering the senator's original question with one word: "No." What's more, Rand had successfully cajoled almost every Republican in the Senate into joining his libertarian crusade, at least for the day. And even though Democratic lawmakers had chosen to skip the filibuster and provide partisan cover to the White House instead, Rand's performance had elicited an outpouring of online support from principled progressives who were alarmed by how Obama was carrying on the terrorist-fighting policies of the previous president. Two American political fringes — the libertarians and the left-wingers — were uniting in common cause, and dragging the entrenched elements of the DC establishment along with them.

Rand felt triumphant. For once, it didn't matter what the old-guard goons of Washington thought of him, or his ideas, or his dad. They now had no choice but to recognize him as a powerful new force in the Republican Party — a troublemaker, yes, but one to be reckoned with.

In the endless loop of filibuster footage that would dominate cable news in the days to come, one scene remained planted in Rand's memory. He had been standing for about seven hours when he noticed Republican senator Mark Kirk wobbling down the aisle in his direction. Kirk had only recently returned to Washington after suffering a stroke, and even with his cane he almost lost balance on his way to Rand's desk. When he arrived he set down two objects: an apple and a thermos of hot tea. The gesture was a reference to the 1939 movie *Mr. Smith Goes to Washington,* whose idealistic titular character embarks on a filibuster to protest DC corruption. Kirk didn't say a word. He just tapped two fingers on the top of the thermos and wobbled back out of the chamber.

The thermos thing really pissed off John McCain. *Seriously?* We were going to compare *this* guy to an iconic symbol of commonsense American populism? *Give me a break.*

Though he'd mostly tried to ignore the filibuster, McCain had caught portions of Rand's performance from his office on the Hill—and he was disgusted with the whole affair. This junior senator, *Ron Paul's kid,* had been in Washington all of about ten minutes, and he was already deigning to tell people like him—veterans of Congress, veterans of war—that they were wrong about how to keep America safe? The longer it went on and the more he saw his colleagues bow to the media pressure, the more irritated McCain was. Surely Rand meant well. He had his convictions, and that was fine. But with this nonsense about drone attacks and San Francisco cafés, he had concocted a preposterous life-and-death hypothetical scenario—and gotten a bunch of Republicans to pay faddish deference to it—when here in the real world there were serious, real-life threats being levied against America and its interests every day. McCain had no intention of keeping quiet about it.

The next day, he delivered a rebuttal on the Senate floor, reading from a *Wall Street Journal* editorial that called Rand's filibuster a stunt meant to "fire up impressionable libertarian kids in their college dorms." But he reserved his true feelings for an interview with the Huffington Post later that day. Asked what he thought about Rand

and his fellow libertarian-leaning lawmakers, McCain paused for a few seconds, contemplating just how far he should go. "It's always the wacko birds on [the] right and left that get the media megaphone," he grumbled, adding that the filibuster had done "a disservice to a lot of Americans by making them believe that somehow they're in danger from their government. They're not."

When Rand was asked later that day to respond to the "wacko birds" dig, he went with the fail-safe statesman pose that he'd been practicing ever since he got elected: disappointed by his colleague's discourtesy, saddened by the toxic tone of Washington.

"You know, I think he's just on the wrong side of history, and on the wrong side of this argument, really," Rand told Mike Huckabee in a radio interview. "I treat Senator McCain with respect. I don't think I always get the same in return."

But in truth, Rand was delighted by McCain's name-calling. He'd had a number of big wins over the past twenty-four hours, from reframing the national debate over drones to unofficially launching his 2016 presidential campaign with a disruptive tsunami of bipartisan support. But driving McCain—smug, self-certain, perpetually wrong Old Man McCain—to such an intemperate outburst of public grumpiness felt so psychically satisfying that it almost trumped everything else. He had just trolled the entire GOP establishment, and they were finally losing their cool.

He couldn't wait to do it again.

When Kristy Ditzler arrived on campus at Baylor University in the fall of 1982, she felt as though she had crash-landed on an alien planet. She was a feminist, a liberal, an eighteen-year-old freshman who had been Berkeley-bound until an injury late in her high school career nixed a swimming scholarship at Cal and sent her scrambling to find a new collegiate landing pad. But almost immediately after enrolling at the Waco, Texas, school, she regretted her decision.

Baylor in the eighties was a deeply conservative place, steeped in devout Baptist culture and old-fashioned gender politics. Coeds were expected to wear skirts to football games; dancing was strictly forbidden; and students of the opposite sex were banned from one another's dorm rooms at all times, with the exception of closely monitored Sunday afternoon visiting hours, when the doors were to stay open and the God-fearing students were to remain upright and vertical. "I walked into this totally unknown universe where I was being told I was a bad person because I wouldn't go to Bible study on Thursdays," Ditzler later told me. Feeling isolated and alone, she almost bailed on the school altogether.

Then she met Randy Paul.

Short and lean, with untidy curls sprouting from the top of his head, the sophomore biology student caught Ditzler's attention with his wry sense of humor and affection for irreverence. They met at swim practice, where Randy and his best friend and teammate, George, spent time in between laps cracking jokes about the school's pharisaical rules and the sheeplike born-again students who fanatically clung to them. Ditzler was relieved to find a couple of kindred spirits on campus. "They were very different from the typical Baylor students," she remembered, adding that Randy "saved me from dropping out."

George and Randy enjoyed brainstorming creative, absurdist ways to subvert campus culture, and for Ditzler, watching them plot their mischief and mayhem often felt like witnessing a live bullfight: it was fun and frightening and charged with the intoxicating sense that anything could happen. George played the role of matador in these bull sessions, always waving some new stunt or prank he'd concocted in front of Randy to get his attention. It didn't always work. Randy, the quieter, more studious of the two, was opposed, on principle, to Baylor's cookie-cutter Christianity and dictatorial administration, but he was not always enthused by silly high jinks.

When George *did* get him to charge, however, there was no telling how it might end. "They were both scary bright," said Ditzler, and when they latched on to some new piece of devilry, they'd go back and forth—eyes lit up, voices rising—as they dared each other to keep pushing the scheme further. "George would start it, then Randy would add in his ideas," Ditzler recalled. "He was the tagalong, George was the mastermind."

Not all of George's ideas were winners. One night, when they were freshmen, he came up with a flimsy, five-beers-in plot to dig up the time capsule buried at the center of campus. Instead, they drunkenly knocked over the monument *on top* of the capsule, and had to flee the scene. When the act of vandalism became front-page news in Baylor's student paper, with various clubs pointing fingers at one another, Randy and George kept quiet and pledged never to speak of the night again.

At his best, though, George was a masterful performance artist. "He was very high-energy," said Ditzler. "If he was going to do something, he was going to be flamboyant about it." When she mentioned one day to George that the rat she had been training all semester in a class was going to be killed and dissected by the biology department, he proposed an emergency rescue mission. They dressed in all black, smeared dark paint on their faces, and broke into the lab in the middle of the night to retrieve the white rodent. "I don't know how he figured out how to get past the lock," Ditzler said. "That was just his thing: make a lot of drama where there is none."

But there was also something strange—even mysterious—about her two new friends. Shortly after meeting them, Ditzler realized she had actually known George many years earlier, when they were kids in the same car pool in suburban Houston. Back then, though, his name was George Schauerte; now he was going by George Paul. Curious and confused, Ditzler began asking around about George's name—but the answer she kept getting from friends and teammates only deepened the intrigue. "The only explanation anyone would give me was that Randy was so cool, and they were so close, that George had decided to change his [last] name to Paul," she recalled. (That Paul used to be George's middle name hardly solved the puzzle for her, especially once she learned that he had actually gone to the trouble of making the name change legal.)

There were other riddles, too. Ditzler started noticing, as she spent more time with them, that Randy and George would often disappear together without explanation. Whenever she confronted them about it, they'd offer vague pretexts and quickly change the subject. Then there was the question of their curiously celibate social lives. Despite their routine mockery of Baylor's chastity police, neither of them ever seemed to be getting any action. Eventually, Ditzler came to the only logical conclusion she could think of: "I thought they were a gay couple."

She eventually disposed of this notion when George started dating one of her roommates, but three decades later she would continue to wonder aloud why "Randy did not ever date anyone."

Ditzler finally did discover the true reason for all their sneaking around—and though it didn't involve a torrid love affair, it would still rank George and Randy among Baylor's biggest sinners.

Unbeknownst to most of their classmates, Randy and George were members of a notorious secret society on campus called the NoZe Brotherhood. Founded in 1924 to make fun of Baylor's fraternities, the organization had evolved over the years into a rowdy rotating cast of mischief-makers and blasphemers who delighted in stuffing their school's sacred cows into meat grinders. "It was about making fun of Baylor and Baptists and...being iconoclastic," said John Green, who was one of Randy's fellow NoZemen. "It appealed to people who didn't fit the traditional Baptist mold, or people who came in that way and were sort of warped while they were there."

The mission of the NoZe Brotherhood was to tweak, troll, irk, rattle, and rile Baylor's administration, and offend the school's more humorless students. As Green would later put it, "We aspired to blasphemy." And, in fact, they were so successful on that front that shortly before Randy was initiated, the university's president booted the group from campus, calling it "lewd, crude, and grossly sacrilegious." Word went out across the school: any student discovered to be a NoZe brother would be automatically expelled.

For Randy and George, the heightened stakes only made it more fun. Driven underground, the NoZe brothers would disguise themselves in Groucho Marx glasses and parade across campus performing elaborate, outlandish stunts. After beauty-queen-cum-culture-warrior Anita Bryant famously condemned oral sex as sinful, the NoZe brothers marched around carrying an enormous picture of Bryant with a cutout circle where her mouth was supposed to be. And when Baylor officials tried to get the liquor license pulled from a local sandwich shop on the grounds that it was too close to campus, the NoZemen showed up with a homemade surveyor's scope and a rope created from rags, belts, and wadded-up American flags. They made a big show of measuring the distance between the restaurant and a campus building before declaring that a meltdown had occurred, "resulting in the expulsion of hot air and dangerous and even toxic levels of Christian atmosphere."

Sometimes the cops would get called on them. Sometimes the cops would show up. And when that happened, the merry band of heretics would joyously scatter—laughing and panting and doubling over as they made their escape.

One favorite NoZe tradition was making up derisive renditions of cherished gospel tunes, like the song "Give Me That Old Time Religion," which they rewrote, replacing "the Hebrew children" in the lyrics with evolutionary descendants of Neanderthals:

It was good enough for Cro-Magnon man,
It was good enough for Cro-Magnon man,
It was good enough for Cro-Magnon man,
It's good enough for me!

During Randy's time in the NoZe, he and his brothers channeled much of their creative energies into a satiric newspaper, *The Rope,* designed to parody and provoke their conservative Christian classmates. (A handful of excerpts from the paper later surfaced during Rand's 2010 Senate race, but the entirety of the archives weren't dredged up until a source provided them to me.) Among the paper's more incendiary items: a story about an eighty-three-year-old man from California admitting he wrote the Bible on a lark ("I don't know what all the fuss is about; I mean, I'm no Tolkien"), a first-person essay in which a teenage Jesus complains that Mary is stepping out on his dad with the Holy Spirit (complete with racist kicker: "Most guys named Jesus don't even know who their father is!"), and a piece dryly lampooning a policy that required underage girls to get parental consent before acquiring birth control ("[This] will effectively end the practice of teenage sex in the United States").

The articles were printed without bylines, leaving it unclear which pieces, if any, Randy was directly responsible for. But several of his Baylor buddies would later tell me that he wrote with some frequency for *The Rope,* and his mug even appeared on the cover of a 1983 issue—albeit masked by a giant fake nose.

Randy fit in comfortably with the troublemaking smart-asses that populated the NoZe Brotherhood, happily joining them as they looked for new lines to cross, new reverences to trample. When they talked about girls on campus, they referred to them as "hairy legs"; the ones who slept with them were upgraded to "Fortunates." They tried to one-up one another with obscure, in-joke nicknames— Randy was SpoonNoze, named after Lysander Spooner, a nineteenth-century antislavery anarchist who was idolized by libertarians—and at the end of each year, they threw a big, boozy underground party with the cash they made selling advertisements in *The Rope.* (For a while, the paper's back page was dominated by an ad offering a "Baylor special" at a local strip club: "Remember, at Two Minnies, every night is family night.")

But while the NoZe Brotherhood was a natural habitat for a non-conformist like Randy, what he took away from his time there had little to do with its disrespect for power structures—he already got plenty of that at home. By the time he got to Baylor, Randy's combative, crusading congressman dad had already taught him the importance of picking principled fights with the powers that be; what he learned from George and the other NoZe brothers was what a win could often look like. Their game wasn't circulating earnest petitions and participating in debates with square-jawed student body presidents. Instead, they aimed to ruffle and offend, to rile and inflame. And when they extracted the unflattering reactions they were looking for from their born-again Baylor targets—flustered and angry and comically indignant—they declared victory. The source of the NoZe brothers' sense of superiority came from their ability to handle their opponents' feelings like Play-Doh.

Randy was never on the same page, politically, as his fellow hell-hound comrades at Baylor—most of them were left-wingers—but he related to them on a deeper level. "We knew he was kind of a right-wing nutjob," recalled Green, who was present at Randy's initiatory "unrush." "He fit in with us because he was antiauthoritarian."

Indeed, if there was one belief that united all NoZe brothers, it was the conviction that they were the enlightened few, the freethinkers, the ones who could look outside the cave and see the world as it was, and who now had a responsibility to drag their unseeing peers up the rough ascent, the steep way up, and never stop until they reached the light of the sun. (Randy was hardly the first NoZe know-it-all to commit a bit of Plato to memory.)

Looking through those Groucho glasses, it was plain as day that the established social order at Baylor was a farce—and that it fell to them to expose it.

At the start of the 1983 winter semester, Baylor pulled the plug on its swim program and filled its pool with cement. While Ditzler brooded over losing her campus sanctuary, George and Randy went searching for distraction, and began spending more time on pot-fueled NoZe adventures. "I was the one who was clearly bitter and suffering," Ditzler said later. "They seemed happy and fun." In particular, she noticed that Randy was getting much more into the spirit of the Baylor baiting. Lacking a more productive hobby, he no longer needed much prodding from George to join in on the antics.

Without daily swim practice, Ditzler drifted apart from Randy and George. She moved to an apartment off campus, where they would visit her sporadically. Then, one day, there was an unexpected knock at her door, and she found Randy and George standing on her front steps, holding a bandanna. They asked her to blindfold herself— which she did—and then proceeded to engage in a sort of mock kidnapping ritual. They stuffed her in their car and drove her to an apartment that reeked of weed, with army tents set up on the floor and clothes piled to the ceiling. "I had heard of guys from the NoZe Brotherhood who would do all their shopping at the Goodwill— wear the clothes a few times and then throw them in some apartment," she told me later. "I thought maybe that's where I was." Randy and George tried to get her to take bong hits with them, and when she declined, they put her back in the car and drove her to a countryside creek outside of town. There, on the bank of the stream, they commanded her to bow down to their god, the "Aqua Buddha."

They never hung out again after that, and soon afterward Randy disappeared from campus without a goodbye. (Ditzler would later learn that he scored high enough on the MCATs to get into Duke without graduating from Baylor.) She didn't bother to keep track of Randy or George, and forgot all about the incident.

But the memory of that strange afternoon returned one day twenty-seven years later when, flipping through channels, Ditzler spotted her old pal Randy on CNN, running for Senate. He was wearing a blue blazer and a power tie — dressed up as if he was going as a Republican for Halloween — and he was delivering some laughably earnest spiel about God, country, and Constitution. Even weirder, the news anchor kept calling him "Rand." It was all so ludicrously out of character that she wouldn't have been surprised to find out the campaign was an elaborate NoZe brothers reunion prank.

Ditzler tried to remember the last time she'd seen Randy, and that's when it came back to her: the image of her curly-haired friend, giddy and weird and probably stoned, shouting out nonsensical things about the Aqua Buddha. "It was like, whoa, you must have changed overnight," she remembered thinking. "Or did we ever really know you?"

But after getting over the initial shock of Randy's new act, Ditzler began paying closer attention to what he was up to. She caught the highlights of his big anti-drone filibuster, and occasionally came across news stories about him picking fights with other Republicans. She was a Democrat, and no aficionada of internal GOP politics, but every so often when she watched him on TV she could catch familiar glimpses of her friend.

"He always made fun of people for following," she said, looking back on their college days. "He made fun of people for not thinking for themselves. He made fun of their beliefs... and he provoked people to cause them to question their beliefs." Ditzler continued to believe that his whole flag-shrouded Republican routine was canned, but in at least one way the guy in the new suit was still the same old Randy.

"I guess that's the only thing that's consistent now with the person I knew," she said. "He still provokes people."

Rand would deploy his trademark provocation at many fellow Republicans as he elbowed and needled his way toward the 2016 presidential race — but few targets would prove more irresistible to him than the governor of New Jersey.

What a bunch of pansies.

It was July 25, 2013, and Chris Christie was sitting at the far end of a row of Republican governors on the Aspen Meadows campus, a playground in the Rocky Mountains for the socially conscious rich and the thought leaders flown in to entertain them every summer at the Aspen Ideas Festival. Tonight's production was a panel, moderated by gregarious *New York Times* reporter Jonathan Martin, featuring four conservative state executives and prospective 2016 candidates. The open-collared governors had spent most of the evening complimenting one another and chatting affably about the policy innovations they were pursuing in their respective states. But for his final question, Martin noted a front-page story in his own paper that day reporting that a surprising number of congressional Republicans, led by Rand Paul, had voted with Democrats to crack down on the NSA's recently exposed domestic surveillance program.

"Is your party becoming more libertarian?" Martin asked the governors.

Christie, his massive frame wrapped in a pink oxford shirt, watched in disgust as, one by one, each of his fellow governors punted on the question. Louisiana's Bobby Jindal drawled that the libertarian surge in the party was "a good thing," and then quickly pivoted away to some boilerplate Obama bashing. Wisconsin's Scott Walker talked about how a "shift overall in the party" toward libertarianism might help the GOP reach younger voters like his college-age son. Indiana's Mike Pence sunnily called the national security debate being driven by libertarians "healthy."

Pansies.

It would fall to Christie, the truth-telling, no-nonsense New Jersey honcho, to put the libertarian rabble-rousers in their place, and stop this silly faux movement in its tracks before they actually managed to put American lives in danger.

"As a former prosecutor who was appointed by President George W. Bush on September tenth, two thousand and one, I just want us to be really cautious," Christie began, "because this strain of libertarianism that's going through both parties right now and making big headlines, I think, is a very dangerous thought."

Christie continued, his voice gathering intensity as he worked up a nice, frothy righteous indignation. "I think what we as a country have to decide is, do we have amnesia? 'Cause *I* don't. And I remember what we felt like on September twelfth, two thousand and one." He was really on a roll now. "And as the governor now of a state that lost the second most people on 9/11 besides the state of New York, and still seeing those families, Jon? I *love* all these esoteric debates that people are getting in . . ."

Martin, realizing that he was one quick follow-up away from a huge political headline, interrupted Christie's monologue.

"Senator Rand Paul, for example?" Martin asked.

Christie briefly considered restraint. "Listen, you can name any number of people who've engaged in it," he started, before deciding, *Screw restraint.* "And he's one of 'em."

"I mean, these *esoteric, intellectual* debates." He paused for a moment, as though overwhelmed by the sheer repulsiveness of all the esotericism. "I want them to come to New Jersey and sit across from the widows and the orphans and have that conversation. And they won't, because that's a much tougher conversation to have."

The panel ended a few minutes later, and in between handshakes with attendees, Martin hurriedly tapped out an email on his Black-Berry and fired it off to Doug Stafford, Rand Paul's top adviser.

In the Republican civil war, Chris Christie had just unleashed an unprovoked broadside aimed at libertarians. And Martin wanted to know: how was Rand going to retaliate?

By the time Rand's advisers in Washington got Martin's email and figured out exactly what Christie had said, it was after 10 p.m. and no one particularly felt like waking up the senator to bring news that the big man from the Garden State had called him a terrorist-loving sissy.

Martin was pressing them for an on-the-record quote to run in his *Times* story, but they said they would have to hold their fire until they got Rand's go-ahead.

He wouldn't need much convincing.

For Rand, finding Christie's comments in his inbox the next morning was like Christmas in July. He'd been riding high ever since his filibuster earlier that year, but the June revelations in *The Guardian* and the *Washington Post* that the NSA was secretly collecting millions of Americans' phone records and emails had turned Rand into a political prophet of sorts. The tidal wave of national outrage that followed the exposés had only buoyed Rand's fight against the hawks in his party, and it had solidified his status as a top tier 2016 prospect. In fact, the same day Christie launched his attack in Aspen, a highly publicized poll showed Rand surging to first place in the field of likely Republican candidates.

Now, this tough-talking oaf from New Jersey was trying to pick a fight with him over the very issue that was fueling the libertarian ascent? It was just too good to be true.

Rand green-lit the counterattack, and by 9:30 a.m. he was calling out the governor by name on Twitter:

"Christie worries about the dangers of freedom. I worry about the danger of losing that freedom. Spying without warrants is unconstitutional."

As Rand's inner circle brainstormed fresh quotes to feed the frenzied political press corps, Stafford suggested using lyrics from a Bruce Springsteen song to tweak Christie, who was famously obsessed with the Boss. After a bit of Googling, they landed on a perfect verse in the 2007 anti-Bush rocker "Long Walk Home." Some on the team thought the quote should be attributed to Rand, but the senator's Springsteen expertise was meager, and there was a concern that he might come off as a poser. In the end, Stafford, the resident E Street Band enthusiast, put his name on it. "In the words of the governor's favorite lyricist, 'You know that flag flying over the courthouse? Means certain things are set in stone. Who we are, what we'll do, and what we won't,'" Stafford was quoted as saying.

According to Washington's traditional rules of engagement for such things, this was considered a proportional response—and a more prudent, polite politician might have ended the spat there. But Rand was just getting started.

At a fund-raiser in Nashville that Sunday, Rand took another swipe at Christie and his ideological allies in the GOP. "They're precisely the same people who are unwilling to cut the spending, and they're, 'Gimme, gimme, gimme—give me all my money now,'" Paul said, referring to the federal funding New Jersey had received after Hurricane Sandy ravaged the state in 2012. "Those are the people who are bankrupting the government and not letting enough money be left over for national defense." Rand was betting this line of attack would drive Christie berserk. The governor's leadership in the storm's aftermath had been the crowning achievement of his first term, and Rand figured that invoking the hurricane was a surefire way to get under his skin.

Rand leaned on his talent for trolling again when New York congressman Peter King tried to get in on the action by comparing Rand on CNN to "the antiwar, left-wing Democrats of the nineteen sixties that nominated George McGovern and destroyed their party for almost twenty years." Rand's pithy comeback on Twitter was notable for both its complete lack of context and its pitch-perfect attempt to turn the flag-waving New York neocon into a sputtering mass of outrage and hurt feelings:

"Peter King, from Dem wing of GOP, wants to send ur $ to places who burn our flag. I don't."

(Rand was comparing his own ideological opposition to all U.S. foreign aid spending to King's more mainstream support for the funding. That Rand would eventually have to walk back his position didn't matter in the heat of battle, and certainly not in the universe of 140-character rejoinders.)

Political gawkers marveled at Rand's deliberate, almost gleeful efforts to stretch out the high-profile intraparty feud for as long as possible. Describing the political rationale later, Stafford would tell me, "We don't look for fights, but if we are attacked, we will go in with overwhelming force, and then get out fast. Just like Rand's foreign policy."

But if Rand seemed especially feisty during the Christie feud, there was a reason. Earlier in the summer, Rand had attended a summit hosted by Mitt Romney for big-time Republican donors and politicos in Park City, Utah. The event was Romney's way of staying involved in the fight over the future of the GOP, and it attracted future 2016 candidates from across the party who didn't want to miss out on face time with Republican moneymen. Mingling for the weekend in the smoky cigar rooms and steamy saunas of the high-end Stein Eriksen Lodge, Rand had gotten one of his first sustained, up close looks at his party's neocon elites in their natural habitat—and what he saw didn't exactly fill him with newfound respect for the crowd.

He had been dragged to the gathering by Trygve Olson, a Republican operative who straddled the gap between the party's establishment and its right wing. The two men had first gotten to know each other in 2010, when Olson was dispatched by GOP officials in Washington to make sure Rand—the surprise Tea Party victor in Kentucky's hotly contested U.S. Senate primary that year—didn't blow it in the general election. Republicans in DC were, then as now, deeply wary of the libertarian newcomer, and it was easy to see why. He was an ophthalmologist by trade who spoke in a creaky voice, and exhibited all the charisma of a parking lot attendant. He was in possession of perhaps the least statesmanlike patch of hair in modern political history—an unruly nest of golden curls that seemed existentially resistant to the taming powers of hair product—and his wardrobe was proudly defiant of regulatory overreach by the fashion-industrial complex. Most damningly, he shared a surname with the kookiest gadfly in the Republican Party. At the time, his campaign was being run by two outsiders that few in the GOP establishment knew or trusted: Jesse Benton, a young Paul family loyalist who was married to the candidate's niece, and Stafford, a former jewelry salesman who worked at a conservative antiunion group. Olson's assignment was to provide some adult supervision to the operation—but he soon hit it off with Rand. Olson, a foul-mouthed hockey player and CrossFit enthusiast, admired the candidate's pugnacious streak, and ever since the 2010 race he had been a friend and informal adviser to the senator, acting as a sort of ambassador to the GOP gentry that Rand so disdained.

Rand knew that if he was serious about 2016, he would have to spend some unpleasant time hobnobbing with the party pooh-bahs, and so he begrudgingly followed Olson to the retreat in the Wasatch mountains. But by the time the weekend was over, Rand was more convinced than ever that these people — many of them architects of the most costly wars in American history — were, among other things, prissy little wimps. For him, the summit's most telling moment came when Dan Senor, who had once served as the Bush administration's chief spokesman for the Iraq War, went skeet shooting with Paul Ryan, and word got around that it was Senor's first time ever using a gun. Afterward, Rand morbidly joked with aides about the namby-pamby neocons who had never before handled a firearm or bruised their knuckles but had no problem sending planeloads of teenagers into Middle Eastern war zones.

"So many of the neocons in our party, they think they're the great defenders of the military," Rand would later complain to me in an interview. "They think, 'Oh, the soldiers must love me because I want to be involved in war.'" The truth, Rand firmly believed, was that most members of the military were not eager to fight. "They will. They volunteered, and they're the most patriotic of our young people. But they're not excited about war. They want to go to war if it's the thing they have to do to defend our country...We could sit in a room with ten GIs and their young wives, or vice versa, and their young husbands, and ask them about it. It's not a chess game to them. It's like, 'My husband's been four times, and still has his arms and legs. I don't want him to go a fifth time'...I think the people eager for war in my party, and the people eager to send troops in to feed people in the Democratic Party, they don't know exactly what it's like because only a very small sliver of our society are fighting these wars. And I think, really, more politicians ought to sit down at the dining room table with our soldiers and just ask them about it."

Beneath all the trolling and the back-of-the-napkin political calculation, this was really what drove Rand to keep hitting Christie. It was one thing for John McCain to publicly ridicule him—the old guy had earned the right to be wrong during his five and a half years of torture and abuse in a North Vietnamese prison camp. But when Rand looked at Christie, he saw an entire class of well-fed, self-satisfied GOP elites who had never seen combat, but still shamelessly wrapped themselves in the flag and used grieving widows and dead soldiers to assert moral superiority. If one of those hypocrites wanted to start a fight with him, he wasn't going to pull his punches.

By the Monday following Christie's remarks in Aspen, Rand could feel the momentum gathering behind him, and he was having a blast. He soaked up every withering word of an editorial in the right-leaning *New Hampshire Union Leader*—an influential force in presidential primaries given its state's first-in-the-nation status—that was going viral in the political world. "If Christie is saying, as he seems to be, that the state should be empowered to take any measures it deems necessary to protect against terror attacks—without any concern for the 'esoteric, intellectual debates' over civil liberties—then he is the radical extremist, not Rand Paul," the editors hissed.

While Rand giddily plotted his next move, Olson worried that the whole thing was getting out of hand. If the barrage didn't stop soon, Rand would risk squandering any credibility he had built up with GOP brass by coming off like an immature, overzealous board game player who keeps obnoxiously gloating as he piles tiny plastic houses on Park Place. They were still two and a half years out from the presidential primaries, after all: didn't Rand know that they were only playing for Monopoly money at this point?

Olson had worked in the past with Christie's chief political adviser, Mike DuHaime, and he was confident that the two could broker a cease-fire. But when he brought the idea to Rand's team, Stafford and Benton replied that the senator was having way too much fun to call a truce now.

You can try, they told Olson. But there's no point. Rand isn't going to stop.

That night, Rand went on Fox News to continue the Christie pile-on. "It's really, I think, kind of sad and cheap that he would use the cloak of 9/11 victims to say, 'Oh, I'm the only one who cares about these victims,'" he told Sean Hannity. "Hogwash!" Rand went on to repeat his "gimme, gimme, gimme" line—slipping into a faint New Jersey accent as he delivered it—and made sure not to get off the air without some more custom-tailored goading. "[Christie] may have heard that, you know, the Republican Party is on life support in the Northeast," he said. "Republicans are in danger of becoming an endangered species. So, it's not real smart for Republicans to be attacking Republicans."

The next day, Christie finally took the bait. At a news conference announcing homeowner grants for New Jersey residents affected by Sandy, the governor said he had nothing personal against Rand, but added that if the senator had a problem with his blunt style, "he can just get in line." Christie went on to note that New Jersey taxpayers sent more money to Washington than the state got back, and suggested, "If Senator Paul wants to start looking at where he's going to cut spending to afford defense, maybe he should start looking at the pork barrel spending he brings home to Kentucky...But I doubt he would. Because most Washington politicians only care about bringing home the bacon so that they can get reelected."

Success!

Rand was elated. After hammering away at Christie for four straight days, he had finally lulled his target back into the fracas. As he mulled how to swat back, Rand had an idea. Some of his more weak-stomached aides might not like it, but it was just too good to pass up.

That afternoon, he went on CNN, and Wolf Blitzer asked him about Christie's accusation of pork barrel spending.

Not even bothering to contain a smirk, Rand quipped, "This is the king of bacon talking about bacon."

Chris Christie.

The king of bacon.

How could anyone pass that up?

The CNN clip went viral instantly, as bloggers and tweeters feverishly spread the news that the junior senator from Kentucky just *went there.* In his ongoing high-wire act of political provocation, Rand Paul had just shown the world that he did not consider fat jokes to be off-limits.

But while Rand was quite pleased with his little act of mischief, it was clear to his inner circle that things had gone too far. "It's time to move on," Olson insisted in an email to the senator. Rand relented with a shrug, and Olson was finally sent to negotiate a truce with the Christie team. But he found them much less interested in the olive branch than they might have been twenty-four hours earlier.

Christie, who had quietly undergone lap band surgery earlier in the year and was steadily losing weight, thought the joke was outrageous, and deemed Rand to be an even bigger joke than he had realized. What started out as a substantive, life-and-death debate over America's national security had devolved, thanks to Rand, into a puerile crack about his weight that any dull-witted third grader could have come up with.

The next day, Rand went on Fox News and invited Christie to have a beer with him. "It's gotten a little too personal," Rand said, in a maddeningly phony tone of reconciliation. "So let's kiss and make up."

But Christie was finished dealing with this ridiculous person. He was never going to be buddies with Rand, and he had no interest in engaging in the Kabuki theater of party unity. "I'm not offended by Senator Paul calling me names. I think it's juvenile, but I'm not offended by it," he told a radio station that same day. Asked whether he would take up Rand on the beer, Christie replied sharply, "I really don't have time for that at the moment."

For Rand, the fight with Christie had been thrilling and, he believed, important. Sure, the Washington handwringers would fret about the trivialization of American politics and express longing for a Great Debate worthy of a Great Nation. But Rand wasn't interested in dryly outlining his arguments on C-SPAN and letting history decide whether he was right. To him, this was more than a mild-mannered contest of policy positions; it was a revolution. In the race toward 2016, Rand would employ every tactic necessary to triumph in this high-stakes battle of ideas, no matter how unorthodox or unsavory or mean.

Fat baiting, Twitter trolling, thirteen-hour filibusters—all of it was fair game, and he would return to the methods again and again in the coming years.

Rand wasn't playing for Monopoly money. For the first time in his life, it looked as if the fates might actually be conspiring to create a true libertarian movement in the Republican Party—and Rand was standing at the head of the line, poised to usher in the new order.

Chapter Seven

"It's Not You, It's Me"

One Republican conspicuously missing from the big, headline-grabbing, intraparty battles was Bobby Jindal. And it was driving him a little nuts.

The Louisiana governor had been so certain this was his moment. With the failure of Mitt Romney's inane campaign causing the Republican Party to cast about in search of a new leader with fresh ideas, Jindal had methodically positioned himself to take advantage. After spending the 2012 presidential primaries stumping for Texas governor Rick Perry and stockpiling goodwill among his grassroots conservative admirers, Jindal became the chairman of the Republican Governors Association at the start of 2013 — a perch that would allow him to hobnob with GOP donors, travel the country, and bank favors in key battleground states.

With those pieces in place, Jindal had set about reintroducing himself as the party's "ideas man." He gave an interview to *Politico* in which he raged against "dumbed down conservatism," called on the GOP to "stop being the stupid party," and urged its leaders to "talk to Americans like adults." He then proceeded to repeat this advice on every TV show that would let him within fifteen feet of a camera.

Jindal's diagnosis of the GOP's woes was largely a self-serving strategy to recapture the momentum he had back in 2007, when he was first elected governor and christened a rising Republican star in short order. On paper, Jindal had possessed many of the same qualities that were just then helping Barack Obama capture the country's imagination with his historic presidential campaign. Jindal was young and idealistic and not white—frequently referred to in the press as the GOP's "great beige hope." Like Obama, he was a second-generation American who had zipped up the meritocratic ladder from humble middle-class roots, on the strength of hard work and diligent résumé building. In one stump speech after another, he had presented himself as a star-spangled manifestation of the American dream (and, implicitly, a walking antidote to the perception that the Republican Party was overrun by old white men).

But Jindal had something else that was even more important to GOP elites circa 2007: he was an Ivy-laureled policy wonk in a party where senior officials and opinion leaders were sick of being stereotyped as drawling dimwits. After nearly a decade of George W. Bush contaminating the party's brand, Acela-riding Republicans in the country's northeastern corridor were eager to show the nation that the new Republican Party would be defined by a fresh generation of sharp-minded leaders with big ideas, not Texas cowboys with stunted vocabularies. They wanted America to know that conservatives could be smart, too—and the "GOP wunderkind" in Baton Rouge was a balm for their neurosis. Every political column about Jindal back then contained a requisite description of his intelligence, often in terms so colorful and extravagant that it seemed as though the journalists were all engaging in the same creative writing exercise. Conservative commentator Kathleen Parker, for example, leaned on *Star Trek* to capture Jindal's otherworldly brainpower, writing that he had "the kind of intellect that makes Vulcans uneasy." And former Bush speechwriter Michael Gerson gushed in a column that Jindal's rise meant that "the hall-monitoring, library-inhabiting, science-fair-winning class president has seized control of the Big Easy. And his coup has been an inspiration to policy geeks everywhere."

Of course, all that had been *before* Jindal was tapped to deliver the Republicans' official State of the Union response in 2009. Looking back on it now, the governor realized that speech could have been a big star-making moment for him. Instead it turned out to be a political self-detonation on live TV. He could still remember the sinking feeling he had while watching the pundits that night savage his performance as "amateurish," and "sing song," and "childish," and "insane," and…

No. Jindal *would not* let himself dwell on that fateful screw-up. He had blown it, plain and simple. But he was determined now to re-ignite the enthusiasm he had inspired back when Republicans were still heralding him as their party's answer to Barack Obama. To do so, he would reestablish himself as the intellectual leader of the GOP—and, consequently, a top tier 2016 presidential prospect.

Jindal already knew he was the smartest guy in the party; he just needed to remind everybody else. Now if only he could get their attention.

It is difficult to pinpoint the exact moment when Piyush Jindal became convinced of his own intellectual gifts. Did it happen in elementary school, when Mrs. Couvillion, a teacher most of his class-mates couldn't stand, launched a read-a-thon to raise money for the class and young Jindal devoured fifty-five books before his father, concerned about how much money he was going to have to donate, told his son, "No, no, stop reading. That's enough. I'll go buy you a prize instead"? Or was it later in his childhood, when he read in a biography of Abraham Lincoln that the sixteenth president was "inquisitive" and, upon looking up the definition of the word, smugly announced to his mother, who had grown tired of her son's constant pestering, "President Lincoln was inquisitive and so am I. And you can't be mad at me for doing what the president did"? It seems likely that the revelation occurred sometime after he precociously decided at the age of four that he was renaming himself after his favorite *Brady Bunch* character, Bobby—but probably before he racked up enough straight A report cards as a thirteen-year-old to land at an elite magnet high school in Baton Rouge.

In any case, these are the stories that hold together the Approved Bobby Jindal Narrative, a self-portrait painted across scores of speeches, personal essays, and a memoir-slash-political manifesto, published in

2010 and titled *Leadership and Crisis*. The book, like so many others written by ambitious politicians looking to introduce themselves to the national electorate, is filled with a candor-like substance that resembles genuine introspection and insight, even though it was vetted by a team of political consultants. Coauthored by Curt Anderson, one of Jindal's closest political advisers, *Leadership and Crisis* lists on its acknowledgments page a bevy of GOP consultants who gave him "input," including his pollster.

What's revealing, then, isn't the story itself, but how Jindal chose to tell it—primarily in a long string of anecdotes about how smart he is. This pattern, which persists throughout his autobiographical writing and rhetoric, is crystallized in the book: when he is aiming for self-deprecation, he jokes about his youthful participation in a math tournament ("Don't laugh"); when he wants to illustrate his critique of America's arrogant elites, he recounts stories from college of besting Ivy League liberals in intellectual debates ("a Baton Rouge education could hold its own"); and when he recounts the chronology of his career—from the Rhodes scholarship he wasn't sure he wanted, to the McKinsey consulting job he fell into, to his ascent to the presidency of the University of Louisiana System at the age of twenty-seven—he does so with the casual self-regard of a brilliant man for whom life is a wild adventure of surprise successes.

Jindal may have always been destined for such intellectual swagger. He was still in the womb when his parents, Amar and Raj, emigrated from India to the United States in 1971 so his mother could pursue a graduate degree in nuclear physics at Louisiana State University. While Raj took classes, Amar took the bus to and from his job at the railroad, earning just enough money to work toward a normal middle-class life for his family and start putting cash away for his kids' education. Amar, who had grown up in third world, stomach-aching poverty, instilled in his kids an immigrant's appreciation for the opportunities America presented—and an insistence that they use every last ounce of their potential to attain the status and wealth that was available to them. In the Jindals' modest neighborhood, where the only two-story houses belonged to doctors, Amar became convinced that Jindal should set his sights on medical school.

With this goal fixed for him early on, Jindal spent his childhood working hard on his homework and excelling in class. He discovered that the work came much more easily to him than to other kids, and he eventually skipped a grade. But while his academic success pleased his parents, it wasn't until he started high school that he found that his intellectual prowess could reap social rewards for him as well.

Baton Rouge Magnet High School offered a unique setting for Jindal's adolescence. The student population was largely made up of the children of LSU faculty, and its relative diversity helped insulate him from the racial tensions that gripped a state that was still grappling with desegregation. "It was a nice mix of people, many of whom had that family pressure of immigrants to succeed," recalled Emilio Mayorga, a Nicaragua native who went to school with Jindal. At Baton Rouge High, the smart kids *were* the popular kids—and Jindal, the habitual hand raiser, the relentless curve ruiner, the terminal know-it-all, was one of the very smartest.

It wasn't long before his academic preeminence started attracting friends and admirers, and by the time he was old enough to join the advanced placement section—which doubled as the school's cool kids clique—he was one of the most popular upperclassmen around, and a star student. When Elaine Parsons transferred to Baton Rouge High as a sophomore, one of the first people she met was Jindal, oozing self-assurance and eager to meet the new coed.

Parsons remembered Jindal primarily as the popular, convivial president of Mu Alpha Theta (the *cool* math club; there were two). "We're getting into pretty dorky territory here, but the math club was a big deal socially," she said. "Our school was an academic magnet school with no major sports...so math club felt to me to be a rather cool thing to do. Most of the most competitive students were in it, and it's where we often hung out before and sometimes after school." By the time he graduated, Jindal had become president of so many clubs that the administration implemented a limit on how many extracurricular organizations a single student could helm at a time.

Although Jindal later wrote in *Leadership and Crisis,* "I had never been a terribly political person in high school," his classmates would remember him enthusiastically immersing himself in the culture of

Reagan's America. He idolized the fictional icons of eighties-era wealth and striving, like Michael J. Fox's character, Alex P. Keaton, the high school Republican with hippie parents in television's *Family Ties,* and the moneyed young investors depicted in the 1987 TV movie *Billionaire Boys Club.* He wore suits to school, sometimes accompanied by a bow tie with a dollar bill pattern, and carried a briefcase through the halls instead of a backpack. When Oliver Stone's blockbuster movie *Wall Street* came out in 1987, Jindal memorized and frequently quoted from the triumphalist procapitalism speech that cutthroat investor Gordon Gekko, played by Michael Douglas, delivers to shareholders of a troubled paper company.

"Greed, for lack of a better word, is good," the teenage Jindal would say, doing his best Douglas impression. "Greed is right. Greed works. Greed clarifies, cuts through, and captures the essence of the evolutionary spirit. Greed, in all of its forms—greed for life, for money, for love, knowledge—has marked the upward surge of mankind."

According to former classmate Reagan Farr, Jindal was drawn to these figures not because he was a rabid ideologue, but because they embodied the only kind of American dream that truly appeals to a teenage son of middle-class immigrants: the potential to become extremely rich. "We just saw the lifestyle of these guys...and we all wanted to go out and make much more money than our parents," Farr said.

On his birthday one year, Jindal arranged for himself and a group of friends to drive to New Orleans, where they spent the night cavorting on Bourbon Street, bobbing in and out of funky shops and jazz clubs, and getting apathetic bartenders to sell them liquor. "It was technically illegal to drink when you were a [teenager], but no one cared because it was a federal rule recently imposed on the state," recalled Parsons, who accompanied Jindal on the trip. And so, in the name of his newfound federalist ideals, Jindal and his friends tipped back their glasses and swigged some of their first gulps of booze. In one club, a performer got word that the lanky brown kid was celebrating his birthday, and she brought him onstage to serenade him. His friends whooped and hollered along with the other revelers, and when it was over they spilled back out onto the cobblestoned streets in a state of joyful delirium.

Jindal was nearing the end of his time in high school by then, and soon he would be off to Brown and then Oxford and eventually Washington, DC. But Baton Rouge High would stick with him as the place where he learned the real value of his superpowered brain. It wasn't just that it could earn him good grades, or parental pats on the head, or maybe even, one day, the rich-enough-to-fly-your-own-jet, rich-enough-to-not-waste-time wealth that Gekko ranted about in *Wall Street.* More important than any of that, his brilliance could win him friends. It could make people like him.

It was a lesson he would keep with him for the next two decades—until one day, all of a sudden, it began failing him miserably.

In January 2013, Jindal got to work revamping his national profile as a brainy conservative policy maestro, beginning with a bold proposal in Louisiana to abolish state income taxes for corporations and individuals. That same month, he wrote an op-ed soberly outlining the ways in which Obamacare's Medicaid expansion would burden state budgets and identifying several ways to reform the program. And as he toured the country, he spoke earnestly about the need for the Republican Party to recalibrate its economic message to emphasize increasing growth, rather than obsess over budget deficits.

In Baton Rouge, Jindal's young, wiry chief of staff, Timmy Teepell, worked around the clock to put legislative points on the board for the governor's agenda. And in Washington, Jindal's rumpled, sardonic media consultant, Curt Anderson, was busy talking up those policy victories—and the big ideas that powered them—with his network of high-powered comrades and insider contacts. But no one was biting.

No matter how many serious-minded op-eds and policy speeches Jindal trotted out, the man who had once been anointed by the Republican smart set as heir to the party's intellectual legacy was now barely making a ripple in the national conversation. He had been relegated to the sidelines while the think tankers, commentators, academicians, and politicians with Beltway zip codes got to drive the debate.

The lack of interest depressed Jindal's inner circle. "If you're in Washington and you can get on the Senate floor, you'll get covered by the national press corps if you say something racy or crazy enough," Anderson grumbled to me. "Or if you're in New Jersey and you want to get attention, you can go to Manhattan—if the bridge isn't closed—and get on national TV." After months of failing to make a national splash, one Jindal adviser glumly concluded, "I'm not sure that someone like Bobby gets enough attention to matter until he decides to get in the race."

But geography wasn't Jindal's only problem. For one thing, the governor's big ideas were sinking him in his home state. By April, his bold tax proposal had become a political fiasco, with state lawmakers on both sides of the aisle revolting against Jindal's plan to raise sales taxes in order to pay for the income tax cut. He was soon forced to withdraw the proposal, and just like that, what was supposed to be the signature policy achievement of his second term was dead. The next month, the school voucher program Jindal had implemented in his first term—already a deeply polarizing initiative in his state for diverting funds to religious charter schools that taught creationism—was found to be unconstitutional by the Louisiana Supreme Court. That spring, his approval rating sank to 38 percent.

Meanwhile, at the national level, Jindal now found himself competing for attention in a crowded field of Republican hero-wonks. When he first came on the scene, his policy acumen was new and somewhat unique among ambitious conservative politicians. But since then, a herd of spreadsheet-wielding, white paper–writing Republicans had stampeded out of political obscurity, and were now dominating the debate over the party's agenda. Paul Ryan had risen to political fame by authoring detailed, deficit-hacking federal budgets, and eventually climbed all the way to the GOP's 2012 presidential ticket. Yuval Levin had launched *National Affairs,* a prestigious journal that published dense conservative policy tracts, and quickly earned prominent placement on coffee tables in GOP offices across Washington. Even Utah senator Mike Lee, viewed in many corners as a Tea Party rabble-rouser, was introducing thoughtful, serious legislation aimed at improving infrastructure and education. Policy wonkishness was now *en vogue* in the Republican Party—and Jindal had done little to significantly distinguish himself from the rest.

Adding to Jindal's problems was the fact that the neuroses of the GOP elites were no longer calibrated toward searching for an anti-Dubya standard-bearer. Whereas in 2009, the conventional wisdom was that Republicans needed a young, whip smart reformer to emerge and dispel the dumb-cowboy stereotypes that plagued the party, now GOP influentials were looking for an anti-Romney to rehabilitate the party's image. In their view, Republicans had lost in 2012 because they were represented by a wealthy, awkward, Wall Street–manufactured automaton who shuffled around on "clean-cut, midcentury capitalist dad" setting, saying things like "Golly" and "Gee whiz" and "I'm not concerned about the very poor." To counteract the damage Romney had done to the GOP's brand, particularly in Middle America, many of the party's leaders thought they should elevate politicians who were personally dynamic, charismatic, relatable—maybe even folksy. And Jindal was, at least the way he was marketing himself now, not one of those guys.

In October, Jindal launched a policy group, America Next, that aimed to come up with innovative solutions to the country's problems. The announcement made a minor splash in the DC trades, but the organization was quickly forgotten—consigned to spend untold years sending little-known academicians to poorly attended panels at conservative conferences.

The longer the governor lumbered along unnoticed by the rest of the GOP, the more convinced he became that brains alone were not going to make him the leader of his party. In what seemed like a cry for partisan attention, Jindal penned a *Politico* op-ed in June 2013 titled "GOP Needs Action, Not Navel-Gazing," in which he complained, rather abrasively, about all the self-analysis and soul-searching going on in his party since 2012.

"It's really getting embarrassing, all these public professions of feelings of inadequacy," he wrote. "Every day it seems another jilted high-placed Republican in Washington is confessing to the voters, 'It's not you, it's me...'"

In truth, Jindal was the one feeling jilted. He had spent months courting the respect and attention of those "high-placed Republicans," chasing them with the hormone-drenched persistence of a teenage boy pursuing his first love—only to strike out again and again. As Jindal surveyed the GOP's field of competing 2016 suitors, he concluded that to win back the affections of his party, brains alone wouldn't be enough: he would need to pull off a grand romantic gesture—a public display of partisan heroics so gutsy and high-profile that conservatives would remember why they fell in love with him in the first place.

And so, with a new plan in place, Team Jindal set out from Baton Rouge in search of a path back into the national limelight. Meanwhile, 1,100 miles away in Washington, one of the most spotlight-soaked stars in the GOP was about to get burned, and badly, by the glare.

Chapter Eight

Daddy Issues

On July 9, 2013, the Washington Free Beacon, a tenacious conservative news site with a knack for troublemaking, posted a story revealing that a staffer in Rand Paul's office had spent years working as a neo-Confederate radio personality who went by the moniker "the Southern Avenger." The site reported that Jack Hunter, who was now serving as the senator's social media director in Washington, had been famous in his home state of South Carolina as a shock jock who donned a Confederate flag luchador mask and spouted off about how "a non–white majority America would simply cease to be America." He had railed against the effects of Mexican immigration and, in one particularly unsettling rant, toasted Abraham Lincoln's assassin, declaring that John Wilkes Booth's "heart was in the right place." To top it all off, he had also served as a local chairman in the League of the South, a fringe group that advocated for the secession of the Southern states.

The story detonated the day's political news cycle, and reporters sprayed the senator's office with phone calls and emails seeking comment. Rand's profile had been rising steadily for months now, and the press was no longer treating him like an entertaining sideshow. He was now an influential political force—the face of America's libertarian ascent—and editors believed he deserved tough scrutiny.

Rand's ideological opponents in the GOP were recalibrating their strategies for dealing with him as well. The party's neoconservative wing—which held that America should assert power and influence in the world through overwhelming military might, and prioritize national defense above virtually all else—saw Rand's noninterventionist message gaining steam in the party, and believed it to be deeply dangerous. The story in the Free Beacon, a neocon outfit with ties to the movement's leading thinker, Bill Kristol, was one early salvo in an amorphous but deliberate campaign to discredit Rand.

Of course, no one believed that the Southern Avenger would single-handedly serve as the senator's undoing. In the course of most every politician's career, there comes a time when he finds out that he has inadvertently hired a deviant—a pervert, a rank homophobe, an unapologetic communist. In Washington's monochromatic political class, there was little room for weirdos or radicals—and whenever it was publicly revealed that one was secretly lurking in the lower ranks of some congressional office, the politician could generally weather the storm by adhering to a widely understood protocol. He would release a statement insisting he was unaware of the deviant's past and assuring the electorate that he held his staff to the highest standards of tolerance and moral fortitude. Then he would unceremoniously fire the deviant and lie low while he waited for the media to move on.

Not Rand. With reporters clamoring to know whether he was going to fire his aide, the senator grumpily instructed his communications director to issue a defiant (but vaguely worded) statement saying only that his office required "all employees [to] treat individuals with the equal protection of the law" and that "we find no evidence that this policy has been violated by any employee."

Translation: Jack Hunter hasn't broken any laws. Now kindly bite me.

When Trygve Olson saw the statement, he was bewildered. Rand could not seriously be thinking of standing by this disposable mid-level aide who was towing behind him thirteen years' worth of racist commentary and radical activism—could he?

Olson called up Doug Stafford in Rand's office and told him what every political operative in Washington already knew: You guys *have* to fire Hunter.

Stafford replied that it wasn't going to happen. Rand had made up his mind; he thought the Free Beacon story was a cheap shot, and he didn't want to give the neocons the satisfaction of a scalp. Besides, he didn't think it was ultimately that big of a deal.

Incredulous, Olson decided to go straight to the source. He had lunch that week with Rand and a couple of his aides, and on the walk back to the Capitol, Olson outlined the myriad ways in which keeping Hunter around would be a disaster. The aide's history would be an albatross around his neck as long as he was on staff. And Rand's failure to get rid of him would send a message to the Republican donor class, whose money he would be begging for ahead of 2016, that his campaign wasn't serious. Why would any multimillionaire write a check to a candidate who wasn't even willing to throw a freak show staffer under the bus to win?

By the time they arrived at his Senate office, Rand had come around.

"Yeah, he probably has to move on," he conceded. "But I don't want to fire him."

Olson assured Rand that he wouldn't have to, that they would persuade Hunter to quietly slink away on his own. Rand signed off on the decision, and finally, almost two weeks after the Free Beacon story went live, Hunter resigned.

It was clear, though, that weeks later, Rand was still smarting from the episode. When he was asked about Hunter during an interview with NPR in August, he lost his composure and began lashing out at the host. "You can go ahead and beat up on an ex-employee of mine, but...don't you have something better to read than a bunch of crap from people who don't like me?" he barked.

L'affaire Hunter left many in the political world perplexed by why it had taken Rand so long to do what obviously needed to be done, and why he seemed to be taking it all so personally.

But inside Rand World, the reason was obvious. Hunter wasn't just any run-of-the-mill secessionist political aide: he was a friend of the family. A libertarian stalwart who was well regarded in the movement, Hunter had been a loyal Paulite for years. He was an early supporter of Ron Paul's 2008 presidential campaign, and at his dad's suggestion, Rand had hired Hunter to coauthor his 2011 book, *The*

Tea Party Goes to Washington. The truth was that Rand had known all about Hunter's Southern Avenger alter ego; it had just never occurred to him that a radical résumé should preclude a talented operative from joining his team.

But that was then. Three years later, Rand was a rising star and leading contender in the early 2016 polls, straining to exhibit serious-ness and escape the tentacles of the libertarian fringe without appear-ing disloyal to his father's legacy. It was a sensitive undertaking rife with familial repercussions. Hunter had come under attack at a time when the relationship between Rand and his dad was growing more fraught with tension and resentment by the day. And while both Pauls publicly slapped down even the faintest suggestion of acrimony, the truth was that their father-son rivalry had been simmering for years.

Rand Paul's earliest political education was gained by eavesdropping on his dad. A slight, quiet kid with shaggy hair, Randy liked to hover near the long, rectangular table in his family's Lake Jackson, Texas, dining room and pretend to read a book while he listened to Ron entertain a rotating cast of libertarian luminaries. He was not an osten-tatiously precocious kid, not the type to butt in. But he was in awe of his father, and fascinated by the philosophical solar system in which his home was increasingly becoming the center of gravity. "I always was more drawn to the conversations with adults than other things," he later told me of his adolescence.

He was thirteen years old and just beginning to take an interest in his dad's incessant talk of monetary policy when the old man was first elected to the House of Representatives, in 1976. Congressman Paul championed a suburban, culturally conservative spin on libertarian-ism that distanced itself from the free love hippies and libertine anar-chists traditionally associated with the ideology, and resonated instead with the type of gun-toting, churchgoing small businessmen who populated south Texas.

The Pauls lived in a big four-bedroom ranch house—paid for with the income Ron made as the only ob-gyn in town—that included a swim-ming pool and a TV set that was always on (even when nobody was watching). Ron and his wife, Carol, had a distinctly laissez-faire parenting style: no firm curfews, no mandatory chores, and absolutely no allowance, which Ron regarded as a handout that might foster dependence. "I don't know that we had any rules," recalled Ronnie, the oldest of the five kids. But while they weren't disciplinarians or taskmasters, Ron and Carol set serious expectations for their kids that made for a brood of high achievers. "We really didn't want to disappoint our parents," Ronnie said.

For Randy's seventeenth birthday, his dad gave him a collection of Ayn Rand novels, which he promptly devoured. The books' heroes—handsome and beautiful capitalists crusading against the evil forces of collectivism—lent romance to his dad's economic sermonizing. At around the same time, Randy fell in love with the Canadian prog rock band Rush, famous for synth-heavy, libertarian-tinged tracks like the 1981 hit "Tom Sawyer," about a free-spirited individualist whose "mind is not for rent / to any god or government."

As his father became a leading light of American libertarianism, many of the movement's most prominent figures became part of Randy's day-to-day life. He drove preeminent libertarian thinker Murray Rothbard to the airport. He watched free market economist Hans Sennholz choke on his first-ever bite of spicy Mexican food. These youthful interactions seemed unremarkable to Randy at the time, but they would become the raw material out of which his ideological worldview was formed.

During summers, Randy interned at Ron's congressional office in Washington. On morning commutes to the Capitol, he would sit quietly in the car and soak up his dad's drive time philosophical musings with chief of staff Lew Rockwell. When the workday ended, Randy would head back to his dad's condo in northern Virginia and the two would chat about the day's political news over dinner. Neither of them could have guessed that two decades later, they would find themselves back in the exact same situation—but as budding rivals.

Shortly after winning his 2010 Senate race, Rand asked his dad if he could move in with him. The senator-elect was taking a hefty pay cut by giving up his ophthalmology practice back home, and he wasn't sure he could afford his own apartment in Washington. He figured rooming with his dad—who was still serving in the House of

Representatives, and still owned the northern Virginia apartment—
would be an easy way to save cash as he transitioned to a government
paycheck.

Ron agreed, and the arrangement soon generated a small flurry of
soft-focus media profiles about the proud father and admiring son
going about the people's business by day, and splitting chores and grocery checks by night. They diligently played up the shtick in interviews, cracking corny jokes about each other's cooking and reminiscing
about the summers they spent together in DC when Rand was a
teenager.

Privately, though, they were both miserable. Ron had bought the
condo when he was first elected to Congress in the seventies, and
Rand discovered upon moving in that the decor hadn't changed in
the ensuing thirty-five years. All wood paneling and retro earth tones,
the place made Rand feel as though he was living in *The Jeffersons'*
"deluxe apartment in the sky," only much closer to earth and about
three decades past its deluxe prime. The younger Paul was also a bit of
a neat freak, and he often caught himself grumbling about the grimy
untidiness of his dad's digs. He wasn't comfortable with his wife
spending the night there when she visited, and he came to loathe his
daily commutes in traffic across the 14th Street Bridge.

Ron, meanwhile, quickly tired of having his forty-seven-year-old son
constantly crowding him. As much as he had always enjoyed spending
time with his kids when he was at home in Texas, Ron long ago grew
accustomed to being a solo operator when he was in Washington. Now,
Rand's inescapable presence was making him claustrophobic.

Rand moved out of the condo after less than six months—but
Ron's claustrophobia never really subsided.

One day early in 2011, Ron met with Jesse Benton—the young political strategist he shared with his son—to break the news that he
wasn't going to run for president again. The veteran congressman was
getting ready to retire, and he felt he had made his point during his
2008 bid. He wanted to wind down his time in office with dignity,
not in the harried heat of another national campaign.

Benton was disappointed, but with Ron out of the picture, he decided it was time to start grooming Rand for a presidential run. He approached the younger Paul and pitched him on mounting an insurgent bid for the Republican nomination in 2012. He was adamant that Rand's polish and pragmatism would make him a far more serious candidate than his dad ever was. Benton argued that, between the fiery base of supporters Ron had built up and the new voters Rand could attract, he would be a real threat to win the White House.

Rand ate it up. He told Benton to start putting out feelers for a 2012 bid, and the strategist moved quickly to schedule a trip to the early primary state of South Carolina. On March 23, 2011, Rand made a surprise appearance at the Charleston Meeting, a gathering of Palmetto State Republican elites, and news of the visit set off sirens in the political punditocracy. Rand fanned the speculation by announcing future trips to Iowa and New Hampshire as well. The buzz was building, the strategy was working, the wheels were in motion—and then, suddenly, it all came to a screeching halt.

A couple of days after Rand's headline-grabbing South Carolina trip, Ron called up Benton. He had been giving some more thought to the idea of a 2012 presidential bid, and he'd changed his mind.

I've decided I'm going to run, Ron said. And I want you to manage my campaign.

Rand, it went without saying, would have to take a seat.

The story of the elder Paul carelessly—maybe even maliciously—sidelining his own son's presidential ambitions was never publicly reported, but it traveled quickly throughout the two men's shared network of operatives and activists, who reacted like dinner guests trapped at a table where a nasty family argument is suddenly erupting: eyes turned downward, fake smiles frozen in place, everyone trying awkwardly to pretend they didn't notice the enormous breach of decorum that had just taken place.

In the weeks that followed Ron's power play, they traded gossip and speculation in hushed tones and discreet text messages. Was Ron jealous of his son's meteoric rise? Resentful that he wasn't getting proper credit for laying the groundwork for Rand's success? Or maybe Rand had jumped the gun without getting his dad's go-ahead? Was this a sign that Ron didn't trust Rand's commitment to libertarian ideals? Or was he only trying to spare his son from foolishly rushing into the presidential fray before he was ready?

Whatever the reason, as the campaign progressed, many in the Pauls' concentric inner circles began to notice a gulf forming between father and son that hadn't been there before.

In December 2011, polls showed that the upcoming Iowa caucuses were—implausibly, unbelievably—within Ron's grasp. The campaign believed that if he simply stuck to his core message of small-government economics for the final weeks of the race, he would win the state. But instead, Ron kept wandering off into unfiltered foreign policy rants that made him sound more like a crazed hobo shouting at a crowded bus stop than a credible contender for the Oval Office. "He kept wanting to talk about how Osama bin Laden had some valid justifications for attacking the U.S., or whatever," one frustrated adviser later complained to me.

Finally, Trygve Olson, who was working on Ron's campaign, dialed up the candidate's eminently more practical son and pleaded with him to stage an intervention, persuade his father to stay on message.

"You've gotta talk to him," Olson said.

"Let me ask you a question," Rand replied. "Do you ever talk politics with your dad?"

"Yeah."

"And how does that usually go?" Rand asked.

"He usually ends up telling me I'm full of shit," Olson cracked.

"What makes you think it's any different with my dad?"

A couple of weeks after losing Iowa, Ron was in the greenroom at a Republican primary debate in South Carolina when Jim DeMint and Lindsey Graham came up to him and began effusively piling praise on his son. They gushed about how Rand was a joy to work with in the Senate, a real contributor, someone with whom they felt they could work productively despite their ideological differences.

Finally, Ron snapped, "Well, if he's so great, he should run for president himself."

DeMint was taken aback by the outburst and quickly shut up. But Graham didn't seem to catch on, because he just kept spurting commendations for Rand in his courtly Southern drawl, as Ron's face twisted into a cranky scowl.

By the time the 2012 campaign ended, the Pauls' shared orbit of allies was quickly dividing into two factions, like middle schoolers getting picked for teams in gym class.

Ron was eager to carve out a choir-preaching perch for himself after leaving office, so he stuck with the most hard-core of the true believers: libertarian scholars at the Ludwig von Mises Institute, and politicos and activists who were either too unpredictable or too rabid in their convictions to work for his son. Many of these purists believed that Rand was watering down his beliefs to suit his presidential ambitions — thus tarnishing his father's legacy and weakening their cause. They didn't mind saying so to Ron either.

This was nothing new for the elder Paul. Ever since Rand had first started running for Senate, Ron had been listening to leading libertarians complain about his son's various disappointments. Once, at a dinner with Walter Block, the Loyola University professor and self-described anarchist rattled off a list of the younger Paul's ideological heresies and demanded, "Can you take Rand out to the woodshed and spank him or something?" Recounting the conversation years later, Block felt bad for being so harsh. As he recalled, "Ron didn't say anything... He just sort of mumbled and changed the subject."

But now the complaints were no longer being restricted to private dinner conversations: they were often out in the open. With Rand seizing his moment on the national stage, Ron found himself stuck in the peanut gallery with the libertarian losers and misfits who weren't invited to join the show, and had nothing left to do now but heckle.

One of the most vocal Rand bashers was Lew Rockwell, a long-serving aide and friend to Ron who had made a habit of using the politician's fame as a vehicle for his own polemics and score settling. In the most notorious example, Rockwell was suspected of authoring a series of racist newsletters that were sent out under Ron's name in the seventies and eighties and came back to haunt him during his 2012 presidential campaign. Antics like this had left many in Paul's circle suspicious of Rockwell. "Lew cuts two ways," said Mary Jane

Smith, Ron's former campaign manager. "Totally, totally loyal to Ron. But Lew had his own ideas, and Ron was such a trusting person."

It was widely understood within the Paul family's orbit that Rockwell detested Rand. He still thought of him as the scrawny, know-nothing teenager sitting in the backseat of his father's car as they commuted to the Capitol all those summers ago—only now the unappreciative twerp was famous and selling out his family legacy every chance he got. Rockwell's seeming contempt was so intense that many people close to the Pauls came to believe he was posting provocative, outlandish statements under Ron's name on social media in an effort to sabotage Rand's political prospects. For example, when @RonPaul tweeted in 2013 that the death of former Navy SEAL Chris Kyle proved that "he who lives by the sword dies by the sword," the public outrage that ensued forced Rand to put out his own statement distancing himself from his dad's provocation and calling the slain sniper a "hero." The episode was a political headache for Rand—and the senator's aides suspected Rockwell was behind it. It wasn't that Ron necessarily disagreed with the tweet, but its tone and timing seemed deliberately designed to tweak his son. (Rockwell denied ever posting on Ron's account, and when he was asked what he thought of Rand, he said he was "agnostic" and "not a fan of the political process.")

"Everyone who works for Ron hates Rand," one of the few operatives who stayed close to both Pauls told me. And while Ron may not have shared his loyalists' animosity toward his son, he could have shut down their trolling any time he wanted to. He didn't.

Rand, meanwhile, surrounded himself with political pros whose explicit mission was to save the senator from following in his father's footsteps. Many of Rand's advisers had worked for Ron in the past, and while they admired his philosophy, they were all too aware of the self-defeating instincts and politically poisonous ideas that might be lurking in Rand's genetic inheritance.

To protect the senator from his own Paulian pathologies, they tried to institute safeguards. For a time, they kept his Twitter password locked away in a filing cabinet, available to only a select group of trusted staffers and hidden from the senator himself. Whenever Rand wanted to tweet something, he would have to send the proposed message to Stafford or another aide. Ostensibly, the process was put in place to give Rand plausible deniability in the unlikely case of a hack or an Anthony Weiner–esque misfire by someone with access to the account. But his social media guardians were also filtering for crazy talk that sounded too much like dear old Dad.

Their concerns weren't unfounded: when Rand used his non-password-protected mouth to communicate, he had a conversational habit of sliding into far-fetched speculation in a manner that could come off as weird and a little nutty, rather than good-natured and gossipy. Once during an off-the-record chat over drinks with a few Washington reporters, the senator matter-of-factly informed them that Hillary Clinton was not going to run for president in 2016.

How do you know? the puzzled journalists asked.

"Because I'm an ophthalmologist and I know what those glasses mean," he said, apparently referring to the eyeglasses Clinton briefly wore after suffering a concussion in 2012.

The reporters pressed him to elaborate, but he would only respond by instructing them, somewhat mysteriously, to "Google it." When they did, they found an outlandish right-wing rumor—widely debunked by mainstream news outlets—that cited Clinton's glasses as proof that she was concealing serious brain damage. Conspiracy theories, it appeared, were a Paul family pastime.

Inside Rand's circle, the senator's father was treated like a kook who needed to be carefully handled. His status as a libertarian cult hero made it necessary for Rand's team to maintain at least an illusion of reverence, lest they further damage their already tenuous relationship with grassroots libertarians. But behind closed doors, Rand's aides generally talked about Ron in terms ranging from irritation and wariness to outright mockery and derision.

One of Rand's strategists even speculated that Ron might have Asperger's syndrome, citing his bizarre interpersonal style and his apparent inability to make friends over the course of his long career on Capitol Hill. And a senior staffer in Rand's Senate office said that after years of trying to dissect the father-son dynamic, he was left stupefied by Ron's antagonism toward his son's career.

"He should be proud of Rand, but he's not," the staffer said. "It's a really weird relationship."

The growing political chasm between his dad and himself took a personal toll on Rand. For his entire life, he had idolized his father and labored ceaselessly for his approval. When he went to medical school he chose his dad's alma mater; when he got engaged he asked his dad to serve as his best man. In the dedication to one of his books, Rand wrote, "From the age of eleven, I followed my father everywhere. I listened to every speech and interview, thousands of them. Are individualists born or nurtured? I think I was both." If, as the pop psychologists like to say, every man is motivated by either defiance of his father or a desire to make him proud, Rand was firmly in with the second lot. They were different people, of course, with distinct sets of opinions and beliefs. But they shared the same foundational philosophy—and when Rand decided to go into politics, he was inspired, in part, by the chance to light up the American sky with the flame his father had first lit.

Of course, to achieve that kind of mainstream influence, Rand had to create some political distance between himself and his dad's world—fire a family friend here, scrub his website of a libertarian reading list there. He didn't *like* doing this stuff. In fact, it often left him feeling conflicted and guilty and defensive. But he thought of these as relatively small compromises—not betrayals, but bricks being laid in a monument to his father's ideas. Surely Dad could understand that   right?

Neither of the Paul men was particularly chatty, and there wasn't much soul baring during their occasional phone calls, but most of the time Rand sensed that his father understood and appreciated what he was doing. Then Rockwell or one of the other kamikaze libertarians in his dad's inner circle would fire off a passive-aggressive tweet or mouth off in an interview, and Rand would have to consciously ward off the wounded feeling that he had let down his dad. "It's hurtful," said one of Rand's aides, describing how the senator reacted to the hostility from Ron's corner.

The relationship appeared volatile enough that by the end of 2013, more than one of Rand's aides believed that he and his father would be estranged if not for the need to keep up appearances.

When I asked Rand's older brother, Ronnie, one day about the apparent rift in the House of Paul, he acknowledged that the political differences between his dad and his brother had grown sharper recently, but insisted that they weren't the source of any family drama. His dad, he said, was an ideological visionary, while his brother was effectively an incrementalist. "But they are both going to the same place." The day we spoke, Ronnie's daughter was preparing to get married at a ceremony in Lake Jackson. He said, "At the end of the day, Rand'll be there for the wedding, and we'll all be together. We'll talk about gardens, and who's the best golfer...They're father and son. They always have been, always will be."

Nonetheless, the cold war between the two Paul camps eventually grew so combustible that Rand's office dispatched Jesse Benton to talk to Ron about toning things down. Benton was working full-time for Rand by this point, but after serving on two of Ron's presidential campaigns (and marrying one of his granddaughters along the way) he was considered the most logical envoy.

Benton knew they would never be able to muzzle Ron, but he thought if he could persuade the old man to keep his public commentary restricted to policy rather than politics—and call off the Paulite freedom fighters, who were actively working to sabotage Rand—they could avoid a full-out nuclear war between the two sides.

Already, some in Rand's orbit were discussing how they might manufacture a "Sister Souljah moment" for the senator—politico-speak that referred to a well-known incident in 1992 when Bill Clinton sharply denounced a controversial rapper to signal his break with the Far Left. Though no one brought it up with Rand because they knew how personally he took the politics of the paternal, some on his team believed there would come a moment in 2016—maybe in the primary, maybe in the general election—when he would have to publicly and ruthlessly repudiate his dad in order to win.

Benton dreaded the idea of such a clash—if for no other reason than the agonizing awkwardness it would cause at his in-laws' family reunions—and he was eager to do what he could to de-escalate the conflict. But he also knew that no matter what he did, the nuclear option wasn't coming off the table anytime soon.

"If we thought it was an insurmountable problem, we would shut it down," Benton said of Ron. "But for now, we think we can deal with it." Besides, as Rand was about to discover, the political hazards lurking *outside* of his family were much more dangerous to his presidential prospects.

Late one day in November 2013, Rand stood surrounded by a coterie of confidants in his Capitol Hill office, engulfed in a crisis with the potential to end his career. The senator was sputtering and spitting and sliding into incoherence as he ranted about the bias and bad faith of the character assassins in the media who were behind this latest unjust assault on his integrity. He was incensed. Furious. Filled with righteous, red-hot rage. And then suddenly, in a fleeting moment of clarity, the words came to him: *hacks and haters.*

Hacks and haters! Yes, that's exactly what these reporters were! A bunch of partisan, no-talent hacks and hopelessly blinkered haters hell-bent on destroying him—and he was going to go on TV and call them out for it.

For the first time in his young political life, Rand Paul was backed into a corner, and he was going to fight his way out the only way he knew how: by closing his eyes and wildly swinging his fists.

It had all started a few nights earlier—October 28—on Rachel Maddow's MSNBC show. Earlier that day, Rand had given a speech about abortion at the evangelical Liberty University that included a lengthy plot description of the futuristic sci-fi movie *Gattaca.* "In the not-too-distant future, eugenics is common and DNA plays a primary role in determining your social class," Rand had explained, before warning that America's culture of elective abortion might lead to a similarly dystopian future. What Maddow and her producers had discovered was that that line—and many more that followed it— was copied practically verbatim from the Wikipedia entry for *Gattaca.* A grinning Maddow had reported the case of plagiarism with discernible amusement and glee, and closed the segment by pronouncing, "Rand Paul wants to be president. But right now, he's just lifting whole sections of this Wikipedia page, hoping that nobody's going to notice, and he can call it his speech."

Across the East River from Maddow's Manhattan studio, Andrew Kaczynski—a political reporter at BuzzFeed with a preternatural talent for Internet sleuthing—noticed. He watched the segment and immediately wondered if the copy-and-paste job was the senator's first offense. Sitting on a couch in his third-floor walk-up in Queens, it took Kaczynski less than an hour to find a second Rand Paul speech that contained text snatched from Wikipedia. (This one, a June address on immigration, had lifted the wording of the plot summary for the 1988 drama *Stand and Deliver*.) BuzzFeed published Kaczynski's story the next day, and a media frenzy quickly ensued.

Rand's office tried, futilely, to kill the controversy in the cradle, calling the allegations "trivial" and claiming it was all just a disagreement over footnoting. But it was no use. For all the sins that were tolerated in the political world, plagiarism was considered all but unpardonable. In 1987, when it was revealed that Joe Biden had knocked off parts of a speech from a British prime ministerial candidate, he had to drop out of the Democratic presidential primary in disgrace—and it took him the better part of two decades before he was ready to reenter the presidential arena.

But while Rand's advisers understood the seriousness of the charges, the senator himself was convinced he was the victim of a fevered witch hunt. He thought the evidence of his supposed lapse in ethics was outrageously thin and nitpicky. He'd been recapping *movie plots* in these speeches, not reciting Tolstoy and calling the words his own. He felt certain that if he could just explain this in a neutral setting, his attackers' petty animus and partisanship would be laid bare.

Yet when Rand tried defending himself along these lines in an interview with Fusion's Jorge Ramos a couple of days into Wikigate, he got nowhere. Reporters were still calling, pundits were still bloviating, and his political enemies in both parties were still calling him a thief and a liar. On Thursday, three days after Maddow's first segment, *Politico* got in on the action with a story alleging that the senator's 2013 State of the Union response included language stolen from an Associated Press report.

The higher the volume got on his critics' attacks, the more indignant Rand became. Was he seriously supposed to sit sheepishly by as

the corrupt, careerist frauds in the political press passed moral judgment on him? When was the last time any of these venal mercenaries
stood up for anything other than their own hides? They could call
him crazy or radical or dangerous all they wanted—the Pauls were
used to such name-calling from the media establishment—but *nobody*
was going to call him unprincipled. By the end of the week, he was so
consumed with outrage that he could hardly wait to get on TV and
call out the reporters who were pushing this preposterous story. If
they wanted a fight, he would give them one.

"I'm not the biggest guy, but when someone is attacking my hon-
esty, whether it's a fistfight or a duel, I'm not going to let them get away
with it," Rand told one adviser, who was left half wondering if the
senator planned to start showing up at newsrooms with his dukes up.

Rand announced to his staff that he was going to take down these
pathetic bullies during his Sunday morning appearance on ABC's
This Week, and since the language he wanted to use wasn't FCC
approved, "hacks and haters" was the line to beat.

As his boss blustered, Doug Stafford was beginning to panic. More
than any other person in Rand's office—including Rand himself—
Stafford was responsible for the writing that appeared under the senator's name. Rand, an acid-tongued iconoclast with dogma-defying
ideas and a penchant for picking on members of his own party, was
constantly in demand—which meant Stafford was constantly writing for him. He wrote at home and on weekends, in between meetings and during dull conference calls, on trains and planes and all
throughout the long daily commute from and to his far-flung Virginia
suburb. From speeches to essays to op eds to books, Stafford was in
charge of it all—and his corner cutting was now costing them.

He knew that Rand, loyal to a fault as he was, would never out
him as the in-house plagiarist. "This stuff went out under *my* name,"
the senator had insisted when someone suggested fingering a staff
scapegoat. But Stafford was queasy about Rand's plan to go on TV
and practically dare the press to dig through every word he'd ever
written. Still, he felt powerless to stop him. Those in Rand's inner circle had never seen their boss quite like this before—so flustered and
foolhardy and emotional. They got the sense that trying to talk him

down would be akin to hurling their bodies onto the Union Station tracks to stop a speeding Amtrak train.

Searching for advice, Stafford invited Trygve Olson into the meeting where they were discussing the senator's planned response, and asked what he thought of the "hacks and haters" line.

Olson said it would be a risky move.

"Look, if this is all that's out there, then you can put that out," he told Stafford. "But if there's more plagiarism out there, whether it's in a book or anywhere else, it's gonna be a huge fucking problem. It's going to be just brutal for you."

As if on cue, the night before Rand's scheduled interview with *This Week,* Kaczynski posted a new story at BuzzFeed revealing that three whole pages of the book Rand cowrote with Stafford, *Government Bullies,* were lifted word for word from a 2003 Heritage Foundation study. The book's endnotes cited the study—which dealt with regulatory overreach in lobster harvesting—but made no effort to indicate that the 1,318 words themselves weren't Rand's own.

The new revelation only further inflamed Rand. The next morning, he went on TV as planned, claiming he was "being unfairly targeted by a bunch of hacks and haters," and declaring, "I take it as an insult, and I will not lie down and say people can call me dishonest or misleading...If dueling were legal in Kentucky, if they keep it up, it'd be [a] duel challenge."

While the gentleman from Kentucky publicly challenged him and his Fourth Estate colleagues to a life-and-death gun battle, Kaczynski was busy loading every word he could find of the senator's into a plagiarism-detecting software commonly used in publishing and academia. Red flags were popping up all over the place. On Monday, Kaczynski posted a story revealing that sections of an op-ed Rand had written for the *Washington Times* about drug sentencing reform were taken without attribution from a similar article in *The Week* magazine. The cribbing was egregious enough that the editor of the conservative *Times* told Stafford that they would have to cancel the regular column Rand had been writing for them. No hard feelings, the editor said, but we do have standards to uphold.

By now Stafford was freaking out. They could no longer argue that this plagiarism nonsense was just the petty obsession of a few ax-grinders. A key ideological media ally—and, frankly, not one known for its Olympian editorial quality—was running away from the senator because of columns everyone in Rand World knew *he* had written.

In an act of desperation, Stafford asked Olson, who used to hang out with BuzzFeed's editor in chief, Ben Smith, when they were both twentysomethings living in eastern Europe, to persuade his buddy to call off Kaczynski.

But Olson was no longer inclined to clean up Stafford's messes for him. As much as he liked Rand, he had grown fed up with the calamitous incompetence that kept tumbling out of his office—and he didn't feel like coddling any of the culprits. He reminded Stafford that he'd warned him not to let Rand go on the attack if there was a chance more plagiarism might surface, and that they did it anyway. Anyone with half a brain could see this was a legitimate story, and he wasn't going to play along in this embarrassing pageant of mendacity by acting as though it was all an unfair media conspiracy.

"I don't have to be a seventh-grade English teacher to tell you that stuff was lifted, and this is plagiarism," Olson told Stafford sharply.

Eventually, the coverage did subside (though not until after vast amounts of additional plagiarism were exposed in *Government Bullies*).

Desperate to get past the scandal, Rand's advisers persuaded him to grit his teeth and publicly promise to be more diligent about citations going forward. But Rand remained convinced that he had been unjustly singled out, and he didn't try to mask his bitterness during interviews. Describing the new speechwriting process his office would implement, he told the *New York Times*, "What we are going to do from here forward, if it will make people leave me the hell alone, is we're going to do them like college papers." Later, while complaining to the *National Review* about the coverage of the plagiarism story, he griped, "It annoys the hell out of me. I feel like if I could just go to detention after school for a couple days, then everything would be okay. But do I have to be in detention for the rest of my career?"

A few weeks after the firestorm died down, Olson found himself in a car with Rand as they drove to a fund-raiser outside New York City.

As the two talked, away from the prying eyes and fragile egos of the rest of Rand's inner circle, Olson offered a blunt assessment of his team's failures in responding to the crises of the past year, and questioned whether they were ready for prime time.

"This is sloppy shit," he told the senator. "If you want to run, my professional counsel to you is, it can't be this sloppy."

The problem, Olson argued, was that Rand was a fast-rising national star loaded with potential but stuck with a cobbled-together team of neophytes, yes-men, and Paul family sycophants. There was talent there, sure, and Stafford had plenty of valuable skills. But the wishy-washy way in which Stafford had handled Jack Hunter and the plagiarism fiasco suggested that he was more worried about keeping his perch at the top of the totem pole than he was with giving Rand the tough-love guidance he needed.

If Rand was going to seriously compete in 2016, he likely would have to take on Chris Christie's professionalized squad of political hit men, and go up against Hillary Clinton's mammoth Democratic machine. He'd have to deftly handle the toxic internal politics of a divided libertarian movement, and find a way to reach out to mainstream Republicans while sharing a surname with a famous crank who counted among his greatest fans 9/11 truthers, and preppers who stockpile ammo and gold in their basements. To pull all this off, Rand would need a crack team of experienced pros who could get him in fighting shape—and right now, he didn't have it.

Olson suggested to Rand that he consider skipping the presidential race altogether, and focus his efforts instead on the Senate. He reasoned that some of the most consequential political leaders of the modern era—from Scoop Jackson to Jesse Helms to Barry Goldwater—had transformed their respective parties not from the White House but from Congress. After all that had happened that year, maybe this was the route for Rand.

The senator listened attentively to Olson's advice as they drove, and then, finally, he made a request: "Don't tell Kelley any of this. She'll never let me run."

Chapter Nine

The Chosen One

On a sweltering midsummer evening in 2013 in America's swampy capital, a who's who of *other* right-wing stars and influential superactivists was quietly crowding into a cramped conference room in Mike Lee's Senate office. Inside, lawmakers including Ted Cruz, Marco Rubio, Jeff Flake, and Pat Toomey stood shoulder to shoulder with senior officials from cash-flush grassroots groups like Freedom-Works and Tea Party Patriots. The off-the-record meeting had been given an after-hours start time so as not to arouse suspicion from unfriendly colleagues, and attendees were told that the gathering was to remain strictly hush-hush. Vast right-wing conspiracies, after all, required the utmost discretion.

The act of rebellion being plotted tonight was an audacious, last-ditch plan to cripple Obamacare before the law went into full effect and became impossible to untangle from the rest of America's social safety net. Defeating the president's legacy-making health-care law had long been an Ahab-like obsession for many Republicans, and it was easy to see why. The law's application was mired in the morass of feckless federal bureaucracy. The parts that did go into effect were a source of consternation for small business owners, many of whom complained that new regulations on employee health insurance plans were forcing layoffs and stunting growth. Polls at the time showed that Obamacare had grown increasingly unpopular almost from the day the White House had jammed it through Congress on a party line vote. And opposition to the law was one of the rare stances that could unite every faction of the GOP. The Affordable Care Act's popular nickname probably played a role, too. As one former political adviser for Cruz told me, "I think there's something about it being called 'Obamacare' that just makes us go crazy, like if we can't get rid of him, we're going to get rid of his law."

But so far, the conservative quest to gut the health-care law had been one long train of failures and disappointments. In 2012, a promising Supreme Court challenge to the law ended in a heartbreaking betrayal, when Chief Justice John Roberts, a Bush-appointed conservative, cast the deciding vote to uphold Obamacare's individual mandate. The Republican-controlled House, meanwhile, had passed dozens of bills repealing the law, but with Democrats still holding on to the Senate, there was a better chance of Harry Reid leading a ritual animal sacrifice on the steps of the Capitol than allowing a vote on the legislation.

Now, however, a perfect storm of legislative crises was on the horizon — and the conservatives gathered in Lee's office were determined to take advantage.

On October 1, the federal government would run out of money and be forced to shut down unless Republicans helped Congress pass a temporary funding bill. About three weeks after that, the United States would begin defaulting on its loans—thus setting off an unprecedented global economic panic—unless Republicans helped Congress vote to raise the debt ceiling. And, as always, the Republicans on the Hill were happy to do their part to steer clear of the apocalypse—for a price.

This had been the modus operandi of Washington's right wing ever since the 2010 wave election sent a militia of Tea Party freshmen storming into the Capitol—and up to that point the high-stakes negotiating tactic had largely worked. Already, conservatives were abuzz about what they would get out of this next round of legislative brinksmanship. Some had suggested demanding the repeal of the unpopular tax on medical devices. Others had raised the idea of delaying the individual mandate.

But Mike Needham, the spiky-haired, thirty-one-year-old CEO of the Tea Party–aligned pressure group Heritage Action, was thinking on a grander scale. Four years ago, in an apparent spasm of Wile E. Coyote envy, Needham had begun drawing up a hypothetical strategy that would leverage the threat of a government shutdown to achieve the wholesale defunding of the president's health-care law. Not chip away at it, or tinker with it, or repeal some fractional piece of it—no, Needham's plan was to bust open Obamacare's federal piggy bank and loot it of every last taxpayer penny, effectively killing the law.

To lead the charge on the Hill, Needham had tapped Lee—a solid, policy-minded conservative with Tea Party roots and a devoted fan base of think tank wonks.

Sitting tonight at the head of the table in a room overflowing with battle-ready allies, the doughy, mild-mannered Utah senator did his best to lay out Heritage's pugnacious plan with flare. Their strategy, he explained, was designed to harness the public outrage that would inevitably accompany a shutdown, and then channel it toward Democrats—eventually piling on so much pressure that they would have no choice but to cave on Obamacare.

As he sat listening to Lee outline the details of the defund plan, Cruz wasn't quite as filled with the same enthusiasm that some of his fellow right-wing conspirators seemed to evince. It wasn't that he harbored any reluctance about annihilating Obamacare by whatever means necessary—that was a no-brainer. But the thing that Cruz found appealing about the defund plan was its potential for high drama: a shutdown fight was exactly the kind of platform he had been looking for ever since Rand's star-making filibuster a few months ago. The voters who had sent him to Washington wanted results, yes—but absent that, they at least wanted to be able to cheer on him and his fellow Tea Partiers as they slugged it out in exhilarating, high-profile brawls on the national stage. And here, it seemed, they might have a problem.

Cruz knew that for this defund plan to take off the way they wanted it to in the fall, their cross-country tour hyping the thing would have to be *the* political spectacle of the summer. The rallies they held would have to be barn burners that conservative activists everywhere would line up around the block to see in person, like

Michael Jordan in his prime. But for all of Mike Lee's many gifts, political theater was not among them. Just that day, Lee had delivered a six-minute speech on the Senate floor designed to build buzz for the coming showdown, but it had been a total dud. For all his policy savvy, Lee lacked gravitas. When he spoke in public, he had a habit of placing his hands just in front of his stomach, and gently pressing his fingertips together in a pose that was reminiscent of a choirboy — or, more fittingly, given his delivery, a mortician. His speech had gone entirely unnoticed — hardly an auspicious beginning to a campaign that was supposed to mark the permanent emergence of the Tea Party in Washington. For this to work, it would have to be *much* more exciting. It would need to be an event, a performance.

Enter Ted Cruz, stage Right.

The bedtime stories Ted Cruz grew up listening to were not the kind with magic beanstalks and fairy godmothers. In his house, story time meant daddy time — and Ted's father never had much interest in gently reciting soporific fairy tales to a tucked-in cherub. A Cuban exile with ironclad ideals and a fighting spirit, Rafael Cruz was drawn to stories with high stakes and lofty themes. At night, when he came home from work, he would swing his son onto his knee and regale him with glorious, true-life tales of tribulation and triumph — epics in which evil clashed with good, and great men met their destinies.

Sometimes these stories would come from Rafael's own days as a young Cuban revolutionary — harrowing yarns studded with gritty details that would stay with Ted forever. The image of bloodstained teeth dangling from Rafael's mouth after three days of torture in an army garrison. The realization that if he didn't flee the country he would risk death at the hands of the ruthless Batista regime. The acceptance letter to the University of Texas, the ferry ride to Key West that felt like liberation, the bumpy two-day bus trip to Austin. And, most memorable of all, the secret pocket sewn into his underwear that carried a hundred dollars in cash — all the money he'd brought to America.

Other times, Rafael's stories would come from the Bible. Together, father and son would sit in their modestly furnished living room as the elder Cruz read to the younger about prophets and kings—about the walls of Jericho crumbling, and the Philistine giant falling, and the Red Sea parting. Stories of persecution endured and miracles performed—and of God's chosen leaders raining down fire and frogs and locusts and lice to deliver the oppressed millions from a power-mad Pharaoh.

But of all the stories Cruz grew up with, there was one that his father told him more often and more urgently than any other. He was just four years old when he heard it for the first time. They were at home, and Rafael had been reading to his son from the Old Testament when suddenly the Cruz family patriarch felt moved by the spirit to prophesy.

"Ted," he proclaimed, each vowel stretched by his Cuban accent, each word punctuated by conviction, "you have been gifted above any man that I know, and God has destined you for greatness."

It was a prophecy that Rafael would go on to repeat—often word for word—every single day until Cruz moved out of the house.

Decades later, an aide and confidant who had worked closely with Cruz for years would point to that moment as singularly formative: "Everything else in Ted's life is explained by his dad saying that."

When Cruz was thirteen his father brought him to Rolland Storey, a kindly and charismatic septuagenarian who ran a conservative foundation aimed at teaching youth about economics and government. Storey educated his pupils about the brightest minds of free market economics: they pored over Friedrich Hayek and Milton Friedman, and marveled at Frédéric Bastiat's denunciations of socialism as legal plunder. A veteran of vaudeville, Storey liked to re-create constitutional conventions and assign students to play delegates in mock debates. Many of his students were gifted, but none could keep up with Cruz in terms of passion and inherent ability. Thrust into some of the momentous scenes from world history, the thirteen-year-old was perfectly at home.

Eventually, Storey invited Cruz to join a traveling troupe of patriotic performers that he called the Constitutional Corroborators. The five students would meet twice a week to study and memorize the Constitution with the help of a mnemonic specialist, and then they took their show on the road, wowing Rotary Clubs and veterans' groups with their mastery of the document: they wrote out entire sections on easels and then answered questions from the delighted crowds. At home, Cruz would practice these performances late into the night, studying himself in the mirror as he perfected each tic and quirk of his delivery.

By the time he got to high school, Cruz was fully accustomed to the adults in his life telling him he was special. But at his small Baptist school, "special" turned out to be alienating, and few of his forty-three classmates bothered to befriend him. "To be perfectly honest, because he was so unusually brilliant, he was a little different," recalled one fellow student. "He was kind of a quirky high school kid." Cruz told himself that the kids who excluded and poked fun at him were jealous, or intimidated, or too slow to keep up with his wit and match his interests. And maybe all that was true.

But he could also be condescending and abrasive—a fact he would acknowledge later in life with one of his aides, in a rare instance of self-reflection. "I think he's deeply okay with it," the aide told me. "He knows who he is, more than I think people realize. He understands people don't like him...We all tell ourselves positive reasons people don't like us. His was that he's special and they're not."

It was late in August 2013, and Ted Cruz was standing on a platform at the far end of a cavernous Hilton Anatole ballroom. "Having spent a little bit of time in Washington, DC," the senator shouted, "it's great to be back in America!" Thousands of restless, well-dressed patriots were sitting in front of him here in Dallas America; a huge blue, rectangular "Defund Obamacare" banner was hanging behind him. The sleeves of his white button-down shirt were cuffed with a precise sort of sloppiness just above his wrists, and a healthy heaping of pomade gave his sharply parted black hair a soft luster under the stage lights.

The production was part of the nine-city tour organized by Heritage Action to gin up grassroots support for its new plan to gut Obamacare, and a brigade of right-wing ruckus raisers had fanned out across the country to make their case during Congress's August recess.

But none of the other spokesmen for the cause were getting the kind of reception that Cruz would get here. Here he was a star. A hero. An icon. An oratorical wizard-warrior who could take any old cluster of words and transform them into a riotous applause line, simply by pausing a beat after the period.

This linguistic alchemy was on full display almost from the moment Cruz began speaking.

"I have publicly committed, along with a number of other senators, that under no circumstances will I vote for a continuing resolution that funds even one penny of Obamacare!" he declared.

The patriots rose in unison, cheering wildly as Cruz planted his feet and nodded his head in the purposeful, macho manner of a pro wrestler. When the room quieted, he surged forward, urging the patriots to ignore the naysayers and the pearl-clutchers who said his strategy would never work.

"Now, why is it that every reporter in the media, and a significant percentage of Republicans, assume with an impasse that President Obama will never, ever, ever give up his principles, so Republicans have to give up theirs?"

More applause, as excitement pulsed through the crowd. Cruz's voice grew louder, his hands, up near his face, formed as though they were clutching an invisible set of stone tablets.

"If you have an impasse... one side or the other has to blink," he said. "How do we win this fight?"

Shouting now and smashing the tablets on the ground:

"Don't blink!"

The patriots rose again, and this time they meant it, whistling and whooping and splashing around in the free-flowing catharsis that the senator had unleashed on the ballroom. And Cruz, caught up in the moment, clapped, too. Because after all, this wasn't about any one senator. It was about the movement. The voters. The "we the people." It was about *America*.

And here in America, they loved him.

Two weeks later, lawmakers returned from their summer vacations to find a Washington awash in defund fever. The crackpot plan floated by Mike Lee a couple of months ago — and ignored by most everyone — was suddenly a full-blown movement thanks to Ted Cruz, complete with hashtags and Hannity rants and a website, enthusiastically touted by the Texas senator and his cohorts, that listed each congressional Republican's stated position on the strategy, and encouraged constituents to call up the ones who were on the "wrong" side of the issue. Right-wing activists were now lighting up Capitol Hill phone lines, and a growing number of House Republicans—some of them genuinely converted, others simply petrified—were lining up behind Cruz, pledging that they would not vote for a bill to fund the government as long as it meant allocating money to Obamacare.

With the prospect of a government shutdown looming over them, Republican leaders in Congress—including Speaker John Boehner, Majority Leader Eric Cantor, and the rest of the GOP babysitters tasked with keeping these Tea Party temper tantrums under control— were frantically searching for a fix. In the past, when flare-ups like this had threatened to derail the basic mechanics of government, the leadership would work out a face-saving compromise of some sort. They'd set up symbolic votes that right-wing lawmakers could take to shield themselves from the wrath of Rush Limbaugh, and then—when necessary—they'd quietly nudge those same members to take the necessary-evil votes in order to keep Washington functioning. This was why, since 2010, the Republican-controlled House had voted more than fifty times to repeal, defund, dismantle, or otherwise destroy Obamacare—even when they knew it would have no practical effect. It may not have been what Madison and Jefferson had in mind, and no one in leadership was particularly proud of the routine, but at least it had kept the lights on through the early days of the Tea Party era.

With this in mind, Cantor dispatched a top staffer, Neil Bradley, to the weekly staff meeting for the Republican Study Committee caucus on Monday afternoon to strategize with the hundred-plus conservative congressional aides in attendance. Bradley's mission was to help figure out a way to sate the right wing's appetite for red meat without shishkebabing the entire party. To do this, Bradley tried to paint a scary picture of the cataclysmic repercussions that could result if a shutdown occurred.

Perhaps the most dire outcome, Bradley told the group, is that our soldiers won't receive their paychecks.

This assertion prompted one of Cruz's lieutenants in the room—an aide named Max Pappas—to stand in objection.

That's not true, Pappas argued. You know as well as I do that if the government shuts down, Congress can simply pass a stopgap bill that pays the troops until it's over. All this destitute-soldier tripe is nothing more than petty scare tactics and typical excuse making from the yellow-bellied establishment.

Pappas might have continued reciting his Cruz-crafted talking points—but all of a sudden, another Republican aide in the room sprang to her feet and cut him off. She introduced herself as a staffer in Texas representative John Culberson's office, and then—without warning—launched into an unbridled tirade against Cruz and his allies. She pilloried the Texas senator for bringing his Shutdown-palooza road show into her boss's district—whipping up local conservatives into a delusional, cultlike hysteria and demonizing any Republican officeholder who was disinclined to guzzle his cyanide-spiked Kool-Aid.

Why, she demanded to know, was Cruz doing this? *Why* was he insisting on making everyone else's life so difficult?

It was a remarkable moment for such a typically staid staff meeting, and soon rumors of the confrontation would hit the Internet, forcing Representative Culberson to release a statement distancing himself from the comments.

But in that instance—as the exasperated Republican staffer let loose a torrent of scorn on Cruz and his narcissistic, nihilistic brand of politics—she wasn't just speaking for her backbencher boss. She was giving voice to the Capitol Hill in crowd's fast-hardening disdain for the self-obsessed freshman who refused to fit in.

"You are not dealing in reality!" she huffed to Cruz's aide, drawing supportive applause from dozens of Republican aides in the room.

And yet reality was an increasingly fluid thing in Washington. The customary decorum and established procedures that once made up the very atomic matter of the Senate had been rapidly dissipating ever since the Tea Party came to town, and the result was a dark and growing void where the laws of the universe no longer applied. As far as Cruz was concerned, these frightened politicos could scurry around trying to reverse the galactic tide all they wanted, but it was never going to work.

He was here now. He'd arrived. This was the big bang.

On September 20, 2013, Cruz notched his first big win since arriving in Washington when the House of Representatives heeded his clarion call and voted 230 to 189 to keep the government open through December 15 on the sole condition that Obamacare's budget was looted of every last dime.

The victory would be short-lived. The House bill was now headed to the Democrat-controlled Senate, where Majority Leader Harry Reid had already declared it would be dead on arrival. Even if the bill did somehow make it to the president's desk, Obama had already pledged to break out his veto stamp.

Meanwhile, hordes of GOP opinion makers were stampeding toward the nearest cameras and keyboards to pile on Cruz and what they called the "Kamikaze Caucus." In the *Washington Post*, conservative commentator Jennifer Rubin eviscerated Cruz and Lee, charging that they were "intent on running into a concrete wall again and again to prove their political machismo."

And on *Fox News Sunday*, Karl Rove took the Tea Partiers to task for flouting even the most basic expectations of partisan courtesy. "You cannot build a congressional majority, in either party, for any kind of action, unless you are treating your colleagues with some certain amount of respect and saying, 'Hey, what do you think of my idea?'" Rove said. "Instead, they have dictated to their colleagues."

While the entire political world coalesced around the conventional wisdom that the defund gambit was a bust, the Texas senator was busy beating the war drum as furiously as ever.

Hold the line!

Don't retreat!

Victory is at hand!

"Republicans have the momentum," Cruz declared three days after the House vote. "All we have to do is have the will to fight."

The senator had the uncanny message discipline of a North Korean propagandist—and his performance was increasingly perplexing to the politicos of the Washington establishment. Cruz was still new to Washington, and many of them had assumed this whole time that he was playing some sort of Machiavellian game with a built-in exit strategy. But now the federal government was days away from running out of money, and there was no sign of an endgame in sight. As this new reality dawned on Washington, some in the political world began to wonder if they had been wrong about Cruz. Could it be possible that he really was the wild-eyed true believer he played at Tea Party rallies? Did he *actually* believe — against all evidence to the contrary — that this cockamamie scheme could work?

And if so, how far was he willing to take it?

Chapter Ten

All In

On September 24, 2013, Ted Cruz stood behind a mahogany lectern on the Senate floor, sporting a dark gray suit, a powder-blue necktie, and a pair of his most orthopedically advanced tennis shoes, as he delivered an important lesson about gambling to his fellow Republicans. "In a game of poker," he said, "if somebody makes a bet and then says to you, 'If you raise me, I am going to fold,' you will lose one hundred percent of your poker games. That is a path to losing."

Cruz had come to the floor just after 2 p.m. declaring his intention "to speak in support of defunding Obamacare until I am no longer able to stand"—and now he was making his case for calling the Democrats' bluff.

The seed for Cruz's filibuster idea had been planted back in March, when Rand Paul gripped the nation's attention for nearly thirteen hours by rambling about habeas corpus and military drones and the dangers of the military-industrial complex. Cruz remembered being impressed by Rand's ingenuity—but he thought he could do better.

The defund-Obamacare movement had caught fire because of him, and conservative revolutionaries across the country now fervently believed they were on the brink of beating back the Obama regime's health-care power grab and finally turning the tide in the fight for America's soul—if only Washington's more weak-willed

Republicans would hold the line. Cruz was intent on keeping his followers riled up, and he had come into the filibuster today armed with an arsenal of made-for-YouTube provocations—viral-ready stunts, one-liners, stories, and jokes—that his office planned to launch into the ether and send ricocheting around the right-wing Web until every true believer with an Internet connection was rallying to their cause beneath the #MakeDCListen banner—and hassling their congress-people to heed Cruz's call.

Now that he had begun to speak, he made no secret of these intentions. "The only way this fight is going to be won," he said, "is if the American people speak so loudly that the politicians in this body have no choice but to listen to the people."

With six days to go before the federal government was forced to shut down, Washington's only hope for averting disaster was a bipartisan compromise hastily hammered out in Congress—and the Senate chamber had been seized by Cruz and his invading army of grassroots guerrillas.

Over the next twenty-one hours, Cruz would cycle through dozens of colorful metaphors and weighty analogies to describe the nature of their fight. At one point, he compared Washington to the World Wrestling Federation, where the matches are "all rigged." At another, he chided the naysayers in his party by taking them through an epic historical journey of doubts defeated and evil vanquished—from the "ragtag bunch of colonists in the eighteenth century" who stood up to Great Britain, to the Nazi appeasers who thought the Germans were indestructible, to the people who said a man would never walk on the moon.

At a little after 8 p.m., Cruz took a break from his lofty oratory to announce that it was his daughters' bedtime and he was now going to read them a story via C-SPAN2. He produced a copy of *Green Eggs and Ham* and spent the next several minutes reading through each page, his voice occasionally lapsing into the same grave, dramatic tone he used in the rest of his speech—like a Sam-I-am burdened by the weight of the world. After wishing his girls a good night, he then turned the Dr. Seuss story into a parable for the hopelessly unpalatable health-care law.

"Three and a half years ago, President Obama and Senate Democrats told the American people, *just try* Obamacare," he said. "When Americans tried it, they discovered . . . they did not like Obamacare in a box, with a fox, in a house, or with a mouse."

The stunt immediately went viral, as Cruz knew it would, and the YouTube video soon became a near-perfect political Rorschach test. To the senator's admirers, it scanned as sweet, funny, and maybe even iconic. To his detractors, it was infuriating and repellant. As for Cruz, he didn't particularly care who or how many ended up in each column. All that mattered to him was that they were paying attention.

When Cruz was a freshman at Princeton in 1988, he liked to start the day with a pump-up ritual. Each morning, before leaving his dorm room, he would flip open his cassette player and pop in a Queen tape. As his favorite song—his ballad, his anthem—reached the chorus, the freshman would crank up the volume and sing along in full voice: *We are the champions! We are the champions! No time for losers, 'cause we are the champions of the world!*

Michael Lubetsky, one of Cruz's few friends at Princeton, was often within earshot during these performances, and the more he got to know the peculiar freshman, the more it made sense. Cruz certainly had no time or tolerance for losers. A star student at one of the most prestigious universities on the planet, he spent his weekends racking up titles at national debate tournaments and his evenings pacing the marble halls in a quiet campus building as he worked on perfecting his rhetorical craft.

Cruz became best friends with his debate partner, David Panton, a sixteen-year-old Jamaica-born prodigy, and the two spent late nights playing Sonic the Hedgehog and gossiping about the internal politics of the debate team. They were lucky to have each other, because almost no one else on campus liked them. Once, when they weren't around, their team held a whimsical mock debate to argue the pros and cons of turning Cruz and Panton into traffic cones. One argument in favor: it would benefit their need for exposure.

But while Cruz tended to rub people the wrong way, those who knew him best said he was desperate to be liked. One Princeton classmate, Craig Mazin, would later recount to the Daily Beast—with an obvious agenda of humiliation—that Cruz used to saunter down to the girls' side of the residential hall decked out in a paisley bathrobe and apparently looking to get lucky. "I would end up fielding the [girls'] complaints," Mazin recalled. "'Could you please keep your roommate out of our hallway?'" But while young Ted's nighttime strolls served to type-cast him with many of his Princeton dorm mates as a creep who couldn't take a hint, the truth was that he was probably just looking for someone to talk to.

Cruz's struggle to make friends wasn't just a product of his know-it-all arrogance—after all, that was not an exotic breed at Princeton. It was that as a conservative, middle-class boy from Texas, he didn't fit in with the typical Ivy League types. And try as he might, he could never convincingly fake it as so many others did. "Part of playing the game involves to some extent schmoozing up with people, sometimes pretending to be something you're not," Lubetsky later reflected. "I think Ted's ability to do that is extremely limited... He comes across as very condescending, very patronizing, because he is what he is. He tries."

Cruz eventually developed a close relationship with his professor and thesis adviser, Robbie George. A nationally renowned scholar who was widely credited as the intellectual leader of Christian conservatism, George spotted Ted's uncommon potential right away. But the professor also recognized how easily the student's particular brand of superiority could put off his peers. "Princeton is a university full of superstars. All the kids were valedictorian, had 1,600 SATs. Concert pianists, high school quarterbacks—they all come in and they're amazing," George explained. "Even in that group, Ted came in and he stood out. Add to that the fact that Ted's views are so politically incorrect, and they're offended by his views, and that's gotta generate a certain amount of jealousy and resentment."

The pattern repeated itself when Cruz got to Harvard Law School, where he quickly became known for his flamboyant snobbishness when it came to matters of intellect. One of his roommates would later claim that Cruz refused to study with anyone who didn't have an

Ivy League undergrad under his belt—and that "he didn't want any-body from 'minor Ivies' like Penn or Brown" either.

But while much stayed the same for Cruz at Harvard Law, one thing did change: he learned how to gamble. As an undergrad, he had once accumulated $1,800 in debt over the course of numerous dorm room poker games, and he had been forced to borrow money from an aunt to pay it back. Many years later, when his Senate press secretary was asked about the incident, she claimed that the humiliating experience had taught Cruz a valuable lesson, and he "promptly quit the game."

In fact, he carried his habit to Cambridge, where he developed quite a reputation at the card tables in Hastings Hall. His Harvard classmates would remember him pulling more than a few all-nighters playing protracted poker games, during which his signature move was to unexpectedly push all his chips forward and declare, through his omnipresent smirk, that he was "all in." In poker, the normal reason for employing such a tactic is to enable a big payout when you think you have an unbeatable hand. But the game's most risk-prone players—the ones with the greatest appetites for danger and drama—were those who gambled everything on a lousy hand just to scare their opponents into folding. It was a precarious strategy, and success required a player with almost unnerving confidence and an impenetrable poker face.

Cruz, it turned out, had both.

As one Harvard card buddy, Alexander Acosta, would later recall, "You'd never know if he's bluffing."

Cruz's Obamacare filibuster was met with a procession of eye rolls, give-me-a-breaks, and general staff-wide snark on Rand Paul's team. From the moment the filibuster began, Rand's advisers pegged Cruz's production as a comically bad sequel to their own boss's filibuster, complete with a B-list leading man; a lame, market-tested hashtag; and an obviously contrived premise. For all of Cruz's phony sermonizing about crusading against the establishment, Rand's Senate aides happened to know that Cruz had actually asked permission from

Senate Majority Leader Harry Reid earlier in the week to put on this little talent show of his. The Democratic leader had agreed, but made sure he retained the power to gavel Cruz's grandstanding to a conclusion whenever he felt like it—making it impossible to even call the exercise a "filibuster" at all.

Now, watching the drama unfold on live television, Rand's aides sniggered among one another at the self-seriousness of it all. *You get 'em, Ted! We need more fearless conservatives like you around!*

But as much fun as they had mocking Cruz, the members of Rand's inner circle were also genuinely annoyed that this display of faux civil virtue would now inevitably be compared to their boss's authentically principled stand.

"There is a major difference," one of Paul's frustrated senior advisers told me while Cruz babbled on into the night. "Rand's [filibuster] was spontaneous and with a goal of achieving something real. The politics of it were unknown. Ted is simply pandering to the conservative grass roots for selfish reasons: to promote himself as an outsider."

As for Rand himself, he thought the entire defund campaign reeked of pandering and performance art.

On the other hand, he knew that if he didn't show up on the Senate floor at least briefly to join Cruz's "filibuster" it would raise a flagrant red flag to Tea Partiers and libertarian activists. And so, at around 5:30 p.m., Rand decided to get it over with. He schlepped from his office to the Senate floor, and when it was his turn to talk, he dutifully congratulated his colleague for "bringing attention" to the disastrous effects of Obamacare. Soon he arrived at his question— one to which he genuinely wanted an answer.

"I would ask the senator from Texas: what are his intentions?" Rand said. "Does he want to shut down the government, or would he like to find something to make Obamacare less bad? I know we would both like to repeal it, but would the senator accept anything in between?"

Rather than answer the question, Cruz responded with an over-the-top outpouring of flattery for and fawning over Rand. Cruz gushed about his "historic filibuster," which had so inspired him that he counted his participation in it "one of the proudest moments of my life." Rand, in full view of C-SPAN and his colleagues, politely made an effort to appear chummy. But when Cruz finally ended his garrulous response with yet another plug for his canned slogan — "Make DC listen!" — Rand couldn't *quite* let him get away with the evasion.

"Would the senator yield for one quick question?" Rand asked, straining to keep up the polite tone of the proceedings. He pressed Cruz again on whether the current standoff could possibly be resolved, and suggested a hypothetical scenario: what if the president acknowledged that his law had serious problems, and requested the Republicans' help in fixing it before any more Americans lost their jobs, or their preferred health coverage? Would Cruz then be willing to accept a compromise?

He can't seriously say no to this, thought Rand.

He was wrong. After some more loquacious beating around the bush, Cruz finally answered, "Personally, no."

Watching the exchange on TV, Rand's advisers were nauseated by the Texas senator's snake-oily smarm. But Rand himself was more dismayed by the implications of his colleague's confession. Cruz couldn't actually stop the Senate from passing a federal spending bill, but as the face of the defund-Obamacare movement, he was consulting daily with the Tea Party caucus in the GOP-controlled House — and they would force a government shutdown in a second if Cruz told them to. But to what end? As far as Rand could tell, Cruz was about to drive Washington off a cliff just so he could prove he wasn't afraid of heights.

The Kentuckian didn't know where his colleague was headed with all this, but he knew for sure that he wouldn't be riding shotgun.

On the first day of October, the beloved twenty-four-hour live cam that broadcast round-the-clock footage of the resident baby panda at the National Zoo went dark, prompting a Twitter-wide outcry from the Internet's vast and vocal constituency of cuddly-animal fans. It was one of the first visible casualties of a federal government that had run out of money—forced to shut down until Republicans and Democrats could reach a détente and turn the lights back on.

Sticking to the plan they had agreed on all those months ago in

Mike Lee's crowded conference room, the right-wing conspirators led by Cruz were refusing to entertain any legislation that included a cent for Obamacare. They reasoned that it wouldn't be long before liberals started to revolt against the president for allowing their cherished big-government bureaucracies to go broke, and forced him to cave.

The next day, panicked Republican senators gathered for a closed-door lunch meeting in the Senate's Mansfield Room and demanded to know Cruz's endgame. They were now thirty-six hours into the shutdown crisis that the Texas freshman had caused, and they were hectoring him for answers: What's your strategy for getting the Democrats to blink? What kind of concessions would you accept to put an end to this? How did you think this would end, Ted?

The truth was that Cruz had always known this gambit had no real chance of defunding Obamacare. He spoke openly about the reality of the situation only within a tight inner circle of trusted aides and allies. But as three of Cruz's confidants would later tell me, very few of the original right-wing conspirators who gathered in Lee's office for that first meeting believed that their shutdown strategy would have the effect they were publicly promising the patriots. "I don't think you could find a single person in that room who really believed the plan would work," one attendee confessed to me.

But Cruz was a gambler, and he was prepared to bank all his chips on the stunt, armed with nothing but several thousand die-hard supporters and his unyielding poker face. Knowing that the exercise likely wouldn't spell the end for Obamacare didn't mean that the Texas senator and his allies believed the whole exercise was without purpose. For one thing, they really did think that angling the massive klieg light of the national media toward Obamacare would reveal its flaws in greater detail than ever before, and hasten public disenchantment with the law. They also assumed their little game of chicken with the White House would at least result in a few policy concessions from the Democrats—a reasonable assumption, given recent history. And, as Cruz would go on to argue in keynote speeches and at fund-raising dinners for years to come, he thought any righteous cause that mobilized the conservative movement was ultimately a plus for the party. The Washington establishment needed a good scare every once in a while, and this had done the trick.

Of course, there were *other,* less noble-sounding reasons for driving the federal government to a shutdown. For example, the crusade was bound to produce a fund-raising windfall for the conservative organizations behind it, like Heritage Action and the Senate Conservatives Fund. For right-wing pressure groups, high-stakes dramas like these were only good for business.

And as for Cruz, standing center stage in the biggest political story of the year posed plenty of advantages. He was now the undisputed king of the Tea Party, having earned the sort of adoring reputation on the right after just ten months in the Senate that lesser living legends took years to build up. His shiny new political brand was sure to help position him for a presidential run in 2016, as would the thousands of activists' phone numbers and email addresses that had been pouring in ever since he seized the mantle of defunder in chief. And even though he had no reason to believe Obamacare would get gutted the way he had been so confidently predicting, he thought his role as an ideological agitator was essential in the grand scheme of things. When debates like this arose, he saw his job as staking out the space on one far end of the spectrum—and then dragging the rest of his party toward him through force of argument and appeals to the conservative movement. If sometimes that meant telling a noble lie here or there to get them fired up, it was all for the cause of freedom. As one adviser in Cruz's Senate office would explain to me, with startling bluntness, several days into the shutdown, "[Cruz] didn't start with 'Delay the individual mandate for a year,' or some more complicated message like that, because that doesn't make for a good hashtag."

Of course, Cruz didn't say any of this in the Mansfield Room, where he did his best to remain unflappable as his colleagues badgered him. In one contentious exchange, someone asked him if he would repudiate the attacks that outside conservative groups had been launching against GOP senators who didn't support the defund strategy.

"I will not," Cruz replied.

*   *   *

Later that day, as rumors of the heated closed-door Cruz grilling circulated throughout Washington, members of Congress received an odd letter from Rand Paul.

"Tension is at an all-time high here at the Capitol," he wrote, in the diplomatic tone of a marriage counselor. "We are all anxious about the shutdown and had to send the bulk of our staff home—worried about their future...Maybe by chatting over coffee together, we can just talk and see if we can get along."

The next morning, Rand showed up for what he had termed a "bipartisan coffee chat" at a designated spot on the steps of the Capitol—in full view of the nearby TV cameras. Sporting Ray-Ban sunglasses and draping his suit jacket casually over one shoulder, he evinced a low-key friendliness that was intended to contrast sharply with Cruz's high-drama theatrics.

Rand had decided to put together this little gathering on a whim, but its underlying strategy had been a subject of much discussion and debate among his advisers recently. For months, political pundits had been predicting that he and Cruz were on a "collision course" for 2016, when the two presidential prospects would inevitably be battling it out for the support of the conservative grass roots. But if Rand decided to run for president, he didn't want to build his campaign around the same elements of the conservative base that had always supported his dad. He had his eye on bigger things: a new, convention-defying coalition of voters. And Cruz's shutdown fever had presented Rand with a perfect opportunity to begin positioning himself as a different kind of conservative.

Only a handful of Rand's fellow lawmakers ended up attending his "bipartisan" powwow—including just one Democrat. But their cheerful thirty-minute huddle got the point across well enough when reporters overheard them joking about singing "Kumbaya."

Over the next two weeks, chaos reigned in Washington. At the temporarily shuttered Vietnam War memorial, military veterans defied orders to stay off the property and police ended up forcibly removing them from the granite tribute that bore the names of their fallen comrades. At the nearby World War II memorial, conservative lawmakers actually joined veterans and demonstrators in storming the gates, leading officials to reinforce the surrounding barricades with wire that bound the fences together. At yet another demonstration, Cruz and Lee joined thousands of veterans as they converged on the White House and the Lincoln Memorial. Surrounded by watchful park police, Cruz rallied the restless crowd.

"Let me ask a simple question," he shouted. "Why is the federal government spending money to erect barricades to keep veterans out of this memorial?" A chorus of boos and shouts rang out while an American flag flew high behind him.

Across the country, meanwhile, the small indignities and injustices brought on by the shutdown continued to pile up. Hundreds of brides who had planned their weddings in national parks like Yellowstone were forced to tearfully change venues at the last minute. Philadelphia runners staged a rowdy protest in Valley Forge Park, while federal workers in Chicago marched angrily behind signs that read "Jobs Not Furloughs."

At the same time, world markets were growing increasingly skittish about the possibility that the two parties would fail to reach a compromise before the U.S. government began defaulting on its debts. As the shutdown neared the end of its second week, financial forecasters handed in glum predictions, shaving multiple percentage points off their GDP projections. Some warned of soon-to-plummet stock prices and devastating disruptions to the housing market, while others said the political uncertainty in DC was already serving as a drag on the national economy, as investors held their breath for the apocalypse. "Even the discussion of default poses great risk to our economy and to our country," warned Randall Stephenson, the chief executive at AT&T.

With the country careening haplessly toward fiscal calamity, the most powerful governing body in the free world had ground to a halt.

And standing amid all the pandemonium was Ted Cruz—reviled and scorned, hated and feared, but for the first time in his life at the center of the action. Washington and the world now turned on a hinge that he held in his palm, just as it was always meant to be.

In the end, even conservatives' most modestly hopeful predictions for how the shutdown would end proved to be overly optimistic. After years of allowing Tea Party lawmakers to extract concessions from the Democrats during manufactured crises such as these, the White House had put its foot down, refusing to negotiate at all on the issue of Obamacare. After fourteen grueling days and a series of failed legislative gambits, congressional Republicans would finally cave without a single victory to point to. Making matters worse, there was evidence that the drama had wreaked havoc on the national perception of the GOP. On October 10, a *Wall Street Journal*/NBC News poll was released showing that the favorability rating for the Republican Party now stood at just 24 percent — the lowest it had been in at least two decades.

But even as the rattled *Journal*-reading GOP establishment publicly fretted about their party's self-impalement at the hands of these unbridled Washington wacko birds, Cruz exhibited no hint of remorse, marching off to a large annual gathering of conservative activists in downtown DC, where the rapturous crowds greeted him like a conquering hero.

Thousands of patriots sprang to their feet as the Texas senator took the stage at the Values Voter Summit, and then a single voice called out from the audience, "If God is with you, who can be against you?" The rest of the patriots roared their approval, and Cruz bowed his head ever so slightly in a gesture of prophetic humility.

"I receive that blessing," he told the crowd reverently.

Two days after the *Journal* poll set off a panic among party elites — and one day before the government would officially reopen, with Republicans having nothing to show for their fight — Cruz won the Values Voter presidential straw poll in a landslide.

He had finally found a place where he belonged. He knew his people, and he knew what they wanted. He was all in.

Chapter Eleven

Gridlock

It was the night before New Jersey's 2013 gubernatorial election, and Chris Christie was spending it in Union City—a gritty working-class town and longtime stronghold for Garden State Democrats, with a population that was 85 percent Hispanic. This was not the kind of place Republican candidates hung out on the eve of an election. But Christie, as always, was proud to be his party's exception. Just before his campaign rally began, supporters spilled out into the street from downtown stores, offices, and apartment buildings, filling a city block. Live salsa music blasted over the speakers, and onlookers munched on cold Cuban sandwiches and bounced up and down to keep warm in the near-freezing temperatures. Spanish-language signs were everywhere: *"Yo Apoyo a Christie el Gobernador."*

Standing on a stage alongside the city's Democratic mayor Brian Stack, Christie told the crowd, "When I asked Brian if we could do this, a couple of months ago, I thought to myself, I wonder what it'll be like. I wonder what it'll be like for me to go up to Union City on the night before my election. I wonder who'll show up."

He paused for dramatic effect, then boomed into his microphone, "Well, *look at you!*"

Christie could barely contain his delight, safe in the knowledge that by tomorrow he would be reelected in a landslide, with polls predicting stunning wins among Hispanic voters, huge gains with African Americans, and even a surge of support from Democrats. Best of all, he knew that the GOP's political priesthood in Washington—more desperate than ever for a 2016 prospect who could save the party from wacko birds—would be salivating over Christie's big win.

It had been just two weeks since the government shutdown ended, and the Republican establishment was increasingly infatuated with Christie, viewing him as a strong, tough, straight-talking standard-bearer who could help erase some of the damage that had been done during this most recent Tea Party fiasco. Not long ago, it had seemed to the moneyed megadonors and moderate politicos who populated the party's pro-business establishment that they would have a dazzling cast of candidates to pick from in 2016. But Ted Cruz had just turned off everyone but the farthest right in the party, Marco Rubio's poll numbers had imploded following the immigration debacle, Jeb Bush was MIA, and Scott Walker, the union-busting Wisconsin governor who had recently survived a recall attempt in his deep-blue state, was facing a tough reelection the next year, and no one knew if he would survive it. The last man standing, it seemed, was Christie.

The New Jersey governor held lots of appeal for the party's pragmatic, pro-business wing. His minority outreach was an obvious plus, but there were also signs that he wouldn't engage in the electorally toxic conservative culture war. He had recently dropped the fight against same-sex marriage in his state, acknowledging that the federal court legalizing the unions in New Jersey should have the last word.

And lately he had been speaking out vocally against the "wacko birds" in Washington who wanted to end the drone program, gut the NSA, and shut down the government. With weeks to go before election night, Christie had blasted the shutdown as "an awful example in governance," the result of politicians who "played chicken with each other."

"If I was in the Senate right now, I'd kill myself," he joked.

Talk like this made the Republican donor class swoon. "He's getting traction with people because people want to win," said megadonor Ken Langone. "After 2012, it dawned on a lot of us that we need to have a better candidate, somebody who can connect, and Christie is the person who can do that." Fred Malek, another prominent donor, said the governor's expected reelection would establish him "as an instant Republican front-runner for 2016."

As Christie looked out over the diverse sea of supporters convened in Union City, he offered a message of cooperation and inclusiveness—one he thought Washington could learn from. "For the last four years, we've worked together to confront every challenge, and now we have one more challenge left in front of us in 2013," he said. "And that challenge left is to prove to all the folks who say we can't come together and work together, that we can't do things together regardless of party...Are you ready to prove them wrong tomorrow?"

The next day, Christie was reelected with 51 percent of Latino voters, 21 percent of black voters, and 32 percent of Democrats. If there was a single microcosm of what the party needed to replicate nationally, New Jersey was it.

And then...

On January 8, 2014, the *Wall Street Journal* posted a story on its website headlined "Bridge-Spat Emails Pose Questions for Christie." Beneath the starchy headline was an explosive revelation: Christie's staff had orchestrated a major, several-days-long traffic jam in Fort Lee, New Jersey—one of the most heavily trafficked areas in the country—to retaliate against the town's mayor for refusing to endorse the governor for reelection. For four days in September 2013, the busiest bridge in the country was reduced to just one access lane. The delays were massive, with emergency workers abandoning their ambulances by foot rather than waiting for traffic to move.

For months, Democrats had been spreading rumors of foul play. And now the damning emails and texts from the governor's staff, which the *Journal* published in full, seemed to confirm the allegations. Weeks before two out of three lanes onto the George Washington Bridge were shut down, Christie's deputy chief of staff, Bridget Anne Kelly, emailed Christie-appointed Port Authority executive David Wildstein, "Time for some traffic problems in Fort Lee."

"Is it wrong that I am smiling?" Wildstein texted in one exchange with Kelly.

"No," Kelly replied.

"I feel badly about the kids," he admitted.

"They are the children of Buono voters," she replied, referring to Christie's former opponent, Barbara Buono.

The revelation set off a national feeding frenzy in the media, and "Bridgegate," as it quickly became known, dominated every broadcast in the country.

On January 9, Christie stepped up to an ornately carved lectern beneath the chandelier of Trenton's statehouse, wearing a discreetly pin-striped suit, a flag pin in the shape of New Jersey, and a contrite face. He was penitent and apologetic, and at times even deferential to the reporters he had made a career out of castigating in public. He seemed drained of the swagger that had long defined his political persona.

"I am embarrassed, and humiliated," he told them, staring straight out into the sea of whirring cameras. And for the next two excruciating hours, he fielded their questions, apologizing over and over for his "failure."

While Christie denied any knowledge of his staff's behavior, the scandal was immensely damaging to his reputation. It made him seem like a bully, instead of a no-nonsense tough guy. It undermined his straight-talk shtick, painting him as yet another shady, corrupt politician.

The days that followed the press conference brought by far the most brutal media coverage of Christie's career. The New York City tabloids were merrily screaming their headlines, overjoyed to have finally found a genuine scandal to match their default populist outrage.

"PATHETIC," sneered one.

"IGNORANCE IS CHRIS," shouted another.

In one particularly on point front page, Christie was portrayed with a thought bubble containing a picture of the White House above his head. The headline: "FAT CHANCE NOW, CHRIS."

As the New York papers derided his "brazen cover-up" and "self-serving, self-pitying display of contrition," the conservative media — which had long ago dubbed the New Jersey governor a traitor and an ideological squish — engaged in open schadenfreude, with Glenn Beck gleefully tweeting "#FatandFurious." "There's more here and it is going to be the problem that haunts Chris Christie," predicted Red-

State's Erick Erickson. And beyond the right-wing pile-on, mainstream political pundits wondered whether Christie might be fatally damaged.

The Republican establishment, meanwhile, was gripped by panic as it watched another favorite son fall from grace. Donors who had been lining up behind Christie were now scattering. "There are definitely people jumping ship," one high-level fund-raiser told me at the time, adding that it had gotten so bad that some of the party's moneymen were now looking back fondly on the good old days of 2012: "You know what a lot of them say to me? 'I think we need Mitt back.'"

Christie's poll numbers slid, both in New Jersey and nationally: the percentage of Republicans who thought he would make a good president sank from 64 to 50 by the end of the month. Republican Ken Cuccinelli, the former candidate for Virginia governor, called on him to resign as chairman of the Republican Governors Association.

Publicly, conservatives knocked the liberal media for giving more play to Bridgegate than Benghazi or the IRS targeting scandal. But privately, donors and kingmakers were quickly backing away from their former anointed one.

Journalists and pundits from Chuck Todd to Bret Baier began citing anonymous donors who declared Christie's 2016 ambitions "done." Another anonymous strategist told *National Review*, "The idea that he's the prohibitive front-runner is over." Media mogul Rupert Murdoch, who owned Fox News and the *Wall Street Journal,* predicted there would be "more stuff coming out" that would further damage Christie's electoral chances. And Bill Kristol—who had quietly met Christie for pizza just a few months before to counsel him on foreign policy and discuss his 2016 prospects—exclaimed during a heated *Crossfire* appearance, "He's not my superstar...He's not the actual favorite among the Republican party. Mike Huckabee would beat Chris Christie right now for the Republican nomination."

Over the following year, Christie would be bogged down by multiple investigations and more allegations of corruption, including probes into whether he mishandled federal funds for Hurricane Sandy relief. More stories would emerge depicting him as a bully. In one, a Rutgers professor who crossed him on a redistricting commission found his program's funding slashed; in another, a Republican state senator who voted against one of Christie's pet projects discovered that plans for a judgeship in his county had mysteriously stalled. There were also stories about Christie's penchant for lavish travel, studded with juicy details, like the $30,000 hotel in Israel to which his family flew in a private jet, or the taxpayer-funded plane tickets totaling $8,156 that enabled his family to attend the Super Bowl.

None of these revelations resulted in indictments or corruption charges, but the conventional wisdom across the party was that Christie was now damaged goods. As the veteran Republican strategist Alex Castellanos put it, "The thing I think about Christie that's hard is that his one trick, which used to be adorable and fun—that he would piss off the news media and speak truth to power—now often comes across as bullying and boorish."

This perception of Christie wasn't limited to cable news chatter; it showed up in focus groups, too. A year after the Bridgegate scandal broke, veteran GOP pollster Frank Luntz addressed a private gathering of top-level donors in California, and presented the latest results from his firm's opinion research on the New Jersey governor. He had been showing footage of Christie's speeches and interviews to groups of Republican voters and asking them to report their opinions of the governor throughout the viewing. He found that Christie's shtick now seemed to wear thin much more quickly than it used to. Five minutes into the video most voters said they liked him; after ten minutes their views began to dim; and by the thirty-minute mark respondents were almost uniformly repulsed by Christie's trademark cockiness and bravado. "They couldn't stand him," remarked one donor after seeing the research.

Chapter Twelve

Seeing the Light

W hat about religious liberty?"

Bobby Jindal was huddled with a small group of advisers in his spacious, sunlit office at the Louisiana governor's mansion, trying to decide what he should say at the Ronald Reagan library in a couple of months. He was scheduled to speak on February 13, 2014, and his inner circle was determined to use the appearance at one of the holiest sites in all of Republicanism to finally shed the malaise that had settled over Jindal's political profile.

But engineering a pitch-perfect breakout performance was proving tricky. The audience inside the room at the Reagan library would be made up of serious-minded Republican elites — the kind who had once fawned over Jindal's wonky smarts and polished credentials. But to be effective, the speech would also need to reach a broader audience of carnivorous conservative activists — people who wouldn't take notice of the governor unless he was serving up a heaping platter of red meat.

There was discussion among the governor and his aides of Jindal recycling the economic speech he had been giving all year. But Curt Anderson, his media consultant, thought the topic was a snoozer.

"That's a really great speech, and you'll give it some more," Anderson told Jindal. "The problem with that speech is, serious people really enjoy it, but it's not something that crowds get fired up about."

That's when Timmy Teepell, an evangelical who was homeschooled as a kid and remained tapped into the Christian grass roots, suggested making the address about religious liberty. The issue had taken on a growing urgency in Jindal's mind lately, as he watched secular liberals adopt an increasingly triumphalist attitude toward traditional Christians, spurred on by a series of gay rights victories. Jindal had been searching for the right venue to voice his concerns about this cultural development, and he thrilled to the idea of making his case at the Reagan library.

Anderson was uneasy about the idea. He told Jindal the topic seemed "kind of obscure" for such a prestigious speech, and he was worried that it would come off as esoteric. After all, Jindal needed to get people talking about him again — and religious liberty was not exactly top of mind in American political discourse at the moment.

But all that changed on December 18, 2013, when *GQ* posted its profile of Phil Robertson online. The bearded patriarch from A&E's monster-hit reality show *Duck Dynasty* — a feel-good series about a family of proud country Christians who got rich selling duck-hunting merchandise — was quoted in the piece crudely musing about the superiority of heterosexual intercourse ("It seems like, to me, a vagina — as a man — would be more desirable than a man's anus") and the sinfulness of homosexuality ("Start with homosexual behavior and just morph out from there. Bestiality, sleeping around with this woman and that woman and that woman and those men...."). The outcry from gay rights advocates was loud and immediate, with the Left threatening boycotts of A&E as long as Robertson was on the air. When the network responded by suspending Robertson indefinitely, religious conservatives pushed back, arguing that the cable star was only expressing a biblical view of sexual ethics, and that left-wing bullies were now punishing him for exercising his right to free speech. Insults were hurled, hashtags were born, chyrons flashed across cable news screens. It was a week before Christmas and, in the spirit of the season, America had fumbled its way into yet another bitter culture war battle.

In Baton Rouge, Robertson's antigay quotes arrived like manna from heaven. Jindal couldn't have scripted a national pageant of umbrage more perfectly suited for him to take a starring role. *Duck*

Dynasty was filmed in Louisiana, and Jindal had been close with the Robertson family for years. He had been searching for the perfect example to illustrate the secular Left's hostility toward conservative Christians, and now it was playing out in his own backwater backyard.

As soon as A&E announced the suspension, Jindal gathered his staff and began drafting a statement in support of Robertson. Not everyone was on board, though. Anderson raised an obvious political concern.

"This may play well in Louisiana, and other places in the South, but we don't know how this will play everywhere else," he said.

Jindal was defiant: "I don't care." The Robertsons were his friends, and he wasn't going to let fears of being seen as uncouth among the country's coastal snobs prevent him from speaking up.

But other aides made a more high-minded case against going out on a limb for Robertson. They argued that the quotes published in *GQ* were coarse, at best, and at worst abhorrent. Not only had Robertson graphically ranked the preferability of certain sex acts; he had also, later in the story, cheerfully shrugged off the history of racial oppression in the Jim Crow south. "I never, with my eyes, saw the mistreatment of any black person," Robertson was quoted as saying. "Not once. Where we lived was all farmers. The blacks worked for the farmers. I hoed cotton with them. I'm with the blacks, because we're white trash ... Pre-entitlement, pre-welfare, you say. Were they happy? They were godly. They were happy. No one was singing the blues."

Did Jindal really want to aggressively defend language like this? the staff contrarians asked. Wasn't this the exact kind of damaging, unthoughtful, "stupid" rhetoric that just a year ago Jindal was calling on his party to purge?

Jindal sympathized with their arguments, but he also knew it wasn't often in politics that an easy pitch like this gets lobbed at you, and he wasn't about to let it sail over the plate.

"That's not the point," he replied. The point was that no one should be banished from public life for expressing an unpopular viewpoint that appears in the Bible.

He tried to appease the holdouts on his team by assuring them that he would make "passing acknowledgment" of the fact that, while he supported Robertson, he wasn't a fan of his friend's choice of words.

But when the statement went out to press the next day, even that caveat was missing.

"Phil Robertson and his family are great citizens of the state of Louisiana," Jindal's statement read. "The politically correct crowd is tolerant of all viewpoints, except those they disagree with. I don't agree with quite a bit of stuff I read in magazine interviews or see on TV. In fact, come to think of it, I find a good bit of it offensive. But I also acknowledge that this is a free country and everyone is entitled to express their views. In fact, I remember when TV networks believed in the First Amendment. It is a messed up situation when Miley Cyrus gets a laugh, and Phil Robertson gets suspended."

(For the statement's kicker, the governor had originally proposed Britney Spears standing in as the symbol of cultural decay, but one of his aides suggested swapping out the aging pop star for the more topical twerker.)

Jindal was the first prominent politician to publicly defend the Robertsons, and his swift, hard-hitting response turned him into a lead cast member in this culture war pageant. While other high-profile Republicans — from Chris Christie to Rand Paul — steered clear of the confrontation, the governor of Louisiana was busy firing off a barrage of tweets, press releases, and made-for-cable sound bites that decried the Left's assault on religious freedom. And when A&E was ultimately forced to walk back its initial statement on the *GQ* story and quietly reinstate their once-shunned star, it was Jindal who received much of the credit from religious conservatives.

In the end, even the staff naysayers had to admit the wisdom in charging full speed into the *Duck Dynasty* kerfuffle. "It was a good nexus of what he believed, and what was politically good, too," one adviser later conceded to me. Jindal was now basking in the celestial bliss of the conservative movement's adoration. By sacrificing a small bit of nuance at the altar of populism, he was once again being elevated as a bold and courageous leader.

He had seen the light, and he was not about to retreat back into the darkness.

Though Jindal didn't hesitate to make partisan hay out of the religious freedom issue while he scrambled toward 2016, the concept of unfettered worship was in fact deeply personal for him—rooted in a tumultuous and dramatic conversion, and a disorienting night in 1987 that would change his life and politics forever.

The lights were lowered in the chapel, and the projector screens high above the stage filled with scenes—taken from a 1979 adaptation of the Gospel of Luke called *The Jesus Film*—of a naked, whip-scarred Savior hanging despondently from a cross. A choir of wide-eyed teenagers below the screen belted out the opening notes of a contemporary Christian electronic-pop song, "This Blood Is for You," and then a soloist leaned into the microphone and began lending graphic description of Christ's suffering with a soulful recitation of the spoken lyrics.

Laced with chips of bone they beat him hard,
From his shoulders to his feet!
And it sliced right through his olive skin,
Just like razors through a sheet.

Sixteen-year-old Bobby Jindal sat in the second row of the audience, taking in the spectacle with a mix of bafflement and wonder. He had been invited to the production, held at a nondenominational church near Louisiana State University called The Chapel on the Campus, by his best friend, Kent, a born-again Christian with a penchant for evangelizing. Jindal, who was Hindu, had taken an intellectual interest in Christianity, mostly to humor his friend, but to him the religion existed primarily as a day-to-day mundanity of life in the Deep South. Christianity for him was LSU football players pointing to the sky after big plays, and omnipresent church marquees lining the streets, and Jesus fish bumper stickers dotting sedans, and pretty girls chattering on Monday mornings about the weekend youth group activities they had attended.

Now, all of a sudden, it felt like much more than that.

In Jindal's accounts of the evening, decades later, he would paper over the specifics of this production, perhaps embarrassed that such a dated, unstylish performance was what planted the seeds of conversion in him. But the Christian God is famously disinclined to bestow tasteful spiritual epiphanies, and he chose this moment to touch Jindal's heart. By the time the choir erupted into the song's chorus, he was overwhelmed with a sense that the violence he was watching Jesus endure was somehow suffered for him personally.

The choir sang, and Jindal's mind raced.

This blood can save the soul!
Heal the sick! Mend the heart!
This blood can give you access,
To the very throne of God!

When the song ended, Todd Hinkie, a square-faced college student who served as the church's youth pastor, stood and invited those who wanted to learn more about Jesus to come talk to him. Jindal sprang from his seat and made a beeline for Hinkie, cutting in front of other audience members in order to grab the pastor's hand. Jindal began talking a mile a minute as he pumped Hinkie's arm in a frenzied handshake.

"Sir, my name is Bobby Jindal; I'm Kent's friend. I really have a lot of questions about Christianity and Christ and the Bible, and to be honest with you, my friends who are Christians, they just can't answer these questions. Can I by chance meet with you?"

A few days later, Jindal met Hinkie at LSU's student union, and the two found a quiet table in the corner where they could talk. Jindal was carrying a long yellow legal pad covered in his own handwriting, and the moment they sat down, he catapulted into his grilling.

"Okay, here's my first question..." Jindal began.

Hinkie, who later recounted the experience to me, was taken aback as he realized that this teenager had scribbled down several pages' worth of theological queries, and he tried to slow him down.

"Hang on, let me tell you the ground rules, dude," Hinkie said.

George H. W. Bush drives a golf cart on a 1983 family vacation in Kennebunkport, ME, accompanied by his son Jeb, who spent his teen years as a pot-smoking prep school kid conflicted about his family's budding political dynasty. *(Cynthia Johnson/Hulton Archive/Getty Images)*

Jeb announces his candidacy at Miami Dade College in Miami, Florida. After deciding to jump into the 2016 race, his lieutenants launched an aggressive, behind-the-scenes campaign to sideline his rivals. *(Johnny Louis/FilmMagic/Getty Images)*

A copy of the gleefully blasphemous underground newspaper published by Rand Paul's secret society at Baylor, featuring a photo of the future senator in Groucho glasses and a false nose. (*The Rope*)

Kentucky Sen. Rand Paul shares a private moment with his father, Ron, a libertarian icon who sources described as privately antagonistic toward his son's political rise. (*Alex Wong/Getty Images News/Getty Images*)

Former vice presidential nominee Paul Ryan attends Pastor Darryl Webster's early-morning religious "boot camp" in Indianapolis as part of his post-2012 tour of impoverished, inner-city America. *(Clare Burns)*

New Jersey Gov. Chris Christie, whose second term was derailed by the "Bridgegate" scandal at the end of 2013 that set off a panic across the national GOP establishment, speaks to constituents. *(Jeff Zelevansky/Getty Images News/ Getty Images)*

Louisiana Gov. Bobby Jindal at church: In high school the Hindu teen secretly converted to Christianity against his parents' wishes; later, as an ambitious governor, he became a conservative culture warrior. *(Courtesy of Timmy Teepell)*

Rafael Cruz spends time with his young son and future Tea Party icon, Ted, whom he often told as a child, "God has destined you for greatness." *(Courtesy of the Cruz Campaign)*

Cruz embraces his father at a victory rally on the night of his election to the Senate in 2012, when he was already eyeing the Oval Office. *(Courtesy of the Cruz Campaign)*

Former Texas Gov. Rick Perry entered the 2016 presidential race looking for redemption after an embarrassing 2012 flameout, but failed to gain traction and became the first candidate to drop out of the 2016 race. *(Courtesy of Ben Price)*

Former Hewlett-Packard CEO Carly Fiorina, the sole woman in the Republican field, sits for an interview with Fox News host Bret Baier. *(Courtesy of Justin Giorgio)*

Cruz and Paul put on a unified front at a conservative "Defund Obamacare" rally, but backstage tensions flared between the two men during the 2013 government shutdown. *(Drew Angerer/Getty Images News/Getty Images)*

Former Florida Gov. Jeb Bush welcomes rising star (and future rival) Marco Rubio to the stage at the Biltmore Hotel in Miami. *(Joe Raedle/Getty Images News/Getty Images)*

Wisconsin Gov. Scott Walker waves to the crowd at the Iowa Freedom Summit, where his fired-up speech turned him into an early top-tier contender for the GOP nomination. *(Scott Olson/Getty Images News/Getty Images)*

Bomb-throwing billionaire Donald Trump shocked the political world and threw the GOP into disarray when he entered the 2016 race. *(Steve Sands/Getty Images Entertainment/Getty Images)*

"This is awesome that you have all these questions, but I know I don't have all the answers. So here's what I'll do: I will do my best to direct you to the answers that are in the scriptures, instead of just giving my opinions. If we can't answer the questions directly out of the Bible, I'll write them down and bring them to people who are smarter than me. Does that work?"

Jindal, impatient and unmoved by this pastorly show of deference to a book he was still quite skeptical of, waved him off. *Yeah. Sure. Whatever.*

"Now, here's my first question..."

To start, Jindal wanted to know about the man he had seen depicted the other night writhing in agony on the cross, and why God had selected such a sadistic and irrational method of achieving salvation for his children.

"Why did that man have to die for my sins?" Jindal asked. "Why couldn't God just say, 'Okay, your sins are forgiven'? I don't get it."

Hinkie took him through the Bible verses that illustrated the competing universal demands of divine mercy and justice, the incompatibility of man's sinful nature and God's holiness, the sacrifice Jesus made on behalf of all mankind. Jindal was mesmerized by the doctrine, and insatiably curious. Up until now, his religious views had been restricted to the Hinduism of his parents; now Christianity was providing him with a whole new theological galaxy to explore.

There was a lot to learn. Jindal was only peripherally aware of many of the most famous Bible passages Hinkie pointed him to, and he frequently had the stories confused with popular fairy tales or children's movies. During the course of their conversations, as Hinkie briefly mentioned the story of Noah's Ark, Jindal interrupted.

"Wait: I thought that was a Disney movie."

When Hinkie showed him that the prophet and his collection of paired-off mammals were, indeed, in the Book of Genesis, Jindal's response was to ask, in all sincerity, if the Little Mermaid was also in the Bible.

The two began meeting weekly to work through Jindal's list of questions. At the end of every session, Jindal would ask for a reading assignment, and Hinkie would give him one—first a few verses from

Mark, and then, when the student complained that it was too short, multiple books in the New Testament at one time.

Throughout the process, Jindal kept his flirtation with Christianity a secret from his parents. He knew they would be devastated, and quite possibly enraged, if they found out he was considering abandoning Hinduism. To avoid the confrontation, Jindal waited until late at night, when his family was asleep, before he slipped into his bedroom closet to pray and read the Bible by flashlight.

For a while, he attempted to reconcile Christianity with the traditions of his parents, once speculating to his friend Elaine Parsons that perhaps he could just believe in Jesus as one of the many gods that Hinduism teaches about. He also tried taking ownership of his native religion, reading Hindu religious texts for the first time. When his grandfather died, Jindal immersed himself in Hindu teachings about the afterlife. But while the idea of Nirvana seemed nice, Jindal was far more compelled by the Christian concept of a just God dividing humanity between heaven and hell on Judgment Day.

While Jindal would spend much of his adult life facing accusations from skeptics who believed his interest in Christianity was a product of political ambition, the truth was that any ulterior motives he might have had were probably more hormonal than Machiavellian. His high school crush-turned-girlfriend, Kathy, was a devout Catholic who was eager to see Jindal convert. On one memorable night, the two sneaked away from their hotel rooms during a regional math tournament and spent hours on the roof, flinging pennies into the fountain below and talking about the future. Kathy said her ultimate ambition was to become a Supreme Court Justice so she could "stop the country from killing babies." Jindal was enthralled by her convictions, and also by her smile, and their relationship was no doubt a driving force in his exploration of Christianity.

One afternoon, Jindal sat with Hinkie in the student union, and during a lull in the conversation, the pastor asked, "What's your next question?"

The yellow legal pad lay untouched on the table between them. Jindal replied emphatically, "I don't have any. I'm done. I've got everything I need." Then he paused just long enough to reveal a chink in the armor of his teenage bravado and asked, "So, what do I do now?"

Hinkie had been schooled in the evangelistic crusades of Billy Graham, who instructed proselytizers in training that the moment a potential convert expresses faith in Jesus, one should take him by the hands and urge him to say the sinner's prayer immediately—thus ushering him into salvation before the devil has time to meddle with his resolve. But when Hinkie proposed such a prayer, Jindal demurred.

"Uh, no," Jindal replied. "That's not something we need to do together. That's something I can do myself."

That night, he knelt in the privacy of his closet and said a prayer that would set him on a new spiritual journey and shape his political destiny—but not before it threatened to collapse his entire world. He accepted Jesus as his personal savior.

The next year, Jindal was driving his father's Toyota Corolla one day when another vehicle slammed into him, sending the teenager's head crashing through the driver's-side window. Miraculously, he endured only minor injuries, and when his parents arrived at his hospital bedside, his mother asked a question any grateful Hindu parent might ask.

"Which god do you have to thank for your safety, Bobby?"

He managed to evade his mother's question in the hospital room, but he could no longer shake the guilt of lying to his mom and dad. These were his parents, after all, not authoritarian rulers—and he was a teenage son, not a conscientious objector. In a fit of frustration and shame, he went to see Hinkie.

"I've got to tell my parents," he said to his spiritual mentor. "I know it's time."

Hinkie tried to offer reassurance. "I'm behind you. And who knows? Maybe the timing is right and their ears will be open."

Jindal was more clear-eyed about the likely fallout.

"They will see this as a total rejection of being Indian," he said. "It's like saying, 'I hate everything about who I am and I reject everything about my family.'"

As they talked, Hinkie was startled by how severe Jindal believed the repercussions of his confession would be. Jindal was so convinced that his parents would punish him by withholding college tuition money that he had secured a full-ride scholarship to LSU as a backup plan. He also seriously believed his parents might kick him out of the house, and he was bracing for the possibility that he would have to finish high school homeless. But he felt he no longer had any choice, so he went home to tell his parents.

A couple of days later, he met Hinkie in his office at the church. The young pastor could tell right away that Jindal was deeply agitated.

"How'd it go?"

"It was really tough," Jindal replied. "They reacted really, really strongly."

Raj, Jindal's mother, was grief-stricken that her son had betrayed their family's faith; meanwhile, his father, Amar, saw this second life as a reckless detour on Jindal's path to medical school. Both parents were irate. Rather than kick Jindal out of the house, they decided to transform their home into a sort of correctional facility for their apostate son. He was told he was not allowed to attend church, read the Bible, or even talk to any of his Christian friends anymore, and that he would be expected home every day within fifteen minutes of school ending. He was forbidden from participating in any activities outside his academic work, and was strictly instructed not to talk to any family members about his spiritual dalliance.

And, of course, he would no longer be allowed to see Hinkie.

"What do I do?" Jindal asked.

Hinkie was at a loss — distressed by the news, yes, but also reluctant to advise a seventeen-year-old to wage holy war against his parents' unrighteous rules. Searching for something to say that would square this pragmatic impulse with a biblical principle, Hinkie felt compelled to open to a verse in Ephesians: "Children, obey your parents in the Lord, for this is right."

The young pastor proceeded with caution. "As I listen to what your parents have told you," he said, "you actually can choose to obey both them and the Lord. I know it would be incredibly hard, but you don't *have* to go to church. You can obey them on that. You don't *have* to talk to those friends you have at school that are Christians. You can obey them on that. You don't *have* to meet with me anymore..."

Hinkie felt a wave of nausea come over him. He couldn't believe he was counseling Jindal—his brand-new convert, his greatest ministerial achievement, his friend—to abandon the trappings of a God-fearing Christian.

He hastened to add, "The only thing they said that you probably shouldn't obey is that you don't read the Bible anymore—because there *is* a higher authority than Mom and Dad. So I would say, figure out a way to keep reading scripture secretively.

"But other than that...God's word says if you are honoring your father and mother, it's going to go well with you."

A pause.

"So, is that what you want to do?" Hinkie asked.

Jindal nodded. "Yes. That's what I'll do."

They said a farewell prayer together and embraced, and then Jindal left Chapel on the Campus for the last time.

As he watched Jindal go, Hinkie said a quiet prayer to himself: "Lord, he's in your hands—and he is completely out of mine."

When Jindal arrived at Brown in the fall of 1988, it was a contentious time for the small, tight-knit Christian community on campus. A year earlier, the student-run magazine *Good Clean Fun* had published a cover story titled "The New Crusaders" that cast Brown's evangelicals as insular, self-righteous, and anti-intellectual. The three-thousand-word feature was rife with caricature—an almost perfect culture war time capsule showing how secular Ivy Leaguers viewed conservative Christians in the late eighties—and it drew vocal outrage from Brown's believers. The magazine dutifully ran several incensed letters to the editor in its next edition, and the episode was largely forgotten by the time the leftover copies were tossed in trash cans. But among the school's Christian students, the feelings of aggrievement lingered well beyond this particular campus controversy.

As a brand-new freshman bulging with pent-up spiritual energy and finally free from his parents' restrictions, Jindal decided his first act of collegiate rebellion would be to immerse himself in campus Christian culture. He populated his social circles with faithful classmates, and seized every chance he got to wage rhetorical combat with the secular student body in defense of his religion. In one emblematic episode early on, he refused to participate in a student orientation program that sought to teach open-mindedness by inviting straight men to identify as gay. When a resident adviser told him the session was mandatory, Jindal shot back, "You can send my dad's tuition money back, but I'm not going."

Jindal's dual interests in highbrow theology and picking fights with campus liberals made him popular among his fellow Ivy League Christians, who gathered in religious clubs that often functioned as salons for high-minded scriptural discussion. Matt Skinner, who was president of Campus Crusade for Christ during Jindal's freshman year, described the club — and Brown's Christian scene in general — as "kind of idiosyncratic... It took on the nature of the college, in the sense that it was primarily more about the kind of stuff going on in our heads."

But during Jindal's freshman year, the friendly, cross-denominational unity that held together the school's conservative Christians was threatened by an unlikely — and jarring — wave of Catholic fervor that was sweeping across the campus. Christian students were turning to the Vatican for spiritual stimulation and in-depth doctrine, attending Mass together, and diving into the catechism. Students who were there at the time later told me this Roman reawakening was driven by Opus Dei, a controversial Catholic organization, known globally for its secrecy and elitism, that was then active on campus. The group, which would later be immortalized (and fictionalized) in the book *The Da Vinci Code* as a cultish secret society, was famous for targeting intellectual elites and prominent conservatives for conversion, and it worked fervently to cull Brown's crop of up-and-coming influentials. Its proselytizing paid off: in 1989 alone, at least a dozen Protestant students converted to Catholicism — a phenomenon that plunged the Christian community on campus into heated sectarian debates.

"A lot of us were really concerned about what was going on," said Michael, a Protestant classmate of Jindal's. "Why were [so many] students converting to Catholicism and taking that really seriously? I had deep concerns theologically."

It is unclear whether Jindal associated with Opus Dei while at Brown, but he was one of many campus Christians who became intensely interested in Catholic doctrine at the time. He was confirmed in the fall of 1989, during his sophomore year. The ceremony took place at a Mass in Providence, where he gave testimony to an audience filled with friends who had helped him along his path to conversion. It was a joyous day, and he felt he had finally reached the destination to which his youthful spiritual journey was meant to take him. It wouldn't be long, though, before his new faith was put to the test one dramatic and unexplainable night; Jindal would wrestle with its events for years to come.

Around the time of Jindal's confirmation, strange things started happening to the Christian students at Brown. There were reports of a sulfuric odor—supposedly a sign of the devil's presence—mysteriously surfacing in dorm rooms, accompanied by confounding sights and sounds. One young woman claimed that a demon had assaulted her, leaving scars up and down her arms. Others complained of night terrors they believed were painted by evil spirits.

These phenomena were not entirely out of place at the Ivy League school. Many of the students came from East Asian countries, where charismatic Christian pastors were famous for speaking in tongues and performing miraculous, forehead-thumping healings. What's more, the past decade of popular cinema had seen a string of blockbuster movies like *The Exorcist, Poltergeist,* and *The Amityville Horror* that lent dramatic weight to the notion of demonic forces reaching into the terrestrial world.

The incidents left Brown's Christian community frightened and flailing, in search of guidance. They sought out help from local priests and pastors, but the staid New England clergy balked at their requests. Feeling helpless, some students began attempting their own exorcism-like rituals to help disturbed peers. Michael recalled one such experience, during which he and three other students laid hands on a young woman they believed to be possessed. As they prayed over her, a larger group of believers huddled in a separate part of campus, pleading with God for a miracle. The exercise was anticlimactic and, looking back on it years later, Michael would acknowledge that it may not have been doctrinally sound.

"If you're really in faith and you really know Christ, the enemy cannot take possession of your soul," said Michael, who went on to become a professional minister after college. "Could he get a foothold in that person's soul and take possession of your voice? Maybe? To be honest, I was twenty-one at the time. What did I know?" He said that if their efforts seemed melodramatic in retrospect, it was only because they were young and grappling with a scary situation. "We were foolish enough to say we cared about these [people] and we were willing to try to free them. I remember saying, 'We're trying to cast out a demon, yes, but what we really want is for her to feel spiritually free.'"

Jindal kept his distance from these episodes at first. For all his religious zeal, he was still a biology major, acquainted with the natural sciences and uncomfortable with the more mystical aspects of his new faith. He had once heard a Rhode Island priest confidently declare that biblical references to angels and demons were not meant to be taken literally, and he was happy to cling to that interpretation. But his aloof attitude toward the darkness that seemed to be settling over many of his classmates wouldn't last long.

Jindal met Susan, a pretty fellow freshman, on a quiet walk to church one Sunday morning shortly after arriving in Providence. "She was beautiful and lost, and I was more than happy to fulfill my Christian duty by showing her the way to church," he later wrote. They quickly became best friends. "Susan" would surface under a variety of pseudonyms in a series of personal essays Jindal wrote for obscure Catholic magazines years later. In them, he described intense, late-night conversations with her that covered everything from past break-ups to abortion policy to theology. They pulled all-night cram sessions together—Jindal double majored in biology, to satisfy his father, and public policy, for himself—and scandalized their see-no-evil Christian friends by frequenting local dance clubs. But despite their intimate connection, their friendship remained stubbornly chaste and romance-free, and Susan eventually grew frustrated by Jindal's inability to make a move.

Their friendship ebbed and flowed over the following months. On one emotional evening, she confided in him that she had been diagnosed with skin cancer and would need an operation; the next day she avoided him altogether. Soon, though, Jindal began hearing unsettling rumors about Susan from mutual friends. She was behaving erratically, her days derailed by sudden emotional outbursts, her nights defined by terrifying "visions." Jindal reasoned that these were natural responses to the stress in her life: in addition to her diagnosis, Susan's Bible study leader back home had recently committed suicide, and the grief was taking a toll on her emotional well-being. Other friends, however, suspected that Satan was striking again.

On the last week of the semester, the University Christian Fellowship called an emergency prayer meeting for Susan on the eve of her operation. When the night of the meeting arrived, about ten students, including Jindal, gathered in a classroom and sat down with Susan in a circle. They sang worship songs and prayed together, but the enthusiasm that typically characterized their meetings was missing. It was finals week, and many were distracted by academics. After going through the motions, a student moved to close the meeting—but he was stopped short. Jindal would recount what happened next in one of his essays a few years later.

"Suddenly, Susan emitted some strange guttural sounds and fell to the floor," he wrote. "She started thrashing about, as if in some sort of seizure." Susan's sister, who had flown in to lend support during the surgery, rushed to her prostrate body and ordered everyone to place their hands on her.

Jindal, horrified and humiliated, felt paralyzed at first. He refused to move. Then, all of a sudden, Susan's incomprehensible growling formed a single, audible word.

"Bobby!" she shrieked.

The exclamation sent a chill down his spine. He moved reluctantly toward the group, and placed a fingertip on Susan's shoulder, "as if afraid of becoming infected with the disease that was ravaging her body." But the moment they made contact, the unfamiliar voice in Susan's throat directed itself at him again: "Bobby, you cannot even love Susan."

He staggered back to the other side of the room. *Why was she speaking in third person?* The voice began lashing out violently at the other students, cursing them one by one, exposing intimate secrets, and verbally assaulting them with a personal cruelty that was entirely out of character for Susan. In a frenzy, they fell to their knees and began chanting:

"Satan, I command you to leave this room!"

"Satan, I command you to leave this room!"

Some of them started sobbing, while others cried out for "demons to leave in the name of Christ!"

Just as they were ready to give up hope, a student leader from Campus Crusade for Christ burst into the room brandishing a crucifix. Someone had called the rival Christian club for advice, and now her presence gave the room energy to keep going. Drawing hope, Jindal reflexively began uttering the Hail Mary—a prayer he had never said before in his life. During his investigation of Catholicism, he had rejected doctrines concerning Mary because they seemed like a form of idolatry. Now, though, it was the only form of prayer he could manage to voice. He said it over and over again, until it became a chant.

The crucifix seemed to have a calming influence on Susan, and her sister seized the opportunity to start reading verses from the Bible. "At first, Susan responded to biblical passages with curses and profanities," Jindal later wrote. "[But] mixed in with her vile attacks were short and desperate pleas for help. In the same breath [that] she attacked Christ, the Bible's authenticity, and everyone assembled in prayer, Susan would suddenly urge us to rescue her."

They encouraged Susan to read from the scriptures, but she choked on the sentence "Jesus is Lord."

"Jesus is L...L...L..." she tried.

At last, a breakthrough: "Just as suddenly as she went into the trance, Susan suddenly reappeared and claimed, 'Jesus is Lord.' With an almost comical smile, Susan then looked up as if awakening from a deep sleep and asked, 'Has something happened?'"

The events of that night toppled the emotional barrier between Jindal and Susan. The next year, they traveled to Europe together as a couple, falling in love as they took in a Viennese opera and walked the streets of southern France.

Jindal never fully came to terms with what happened that night, but it served to cement his faith in Catholicism and convince him of the reality of supernatural "spiritual warfare." He also came away with a stronger conviction than ever that people should be free to worship and talk about their faith—no matter how far outside the mainstream it may be—without fear of retribution. Decades later, it would become the bedrock of his political career—and the driving force in his presidential campaign.

On the night of February 13, 2014, Jindal walked out onto the stage at the Ronald Reagan Presidential Library to deliver what had become a highly anticipated speech. In the two months since he had entered the fray of the *Duck Dynasty* battle, Jindal had become a heroic figure to many on the religious Right. Now he had come to California to issue a dire warning to believers everywhere.

"The American people, whether they know it or not, are mired in a silent war," Jindal declared. "It threatens the fabric of our communities, the health of our public square, and the endurance of our constitutional governance."

He continued, "The war is waged in our courts, and in the halls of political power. It is pursued with grim and relentless determination by a group of like-minded elites, determined to transform the country from a land sustained by faith into a land where faith is silenced, privatized, and circumscribed."

He predicted that it wouldn't be long before liberals passed laws targeting churches that refused to perform same-sex marriage ceremonies, and he bemoaned the fact that religious business owners were being forced to violate their consciences by serving same-sex couples.

"Under the Obama regime, the president and his allies are intentional in pursuing these conflicts from the perspective that you must sacrifice your most sacred beliefs to government the instant you start a business."

He also spoke up, once again, for the *Duck Dynasty* family.

"I defended them because they have every right to speak their minds, however indelicately they may choose to do so. The modern Left in America is completely intolerant of the views of people of faith. They want a completely secular society where people of faith keep their views to themselves."

The 4,500-word address was deeply researched, carefully annotated, and thoroughly fact-checked — substantive enough to impress the elites in the room. But the thrust of the speech — its abundant combat metaphors, its description of sinister plotting within the "Obama regime" — was designed to stoke the righteous outrage of millions of aggrieved Christians. Jindal was aiming his message at social conservatives across the country who felt as though the modern GOP — with its sudden insecurity over not being on the "right side of history" — had abandoned them. He wanted them to know that in the governor of Louisiana, they had a champion.

Jindal had always relished making rigorous, intellectual arguments in defense of his faith, and even though all this had started with a reality TV star popping off with some decidedly ignorant comments, his aides could tell he was enjoying this new role more than many would have guessed. "There is an elitist presumption in the Boston-to-DC corridor that you can't really be smart and a Christian who believes these things," one adviser later explained. "Bobby really enjoys taking that on. He says, 'Throw me in that briar patch.' I think some reporters look at him and say, 'Okay, this guy's really smart, I accept that,' and in the back of their minds they're thinking, 'His parents are from India, so he's probably good at math, too.' But they forget something. He's not from India. He's from the Deep South. His faith is a big part of him."

More to the point, this new tack of his was working. For the first time in a long time, Jindal had conservatives buzzing, fawning, cheering — saying his name.

PART III

WANDERING

Chapter Thirteen

Coalition Building

The drive from Jerusalem to the kibbutz by the Sea of Galilee was only supposed to take two hours. But then the rain started falling, and the flash floods started forming, and the hail pellets started ricocheting off the windshield, and before there was time to repent and petition Yahweh for deliverance, rockslides in the West Bank washed out the road, making it impossible to proceed. The chartered bus in which Rand Paul was riding was packed with enough Orthodox rabbis and evangelical ministers that a minor miracle wouldn't have seemed entirely out of order—a parting of the stream, perhaps, or a small ark to float them across the sinkhole that blocked their path. But today the vengeful God of the Old Testament wanted his tribe to wander.

As their luxury coach turned around and began its long, slow, winding detour, Rand was reminded briefly of the Bible camp his parents had sent him to as a kid, when the church's rickety old bus would invariably break down and he and his fellow campers would wind up at a roadside Stuckey's somewhere, gnawing on Pecan Log Rolls as they waited for the tow truck to arrive. Truth be told, Rand had felt at times during this little excursion to Israel as if he was participating in another obligatory display of prefab devotion—like teenage church camp, but with higher stakes and a nicer bus.

The trip had been organized and paid for by David Lane, a former

Bible salesman who now marshaled millions of born-again activists and clergy in the United States, and had made it his mission to yoke the GOP's presidential aspirants to the religious Right as firmly as possible. But many of the conservative faith leaders Lane had invited on this trip were suspicious of the curly-haired libertarian in their company, particularly when it came to his views on Israel. Rand's father, Ron, had spent much of his career in Congress and on the campaign trail raging against the bulletproof nature of America's alliance with the Jewish state. As an avowed isolationist, Ron strongly opposed U.S. meddling in the Middle East, and as a fiscal libertarian he believed the American government had no business sending tax dollars to its allies overseas. He was so outspoken over the years that some American Jewish leaders had branded him an anti-Semite. The younger Paul had not been quite so bellicose as his dad on this issue, but he had nonetheless called for putting an end to all U.S. foreign aid payments, including money that went to Israel.

To the Republican Party's hawkish donors and foreign policy luminaries—who widely viewed Israel as an essential partner in the global fight for Western ideals and free markets—Paul's position amounted to political heresy. And to the party's base of conservative Christians—who fervently believed that the establishment of Israel had been a divine fulfillment of biblical prophecy—his stance looked an awful lot like *actual* heresy.

And so here Rand found himself, rolling slowly down a highway somewhere between the sepulcher Jesus escaped from and the water he walked on, trying to keep spirits high while a busload of cold, tired, hungry clergymen silently rendered their judgments of his apostasy. The tone of the trip had been mostly polite and positive up to this point, but now their two-hour bus tour had turned into seven, and some of the senator's political aides worried that the fragile diplomacy in their little group was at risk of collapsing beneath the weight of frayed nerves and clashing ideologies.

The tour guide, looking to brighten the mood, suggested a wholesome distraction. "How about a gospel tune?"

But Rand had a different idea.

"Do we have 'Knockin' on Heaven's Door'?" he called out. "The Guns N' Roses version?"

No one on the bus knew whether he was serious at first, and some wondered whether a glam-rock ballad was appropriate for the occasion. But Rand, feeling punchy, wouldn't let up.

"Come on!" he shouted. " 'Knockin' on Heaven's Door'!"

Finally, the tour guide tinkered with the bus's sound system until Axl Rose's vocals began screeching out of the speakers.

"There we go!" Rand exclaimed, before gleefully belting out the lyrics: *Knock-knock-knockin' on heaven's doo-oo-oor!*

"We need to change the name of this bus," Rand declared during a pause in his performance. "It's not the David Lane Tour anymore. It's the Plague Tour. We've got hail, we've got darkness—all we need now are the frogs!"

Bleary-eyed rabbis and ministers dissolved into laughter, and as the high-pitched harmonic squeal of Slash's guitar solo blared out of the speakers, their bus finally began its descent into the valley where the Sea of Galilee sat.

It was a quintessential Rand Paul moment—unorthodox, irreverent, and a little bit goofy—but it succeeded precisely because of its eccentricity. By sheer force of personality, he had kept his little tribe together and shepherded them safely to the promised land, if only for a day. The question now was whether he could pull off the same trick for the entire Republican Party.

The senator's pilgrimage was one part of a far-reaching, and audacious, bid to answer the single most critical question that faced Republicans as they barreled haplessly toward 2016: how could they rebuild a winning national coalition of voters before the next presidential race?

Every White House contender in the party had his own theory of the case—the GOP's primary focus should be to close the gender gap, or convert more Latinos, or recapture the Midwestern blue-collar vote—but Rand's idea was the most radical. He envisioned a Republican Party whose very molecular makeup was mutated beyond recognition, a party comprising the sort of motley crowds that used to turn up at his dad's campaign rallies, where young, tree-hugging vegans stood side by side with middle-aged, jerky-chewing gun nuts because they both found something in the libertarian cause to cheer about. Rand believed the 2016 presidential primaries posed a once-in-a-generation chance to make this a reality.

He knew that his idiosyncratic views meant he would never pass as an archetypal Republican candidate. He was not the Bible-thumper, or the businessman, or the war hero. But he believed that for every one of the disparate tribes in the GOP, there was at least one unique ingredient in his platform that was perfectly suited to their respective political palates. He just needed to give them a taste. This had been the rationale behind Rand's Israel trip: to show the neocon elites and the evangelical Zionists in his party that even if they didn't like his views on *this* issue, surely there was something else he could offer them.

Ever since his 2013 drone filibuster, Rand had been working on a manifesto that detailed his vision for the "New GOP" he was trying to build. Many in the senator's orbit had privately urged him to find a different ghostwriter for his upcoming book after the egregious cribbing in his last title set off a media firestorm. But Rand, defiant and loyal as ever, stuck with repentant plagiarist Doug Stafford as his chief scribe. Stafford labored over the manuscript as if it were his own masterpiece: researching, writing, rewriting, carefully — *very* carefully — compiling citations, submitting the drafts to Rand, and then starting all over again once the senator returned the pages with handwritten notes scribbled across the margins.

One key passage that emerged from this process would eventually wind up in a chapter titled "Tree Hugger," in which Rand iconoclastically identifies as a "crunchy conservative" and details his comically cursed efforts to grow a giant sequoia tree in his yard, before describing the subversively pluralistic party he hopes to build.

The New GOP has a place for those who want to preserve and protect and provide for a cleaner, brighter future for our planet.

In the New GOP, it will be okay to watch Jon Stewart or read Barbara Kingsolver, perhaps just not both in the same day. In the New GOP, it will be just as admirable to defend the Fourth Amendment as the Second Amendment.

In the New GOP it is cool to compost, shop at the farmer's market, and maybe, just maybe, okay to commit civil disobedience and drink raw milk transported across state lines... That's the GOP I hope to lead.

As soon as these paragraphs came together, they knew they'd found the section that book critics and political reporters would seize on. Rand's plan was to time the release of the book, called *Taking a Stand,* to his presidential campaign kickoff, believing it would infuse his candidacy with a high-toned, and even historic, sense of mission that would make his rivals look like the small-ball partisans that they were. But as he entered 2014, Rand's vision for a new kind of Republican Party suddenly became less abstract—and much more politically urgent.

Ted Cruz had emerged from his failed crusade to dismantle Obamacare as a fully canonized conservative saint. Less than two weeks after the government shutdown ended, he was stoking presidential buzz in Iowa. Sitting at the head of a ballroom in Des Moines, the Texas senator had bowed his head reverently while a Republican activist pleaded with God to send more principled leaders like Cruz who were willing to "be crucified for their belief system." Six hundred conservatives sang out their "Amen"s in unison—and just like that, the Tea Party had found its new hero.

It now seemed clear that Rand's 2016 presidential bid wouldn't be able to count on the same alliance of Tea Party conservatives and libertarian activists that had swept him into the Senate. Cruz was leaving little doubt about his presidential aspirations, and he would likely siphon off substantial Tea Party support in the primaries. Rand would have to pesuade a new conservative constituency to unite with his grassroots libertarian fan club.

But who?

Inside the senator's inner circle, a long-standing disagreement about 2016 strategy soon curdled into a bitter divide over how to respond to Cruz's rise. On one side were the advisers who argued that Rand's best bet was to bring conservative Christians into the libertarian fold. Stafford was a key proponent of this strategy, as was Rex Elsass, a cigar-chomping media consultant out of Ohio who had gotten enough born-again culture warriors elected over the years to buy himself a private jet. Their hypothesis was that the religious Right—with its unfashionable politics and growing estrangement from the party's moderate elites—would relate to libertarians' long-held sense of persecution at the hands of the political class. Rand could win the nomination, they argued, by cobbling together a coalition of Republican outcasts and outsiders.

But on the other side of the internal divide, Rand's establishment emissaries were working fastidiously for over a year to build goodwill among the GOP's megadonors and power brokers—and they balked at what some privately referred to as Stafford's "Island of Misfit Toys" campaiga strategy. This camp of advisers—led by Olson, Jesse Benton, and Virginia-based GOP fixer Chris LaCivita—believed that Rand could win over the Republican Party's business wing with his deep ideological commitment to tax cuts and deregulation, as well as his potentially game-changing appeal to younger voters. When it came to courting the denizens of the political establishment, Benton told me at the time, "It really helps that he doesn't want a culture war." But if Rand suddenly tried to transform himself into a fire-breathing family values crusader, he would instantly wipe out any inroads he had made with donors and party officials.

As the debate raged inside Rand's inner circle, the senator tried to broker peace by insisting he didn't have to zero in on just one group of voters. After all, if his New GOP was ever going to be nationally dominant, it would need *everyone*—not just the tattooed libertarians, but the chinos-clad chamber of commerce crowd, and the evangelicals, and the Tea Partiers, and the left-leaning college kids, and probably a good portion of black and Latino voters as well. He was going peddle his pitch everywhere—and he was certain that, given the chance to lay out his vision, none would be able to resist his persuasive powers.

With grand electoral conquest on his mind—and 2016 on the horizon—Rand hoisted the black sail of his pirate ship and headed for hostile political waters. And if he seemed overly confident in his mission, it was only because he had been here once before, just five years earlier.

On May 14, 2009, Rand Paul sat perched on a stool in front of a low-tech, orange-and-purple backdrop at a remote TV studio in southern Kentucky, waiting for his cue to launch the revolution. When it came, it was in the unlikely form of a question crackling through his earpiece from a left-wing cable news personality.

"Dr. Paul, I understand that you yourself have some political ambitions," said MSNBC host Rachel Maddow from her studio in New York. "I was hoping you might talk about those tonight on the show."

"Yeah I do," Rand replied, speaking deliberately to convey the gravity of the occasion. "I'm happy tonight to announce, on *The Rachel Maddow Show,* that I'm forming an exploratory committee to run for the U.S. Senate."

It was an unorthodox way to kick off a Republican Senate bid in a deep-red state—and truth be told, MSNBC had not been his first choice. Earlier that month, Rand had asked Benton to shop his big announcement around to cable news producers in New York. "We tried CNN, we tried Wolf [Blitzer], we tried Fox, but other folks weren't interested," Benton would later tell me.

Benton suggested that Rand consider a more conventional platform to launch his campaign, like a rally in his hometown or an appearance on local talk radio. But the candidate wasn't having it: he insisted that it take place on national television. The political elites in Kentucky were laughing at the prospect of his candidacy—he just knew it. They thought of him as a punch line. A stooge. And he couldn't think of a more satisfying way to wipe the doltish grins off their faces than by going on prime-time TV—precisely which show, it didn't matter—to announce his bid to explode their monopoly of power in the state. The Maddow appearance, he told Benton, would give him "an image of legitimacy."

If Rand was spoiling for a fight with the Republican establishment, there was no better battleground in the country at the time than the 2010 Kentucky Republican primary, where party bosses were transparently working to bypass the whims of the electorate and install their own chosen candidate. The only reason the Senate seat was even open was because Senator Jim Bunning, a retired baseball player and conservative populist, had wounded the ego of the state's sharklike senior senator, Mitch McConnell, by defying his express orders to support the bank bailout legislation. When Bunning voted his conscience instead, McConnell, who was Senate Minority Leader, put out word to the Republican Party machine in Kentucky and DC that no one was to lift so much as a pinky in support of Bunning's reelection bid. The ominous *or else* was implied, as it always was with McConnell and his gang of partisan enforcers. Bunning was compelled to bow out, and McConnell quickly anointed thirty-seven-year-old Trey Grayson, a well-bred Harvard alum and Kentucky's secretary of state, to be his replacement.

Oh, how Rand *loathed* this sort of antidemocratic big-footing. He was practically jumping out of his hiking sandals at the chance to blow up the plans of McConnell and his good ol' boys.

But with little money and few resources to start with, his initial campaign operation was cobbled together with the political equivalent of duct tape, populated by a hodgepodge of earnest, eccentric devotees of his dad. For all the family dinners he'd sat through, Rand didn't know much about the mechanics of professional campaigns. During one early meeting, while a team of professional political consultants tried to pitch him on a communications strategy complete with media market breakdowns and potential ad buys, Rand interrupted. "What do you guys do exactly?" he asked. "Write press releases?"

What he lacked in operational expertise, however, he made up for with an unwavering confidence in himself, and in the superiority of his ideas. He was not going to squander this chance to pit his absolute rightness against the unsalvageable wrongness of GOP leaders.

Rand built early grassroots buzz by granting YouTube interviews to libertarian bloggers and drumming up support on *Infowars with Alex Jones,* a national radio show hosted by the infamous conspiracy theorist. But to win the primary, Rand would need to expand his appeal beyond libertarians and Tea Partiers and convince a wider cross section of Kentucky Republicans that he was Senate material. This was a tall order. Across the state, Republicans were already whispering that the libertarian eye doctor from Bowling Green might be a secret supporter of abortion rights and gay marriage, and that his opposition to Guantánamo Bay made him a soft-on-terror peacenik.

Rand wished he could sit down every voter in the state and explain to them, one by one, why they were wrong to believe the smears. He knew that if only he had the time to walk them through the unimpeachable logic of his positions — step by step, point by point, repeating himself when necessary to make sure they *truly* understood — the power of rational argument would win the day. If he lost this election, he believed, it would only be because he didn't get a chance to adequately explain why he was right and his antagonists were wrong — and he longed for a more substantive medium for persuasion than press releases and abbreviated interviews.

Enter Doug Stafford.

Rand had first met Stafford on a trip to Washington in the spring of 2009, when he was still mulling a Senate bid, and a friendship quickly formed. The candidate felt as though he had found a kindred spirit in Stafford: a genuine political nonconformist. And Stafford, meanwhile, was impressed by Rand's command of policy and political history, and the quiet certitude with which he expressed his opinions. When Stafford, who was afflicted with a lazy eye, told Rand about a surgical procedure he was thinking of having to improve his vision, the ophthalmologist asked a series of questions and then rendered his prognosis.

"I would consider it malpractice to operate on your eyes," Rand said matter-of-factly. Stafford didn't need a second opinion. He never got the operation.

One day, after Rand got into the race, he was on the phone with Stafford, complaining about the mind-numbing conventions of campaign messaging, when the strategist proposed an idea. Why not make his arguments and respond to false charges with a series of long, detailed, well-argued essays and then mail them to voters across the state? Stafford, who worked in political mail advertising, made the case to the candidate that such a strategy would be relatively cheap — and *much* more substantive! — compared with putting up thirty-second TV spots during *Seinfeld* reruns.

Rand loved the idea, and soon his campaign was shipping out thousands of newsletter-style documents that were aimed at selling his libertarian platform to Kentucky's average Republican voters. One of the mailers featured a photo of Rand admiring rows of shotguns and rifles, and it couched his pro-gun rhetoric in a broader, more libertarian-tinged argument: "It's important that you and I send people to Washington who not only understand the Second Amendment, but who follow the entire Bill of Rights," he wrote. For example, "how many supposedly pro-gun politicians voted for the Patriot Act, which gives the government the right to search your home without a warrant, leave listening devices, and use any and all information to prosecute you on any charge, regardless of their original reason for the search?"

Many in Rand's orbit at the time questioned whether voters were actually reading all these long-winded opuses that the campaign was cramming into their mailboxes. But it didn't matter. The strategy was perfectly calibrated to the candidate's conviction that superior ideas (meaning, of course, *his* ideas) would always win the day as long as he had sufficient space and time to fully articulate the arguments.

Though he didn't know it then, Rand was just a few years away from putting that assumption to the test on the biggest stage in American politics.

Shortly after Senator Rand Paul's presidential coalition building commenced in earnest, the libertarian found himself sitting down to lunch at an upscale Washington eatery for a first date with Karl Rove. They were joined at the table by Stafford, Olson, and veteran GOP fund-raiser Ron Weiser. Everyone was bracing for a disaster — and there was good reason why.

Rove privately regarded Rand as a political flash in the pan whose career in Republican politics was incurably burdened by wacky libertarian ideas and a cuckoo-bird father. Rove didn't care how many columnists and magazine covers were breathlessly touting a supposed "libertarian moment" in their party: he firmly believed the junior senator from Kentucky was headed for a crash and burn. Rand, meanwhile, saw Rove as an avatar of the corrupt old-guard GOP—the George W. Bush spinmeister who'd hawked the Iraq War to the sleepy American masses like a late-night infomercial pitchman and then left the White House to enrich himself with his connections. Rarely had a Washington power lunch featured two diners more predisposed to disliking each other.

But Olson, who did consulting work for Rove's American Crossroads in addition to advising Rand, had taken the risk and set up the meeting anyway. Whatever animus Rand harbored toward Rove, the fact remained that he was one of the most influential gatekeepers and opinion makers in the GOP's moneyed set. He was a regular columnist for the rich-guy paper of record, the *Wall Street Journal,* and a Fox News pundit who routinely appointed political winners, losers, and rising stars from his perch in prime time. Any ambitious Republican hoping to raise enough money for a serious presidential bid knew that Rove's stamp of approval was enormously important, and Rand was no exception.

The lunch began as a study in contrasts, with the lean libertarian meekly nibbling his way through the meal while the carnivorous superconsultant greedily gorged himself. But then somebody mentioned that the two men had both been raised in Texas, and before long they were reminiscing, and roistering, and reveling in the unparalleled greatness of their native state—a beloved tradition for Texas supremacists everywhere.

By the time the check arrived, Rove was impressed with Rand's palpable self-confidence and his ability to play nice with other Republicans—two attributes the batty elder Paul had never possessed.

"Man, he's the only politician I've ever met that's as comfortable with himself as Dubya," Rove marveled to associates after he left the meeting. "I mean, he's really confident. I don't agree with him on some stuff, but boy, he certainly isn't his old man, is he?"

Mission accomplished, thought Olson.

Soon, the doughy-cheeked talking head was mentioning Rand in his punditry alongside other top presidential prospects, and holding him up as a model for the sort of movement conservative the GOP should get behind. During one appearance on *Fox News Sunday,* Rove even declared that the party needed "more Rand Pauls."

With the Republican Party's most influential billionaire whisperer singing the senator's praises, Rand's team moved to take advantage. In the months that followed, they trotted out Rand at countless well-appointed boardrooms, VIP retreats, and extravagant penthouses, where he flattered and pitched to every deep-pocketed donor who would listen—regardless of what he or she believed. He met privately with the Omaha-based founder of TD Ameritrade, and genuflected before Wyoming's richest conservative Christian. He trekked to Boston's Newbury Street, where Mitt Romney's former fund-raising chief, Spencer Zwick, assembled a small gathering of curious millionaires to hear out the senator. And when summer came, Rand dutifully trudged to another one of Romney's loathsome Park City summits, where he stayed on his best behavior all weekend. He even got a hearing from the board of the staunchly pro-Israel Republican Jewish Coalition, telling stories about his trip to the Holy Land and subjecting himself to an aggressive grilling from the party's most prominent hawks and Zionists. After the meeting, Ari Fleischer told the *New York Times* that he appreciated Rand's efforts, regardless of their disagreements. "He's thinking about these issues," Fleischer said. "He's trying to learn."

The senator's mad cash dash was generating glowing reviews from donors and party elites across the country. Olson often found himself on the other end of a phone call with one multimillionaire or another who had just met Rand, and wanted to gush about how compelling the senator's unique 2016 pitch was. Team Rand's establishment charm offensive was going better than they could have possibly expected.

There was, however, one glaring obstacle: Doug Stafford. The strategist had never been fully on board with the campaign to win over the party pooh-bahs, and now he was proving to be disastrously ill suited for the task.

Washington bigwigs and political benefactors expect a certain degree of poise and polish from the operators who come to schmooze them—and Stafford, with his ill-fitting blazers and off-putting personal quirks, didn't fit the ticket. His background as a Beltway outsider was what had first endeared him to Rand, but now his lack of experience with the modes and manners of the 1 percent was proving disruptive.

In one emblematic mishap, Stafford bailed at the last minute from accompanying Rand to an elite fund-raiser held at the Manhattan penthouse of New York Jets owner Woody Johnson. While the other presidential aspirants in attendance, like Marco Rubio and Scott Walker, spent the night promenading around the premises with their well-connected strategists at their sides to make introductions, Rand was left to wander aimlessly through the crowd and strike up conversations on his own with major party donors. The senator managed to salvage the evening and hit it off with several of the attendees—but when Olson heard what had happened, he grumbled that it was "bush league."

It often got worse, though, when Stafford *did* show up for donor pitches. The strategist spent so much time grandiloquently prattling on that Rand had to fight to get a word in edgewise. Once, after suffering through such a performance by Stafford, a megadonor remarked, "That guy needs to shut up."

Olson, Benton, and others tried to broach the subject with Stafford, but when they did he seemed to grow paranoid that they were plotting against him. He jealously guarded his status as Rand's political Svengali, and he was determined to prove he was up to the task of running a presidential campaign. He took to sending unprompted emails to the senator in which he touted his abilities and tallied his recent successes, sometimes cc'ing other advisers so they would appreciate his talents. He often compared himself to legendary campaign operatives like James Carville and David Axelrod, whose humble career beginnings, he claimed, were just like his. He began boasting that he was "the Karl Rove of Rand World."

But the lofty comparisons were slow to catch on in some quarters of Washington. One evening, at a reception following an American Crossroads board meeting, Stafford cornered the actual Karl Rove and proceeded to talk his ear off about campaign strategy and the 2016 electoral landscape. He held forth at great length, barely bothering to mask his self-regard and missing several social cues from his eager-to-escape captive.

When Rove did finally manage to extricate himself from Stafford's conversational maw, the baffled consultant waved down Olson.

"Who *was* that?" Rove asked, apparently having forgotten the strategist.

Olson would later joke to colleagues that it took everything within his power not to respond, "You don't know? He's the next Karl Rove!"

At the same time that Rand was crisscrossing the country in a frenzied game of millionaire matchmaker, he was also working to court another key component of every Republican primary coalition: God. That mission led him, one afternoon in February 2014, to a downtown Dallas hotel suite, where he met with Pastor Brian Jacobs, a plugged-in player in national conservative Christian politics. Rand's goal was to recruit Jacobs to join his fledgling team of evangelical outreach advisers—but before he could even begin his pitch, the pastor issued an ultimatum.

"Listen, Senator Paul, I don't want to waste your time," he said, "but I just want to say now: if you have a *Karl Rove* on your team, then there's no reason to continue this conversation."

The pastor had served on the 2004 Bush campaign, and he had come away convinced that Rove was a cynical, win-at-all-costs mercenary who cared about people of faith only when they could help him win elections. Jacobs wanted to make absolutely sure he wasn't dealing now with the kind of politician who surrounded himself with a hive of corrupt, godless mini-Roves.

Rand smiled at the pastor's demand. "I assure you, there's not gonna be any Karl Roves around me," he said.

With that settled, the senator went on to solicit help in getting to know some of the key figures in the evangelical movement.

Have you met with Dr. Moore yet? Jacobs asked, trying to get a sense of how much progress Rand had made.

His question was met with blank-faced silence.

Dr. *Russell* Moore, Jacobs clarified. From the Southern Baptist Convention?

Nothing.

What about Bishop T. D. Jakes? the pastor tried.

Not even a flicker of recognition.

Franklin Graham? Gary Bauer?

Jacobs continued to rattle off the names of some of America's most prominent Christian leaders until finally it dawned on him: the senator sitting before him had no idea who any of these people were. Jacobs was shocked. He had spent a lot of time with politicians, but he had never seen a serious Republican with national ambitions exhibit this level of ignorance. "I had to pick my jaw up off the table," Jacobs later recalled to me.

Rand, realizing his faux pas, became contrite. "I've lived in the Washington bubble for years, and I apologize that I don't know who these people are," he said. "But that's why I need your help. Number one, I want to understand who these people are. And number two, I want to understand what they do."

Jacobs sized up the senator, and decided his humility was authentic. "Wow," the pastor said. "We've got a long way to go."

He didn't know the half of it.

Inside the tight-knit coterie of evangelical ambassadors that Stafford had already assembled on Rand's behalf, a quiet but urgent effort was under way to give the libertarian contender a crash course in conservative Christianity. The man leading this endeavor was Doug Wead, a Christian historian and longtime GOP strategist who had been a key player in building the Bush family's winning alliance with the religious Right in the eighties and nineties. A former multilevel marketing magnate with an easy smile and grandfatherly charm, Wead had a keen talent for tailoring a pitch to a target audience. So, shortly after he was recruited to join Rand's team, he wrote an eighty-page memo that outlined in blunt, clinical detail exactly what the senator would need to do to win over evangelical voters in 2016. The memo was circulated only among Rand's most trusted advisers, with strict instructions to keep it far away from the press. (It is being described here for the first time publicly.) But it quickly became the central playbook in Rand's campaign to woo conservative Christians.

The first step in Wead's plan required Rand to learn a new religious vocabulary. "Everyone has their own language," Wead later told me in an unexpectedly candid interview. "Catholics speak a language.

Mormons speak a language... and so do evangelicals. So, part of this was to learn the language." Rand's own religious experience was limited to moderate, mainline Protestant denominations—baptized Episcopalian, practicing Presbyterian—and the distinct dialect of right-wing born-agains was as foreign to him as Swahili. To fix this, Wead assembled a list of creedal buzzwords that would signal to evangelical voters that Rand was one of them—a sort of Rosetta Stone for Evangelicalese. Soon, with some tutoring, Rand was conversational.

As evidence of Rand's progress, Wead would later point me to a 2014 interview the senator had given in which he recounted his teenage conversion to Christianity. "When [Rand] said, 'I accepted Christ as my savior,' an evangelical was hearing that he was born again," Wead explained. "But that's not what he's actually saying... In fact, he didn't even say Jesus is divine. He didn't say any of that! But that's what is *heard*."

To Wead, the question of whether Rand had misrepresented his beliefs in the interview seemed beside the point. The senator's answer, he told me, was "terrific, very powerful."

The truth was that within Rand's circle of Christian-courting advisers, nobody was quite sure *what* he believed when it came to matters of faith. To some of them, he seemed spiritually detached from religion altogether. It wasn't that he was biblically illiterate; it was that he seemed to treat doctrinal teachings as a source of intellectual stimulation—on par with Dostoyevsky or Ludwig von Mises—rather than as the key to salvation. When I put the question of Rand's religiosity to Wead, he paused for a long time and then launched into a lengthy meditation on the many presidents he had either studied as a historian or gotten to know personally over the course of his life. "What I've found is that very few of them get all the way to the White House with their provincial faith intact," he told me, adding that based on his conversations with George H. W. Bush, the former president's faith was a "Pan-Christian-Buddhist-Muslim sort of thing—and yet he was smart enough not to articulate that publicly."

And what about Rand? Was he, in fact, a believing Christian?

"My point is, I don't know," Wead finally said. "I don't think we can know. I don't know if *he* knows."

Still, Wead had worked in politics long enough to know that a lack of Christian devotion didn't necessarily doom a candidate to a lack of Christian votes: it was all about the messaging. And so, as they marched through 2014, Rand and his team continued to follow the strategy laid out in Wead's memo. They compiled an expansive directory of evangelical power brokers and then methodically worked their way down the list with Jacobs's help, meeting with more than two dozen Christian leaders across the country by the end of the year. The senator also granted a number of sit-down interviews to evangelical media outlets, and attended numerous pastor luncheons in Iowa.

Rand's mission to the religious Right also extracted a personal sacrifice when he and his family had to leave the Presbyterian church in Bowling Green that he and Kelley had been attending since they got married. Kelley had been a deacon at the church for eighteen years, and their kids had grown up going there on Sundays. But the congregation was part of the national Presbyterian Church (USA), a denomination that had recently begun ordaining gay clergy and embracing same-sex marriage—two stances diametrically opposed to the orthodoxy of the Christian Right. Rand's advisers warned that his church could become a major liability in the 2016 primaries, and so one Sunday the family said goodbye to their longtime pastor and quietly transferred to a Methodist church in town. When I later asked an adviser for the senator why the Pauls had changed churches, he said simply, "Their old church had gotten too liberal and they felt more comfortable somewhere else."

As he traveled the country speaking to religious conservatives, Rand sought to reframe his libertarian platform as an extension of the Christian gospel. He pitched loosening drug regulations, softening criminal sentences, and curbing aggressive police tactics in minority communities, arguing that such positions were rooted in Christlike forgiveness and compassion. He routinely reminded his audiences that " 'libertarian' doesn't mean 'libertine,' " and insisted that radically reducing the government's reach would better enable Christian morality to govern the country. And he made the case that his anti-interventionist foreign policy came closer to passing the "What Would Jesus Do?" test than the hawkish neoconservatism that permeated his party. "I do think it is unacceptable not to hate war," he said, adding, "I don't believe Jesus would've killed anyone, or condoned killing."

The success of these offbeat arguments sometimes galled his fellow 2016-bound Republicans. One morning, at a large conservative political conference in DC, Marco Rubio sat backstage and watched as Rand drew fervent applause from the crowd with calls to stop sending American tax dollars overseas to countries that systematically persecute Christians.

Rubio was in awe at the audacity of the argument. He leaned over to Stafford, who was also in the greenroom, and said, "You guys just made foreign aid anti-Christian, didn't you?"

The strategist smirked. "Yeah, I think we did."

Rubio sighed, shaking his head in exasperation. "You guys..."

As unorthodox as some of these appeals were, Rand felt he was beginning to find his footing with the evangelicals. At the Values Voter Summit on September 26, 2014, he strode onstage in front of thousands of conservative Christians while images of a fetal ultrasound filled giant TV screens and the thrum of a baby's heartbeat echoed through the ballroom. He touted his record as a lifelong opponent of abortion, and concluded his speech with a verse from 2 Corinthians: "Where there is the spirit of the Lord, there is liberty."

His performance won a rave review from Tony Perkins, president of Family Research Council and host of the summit. "He put forward a very strong foot here," Perkins told reporters. "He clearly knew who his crowd was."

Rand also knew who his crowd was a week later, when he turned up at the College of Charleston—wearing blue jeans and a rumpled white oxford shirt—attempting to court yet another distinct constituency he considered vital to his 2016 coalition: liberal college kids.

He had watched in the last two presidential elections as his dad marshaled an amped-up army of libertarian students across the country. And now that he was taking command of that army, Rand planned to expand its numbers by seizing on millennials' widespread generational disillusionment with President Obama. "We need to have people with ties and without ties; with tattoos and without tattoos; with earrings, without earrings," Rand liked to say when describing his vision for the new Republican Party. And so he had gone in search of them—at Howard and Berkeley, at Harvard and Bowie State.

For a libertarian like himself, there was a simple formula to devising a message that would resonate with students. Obama had spent two terms in office sending their friends and classmates into foreign wars, so Rand would preach anti-interventionism; Obama had unleashed a massive surveillance state, so Rand would promise to crack down on the NSA. Any talk of decriminalizing pot was always a winner with the campus tokers, and his general penchant for bashing the leaders of his own party made him seem, to many students, honest and even a bit subversive.

His one rule for college visits was to steer clear of the two culture war issues that most alienated the millennial generation from the GOP: gay rights and abortion. In Charleston, though, he broke this rule—and the ensuing fallout would highlight just how tenuous his unique campaign of coalition building really was.

The question that started it all came during a student Q & A, from a young woman sporting a seersucker baseball cap. "If life starts at conception, should medicine that prevents conception like Plan B be legal?" she asked.

"I am not opposed to birth control," Rand replied reluctantly, shifting his weight from one foot to the other. "That's basically what Plan B is." He cast his eyes down. "Plan B is taking two birth control pills in the morning and two in the evening, and I am not opposed to that."

The video of his response was online within hours, and it immediately set off a backlash from the religious Right. To pro-life conservatives, emergency contraceptives like Plan B—more commonly known as the morning-after pill—were considered tantamount to surgical abortion, and Rand had just endorsed them. All of a sudden, the same conservative Christians who had been exalting him just days before were now ready to burn him at the political stake. Right-wing radio host Bryan Fischer declared that the senator had "jeopardized his pro-life credentials and his 2016 chances." Pro-life bloggers suggested that the quote should "disqualify" Rand from the presidency. Perkins even took to Twitter to needle the senator, writing, "W/ due respect to @SenRandPaul, Plan B isn't 'basically' birth control. Its function is to create conditions hostile to human life in utero."

When Rand saw Perkins's tweet, he was infuriated. It was bad enough having a mob of self-righteous flat-earthers who hadn't cracked a science textbook since twelfth grade question *his* medical expertise. But for a high-profile Christian power broker to deliberately fan the flames just a week after Rand had done him the courtesy of speaking at his conference — well, he wasn't going to stand for it.

He instructed his staff to fire back, and soon Stafford was on the record accusing the senator's conservative critics of relying on "outdated science" and doing "harm to the pro-life cause." Though Rand himself didn't voice the words, the quotes were shaded with his signature self-certainty. "Contraception does not cause an abortion," Stafford told the Daily Beast. "There is ample, current science to back this up...Senator Paul will take a backseat to no one in his defense of human life, but also, as a medical doctor, won't allow bad information to force people to discuss something that should not even be an issue."

Some of Rand's evangelical outreach advisers had encouraged him not to inflame the situation, to just let the whole thing go. But Rand refused to let Perkins get the last word. For more than a year, he had been bending over backward to get in the good graces of the religious Right, and now after one perceived transgression they were ready to condemn him to hell. This was no way to conduct business, he thought — and it wasn't very *Christian* either.

Rand's feud with the pro-lifers only increased his drive to widen the Republican tent — to build a party big enough that its aspiring leaders weren't held hostage by the dogmas and demands of just one religious sect. So, a few days after his clash with Perkins, the senator continued on his coalition-building quest by parachuting into a place that had recently become ground zero for racial tensions in America: Ferguson, Missouri.

By the time Rand arrived in Ferguson on October 10, 2014, the city had already been gripped with demonstrations and riots for two months, ever since a white police officer had shot and killed an unarmed black teenager named Michael Brown. Witnesses on the scene said Brown was trying to raise his arms in surrender when the bullets began flying, and his death soon became a national flash point in the long-simmering tensions between police and people of color. The day Rand got to Ferguson, organizers were launching a "weekend of resistance." Hundreds of protesters marched through the streets chanting "Hands up, don't shoot!" and lined up outside the police headquarters, standing toe-to-toe with stone-faced officers while an official with a megaphone warned, "If you touch a police officer, you will be charged with assault."

Rand was the first presidential hopeful from either party to visit the volatile scene, and some of his allies and advisers thought the trip was too risky. But Rand was uniquely positioned to contribute to the combustible debate surrounding Ferguson. Back in August—when white police in riot gear first started clashing with black protesters, firing tear gas and turning an American suburb into something that looked like a war zone—the senator had written a bold op-ed for *Time* titled "We Must Demilitarize the Police." Citing an array of libertarian scholars and writers, he blamed the federal government for helping local police precincts "build what are essentially small armies" elaborately equipped with "military gear that goes far beyond what most of Americans think of as law enforcement." He wrote that the trend was particularly dangerous for people of color: "Anyone who thinks that race does not still…skew the application of criminal justice in this country is just not paying close enough attention."

The op-ed drew some criticism from some law-and-order conservatives who looked at Ferguson and saw little more than looters and thugs. But Rand saw it as a perfect instance where his libertarianism intersected with the interests of a constituency—in this case, African Americans—that hadn't supported the GOP since its most prominent leader was wearing a stovepipe hat. His op-ed was impressive and surprising enough to open doors with some of Ferguson's black preachers and civil rights leaders. But not all of his attempts to connect with minorities had gone so smoothly.

A year earlier, during a visit to the historically black Howard University, Rand had slipped into his hard-to-shake habit of lecturing those who disagreed with him. At one point, he asked the students in the lecture hall if they were aware that the NAACP had been founded by Republicans, and the all-black audience burst into laughter at the condescension of the question.

"I don't mean to be insulting," Rand tried to clarify. "I don't know what you know. I mean, I'm trying to find out what the connection is."

But after another twenty minutes of explaining various chapters of the civil rights movement to the audience, his sermonizing was given a name: "Randsplaining."

As with every other outreach effort he had undertaken, these attempts at courting the black community were the subject of disagreement and division within Rand's team. Elroy Sailor, an influential black Republican lobbyist in Washington, was responsible for arranging many of the senator's meetings with key black leaders across the country, and he said they were making an authentic, good-faith effort to win black voters. "If he runs in 2016, you might not see a lot of African Americans switching over to becoming Republicans," Sailor told me. "But I think what you're going to see is a lot of Paul Democrats."

Benton, on the other hand, saw a more realistic political rationale for Rand's black outreach efforts: it gave him a veneer of national electability that helped raise money and impress party elites. "All that stuff is really a play for the establishment Republicans," he told me flatly.

But even as his advisers debated the political pros and cons, Rand found himself sincerely learning as he spent more time listening to black leaders. When right-wing rock star Ted Nugent drew national ire for calling President Obama a "subhuman mongrel," some prominent conservatives like Rick Perry initially came to his defense, while others dodged media questions about the racially charged insult. But after months of "listening sessions" with African American civic leaders, students, and government officials, Rand had come to appreciate how hurtful comments like those could be, even when coming from unserious celebrity provocateurs. One night after Nugent made the comment, Rand emailed Stafford saying he wanted to denounce the remark.

Stafford was sympathetic, but he cautioned that, politically, it could cause problems on the right.

As a father, doesn't it offend you? Rand wrote back.

Stafford glanced up from his phone at his adopted daughter, who was black, and then at his wife, who had been fuming about Nugent's comment ever since she heard it. "You're right," he told Rand.

That night the senator tweeted, "Ted Nugent's derogatory description of President Obama is offensive and has no place in politics. He should apologize."

The trouble for Rand—and, more broadly, the Republican Party—was that after a year of competing for new votes and showing up in new communities, there was little evidence of a broad new national coalition emerging in support of the GOP.

In fact, if Rand's grand experiment had shown anything, it was that no matter *who* the party nominated in 2016, it would take a herculean effort to cobble together enough disparate demographic groups and ideological tribes to win a national election. The GOP had let its pool of partisan supporters stagnate for so long that any attempt to lure new voters—whether they were white, liberal college students or black, low-income Southerners—would take a huge investment of time and an enormous amount of effort. In the meantime, the constituencies that had long made up the foundation of the Republican Party—from the religious Right to the wealthy business wing—seemed dead set on clinging to their influence within the party and keeping their candidates in line with strict demands and acid litmus tests.

For Rand, these tensions began to come into focus one week in the summer of 2014, when all his coalition-building compromises and competing promises collided in one hectic, three-day swing through Iowa. He was in the state to stump for Representative Steve King's reelection bid, but his main objective was to get face time in the all-important, first-in-the-nation caucus state. Amid a year of venturing into unexplored political terrain, the Iowa trip should have been a familiar jaunt in friendly territory. King was a right-wing congressman whose supporters included the sort of rank-and-file Tea Partiers that had first gotten Rand into office.

But the trouble began the very first day, when a journalist asked the senator if he still thought the United States should phase out aid to Israel given the recent violence in the region. Rand immediately became defensive. "I haven't really proposed that in the past," he asserted, before accusing the reporter of misrepresenting his position. The truth, of course, was that cutting aid to Israel—and every other foreign country—had been part of his platform for years. But that had been *before* he was begging neocon millionaires for super PAC donations every week. In any case, Rand's answer to the Israel question was widely reported in the news media as a flip-flop.

The next day, Rand was sitting down to dinner at a lakeside tiki bar with King when a couple of young immigration activists confronted the Republican duo—with cameras rolling. Rand politely shook their hands, but when one of the activists began peppering King with questions about his hard-line immigration positions, the senator jumped to his feet and scurried away—leaving his hamburger untouched, and his congressional comrade to fend for himself in what soon became a hostile debate with the activist. When the video of the exchange hit the Internet, Rand was widely mocked for appearing to flee in fear of an opinionated Latina immigrant. (In fact, one of his aides would later tell me, he was fleeing King, because he didn't want to get caught sitting next to the congressman in case he said something xenophobic.)

As Rand completed his tour of Iowa, he was forced to contend with an endless stream of conservative voters who seemed delirious with cases of impeachment fever. In recent months it had become *en vogue* on the Far Right to argue that President Obama had so brazenly abused his powers that he deserved to be tossed out of office. Now, everywhere he went, Rand was fielding questions from conservatives who wanted to know when he planned to get the president impeached for his crimes against the Constitution.

Rand had no interest in associating himself with the crackpot

impeachment movement. It was laced with all the strands of grievance, anger, paranoia, and prejudice that he knew alienated young
voters and minorities from the GOP. At the same time, there was
something he couldn't quite place about the impeachment buzz.
While he knew that a couple of Republican officials had floated the
idea, the vast majority of the party's leaders—and, for that matter,
most of the big right-leaning media outlets—had ignored or rejected
the idea. So where was it coming from? Who was fueling it so effi-
ciently? Why wouldn't it go away?

The answers to those questions—and the source of many of the
Republican Party's most acute electoral problems—lay deep in the
right-wing fever swamps.

Chapter Fourteen

Into the Fever Swamps

Donald Trump was on a roll. He could *feel* it. Hunched like an ape over the podium at the January 2014 Politics and Eggs forum, the billionaire was regaling a room full of New Hampshire Republicans—*Biggest crowd they ever got...HUGE crowd!*—with a killer story about the beginning of his long-running hit reality show, *The Apprentice,* and all the losers who predicted it wouldn't succeed. He told them about the pathetic TV critic who said it would flop because women viewers wouldn't like him. And then he told them about the "biggest agent in Hollywood" who tried to make him pay four million bucks as commission even though the guy had strongly advised *against* the project. And then, finally, Trump arrived at his iconic, crowd-pleasing catchphrase—the one thing that never failed to make his audiences go nuts.

"Let's say the agent's name was Jim..." Trump said, teeing it up.

He paused a beat, and then, with great gusto: "I told him, 'Jim? *You're fired!*'"

And sure enough, the few hundred Granite State politicos gathered that morning at the New Hampshire Institute of Politics *did* laugh at the line—but the response was different somehow. Muted. Distracted... *polite.* Trump, caught off guard, hurriedly moved along to a new subject.

He spent the rest of the hour aiming his rambling remarks at the reporters in the back of the room—peppering his speech with Twitter-tailored bursts of bravado ("I wish I would have run [in 2012] because *I* would have won!") and provocatively bizarre opinions ("Whether you liked Saddam or not, he used to kill terrorists").

But no matter what Trump threw at them, every time he glanced back at the press section he saw the same bored gaggle of blank-faced cameramen and sleepy local reporters. They were chatting with one another...swiping at their iPhones...ignoring him. *Him!* The Donald!

Try as he might, he just couldn't seem to set off the same sort of frenzy he had routinely generated in the news media during the 2012 election, back when he had thundered onto the national stage during the Republican primaries with the unparalleled media instincts of the best-paid reality TV personality of all time—and bombastically declared he was very seriously considering tossing his hat in the ring.

This wasn't anything new for Trump. He had been publicly flirting with a presidential bid on and off for a quarter century, since he first collaborated with a New Hampshire Republican activist named Mike Dunbar to launch a "Draft Trump" campaign in 1987. After a single speech at a Portsmouth restaurant prompted a spasm of national press coverage, the pathological attention seeker was hooked—thus beginning a decades-long career in political noisemaking that would gobble up thousands of journalistic man-hours as he continually pretended to consider running for office before inevitably bailing out.

To make sure the cameras stayed on him in 2011, Trump pulled his most effective political stunt yet by embarking on a months-long crusade to expose the "cover-up" of Barack Obama's true birthplace. The fringe conspiracy theory to which he was adding his bellicose baritone held that Obama and his backers had colluded to conceal his secret Kenyan nationality in order to be constitutionally eligible for the presidency. The rumors were actually rooted in the contentious 2008 Democratic primaries, when rabid Hillary Clinton supporters lit up online message boards and furiously forwarded chain emails with subject lines like "Obama May Be Illegal to Be Elected President!" The idea was promptly discredited when the Obama campaign released a certificate of live birth proving he was born in Hawaii—but ever since 2008, the theory had lived on among a strain of right-wing proponents known as "birthers," who donned virtual tinfoil hats and gathered in online bunkers to compare notes and peel back new layers of the "conspiracy."

Trump aggressively championed the nutty notion everywhere he went, demanding to see the president's *real* birth certificate, and claiming that he had dispatched investigators to Hawaii to unearth the truth. "You won't believe what they're finding!" he declared. Ever the showman, he eventually tried to up the ante by publicly offering to donate $5 million to a charity of Obama's choice if he would release his college transcripts and passport paperwork. The performance proved irresistible to TV news bookers for its outrageous entertainment value—but to many conservatives it had a ring of truth to it. In April 2011, after beating the birther drum for months, Trump had climbed to the top of a GOP primary poll—and, along the way, turned what had once been an Internet conspiracy theory into a political litmus test for millions of conservatives. The same poll that found Trump leading the primary pack also reported that a full 23 percent of Republican voters would not even entertain voting for a candidate who clearly stated that Obama was born in the United States.

Those were the days.

To Trump's deepening dismay, many in the political press now seemed impervious to his hint dropping about future political plans. For the past few weeks, his focus had been on fanning speculation that he might run for governor of New York later in 2014—but after spending an entire morning glad-handing students, activists, politicos, and reporters in Manchester, no one seemed even remotely interested.

"They didn't ask one question about running for governor," Trump lamented to his yes-men in the SUV after the event, as he slathered on hand sanitizer. "They didn't care."

There was a tense moment of silence before the driver offered, "They probably think you're already past that."

Trump liked this theory.

"That's interesting," he said, raising his voice so that everyone in the car was listening. "Did you hear what he said? He said they think I'm past that. I can't tell you how many people have said that to me. They say, 'What are you doing running for *governor?*'" he said. "It's a good point."

The notion that he was simply too big—too *presidential*—for a measly job in the Albany statehouse had temporarily cheered him. But the morale boost only provided a brief respite from Trump's slow-burning sense of panic. It wasn't that he lacked for attention. He still had his reality show (*TREMENDOUS hit show!*), and NBC was still paying him an A-list salary (*BIG money... more than Jennifer Aniston got!*). And he still roamed the world in a protective bubble of adoring mini-Trumps who functioned as automated affirmation dispensers. But even amid all the "Yes, Mr. Trump"s and "You were great, Mr. Trump"s, he could still hear the din of guffaws from the political class and party establishment—and it was driving him crazy.

This was The Donald in winter. He didn't just want attention from the TV-watching masses, or praise from people on his payroll: he wanted respect from serious people. He deserved it. Needed it. Lusted after it as though it were a long-legged Slavic supermodel. And so, as his SUV wound through the snowy streets of Manchester this January morning, he decided to return a phone call from the one news outfit that actually treated him with the seriousness he deserved.

He announced from the passenger seat that he was ready for the call, and soon one of his aides had punched the number for Breitbart News reporter Matt Boyle into Trump's flip phone. (He preferred the ancient model because he liked how the shape placed the speaker closer to his mouth.) He spent a few minutes answering questions about serious policy issues—and, to his relief, his political plans—and a couple hours later, the site would blast out its all-caps "exclusive": "TRUMP: SELECT COMMITTEE NEEDED TO INVESTIGATE BENGHAZI SCANDAL."

Boyle was a rising star of the far-right Web, where Breitbart served, for a fringe of the conservative blogosphere, to set the agenda, introduce new narratives, and shape the common wisdom within a narrow, hyperaggrieved class of conservative activists. During the 2013 immigration debate, Boyle had been the lead reporter pushing both the "Marcophone" myth and the Menendez hooker scandal, and if there was any confusion as to why his site never published corrections on those stories, one needed only to look at its unofficial mission statement, comprising a hashtag and three letters: #WAR.

The site was only the most recent incarnation of an ideological fever swamp that had long festered in American conservatism—from the John Birch Society newsletters of the seventies and eighties, to the AM talk radio shows of the nineties, to the chat rooms and email chain letters around the turn of the millennium and the vibrant, frenzied blogosphere of amateur muckrakers and conspiracy hobbyists in the mid-2000s. The fever swamps were where like-minded kooks, crazies, and radicals mined the news for world events, and then twisted and redisseminated them in service of their dogmas and in opposition to their foes.

These sorts of delusional fringes existed on both sides of the political spectrum, and they tended to thrive when their respective parties were out of power. In the conservative fever swamps of the nineties, a decades-old investigation into Bill and Hillary Clinton's finances turned into a fanatical conviction that the First Couple had pursued a massive cover-up of past corruption, leaving a trail of corpses in their wake. During George W. Bush's presidency, the left-wing fever swamps teemed with crazed speculation about the White House orchestrating terrorist attacks on American soil. And in the Tea Party fever swamps of the Obama era—which comprised a corps of professionalized, well-funded websites—crusading swamp warriors fought to purge the GOP of ideological traitors, while also flooding social media with rumors of Sharia law in suburbia, or a fast-approaching "race war" in America targeting whites, or secret crimes committed by the president that called for his impeachment.

Since 2012, the GOP's presidential aspirants and ambitious reformers had been forced to navigate one fever swamp flare-up after another as they tried to implement their grand visions. There was the right-wing backlash that helped sink Marco Rubio's immigration bill with misinformation; the pressure to pander, causing Bobby Jindal to back off on his "stupid party" critique; the libertarian trolling from Ron Paul's guttersnipes that got in the way of Rand's outreach efforts; and of course Cruz's crusade—powered by the engine of the fringe—to defund Obamacare or shut down Washington trying.

But for Trump, the fever swamps were a place where he could still get the respect and validation he thirsted for in the political realm—all he had to do was put on a show for them. By and large, GOP leaders at the time weren't very worried about Trump's little torch-juggling act. Some of them even thought it was better for him to spend his time entertaining a tiny online fringe composed entirely of pixels and plasma—it made it that much easier to keep him away from the party's main stage and its serious actors.

But as it would turn out, the party elders were vastly underestimating the degree to which the viral fever had already spread from the online swamps and into significant swaths of the Republican base. And though no one in the party or the media realized it in the winter of 2014, Trump was doing more than putting on a frivolous performance. He was assuming command of a riled-up and surprisingly powerful army of avatars that he would soon begin dispatching to harass the establishment losers who had wronged him, derail the coming 2016 primaries—and, more immediately, try to take me down.

On that cold morning in January 2014, I had arranged to interview Trump on the flight back to New York after the Politics and Eggs summit. So when his speech was over, I squeezed into the SUV with Trump and four of his well-dressed yes-men, and we set off for the nearby runway where his $100 million private jet was idling. On our way there, the pilot called to report that a blizzard was shutting down LaGuardia Airport. Schedules were rearranged, flight plans rerouted, and before I had time to think it through, I was strapped in with a gold-plated seat belt in Trump's 757 as we soared toward our new destination: Palm Beach, Florida, home to the billionaire's sprawling beachside compound, Mar-a-Lago.

As we ascended, the large flat-screen TV in my section of the plane, which was connected to the one in the bedroom to which Trump had retired, flipped back and forth between Fox News and MSNBC, as he searched for coverage of his New Hampshire visit. But The Donald was nowhere to be found, and after about an hour the channel stopped changing. He had given up and gone to sleep.

My interview with Trump took place later that day in Mar-a-Lago's "living room," a cavernous, ornate structure located at the center of the 17-acre estate, with big chandeliers and high gold ceilings. After showing off the place for a while, Trump led me to a dimly lit den off the main room with walnut-paneled walls and a large portrait of a young, sweater-clad Trump staring down at us. Trump sat slouched in his chair at the other side of a small circular table. He was sporting an uncharacteristic open collar that gave his thick neck, orange-dyed noggin, and famous mane a certain disproportion to his body that called to mind a celebrity bobblehead.

Our conversation started out fine, but soon Trump began veering off into fevered discourses on forged birth certificates and presidential cover-ups, and no matter how many different questions I asked, he kept finding ways to maneuver back to the subject. After a few minutes of ranting along these lines, he seemed to realize he was losing my attention, so he began speaking in a slower, more deliberate manner in order to connect the dots for me. "We have seen a book of [Obama's] as a young man that said he was from Kenya, okay?" Trump said, pausing to squint at me. "The publisher of the book said at first, 'Well, that's what he told us.' But *then* they said, 'No, that was a typographical error.' But you know what a typographical error is?"

I couldn't quite tell whether the question was rhetorical, so I said nothing, which apparently he took as a cue to explain typographical errors.

"That's when you put an *s* at the end of a word because you—"

I nodded.

"You understand that," Trump said, waving a hand. "So, he has a book where he says he is from Kenya and they say that's a typographical error? I have a whole theory on it and I'm pretty sure it was right..."

As he launched into his probably right theory, I listened to him relitigate and relive the whole 2012 birther episode. I realized he was trying to deliver an encore performance—hoping, perhaps, that if he could just get me and my colleagues in the press interested again, he would be catapulted back into political relevance.

"What do you think of the critics who say all the birther stuff was racially based?" I asked, deciding to humor him. "Was it?"

"No," Trump replied emphatically. "Not at all."

He paused, seeming to consider what vein he should continue in, before landing on his old standby: incendiary.

"Don't forget," he said. "Obama called Bill Clinton a racist, and Clinton has never forgiven him for it. Every time someone disagrees with Obama he calls them a racist, so there have been many people called a racist. But it never stuck in my case at all.

"You know why it never stuck?" he asked. "I am so not a racist, it's incredible."

Eventually, he moved on to other subjects, and before the interview ended, Trump shared with me his philosophy of how to treat fans. He said that Michael Jordan ("a friend of mine") was often dismissive when people approached him asking for autographs. Not Trump. "You know, it's a lot of work to smile for an hour and a half," he told me, recalling the people who had surrounded him in New Hampshire earlier that morning asking for pictures and autographs. "At the same time, I always say to myself, how would it be if I stood there and there was nobody wanting it? That wouldn't be so nice either."

A few weeks later, my story was published at BuzzFeed under the headline "Thirty-Six Hours on the Fake Campaign Trail with Donald Trump." It focused primarily on what I called the "long con" of his supposed political career, and explored why he seemed so driven to keep it going. The story channeled a widely held sentiment in the political-media complex at the time that had been eating at Trump, and he quickly declared a fatwa on my head. The war that he and his online followers waged on me in the weeks and months to come presented a tiny microcosm of the influence Trump could still wield within politics—and it would foreshadow the wild, disruptive, scorched-earth assault he was planning for 2016.

It began simply enough with Trump firing off tweets denouncing me as a "slimebag reporter" and "true garbage with no credibility," and soon his followers were also hurling angry, all-caps insults my way, while posts on obscure right-wing blogs and message boards derided me as a corrupt media "libtard," and cryptic emails from apparent Trump allies landed in my inbox—including one admirably economical missive from Carl Paladino, the Republican nominee in New York's 2010 gubernatorial race, who wrote simply, "Big joke. Fuck you, asshole." To exert financial damage, Trump's office sent me an addendum to the $850 bill BuzzFeed had already paid for my stay at Mar-a-Lago, claiming that they'd neglected to tack on the cost of the flight: $10,000. Meanwhile, a Buffalo-based public relations employee with ties to Trump named Michael Caputo began circulating an email to every Republican press secretary in Congress, accusing me of being a "partisan flibbertigibbet" and warning that I was not to be trusted.

Next, Trump turned to Breitbart, which began publishing stories about me, kicking off the series with a masterpiece of its genre, right down to the pitch-perfect headline: "EXCLUSIVE—TRUMP: 'SCUMBAG' BUZZFEED BLOGGER OGLED WOMEN WHILE HE ATE BISON AT MY RESORT." Written by Boyle, the 2,100-word yarn relied on interviews with Trump and his yes-men to chronicle a vivid alternate-reality version of our trip to Mar-a-Lago, starring myself as a "quiet, reserved, and nervous" geek of a reporter who spent the flight to Florida cowering in the presence of The Donald's gravitas—and then promptly mutated into an untamable lout upon arriving at his estate, crudely hitting on every pair of legs that sashayed across the carefully manicured grounds. In one particularly colorful passage, a hostess at Trump's club identified as "Bianka Pop" recounted the vulgar tactics I had employed in my efforts to seduce her. "He was looking at me like I was yummy... [like he wanted] a cup of me or something," she said, adding that my come-ons were "a little bit nasty" and that she was "not feeling comfortable." One of Trump's yes-men regretfully recalled having to apologize to waitresses for my creepy "ogling" as we dined on bison burgers. And toward the end of the piece, Trump himself took the opportunity to shake his husbandly head at my wandering eye: "There were two beautiful girls walking around Mar-a-Lago. He said to me, 'Boy, I wish my wife looked like that,' while he was gawking at them. Unbelievable. What a scumbag."

For the next two weeks, the site's editors scoured the archives for past hit pieces they had published about my stories at BuzzFeed, and splashed them across the home page. They began calling up advisers to prominent Republicans, and tried to get them to bash me on the record. Most of them, it seemed, declined or demurred, but several days into Breitbart's crusade, the editors struck gold: "EXCLUSIVE—PALIN CALLS FOR BOYCOTT AFTER BUZZFEED HIT PIECE ON TRUMP." There was her quote in black and white: "This nervous geek isn't fit to tie The Donald's wing tips. Don't ever give him attention again."

But the most disquieting moment came when I was up late one night working in my apartment. A notorious right-wing blogger and opposition researcher popped up in my Gchat with a brief, cryptic note reporting that someone had tried to enlist him for a "project" in which I was the target. Somewhat startled, I prodded him for more information, but he wouldn't give much. He had turned down the offer, he said, but he knew there were "others." The goal was to dig into my personal life until they unearthed something scandalous enough to "finish" me. He logged off.

Over the next few days I found myself growing increasingly paranoid—looking around in an agitated, twitchy sort of way and trying to figure out how to know if someone was tailing you. It was fairly embarrassing. I wondered if this was what it was like to be a full-time citizen of the fever swamps.

Trump's earliest political experience came when he was a young entrepreneur working to expand his father's New York City real estate empire from the outer boroughs into the glitzier, more competitive Manhattan market. As he went about the requisite favor trading with city bureaucrats who got to decide how tall his skyscrapers could be, Trump came to understand political loyalties as bargaining chips. "When you need zone changes, you're political . . . You know, I'll support the Democrats, the Republicans, whatever the hell I have to support," he later explained. Now, with Trump stewing over his dwindling political relevance, he spent much of 2014 trying to buy some loyalty of his own. He forked over cash to the Republican National Committee, headlined fund-raisers for state parties, wrote checks to conservative candidates, and offered support to a variety of right-wing outfits.

Inside Breitbart News, employees privately complained that the company's top management was increasingly turning their outlet into a Donald Trump fan website. Staffers told me Trump and his yes-men would often place calls to Breitbart executive chair Steve Bannon to discuss the site's coverage, and that those calls were treated with the utmost seriousness. Indeed, a search of Trump's name in the site's archives yielded thousands of articles hyping his political prospects, attacking his enemies, and breathlessly covering his every politically tinged utterance — including a series of perfectly credulous stories about his years-long birther crusade. Trump's typical coverage tended to center on his serial flirtations with running for office, staffers told me, but his constant presence on the homepage and knack for pandering to the fever swamps had won him a true following within the site's readership.

One Breitbart editor, who considered Trump a fraud when it came to the conservative cause, called his site's water carrying "despicable" and "embarrassing." He and others in the editorial ranks came to believe the billionaire had a financial interest in the company that explained the fawning coverage. Bannon denied the allegation, telling me in a statement, "We have no financial relationship with Donald Trump as an investor, advertiser, or in any other capacity at this time — nor have we ever. The insinuation that we do — or did — is a lie." (As a privately held company, Breitbart doesn't make the sources of its financial backing public.)

Meanwhile, Trump generously contributed to conservative groups that hosted the sort of high-profile political conferences that were populated by TV cameras. Because these organizations generally weren't required to disclose their donors, Trump was able to claim that organizers were constantly clamoring, pleading, *begging* for him to grace the stage at their events — simply because he was such a big-time star.

Back in 2013, many on the right had been dismayed to see Trump with such a plum speaking slot at the Conservative Political Action Conference in Washington. With the exception of a small die-hard fringe, most Republicans were by that point frustrated with The Donald's exhausting self-promotion and birther drumbeating, and the speech he gave was not well received. The next year, when organizers began planning the 2014 conference, some on the board strongly opposed inviting him back, arguing that he was "not a serious movement leader." But then Trump wrote a $50,000 check to the group that put on CPAC—and hosted then-chairman Al Cardenas at Mar-a-Lago—and the billionaire was back in the lineup. Cardenas would later confirm the donation to me, but he denied that the money bought Trump a speaking slot. "He's entertaining," Cardenas said of The Donald, comparing him to Ann Coulter and arguing that CPAC had always featured "personalities that I didn't consider serious, thoughtful leaders."

But Trump expected more than backhanded compliments and half-hearted support from the allies he procured. For all of the investments he had made in the Right, the returns in political clout were unacceptably puny. If The Donald was going to get the attention and respect he deserved, he was going to have to do something big.

Chapter Fifteen

Inner-City Education

After an early workout on the morning of March 12, 2014, Paul Ryan called in to a nationally syndicated talk radio show hosted by one of his many old mentors, Bill Bennett. Ryan had recently given a speech on what he had learned so far during his poverty tour, and he'd agreed to come on Bennett's show and elaborate on his observations. He was still struggling with his transition from the role of modest, observant student during his visits with Woodson to authoritative poverty expert in Washington, and the uneasiness came through on the radio. It wasn't long before Ryan's sensitive tone began to strain under the demands of a skilled partisan interviewer.

"You lost your dad at an early age," Bennett said during the show. "Who taught you how to work?"

Ryan replied by talking about his mother's strong example, and the influence of his tight-knit family and network of friends in Janesville—but that wasn't the answer Bennett was looking for.

"But, I mean, a boy has to see a man working, doesn't he?"

"Absolutely," Ryan responded. "That's the tailspin or spiral that we're looking at in our communities...We have got this tailspin of culture, in our inner cities in particular, of men not working and just generations of men not even thinking about working or learning the value and the culture of work, and so there is a real culture problem here that has to be dealt with."

The assault from the Left began immediately. The liberal website ThinkProgress posted a portion of the transcript under the headline "Paul Ryan Blames Poverty on Lazy 'Inner City' Men." Eager to advance its scoop, the site then began sending its story to Democratic congressional offices, asking for reaction quotes. Soon Representative Barbara Lee, Ryan's Democratic colleague on the House Budget Committee, released a blistering statement calling the congressman's comments "a thinly veiled racial attack," and charging that "when Mr. Ryan says 'inner city,' when he says 'culture,' they are simply code words for what he really means: 'black.'" Nancy Pelosi's office piled on, dubbing Ryan's quote "shameful, disturbing, and wrong."

Ryan was stunned by the force and violence of the reaction. When he consulted the transcript of the interview later that day, he could see how he should have been more precise in his language—but did all these people really believe he was a racist?

Ryan's phone rang, and he answered to find Woodson on the line, chuckling.

"Well," Woodson said, "what you said was true, but I'm not so sure you're the one who should be saying it."

Ryan was defiant at first, so Woodson tried to explain the gaffe in terms that the congressman might understand: "It's the difference between a coach berating a player and a fan berating a player. They can both have the same message for the same reasons, but with one, the player's head is hung down, while the other gets punched out."

At around 5:30 a.m. on a cold April morning a few weeks later, men began filing into Indianapolis's Emmanuel Missionary Baptist Church. They were ex-convicts and reformed drug dealers, recovering addicts and at-risk youth—a proud brotherhood of the city's undesirables. Some of them liked to joke that if he were around today, Jesus would hang out with reprobates like them. On this cold April morning, they were getting Ryan instead.

He had been to this church early on in his poverty tour, but that was before his "inner-city" gaffe turned him into a poster boy for right-wing race-baiting. Now he stood self-consciously in the lobby, just trying not to screw up. Sporting khakis and a new-haircut coif, he clutched a coffee and chatted in a subdued manner with three besuited associates. Despite his discomfort, most of the men rambling in through the front door didn't seem to recognize the wiry white guy loitering in their church. A few parishioners came up and introduced themselves to him, but most passed by, exchanging quizzical glances and indifferent shrugs.

After several minutes, a sturdy, smiling pastor named Darryl Webster arrived and greeted the church's guest of honor.

"I appreciate you coming," Webster said as he clasped the congressman's hand. "You know, when you get up this early in the morning, it's intentional."

"Usually when I get up this early, I get up to kill something," Ryan cracked.

The words hung uncomfortably in the air for a moment, this not being a congregation of bowhunters. Ryan hastened to clarify.

"This is the first time I'm getting up this early without wearing camouflage," he explained.

The joke landed, the group chuckled, and Ryan shuffled toward the chapel, looking weary and uncertain.

Since his ill-fated radio interview, Ryan had endured an onslaught of criticism. Many on the left argued that Ryan's comments were rooted in bigoted stereotypes about black men being lazy, and exposed a sinister streak of racism lurking beneath his Homecoming King of Congress act. Others accused Ryan of cynically using the remark as a "dog whistle," meant only to be heard by his target audience of racist white conservatives. Ryan's office had been flooded with press inquiries as serious Washington reporters asked communications director Conor Sweeney whether the congressman "really hates black people."

In truth, what Ryan's foot-in-mouth moment revealed wasn't bigotry but a debilitating lack of experience in interacting with the urban poor and people of color—a problem that afflicted his party at large. Ryan wasn't racist, nor was he trying to curry favor with racists; he was a tone-deaf white guy who had never developed the vocabulary required to talk about race and urban issues, because as a professional Republican he never had to. While he had always gone through the motions of minority outreach, Ryan still hailed from a hometown where "diversity" meant neighbors swapping genealogical trivia about their Swedish and Norwegian ancestors. (According to the 2010 census, the population of Janesville was 91.7 percent Caucasian.)

Now Ryan was receiving his sensitivity training on the job—and it was a frustrating experience. *"Dog whistle,"* he grumbled to me at the time. "I'd never even heard the phrase before, to be honest with you... When I think of 'inner city,' I think of everyone. I don't just think of one race. It doesn't even occur to me that it could come across as a racial statement, but that's not the case, apparently."

If the outrage over his gaffe had brought Ryan a heightened degree of self-awareness, it had also infected him with a persistent strain of insecurity. At Emmanuel Missionary, he was endlessly preoccupied with his diction, prone to halting self-censorship, and acutely conscious of his own out-of-placeness. Like a singer who suddenly discovered his lack of relative pitch while onstage, Ryan was now worried that every note he belted out was off-key. It was a humbling experience to a guy who had been a few hundred thousand swing state votes short of the vice presidency.

The congressman followed Pastor Webster and Woodson into a spacious, warmly lit chapel, where about a hundred men were sitting in pews, cheerfully chattering as they waited for the proceedings to begin. Woodson introduced Ryan to Ken Johnson, a stout man with an eye-popping cross swinging from his neck, who served as the chaplain for the Indianapolis Colts.

Johnson's eyes narrowed as he came face-to-face with Ryan. "I know you," he said, trying to remember from where. "Are you..."

"I'm Paul."

Nothing.

"I'm in Congress," Ryan tried.

"Oh," the chaplain said tentatively. "Yeah. Okay. I guess that's how I know you."

"Back home, I just tell people I'm the weatherman."

When it came time for the service to begin, Ryan took a seat in the front row next to a small gaggle of aides and allies. They were there to observe a "boot camp" that Pastor Webster hosted for the men of Martindale-Brightwood, a rambling stretch of concrete and crumbling houses on the northeast side of Indianapolis. Like many of the places Ryan had been visiting, the neighborhood had long ago been poisoned by drugs, bloodied by violence, and starved of cash. Webster's ministry focused on helping the community's underachieving dads, husbands, and sons to get off drugs, fix their marriages, write résumés, and (with the ministry's vouching) land jobs with suburban business owners. Every couple of months, Webster invited the men to a series of early-morning spiritual workouts, where they shared testimonials, listened to uplifting sermons, and chanted refrains in unison, like "You've got to know yourself to grow yourself" and "Life is in session. Are you present?" Since 2005, Webster had put nine hundred men through the program, and nearly 70 percent of them had overcome an addiction, according to the church.

Ryan sat practically motionless as the service progressed, one of his long arms draped over the back of the pew, his eyes fixed intently on whoever was speaking, his angular face registering only the faintest reactions to the sermons.

Woodson delivered an impassioned speech about African Americans taking responsibility for their communities. "In black America, we have a 9/11 every six months," he declared. "Which means that three thousand young black men are being killed every six months."

As the audience erupted with "Mm-hmm"s and "Yeaaah"s and "That's right"s, Ryan turned his eyes downward and mouthed, "Wow."

Woodson continued, "And that's not gonna change by changing whoever's president. It's gonna be changed on the ground, by boot camps like this around the country."

Later, in a sermon about redemption, Pastor Webster illustrated his message by encouraging the congregation of former criminals and gangbangers to remember their lives on the street. "How many of y'all have got some nicknames?" the pastor asked. "You got some nicknames you used to live by. What was your nickname, Thomas?"

A man shouted out from one of the pews, "Cat!"

"Aw, no," Webster responded, grinning. "I never knew that. Does that mean you was a cat daddy?"

The men laughed knowingly, and Ryan laughed carefully.

At one point, Ryan was invited to speak. He kept his remarks brief. "Look," he said. "I have a lot of humility right now. I just want to— I'm here to learn. I'm here to listen."

Near the end of the service, Webster invited the audience to stand for a song, and Ryan rose with them. A two-man band on the stage began to play as lyrics scrolled across projector screens hanging on the walls. Most of the men were familiar with the routine; Ryan clearly wasn't. Still, he bent his arms in the position of "receiving" like everyone else, and began gently swaying back and forth, as though he was slow dancing in middle school. He opened his mouth ever so slightly—just wide enough to let the words seep out—and started to sing.

> *Here's my hands, oh Lord.*
> *Here's my hands, oh Lord.*
> *I offer them to you.*
> *As a living sacrifice.*

The song had several verses, and with each stanza the chapel full of amateur baritones swelled with fervor. Ryan remained stone-faced, his eyes dutifully locked on the projector screens. And when the band eventually stopped and the pastor closed the meeting with a prayer— that God would bless Ryan with "understanding as he crisscrosses the country"—the congressman's voice seemed to grow louder than it had been all morning as he said "Amen."

Hours after the service, Ryan was still self-conscious about how he had performed during the devotional. "I'm so goofy with that stuff," he said. "It's just not my thing. I'm Catholic!"

The uproar over Ryan's "inner-city" comments threw into sharp relief the sheer audacity of his mission to transform the GOP into champions of the poor. He felt as though he had charged headfirst without a helmet into a bitterly entrenched battle on unfamiliar terrain, zealously and clumsily fighting for a segment of the American public that Republicans hadn't reached in generations. And he was concerned that all the demagoguery he was now experiencing would prevent his fellow Republicans from joining the cause.

"He knows this kind of crap is the price of admission when you challenge the Left's perceived political monopoly," one Ryan adviser told me amid the hailstorm of criticism. "But the 2012 experience was very helpful in thickening the body armor. I think the bigger worry is what sort of signal it sends to would-be reformers...It can be really dispiriting."

What made it more daunting was Ryan's realization that this probably wouldn't be the last time he said something dumb or insensitive as he tried to build inroads to the urban poor. It was just the nature of the project: if he had any chance of advancing a conservative antipoverty agenda, he would have to fight and fumble his way through a thousand little gaffes, missteps, and screwups. "What I learned is that there's a whole language and history that people are very sensitive to, understandably so," Ryan told me. "We just have to better understand. You know, we'll be a little clumsy, but it's with the right intentions behind it." It would be frequently awkward and occasionally humiliating, but it was also better than staying on the sidelines.

This was Ryan's attitude when he walked into a closed-door meeting with members of the Congressional Black Caucus on April 30, 2014. The caucus had invited him to its meeting shortly after his radio interview, and his initial instinct had been to make peace with his colleagues by profusely apologizing and lathering on his trademark flattery.

But when Woodson heard about the invitation, he urged Ryan not to waste time with mea culpas. This was a rare opportunity to talk to his partisan opponents about poverty, outside the reach of TV cameras and buzzthirsty pundits. He should embrace the inherent ideological friction and speak his mind bluntly—not reach for a "Kumbaya" hugfest.

"He was expecting to get his ass kicked, and I told him, 'Don't go in there with your hat in your hand,'" Woodson later told me. "I coached him on that. I said, 'You know, first of all, you need to recognize that you have visited more poor black communities than any of them have.' I told Paul, 'Never play defense.' I don't have any defensive plays in my playbook. I'm all attack, all the time."

Ryan took his advice, and began girding himself for a knockdown, drag-out fight with a bunch of lawmakers who had spent the past several weeks calling him racist on MSNBC. He wouldn't defend the phrasing of his now-infamous comments, but he decided he wouldn't apologize for them either. Instead, he was prepared to offer a vigorous defense of his conservative vision for fighting poverty—and that included addressing the toxic culture created by society's isolation of the poor.

To Ryan's surprise, though, the tone of the meeting was decidedly subdued. After offering some mild criticism of what he had said on the radio, the lawmakers dropped the subject—and the made-for-cable bluster—and earnestly questioned him about his trips into poor urban neighborhoods. Ryan was able to plead his case for decentralized, homegrown poverty cures, and tell some powerful stories about the people on the ground making a difference in the communities he'd visited.

Still, he and his black Democratic colleagues couldn't find much common ground on policy. The lawmakers remained dismayed at the deep cuts to federal social programs Ryan called for in his budget, and they believed his austere fiscal proposals represented an irreconcilable tension with his stated concern for the poor.

Describing the meeting afterward to reporters, caucus chairwoman Representative Marcia Fudge said that while Ryan claimed his observation about inner-city culture was merely inarticulate, "his policies belie that and basically say that he believes what he said."

The question of what Ryan truly believed was at the heart of the controversy surrounding his outreach and his "inner-city" gaffe, and it was one that had trailed him through his entire career. But now, after years of having his personal motives dissected and held up for public inspection by all of Washington, he was growing tired of it. What Ryan *believed* was that the best way to help the poor was to scale back the massive federal programs and empower a diverse constellation of

Emmanuel Missionary–like programs, each one of them tailored to its specific community. *Was that really so sinister?*

Later that year, when the House committee that Ryan chaired released the Republicans' 2014 budget without any of his antipoverty proposals factored in, his critics pounced. The liberal *New York* magazine writer Jonathan Chait, one of Ryan's most prolific antagonists in the commentariat, wrote that the omission "reveals something very deep" about him: "His policy vision is fundamentally impossible."

Ryan defended himself at the time, telling me, "I've got two roles. I'm chairman of the House Budget Committee, representing my conference...and I'm a House member representing Wisconsin, doing my own thing. I can't speak for everybody and put my stuff in their budget. My work on poverty is a separate thing."

But many found this argument unconvincing—including his own poverty Sherpa. The truth, Woodson believed, was that Ryan was growing tired of the limitations imposed by the budget process—and the politics of Capitol Hill—as he spent more time visiting with the poor outside the Beltway. "He wants to spend less time with budgets, less time arguing in Congress, and he's desperate to spend more time with us," Woodson said. "I think he's tired of it; I think he finds it a little tedious. It's just not how Paul defines who Paul Ryan is anymore."

As 2016 neared, Ryan would continue to answer questions about whether he planned to run with vague, I'm-thinking-about-it language that left the door open. Polls showed him in the top tier of Republican presidential prospects, and many assumed that if he entered the race the nomination would be his for the taking. And yet, for the first time in his life, Ryan was starting to think about getting out of politics altogether.

Chapter Sixteen

Double Bind in the Greenroom

While Paul Ryan was planning his exit from the political carnival once and for all, Carly Fiorina was ardently searching for a way in. Which was why she spent the week of the Conservative Political Action Conference in March 2014 bobbing in and out of a testosterone-soaked greenroom. The small, curtained-off enclave in the Gaylord Hotel in National Harbor, Maryland, was where the Right's big wheels, big deals, and bigheaded alpha males converged to sniff one another and assert dominance before stomping onto the stage and triumphantly beating their chests in front of a roaring crowd of conservative activists. Nowhere was Fiorina more acutely aware of her middling place in the Republican food chain than here.

In other rooms, and in another era, Fiorina would have easily commanded the attention of the cheap suits milling around her. As a trailblazing executive whose meteoric rise had once made her the most powerful businesswoman in U.S. history, she had spent her fair share of time busting up boardroom boys' clubs. Once, she had gone so far as to stuff wadded-up athletic socks down her pants and then flaunt her bulging crotch at a high-stakes sales meeting as she declared, "Our balls are as big as anyone's in this room!" "It was an outrageous thing to do," she would later concede, but "effective communication means speaking in a language people understand." And to the cocky, irreverent, foulmouthed sales bros in that 1999 meeting, the message of her brash stunt had come through loud and clear.

243

But the VIP sausage fest on display backstage at the conservative movement's marquee annual gathering was not so easily won over. Here at CPAC—where thousands of activists had descended on a riverside convention complex in Maryland for four days to cheer on a star-studded lineup of Republican speakers—Fiorina was not a star. She was not in charge, nor was she one of the guys. Her pioneering private sector career might have earned her an eight-figure net worth and a case study carve-out in management textbooks, but in the insular world of conservative bigwigs, she was just a failed Senate candidate whose most valuable proven skill was soliciting political donations from her fellow millionaires. She was well regarded and well liked, sure, but certainly not feared. Brimming with competence, but lacking in clout. And while her perch on the board of the American Conservative Union, which put on this conference each year, guaranteed her a speaking slot this week, no one was expecting much of a performance. Among the few political reporters who had spotted her name in the program, it was widely assumed that she was there to fill some kind of double X chromosome quota.

Fiorina knew all this. She was clear-eyed about her D-list standing in the conservative statusphere, and she had *mostly* made peace with it. But then, at a meeting on the eve of the conference's kickoff, a fellow board member of the ACU blindsided her with a strange suggestion.

"Carly," he said, "I want to talk to you about running for president."

She was taken aback by the suggestion. "It was sort of out of the blue," she would later tell me. Fiorina knew that the Washington wise guys who were already busy handicapping the 2016 primaries would deem the notion laughable—and, frankly, she couldn't entirely blame them. She had never held elective office, and her foray into electoral politics had ended in 2010 with a double-digit defeat to her Democratic Senate opponent in California. But when a prominent member of the ACU board, no small figure in the party, says you'd make a good commander in chief, you don't just shrug him off.

Fiorina had responded tentatively: "Okay, let's talk about that." And then they agreed to table the topic until after the conference was over.

And so she had spent the week cheering on the CPAC parade of superstars while this crazy "What if?" ping-ponged around in her head. Fiorina had no doubt that she was every bit as smart, gutsy, and qualified for the presidency as political peacocks like Ted Cruz and Chris Christie. The notion that presidents had to be picked from such a small pool of politicos was preposterous to her, and she believed it flew in the face of the citizen government the Founding Fathers had set up. She had also been itching to get back in the arena ever since 2012, when Democrats had spent the entire election using wedge issues like abortion and birth control to weave an audaciously dishonest narrative about conservatives waging a "war on women." She wanted to pull out her hair as she watched her party's feeble, bumbling response. On Election Day, Mitt Romney had lost women by a whopping eleven-point margin, and single women had voted against him two to one. The fiasco had convinced her that the men of the GOP were either too sissy to fight back or too stupid to do it right—and it had left her with lots to say on the subject. But would anyone listen?

On the final day of the conference, a plugged-in Republican strategist named Mercedes Viana Schlapp took the stage ahead of Fiorina and delivered an unexpectedly lofty introduction for someone who was a virtual unknown to most in the audience.

"It is my honor to introduce a true leader," Schlapp said. "She has led in the private sector. She leads in the charitable world. She is leading in the debate of ideas. She bravely took on liberal Barbara Boxer in California. That's right—she ran against a liberal woman in the most liberal state in the country." Schlapp paused for some lukewarm applause and then delivered the kicker: "Wouldn't it be *interesting* if she took on another liberal woman in 2016?"

This was the first time anyone had publicly mentioned Fiorina as a potential 2016 presidential candidate, and the idea was not exactly greeted as a stroke of brilliance even by the ebullient crowd of happy partisan warriors. Schlapp's line was met with scattered laughter that morphed into tepid applause as the attendees seemed to realize she was being serious.

But Fiorina wouldn't be a joke for long. When the introduction concluded, she strode across the stage in a royal-purple skirt suit and launched into her feisty speech with an opening line that was sure to grab the crowd's attention.

"You know what makes me *mad*?"

The rhetorical question was followed by a litany of Republican-approved answers: environmental regulations that were hurting California farmers; mayoral crusades against charter schools in New York City; climate change alarmists hyperventilating about the weather; economic ignoramuses calling for hikes to the minimum wage. These were standard clap lines at CPAC, and the audience politely applauded through the first half of her speech.

But then she arrived at the grievance that would ultimately serve as her presidential launching pad.

"And one last example," Fiorina said. "I am a proud, pro-life woman...I am prepared to accept and respect that not all women agree with me. I know how lonely a woman can feel when she faces a terrible decision. What we are *not* prepared to accept is that we are waging a *war on women* simply because we know that an abortion at five months is inhumane to mother and child."

The audience erupted, as Fiorina expertly adjusted the volume of her voice to speak just above the din, building on the room's energy.

"We are not waging a *war on women* simply because we believe there is no reason for birth control to be free!"

There were more cheers, and Fiorina charged forward.

"We respect *all* women and we do not insult them by thinking that all they care about is reproductive rights!"

The crowd was growing noisier now, the enthusiasm was frenetic. This was a ballroom full of conservatives who had spent much of their lives angrily, indignantly, and desperately fending off the Left's accusations of misogyny. And now here was Fiorina, a prominent, successful, career-driven woman—the kind of glass-ceiling shatterer that liberals and feminists loved to celebrate—telling them they had nothing to be ashamed of. Not only was she absolving them of their supposed war crimes, but she was calling out the *other* side's intolerance and condescension. And while she wasn't saying anything her audience didn't already believe, there was a psychic satisfaction in seeing an impeccably credentialed woman like Fiorina say it.

"All issues are women's issues!" Fiorina proclaimed as the crowd roared. "We are half of this great nation!"

The speech generated few headlines in the mainstream press — many reporters didn't even bother to watch it — and the ground-level buzz around Fiorina would soon be drowned out by the populist ramblings of CPAC's grand finale speaker, Sarah Palin.

But that brief jolt of enthusiasm was all Fiorina needed to begin seriously entertaining a long shot presidential bid.

"What I remember most was young men — and young women, especially — coming up to me and saying, 'I loved that speech! You have to stay out there!'" she would later tell me. "So that really made me pause and think. Because it was obvious that what I had said and the way I had said it was different, and broke through for a lot of people."

For most of her climb up the corporate ladder, Fiorina had tried not to play the lady card. In conference rooms and on corporate retreats, she affected with her male colleagues the manner of a good-natured towel snapper rather than an HR tattletale. She encountered the same routine slights and petty prejudices endured by every woman in the workplace — and they often drove her nuts. But she adhered strictly to a Lent-like abstention from victimhood, grinning gamely through cracks about her wardrobe and menstrual cycle, and refusing to react emotionally when competitors and coworkers called her a "bitch."

Once, early in her career, a group of male coworkers — apparently threatened by her success — conspired to move an important meeting with one of her clients in DC to a strip club called the Board Room.

"The thing is," a colleague said while informing her of the change, "they have a favorite restaurant here in DC, and they've requested that we meet there. You know, I always do what the customer wants, and so I don't think you'll be able to join us."

Fiorina spent a couple of hours agonizing over the power play before finally deciding, *Screw it.* She donned a power suit and bow tie and charged into the strip club on time for the meeting. To get to where her coworkers were seated, she had to walk the length of a stage where a live striptease was taking place. "I looked like a complete idiot," she later recalled. But when she arrived at the table, she found her coworkers and clients shocked—but at least a little impressed. Fiorina attended to her client while strippers in see-through baby doll negligees danced on tables all around them, and by the time the meeting was over, she had won over the group.

"My male colleagues never did that to me again," she said years later. (She also noted, with a satisfied grin, that despite the men's best efforts, they couldn't persuade a single stripper to mount their table as long as a lady was present.)

Sure, Fiorina could have caused a stink about this slight from her male coworkers. She could have reported the lot of them to human resources, or, if she was feeling especially ambitious, she could have called up Gloria Allred and held a press conference outside the Capitol announcing a multimillion-dollar sexual harassment suit against her employers. But she believed the only way for a woman to win in corporate America—and to really take pride in the win—was to refrain from working the refs and instead play twice as hard as anyone else on the field.

And that's what she did, starting out as a secretary for a real estate company, and eventually working her way up from sales to vice president at AT&T. In 1995, she managed the spin-off of a new company, Lucent, where she launched an aggressive $90 million rebranding campaign that transformed the humdrum telephone manufacturer into a sensation of the high-tech new economy—and made her into a corporate star. During her tenure, Lucent's revenues increased a whopping 58 percent, and Fiorina was soon offered the job of CEO at Hewlett-Packard. At the press conference announcing her hire at HP, reporters peppered her with questions about what her ascent meant for womankind, and she replied with a curt rejection of the premise.

"There is no glass ceiling," she said.

But now, at the head of one of the biggest tech companies in America, Fiorina felt empowered to start reaching down and pulling her fellow corporate sisters a few rungs up the ladder. As she studied the sprawling organizational charts at HP, she found that despite the company's rather vocal claim to enlightenment and diversity, the patterns of advancement for women were not much better than at other companies. "We had a lot of women coming in at the entry levels, and then they sort of thinned out at middle management, and by the time you got to senior levels of business they weren't prepared."

To rectify the problem, she told her direct reports at HP that, going forward, for every manager-level job opening in the company, they would have to put in the time and effort to produce a list of potential hires that was not composed exclusively of their pasty-faced drinking buddies. "We didn't have quotas, we didn't have goals, but we insisted that we consider a diverse set of qualified candidates for every job," she told me.

The process didn't go smoothly at first. "Initially, what would happen is, people would come back and say, 'I can't find a woman,' or, 'I can't find an African American,' and I would say, 'Yes you can. Go back and look.' And inevitably they would."

But even as Fiorina embarked on a mission to empower Silicon Valley women, she was careful to couch the rationale in terms of dollars and cents, not right and wrong. "Enlightened managers and leaders don't think about this as an issue of diversity," she would tell me later. "They think about it as a business imperative. It's a business imperative to take advantage of all the talent that exists. It's a business imperative to hear different points of view and perspectives around the table because when everybody thinks alike, you're going to miss something really important."

Fiorina's five-and-a-half-year tenure at HP was marked by tumult, as the dotcom bubble burst and panicked board members battled her at every turn. Even as she presided over a 50 percent drop in the company's stock prices and massive layoffs amid industry-wide calamity, she engineered a controversial acquisition of Compaq, which would ultimately bring her a measure of vindication when markets deemed the merger a success. At the same time, though, Fiorina's newfound status as a celebrity CEO in high heels drew an onslaught of gendered indignities that chipped away at her grand ideals of a gender-blind corporate world. And by the time her board ousted her in 2005, she was ready to call out the sexism of Silicon Valley and the media.

In a score-settling 2006 memoir, *Tough Choices,* she wrote about a

BusinessWeek editor whose first interview question was, "Is that an Armani suit you're wearing?" She debunked insulting rumors that she traveled full-time with a hairdresser and a makeup artist, and that she had spent thousands of dollars to build a pink marble bathroom in her office. She recounted frequent descriptions of herself in the press as "flashy" and "glamorous" and "diamond studded"—and expressed dismay at speculation that she never had children because she was "too ambitious."

"I was routinely referred to as either a 'bimbo' or a 'bitch'—too soft or too hard, and presumptuous, besides," Fiorina wrote.

She also said she had gone to great lengths to prevent the media from dwelling on her gender.

"Whenever I agreed to an interview, I'd set ground rules: I won't talk about the glass ceiling, I won't talk about myself, I'll only talk about the company," she wrote. "Over the years that followed I turned down numerous requests from *Glamour, People, Vogue,* Diane Sawyer, Oprah Winfrey, and more. These were great ventures and personalities, but they weren't interested in the company; they were interested in me."

That may have been a sound strategy for a corporate chiefstress, but the world of conservative politics awaited her—and there, Fiorina would learn, getting people interested was the whole ball game.

In 2008, Fiorina, who had been busying herself with philanthropy since leaving HP, signed on to the McCain campaign as a fund-raiser and surrogate. Soon she became a go-to talking head whenever it was necessary to defend Sarah Palin in the media.

It was clear to Fiorina from the very beginning that the Wasilla-bred veep candidate was blazing a new path for conservative women when Palin praised Hillary Clinton at her very first rally for having "left eighteen million cracks in the highest, hardest glass ceiling in America."

"It turns out that the women of America aren't finished yet," Palin had declared to an electrified conservative audience that day in Dayton, Ohio. "And we can shatter that glass ceiling once and for all!"

This was not the sort of language conservatives were used to applauding, but Palin made it work. And as the election progressed, the McCain campaign took the strategy further, deflecting attacks on Palin's lack of experience and unsteady grasp of policy issues with full-throated accusations of sexism.

Within weeks of Palin's pick, the McCain campaign was up with a TV ad in swing states depicting a desperate Obama, his celebrity waning, who had "lashed out" at the running mate — "dismissed her as 'good-looking'...said she was doing 'what she was told'...How disrespectful."

When *Us Weekly* splashed "Babies, Lies, and Scandal" across its front page, alluding to rumors that Palin had faked her pregnancy with her four-month-old son, Trig, in order to cover up her own daughter's out-of-wedlock pregnancy, Cindy McCain called the magazine's antics "insulting" and "outlandish," and declared, "The media has decided to treat her differently...I believe, because she's a woman." And when a watchdog group filed a campaign finance complaint over Palin's infamously pricey wardrobe, she deftly compared herself to Hillary Clinton: "Do you remember the conversations that took place about her? Say, superficial things that they don't talk about with men, her wardrobe and her hairstyles, all of that? That's a bit of that double standard."

In a movement that had long rejected liberals who couched every point and counterpoint in the culture wars with that much-loathed argument ender *"As a woman...,"* Palin had decided to seize the rhetorical weapons of political correctness, and she was brandishing them to great effect. Conservatives delighted in how Palin gleefully beat the Left at its own game, and she quickly became the biggest star on the right — far outshining the party's white male septuagenarian nominee.

Fiorina was not especially close with Palin, nor was she involved in crafting the campaign's strategy, but she got to see its success up close, and occasionally got in on the action herself. On the campaign's behalf, she appeared on MSNBC to tell Andrea Mitchell that Tina Fey's caricature of Palin on *Saturday Night Live* was "sexist" and "disrespectful in the extreme." And Fiorina, too, took to comparing the sexism the media aimed at Palin with that suffered by Hillary Clinton. "Both of these women are courageous, out there on a firing line," she said. "And they are spoken about in a way that we would never speak about a man." Fiorina complained that the media treated Palin like a "nice little girl, a good show horse, but not qualified."

But even as Palin delighted the Republican masses with her charismatic assaults on liberal hypocrisy and sexism, a low-pitched, little-noticed grumble persisted throughout the 2008 election among the elites in the conservative commentariat, who worried that the fresh new face of the party was buying into the Left's framing of American gender politics to score a few cheap points. Writing for the esteemed conservative *City Journal,* Heather Mac Donald mocked Palin's veep pick as "a diversity ploy" full of "hackneyed feminist bromides." "I thought that conservatives scoffed at the idea that American society systematically blocks accomplished women from advancement," she wrote. "It's a sad day when Republicans decide to match the Democratic predilection for chromosomal consciousness, since there will be no turning back."

These complaints would only grow louder once the election ended and Palin expanded her trademark politics of identity and aggrievement. When a 2009 *Newsweek* cover featured Palin, hip popped and clad in running shorts, she blasted her portrayal as "sexist," "unfortunate," and "oh-so-expected by now." During the 2010 midterms, she traveled the country anointing a cast of conservative candidates she referred to as "mama grizzlies"—Tea Party moms awoken to the ails of Obama's America—as the ones who could "take this country back."

"You don't want to mess with moms who are rising up," she warned. "If you thought pit bulls were tough, you don't want to mess with mama grizzlies."

Remarkably, Palin even flirted with embracing the *f* word: feminism, which had long functioned as a sociopolitical profanity in conservative circles. In a May 2010 speech in front of the pro-life political group the Susan B. Anthony List, Palin declared that she and her fellow mama grizzlies would champion "an emerging, conservative, feminist identity."

This was not taken to kindly in the overwhelmingly male corridors of the conservative elite. The columnist George Will fretted that Palin's rise—and the model she was presenting to a new breed of Republican women—had become a "problem" for conservatism. Charles Krauthammer chimed in that Palin was dangerous to the movement because "when populism becomes purely anti-intellectual, it can become unhealthy and destructive." And the *Weekly Standard*'s Matt Labash lashed out at Palin in a blog post for the Daily Caller, dubbing her an "impish little media-bias monitor," and demanding to know, "When did conservatives turn into such a whiny lot of needy, politically correct meter maids, issuing citations for every perceived slight?" He called on the Palinistas to "sack up" and "quit being what you've always professed to despise, which is a bunch of thin-skinned weenies who take grievous offense at any and all provocations."

But for all the weeping and wailing and gnashing of teeth from think tank scolds and crotchety bloggers, the rank and file of the conservative movement ate up Palin's shtick—and her success helped spawn a new generation of Republican women who drew unabashedly on the power of their gender to sell their message and fend off criticism. When the gossip site Gawker published an anonymous account from a man who claimed to have had a one-night stand with a Palin-backed Delaware Senate candidate named Christine O'Donnell, her campaign stoked national outrage with a statement decrying the report as "another example of the sexism and slander that female candidates are forced to deal with." And in an ugly gubernatorial primary in South Carolina that year, candidate Nikki Haley fought off eleventh-hour accusations of adultery from local political foes with Palin's help by recasting the charges as a desperate, flailing attempt by the Palmetto State's good-ol'-boys network to keep a reformer—and a woman—out of office. The line worked, and Haley won the primary handily, winding up on the cover of *Newsweek* as "The Face of the New South" four months before she was even elected.

Fiorina differed in meaningful ways from the rest of the mama grizzly crop, but her 2010 Senate candidacy ensured that she was often lumped in with the other women in Palin's roving pack of grizzlies. And while Fiorina ultimately lost her race, that election cycle saw enough successes that it cemented the new strategy.

On June 30, 2014, Fiorina announced the formation of the Unlocking Potential Project, a political action committee that she would lead to help the Republican Party appeal to female voters ahead of the midterm elections. The GOP was, of course, already lousy with Washington-based outreach initiatives of this sort. The party's dreadful performance among women in 2012 had created an appetite among donors and politicos for new gender-gap closers to throw money at, and a small group of enterprising Republicans had responded with enthusiastically acronymed organizations. The National Republican Congressional Committee had launched something called Project GROW (Growing Republican Opportunities for Women), designed to recruit and groom potential female candidates, and former George W. Bush aide Marlene Colucci was now at the helm of RightNOW Women PAC, which aimed to draw young women into the GOP fold. Fiorina's group distinguished itself with a focus on building and organizing female activist groups in battleground states with competitive Senate races, like Iowa, New Hampshire, and Virginia.

The most immediate result of Unlocking Potential, however, was that it provided Fiorina with a vehicle for staying at the forefront of the urgent intraparty discussion over how to appeal to women. She strongly believed that the only way her party would ever win back women voters was to elevate conservative spokeswomen like herself. Republicans wouldn't get anywhere as long as the national debate over so-called women's issues was taking place, as it was in 2012, between the savvy message mongers on the left who came up with "war on women" and the foot-in-mouth morons on the right like Todd Akin, a Republican Senate candidate in Missouri who became the face of conservative misogyny after musing on television that women couldn't get impregnated by "legitimate rape."

And so Fiorina assembled a small political team and went about crisscrossing the country, pitching her cause and herself to elite Republican donors and power brokers, and stumping for women like Iowa Senate candidate Joni Ernst. Everywhere she went, her simple message stayed the same. All issues were women's issues. Women were worse off under Obama. Republicans had the answers. And most popular of all: liberals, not conservatives, were waging the *real* war on women.

But something funny was happening as she spent the election standing up for her party's female candidates: prominent Republican men kept urging her to run for president. It started in August, when Newt Gingrich, the former Republican House Speaker and emeritus Sunday morning talking head, pulled her aside backstage at the American Legislative Exchange Council meeting in Dallas and told her she would make a great addition to the 2016 field. He wouldn't be the last one. Elite Republican fund-raisers who had already committed their efforts and dough to Jeb Bush if he got in the race nevertheless pushed Fiorina to toss her hat in the ring as well. Ditto Chris Christie's donor crowd. The more the merrier, they said. The party needed her voice, they said.

Even Mitt Romney, in a private conversation just weeks before he began his own public flirtation with a third campaign, told Fiorina she should enter the primaries.

"I'm not running, but no matter what I do, you should run," he told her with typically Romneysian hedging.

Fiorina and her small political team were savvy enough to know why all these otherwise 2016-committed Republicans were clamoring for her to enter the race. On the Democratic side, Hillary Clinton's coronation as the nominee seemed all but certain, and so far the prospective Republican field was composed entirely of men. Everyone felt the inevitable barrage of media questions coming. Why can't Republicans field a serious woman challenger for the presidency? they would demand to know. What does it say about the GOP that the primaries are so lacking in estrogen?

Fiorina's presence in the 2016 primaries would undercut that damaging line of questioning and prevent the nightmare image of a debate stage filled with Republican men, as moderators baited them into musing about the mommy wars or abortion or birth control. What's more, her ties to the GOP's more staid, responsible business wing and her party-wide reputation for being a good soldier unprone to mischief making meant that she was unlikely to make any serious trouble or cause any problems for the top tier candidates. She would, most of the likely candidates believed, spend the primaries parading around Iowa and New Hampshire, putting on her GOP girl-power show and bashing Hillary—all while the real candidates slugged it out for the nomination. Heck, if she really caught on, they might actually even put her on their veep short list when the time came.

The underlying belief that pervaded this thinking, of course, was that Fiorina didn't have even a remote chance of winning. No one in the party believed she would be a real threat; she would be a cheerleader dressed up as a player—acting like a candidate, but truly just there for moral support while the real candidate slugged it out for the nomination.

Fiorina understood that this was how her party saw her, but she didn't let it deter her. After her bruising defeat in the California Senate race, her search for postelection solace had led her to where many also-rans before her had ended up: the comforting belief that campaigns can stand for something greater than winning or losing.

"While the point is to win, of course—the goal is to win—there is no value in the race unless you're making a set of arguments, and a set of points that you actually believe in and that you actually think people need to hear," she would later explain to me. "I mean, I will run to win...But I think it's important that my perspective, my experience, and my voice are in this process."

By the end of 2014, Fiorina was ready to start actively preparing for a presidential run. She expanded her political team, bringing on the talented Sarah Isgur Flores from the Republican National Committee to help with communications, and told them to start laying the groundwork for a campaign. Her hired guns weren't quite willing to acknowledge that Fiorina was effectively positioning herself as a token—they believed that doubts about her electability were simply symptomatic of a lack of "electoral imagination"—but Fiorina was clear-eyed about her role. She was willing to play the partisan cheerleader as long as it meant her message got the attention from the rest of the team that it deserved.

But she would soon learn that the stunt she was trying to pull off was trickier than she had realized.

As 2014 drew to a close, Fiorina began to make noise about a presidential bid, launching a miniature media tour in which she did not shy away from her role as the GOP's woman truth teller; she took on the Left's lame lady pandering and the partisan sexism of the mainstream media. One early example of her talent for Palinian posturing came when she appeared on HBO's *Real Time with Bill Maher,* a political gabfest known for its signature irreverence. Fiorina was the sole woman on a roundtable that otherwise featured Jay Leno, Democratic pundit Paul Begala, and author Salman Rushdie joking with the host about Kim Kardashian's backside and Jeb Bush's mother before devolving into fits of laughter at their own cleverness. Fiorina's breaking point — and opportunity — came when Rushdie began discussing the liberal "fantasy" that Hillary Clinton would tap Massachusetts senator Elizabeth Warren as her 2016 running mate, creating an all-woman Democratic ticket.

"What happens in your fantasy?" Maher quipped to Rushdie, drawing naughty laughter from the men around the table.

"You know, how do I put this?" Rushdie responded. "They're a little old for me."

"Oh no you didn't!" Maher responded, waving an index in a show of mock sassiness.

Fiorina finally interjected, "It's pretty clear I'm the only conservative and the only woman on this panel, based on that last set of comments."

The in-studio audience suddenly went silent as liberal guilt seemed to wash over them, and the dude-studded panel froze for an agonizingly awkward beat of silence. Fiorina felt like pumping her fist.

Take that.

She seized the moment again during an appearance on Bloomberg TV the night before the State of the Union. Mark Halperin, the cohost, was pressing Fiorina to name "two or three Republican women who are qualified to be president." She tried responding by road testing a stump-bound spiel about the need for a return to citizen government, but Halperin wouldn't back down. Finally, Fiorina saw her opportunity, and she pounced.

"Let me just ask you, Mark," she said. "Would you ask the question, how many men are qualified to be president? I don't think so."

Halperin tried a halfhearted comeback, but the trump card had been played and the game was lost. His cohost, John Heilemann, quickly swooped in and changed the subject, while offstage, a female producer cheered on the feisty line to a Fiorina aide. "I'm so glad she called Mark on that," she said. "He never asks questions like that about men."

The next morning, Fiorina was at it again, this time appearing on MSNBC's *Morning Joe.* The night before, President Obama had plugged in an applause line calling for legislation that would ensure equal pay for men and women—one that prompted a standing ovation from the chamber's Democrats and statue-like silence from Republicans—and now senior White House adviser Valerie Jarrett was on TV spinning for the proposal. While the MSNBC panelists took turns lobbing softballs at Jarrett, Fiorina waved at cohost Mika Brzezinski off camera and asked for a chance to get in a question.

When the camera turned to her, Fiorina told Jarrett, "I am struck by the fact that the president hasn't really led in this regard. He's not paying women equally by his own measures in his own White House... Why wouldn't the White House take on the seniority system and say, 'Let's pay women by merit and their results'?" The clip of Fiorina puncturing Jarrett's spin spread rapidly on the right, popping up on conservative sites like Breitbart.

But even as Fiorina's made-for-cable performances surrounded her with that ever elusive "buzz"—and helped her stake a claim on her niche in the media—they also made her political team slightly nervous. True, making liberal bogeymen like Maher squirm with accusations of sexism was a slam dunk in conservative circles, and calling out the stewards of the always villainous mainstream media like Halperin would make her look tough on the right. But Fiorina's strategists also knew she had to be careful. Pull one too many of these stunts, and their candidate could transform in an instant in the eyes of conservatives from the tough, truth-telling Amazon of the Right to the shrill, bossy PC police—a Hillary clone with an *R* next to her name.

Such was the double bind for the ambitious conservative woman in the post-Palin era. In a male-dominated movement, her gender was what made her unique and gave her a chance to break out—precisely with the sort of rhetoric reffing of the Left that Fiorina had been practicing. But if she allowed herself to become defined by her womanhood, she risked marginalization within the party. Conservative elites would dismiss her as a lightweight token, only interested in populist drumbeating and political celebrity—not issues or ideas. What's more, if she kept up the girl-power talk for too long, she risked accidentally crossing the line from Sarah Palin to Sandra Fluke. For example, as much as Republicans thrilled at watching Fiorina make Jarrett squirm, those who took a moment to more closely study the exchange might have found her buying into a premise that was anathema to their idea of fairness. She was free to call Obama a hypocrite, but acknowledging that there are real, systemic biases behind pay inequity was a much riskier proposition. They told her to be careful.

"We can't be the campaign that's always calling balls and strikes," one Fiorina adviser told me.

Fiorina's embrace of Palinian gender politics positioned her as a rising star in the conservative movement as she headed toward 2016. But it also installed a ceiling—entirely visible, not made of glass—that kept her from rising too far, and that no Republican woman before her had figured out how to break through.

Chapter Seventeen

From Teacher's Pet to Troll

Bobby Jindal, striving for a breakthrough of his own, looked out over the sea of seersuckers that had convened in Columbia for the annual Silver Elephant Dinner on June 6, 2014. He knew what he had to do. The field of likely GOP presidential candidates was ballooning. Beltway pundits were floating new prospects every day, and would-be contenders were coming out of the woodwork. (*Carly Fiorina? Really?*) To stay relevant, Jindal needed to seize every chance he got to make a splash—and here at the South Carolina Republican Party's biggest fund-raiser of the year, the pressure was on.

Jindal had forty-five minutes to earn his keep as the event's headliner, and he did not intend to waste it on caveats or carefully worded hedging. This wasn't the venue to try out some new stuff he had been working on in the studio; it was an audience of liquored-up donors looking to have a good time on a Friday night, and they wanted to clap along to the greatest hits.

Jindal was happy to oblige.

He started the set with a catchy single: "I think President Obama should sue Harvard Law School to get his tuition back. I'm not sure what he learned!"

Laughter.

Then, an oldie but a goodie: "You may remember that this is a president who, when he was campaigning in California, accused the country of clinging to our guns and religion." Pause, smirk. "Now, I know that was supposed to be an insult, but as the governor of Louisiana, I'm proud to report to you that we've got plenty of guns *and* religion!"

Hoots, hollers.

Finally, an anthem of outrage that was burning up the charts just this week, as news broke that the Obama administration had given up five Taliban prisoners in exchange for the release of a disillusioned U.S. soldier named Bowe Bergdahl: "Apparently, our president has adopted a catch-and-release policy toward terrorists." Then, inviting the audience to sing along with the chorus: "I've got three simple questions for you.

"Do you think it makes sense for the president of the United States to be negotiating with terrorists?"

No! came the response from the veterans and military moms looking up from their plates.

"Do you think it makes sense for the president of the United States to have the unilateral right to simply break and ignore American law whenever he chooses?"

No! bellowed the portly job creators and women in pearls.

"Do you think it makes sense for the president of the United States to release five Taliban members who may make it their lives' mission to attack not only Americans but our way of life, our values, what we believe in—does it make sense for the president of the United States to let these terrorists go?"

No! yelled the freedom-loving South Carolinians who would soon leave this ballroom and tell their friends and neighbors to keep an eye out for that Jindal fella because he sure seems to know what he's talking about.

By the end of the performance, the audience was on their feet, showering Jindal with validation. This new rhetorical approach of his—less bookish, nerdy, and earnest; more noisy, caustic, and sharply partisan—was a welcome transformation.

Twenty-two years earlier, Bobby Jindal—the stick-skinny Indian American kid sporting an oversize suit and a part in the middle of his hair—stood at the head of an august lecture hall on Oxford's centuries-old campus and started to talk. He had a forceful, high-velocity style of speaking that caused consonants to bang into each other, frequently damaging the words beyond recognition. But it wasn't long before the students in the audience realized what their classmate was up to: Bobby Jindal, all of twenty-two years old and a recently enrolled Rhodes scholar, was telling the world famous political theorist seated in the front row that he was wrong about everything.

At the start of the semester, Jindal had been the first to raise his hand when the professor, Ronald Dworkin, asked for volunteers to give class presentations. It wasn't until Jindal went to the library after class that he discovered Dworkin was one of the most influential legal philosophers of his generation. Jindal spent hours perched at a quiet desk surrounded by towering bookshelves as he pored over Dworkin's work. The more he read, the more he found to disagree with. The theory for which his professor was most famous contended that human rights were guaranteed by a "seamless web" of legal principles and precedent, that every question had one "right answer" that could be determined by examining the constellation of contracts that man has created over the centuries. Jindal thought that Dworkin was giving credit for the moral framework that governed humanity to a bunch of judges, scholars, and lawmakers, rather than acknowledging the fact that morality was absolute, objective, and God-given.

Deciding to say so in front of his entire class was more than a routine flourish of grad student bravado. Jindal had little academic training in political philosophy, having spent his undergraduate years at Brown diagramming prokaryotic cells and studying regulatory models for health insurance subsidies. But his personal study of Catholicism had led him to read legions of theologians and conservative philosophers, and he had built for himself a uniquely well-informed, scholarly orthodoxy. Inasmuch as he experienced ideas that challenged his worldview, it was typically through the eyes of Aquinas and Hayek, or in feisty dorm room debates in which the only goal was to win. It was in this spirit that Jindal set about outlining his arguments against Dworkin's philosophy, using health-care policy as his frame because he was familiar with the material.

When the day of the presentation arrived, Jindal stood before the class and vigorously made his case. His central thesis was that a righteous health-care system could succeed only if it was based on the religious principle of "human dignity," and would fail if it relied solely on the "neutral" liberal values outlined by Dworkin.

Jindal held forth for the better part of an hour, delineating the myriad ways in which Dworkin's thinking was misguided. It wasn't until he concluded his presentation and saw that his classmates were sitting in stunned silence that he realized he may have committed a faux pas. For several excruciating moments, nobody made a sound. "You could hear a pin drop," he later recalled.

Finally, Dworkin dismissed the class, but before Jindal could slip away, the professor pulled him aside. Jindal braced himself for a reprimand. Instead, Dworkin asked if he would join him for lunch. He had been impressed by his student's arguments — and his intellectual guts — and he wanted to talk about recruiting him to assist with research for his next book.

A couple of decades later, in *Leadership and Crisis,* Jindal would cheerfully gloss over what happened next. "It turned out [Dworkin] was writing a book on health care and asked me to help him," he wrote. "It was a great learning experience, and while we never managed to agree on the issue, it was a wonderful opportunity to debate important ideas and policies, policies I'm still dealing with today."

But Jindal's relationship with the professor had a far more profound impact on the way he thought — and his approach to public policy — than he was willing to let on in a political memoir. Dworkin, a rakish, bespectacled superstar of the academy well-known for his wit and verve, took an interest in Jindal after his audacious class presentation, and the young student was soon pulled with unbending gravitational force into his orbit.

The project for which Dworkin enlisted Jindal's help was not so much "a book on health care" as it was an enormously controversial and ambitious attempt by the liberal icon to reframe the charged public debate over abortion and euthanasia. Jindal spent months engaged in heady meetings at the professor's office, providing research and talking through everything from American health policy to the Catholic catechism. Under Dworkin's tutelage, Jindal was cast into a deep and vast sea of ideas that he had previously experienced only as he sliced through them in the high-powered vessel of orthodoxy.

The eventual result of Jindal's research was *Life's Dominion,* published in 1993, in which Dworkin argues that the pro-life and pro-choice camps are not actually ideological enemies, and that a proper examination of their positions reveals that they share the same values, both viewing human life as an "intrinsic" good. To get there, Dworkin reaches a number of conclusions that would rile any group of Christian conservatives, including a rather patronizing premise that, no matter what pro-life advocates might say, they can't possibly believe that a fetus is a human being with the same "right to life" as a born child because many of them still support abortion rights in cases of rape and incest. The book made a splash in the United States, earning rave reviews from the likes of Susan Sontag and Joan Didion and many heated takedowns from Christian intellectuals. The venerable conservative Catholic journal *First Things* skewered *Life's Dominion,* listing among its many complaints that "the position of the Catholic Church...is so misrepresented by Dworkin as to be almost unrecognizable." Had Jindal known his presidential aspirations might one day hinge on his popularity among *Duck Dynasty* viewers, he might have asked the professor to keep his name off the acknowledgments page.

Jindal never did come around to Dworkin's philosophical worldview, but the professor's fingerprints were left all over the master's thesis he wrote before graduating. Titled "A Needs-Based Approach to Health Care," the 187-page document—which would remain tucked away in Oxford's library for decades, largely forgotten and unread, until I came across it—was laced with Dworkin's terminology even as it argued from an opposing philosophical standpoint: while Dworkin believed that health-care resources should be allocated according to human rights derived from man-made law, Jindal argued that only a societal belief in "human dignity"—detached from the law, and probably born of the Creator—could drive a just health-care system.

More revealing than the specifics of the philosophical debate, though, was the sophistication on display in Jindal's discussion of justice and equality—a depth he had achieved, in large part, while studying under Dworkin. Indeed, Jindal had come a long way since reciting Gordon Gekko's "greed is good" speech as a high school conservative.

> All cohorts benefit from the contributions of past generations and create a wealth of resources and ideas which benefit future generations...However, each individual is not in an immediately reciprocal relationship with society. The argument that each individual must receive benefits from society equal to his contributions contradicts the policy suggested here and the underlying principles...
>
> Though rationing is necessary to control overall expenditures, human dignity invests individuals with inviolable rights which cannot be trumped by such considerations...Regardless of economic contributions, all humans have a right to adequate housing, food, clothing, and health care.

As a devout Catholic, Jindal's arguments for a robust social safety net are not entirely surprising, but this rhetoric would likely sound alarm bells among the right wing he found himself courting ahead of 2016. Even more striking, in the final pages of his thesis Jindal outlined some proposed health-care policies he believed would help guarantee a more just system.

> The government could require every American to purchase long-term and catastrophic health-care insurance to provide for overwhelming needs, such as chronic illness and nursing home expenses. A federal regulatory board would operationalize the efficacy requirement, i.e., indicate when particular treatments

must receive funding. Both premiums and extent of coverage would vary according to an individual's income and needs; the government would subsidize premiums so that every individual could afford the necessary coverage. Young adults and the wealthy would pay more for their coverage than they would receive in benefits; the elderly and the poor would receive more in benefits than they paid in coverage. Obviously, premiums would not fluctuate with age or health and would thus be based on community, instead of experiential, rates; insurance companies would be obligated to issue and renew coverage, regardless of preexisting conditions.

While some of these ideas were kicking around right-leaning think tanks at the time, the basic contours of the policies Jindal was proposing—a personal health insurance mandate, a government regulatory board that decided which treatments should be subsidized, the preexisting conditions clause—would later become anathema to conservatives in the Obamacare era.

Jindal didn't know it at the time, but his months at Oxford set him on a collision course of conscience. Under Dworkin, he had gone from being a smart kid who wielded his intellect like a weapon to a genuinely thoughtful student of ideas—not without convictions, but willing to submit them to interesting challenges from all quarters of the intellectual world. He came to love working alongside ideological adversaries, and he developed a deep appreciation for nuance. But he also decided he was destined for a life in politics. He found his personal ambitions shifting away from practicing medicine and towards policy making, reasoning that he would be able to help millions in government as opposed to treating sick people one by one.

Compared to the many aspiring officeholders who populated Oxford while he was there, Jindal seemed like an unlikely political prospect. Whereas his self-confidence manifested itself in more bookish pursuits, his fellow Rhodes scholar Cory Booker, for example, oozed candidate-like charisma, strutting around campus with his arm around a rotating cast of pretty coeds. (When the unmarried Booker later faced gay rumors as he ran for U.S. Senate in New Jersey, Jindal was skeptical. "If that's true," he would later joke, "then he had *a lot* of beards. He was really overcompensating.")

But Jindal was just as ambitious as anyone, and when the time came decades later for him to overhaul his personality in pursuit of the presidency, he wouldn't hesitate.

The new and improved—and nosier—Bobby Jindal of 2014 was the product of months of behind-the-scenes deliberation among his advisers. Shortly after the *Duck Dynasty* episode, with Jindal riding a wave of populist glory, his team decided it was time to punch up the governor's rhetoric—but how?

To those who worked with him, it was no secret that beneath Jindal's wholesome, well-mannered earnestness was a barbed wit that he was liable to swing at you in moments of frustration or boredom, or even just for his own amusement. "If you start trading insults with him, it's not gonna go well for you," one close adviser said. Everyone on Jindal's team had a story about falling victim to one of his acerbic put-downs. Once, when he was visiting the Old Town Alexandria offices of Curt Anderson's consulting firm, OnMessage, he noticed that the shelves of industry awards on display included one for the radio ads the firm had produced during his failed 2003 gubernatorial campaign. "Oh, that's nice," Jindal murmured. "Kind of like the juice boxes and trophies they give to every kid after they lose a soccer game." Later, as Anderson and his colleagues pitched to him on why they should be hired to work on his next campaign, Jindal quipped, "I'd like to congratulate you guys. You had the cojones to come in here and tell me how good you are right after we just lost." Another time, after his staff insisted that he sit for a briefing from his pollsters, he impatiently announced, "My calendar says that the next fifteen minutes are devoted to y'all presenting some junk science that is as useful to me as voodoo."

Jindal's aides mostly enjoyed his swaggering sarcasm, but they also recognized that it might not be received well outside the quarters of the foulmouthed, overcaffeinated political class. Anderson, in particular, worried that Jindal would come off as a condescending smart-ass if he revealed that side of himself to the public, and whenever it flared up during debate prep sessions or mock press interviews, the operative actively worked to tamp it down. "I always thought it was a little bit dangerous," Anderson said.

But Jindal was no longer merely contending for votes in the Bayou State. He was vying for attention from a national conservative media complex that often appeared as though it valued political trolling above all other forms of persuasion. Proving your argument right was nice, and defeating your ideological enemies was great. But successfully whipping up the Left into an indignant, frothy-mouthed frenzy by saying something strategically provocative—that was the gold standard. And for a Republican who wanted to be a champion of the conservative movement, it was a craft that had to be mastered.

Over the next few months, Jindal punctuated his speeches with increasingly razor-edged partisan barbs. At the Saint Patrick's Day Wild Irish Breakfast in Nashua, New Hampshire, he earned roaring applause and laughter with a line that would turn into a mainstay of his rhetoric. "Are we witnessing the most extremely liberal, ideological administration in our country's modern history? Or are we witnessing the most incompetent administration in our country's history? Well, to quote Secretary Clinton, what difference does it make?"

His writing became more fiery as well—not to mention more abundant. To overcome his distance from the DC press corps, Jindal began cranking out op-eds at a stunning pace, firing off more than twenty different articles in the first half of 2014, and sending his staff scrambling to find publications that would take them. No newspaper was too small, and no issue too obscure, to disqualify itself from Jindal weighing in: what mattered was that he was everywhere. There he was in the *Ouachita Citizen,* demanding to know what the liberal advocacy group MoveOn.org had "against individuals with disabilities." Here he was in the *New York Post,* comparing New York City's mayor to a "petulant tyrant holding low-income students hostage." There he was on some website called NetRightDaily, accusing the Obama administration of sending the IRS on a political witch hunt, or "jeopardizing the freedoms of billions of citizens the world over," or any number of other transgressions. As with any weekly columnist— because that's effectively what he had become—Jindal's body of work varied in quality and tone. But the pieces often read as though they were written by the governor's hyperaggressive alter ego, a right-wing Mr. Hyde.

He continued to roll out new policy proposals, but his efforts seemed pro forma, and his ideas were greeted unenthusiastically by the conservative wonk crowd. In the spring, Jindal's policy group, America Next, introduced a proposed health-care plan that would repeal Obamacare, dramatically shrink costs, and reduce the number of Americans who were insured. The plan was missing many of the ideas he had written about at Oxford—it would eliminate the insurance mandate, provide no tax relief for catastrophic care, and lift regulations aimed at protecting people with preexisting conditions—and even many conservatives found it to be too austere. In April, when Jindal traveled to Washington and met with a small group of right-leaning policy writers and scholars to pitch the plan, he received strong pushback from conservatives who thought the kind of cuts he was calling for would be devastatingly unpopular in a post-Obamacare world. Writing about the plan after the meeting, conservative *New York Times* columnist Ross Douthat summed up, in his perpetually polite manner, the real logic of Jindal's plan: "Politically, I don't think there's any question that Jindal's argument...would play well with at least *part* of the GOP electorate in a primary campaign."

The overhaul to Jindal's political persona was jarringly obvious to many in the press, but his team dutifully spun his new act as perfectly in sync with the old, wonky, thoughtful, "stupid party"–bashing governor. "He's not a dog who'll take a kicking," an adviser told *U.S. News* when a reporter asked about the change in tone. "We are not hiding it anymore."

In late April 2014, Jindal published an op-ed on CNN's website titled "The 'Stupid Party,' Revisited" in which he sought to dispense with any lingering perception of himself as a smarty-pants scold trying to make his party more thoughtful and intelligent. "While it is true that we as Republicans need to do a better job articulating our principles and being the party of bold new ideas, the Democrats have a far worse problem," he wrote. "Democrats need to stop being the party that thinks Americans themselves are stupid." Never mind that less than two years earlier, one of his central prescriptions for his own party was to "stop insulting the intelligence of voters." The new Jindal was a happy partisan warrior, doling out affirmation for Republicans and withering criticism for Democrats every chance he got.

This pose wasn't entirely new for Jindal. He was a politician, after all, and black-and-white partisanship was always part of the gig. But for years, Jindal had been speaking to conservatives in two different languages, simulcasting brains and policy sophistication to the GOP elites, and a brash, rowdy zest for culture war to the right-wing base. The result was that his message had always been muddled—a sort of Spanglish that both groups could make out, but neither found particularly inspiring.

Now it was quite clear that Jindal had chosen the guttural growl of the conservative movement as his first language. His most ungenerous critics said he was a sellout, that he had dumbed himself down and become the embodiment of everything he once wanted to purge from his own party. But Jindal didn't care. He had been blessed with the gift of tongues, and his fluency was winning converts—converts who might stick around for a presidential run. Who could possibly say *that* was dumb?

Four days after Jindal's raucous performance in South Carolina, a small contingent of right-wing elites gathered for an intimate dinner party at the Great Falls, Virginia, home of conservative superactivist Brent Bozell.

The evening's guest list comprised leaders of the country's most influential Tea Party organizations and right-wing pressure groups—people whose shared mission was to burn down the Republican establishment and install a new regime of brash, populist hard-liners in its place. They included Heritage Action's Mike Needham, who had masterminded the 2013 government shutdown; Family Research Council's Tony Perkins, who could sic a mob of culture warriors on any Republican who signaled disloyalty to the religious Right; Tea Party Patriots founder Jenny Beth Martin; Andy Roth of the Club for Growth; David Bossie of Citizens United; and prominent conservative fund-raiser Richard Norman. These were four-star generals in the conservative movement, and together they commanded millions of pavement-pounding activists and many tens of millions of dollars.

They were just starting in on the ceviche hors d'oeuvres when Martin glanced at her phone to check the early returns in House Majority Leader Eric Cantor's primary race. Like her dinner companions, she viewed the Virginia congressman as emblematic of the Republicans' corrupt, compromising congressional leadership—but she wasn't holding out hope for him to lose tonight's contest. Cantor was running against an obscure conservative economics professor named David Brat, who had little money and no discernible campaign structure. Last she had heard, his entire operation consisted of two part-time aides who shared a flip phone for campaign business. Just a few days earlier, the *Washington Post* had reported that the Cantor campaign's internal polling showed him cruising to a thirty-four-point victory in the primary.

At the moment, Martin saw, Brat was slightly ahead in the vote totals—but only two precincts had reported so far. She shared the news with the dinner party.

"Cantor should give his concession speech now!" Bozell joked.

Everyone laughed, but it wasn't long before their phones started buzzing with the startling news that Cantor, the second most powerful Republican in the House of Representatives, was actually about to go down to a grassroots insurgent.

The development upended the friendly dinner party, as attendees began hurriedly placing calls to activists and scanning their phones for updates. Somebody turned on CNN, and they watched, awestruck, as the race was officially called for Brat.

"Can you think of a greater political upset in your life?" Bozell marveled. "I can't think of one. This is stunning. This is the conservative movement *on fire.*"

The mood at the party quickly evolved from shock, to ebullient celebration, and finally to defiance. All through the midterm primary season over the past few months, the people in this room had seen their efforts to engineer another 2010-style Tea Party insurrection fall

flat. There was a reason for this: after watching Ted Cruz and his brigade of bomb throwers shut down the government a year earlier, the
GOP's establishment forces had redoubled their efforts to beat back
right-wing challengers in primary races across the country and bolster
electable, reasonable-sounding Republican candidates. With the help
of groups from the chamber of commerce to Karl Rove's American
Crossroads, they had largely succeeded—and lately the national
political press had been permeated with obituaries marking the
demise of the Tea Party.

Now Bozell and his comrades couldn't help but indulge in a little
gloating.

"Is the establishment going to get questions for the next week and
a half asking whether *they're* dead?" Martin joked sarcastically.

"Damn right we won!" Bozell exclaimed. "Damn right the movement is still alive!"

The irony was that none of the groups represented at Bozell's dinner table had actually supported Brat's campaign, all having deemed
it a lost cause. Cantor, determined not to get caught flat-footed by a
primary challenger, had actually sunk himself by spending $2 million
on a negative ad campaign that inadvertently elevated his opponent
and touched off a last-minute conservative backlash.

But even if it was a fluke, no one in Great Falls that night seemed
to care. They had Cantor's head on a pike, and they planned to hoist it
in the air as they paraded through the streets reenergizing the right
wing and reclaiming the momentum in the Republican civil war.

Over wine and vegetable lasagna, the group looked past the midterms and began plotting for the next presidential race. The question
at hand was how they could use tonight's coup to embolden the Tea
Party, and make sure a true conservative triumphed in the 2016 primaries. Ted Cruz's name came up. Rand Paul's did, too. Somebody
mentioned that Jindal was showing promise. They weren't ready to
coalesce around a single populist contender—at least not yet—but
they all fervently agreed that they *could not* let the party nominate
another milquetoast moderate like Mitt Romney.

As the room buzzed, Bozell briefly retreated from the dinner with his public relations consultant to craft a press release that ominously warned of the war on the horizon.

"Eric Cantor's loss tonight is an apocalyptic moment for the GOP establishment," the statement read. "The grass roots is in revolt and marching."

PART IV

PROMISED LAND

Chapter Eighteen

Ball and Chain

Almost as soon as *he* became a credible presidential prospect, Rand Paul began cheekily referring reporters' questions about his 2016 plans to his wife, Kelley. "There's two votes in my family. My wife has both of them," he joked to the Detroit Economic Club in December 2013. Nine months later, he reported to inquisitive attendees at a New Hampshire fund-raiser that "my wife is not completely convinced of it." And in November 2014, he responded to 2016 queries shouted across a campaign rope line in Kentucky by instructing reporters to "ask my wife."

Washington's smart set didn't give any of this much thought. Rand seemed to be playing the shtick in the winking, sitcom-y way of a suburban husband who says he's got to "ask the boss" before he can join his buddies for poker night. It was a well-worn bit in politics—a little smarmy, maybe, but popular across time zones, and particularly effective with swing state soccer moms. The fact remained that no politician in recent memory had been more brazenly transparent about his presidential ambitions than the junior senator from Kentucky. He was staffing up his vast and growing shadow campaign, networking with Iowa power brokers and Manhattan moneymen, and posing for one magazine cover after another. As far as the political class was concerned, Rand Paul was running for president. As for his routine display of deference to his wife, they chalked it up to the faux coyness in which every candidate cloaks himself before eventually entering the race, hand in hand with a prim and smiling spouse.

It wasn't that.

Behind the closed doors of their redbrick colonial in Bowling Green, family confidants told me, Rand had been engaged in a carefully orchestrated and increasingly desperate lobbying effort to get his wife on board with the idea of a presidential campaign—and the whip count of one was proving stubbornly resistant to his efforts. By the fall of 2014, rumors of Kelley's reluctance had begun to spread within Rand's orbit, and many became genuinely worried that she might actually pull the plug at the last minute on the operation they had been building for years.

"Think of it from her perspective," one adviser told me in October 2014. "You're comfortable. You're happy. You've got a kid still in high school, two in college, and your husband could run for reelection in Kentucky and probably win hands down." The adviser then added, with a sigh suggesting defeat, "Would *you* want to put yourself through a presidential campaign?"

Kelley took some pleasure in the mild panic she had set off among the colony of worker bees that was constantly buzzing around her husband. This was *her* family, after all. Her life. And no matter how confident and in control Doug Stafford and the rest of Rand's DC operators pretended to be, this was still *her* decision—and she wanted them to know it.

It's not that she was unsupportive of Rand's political ambitions. She had spent her entire marriage watching her husband bob in and out of his father's inner circle, and she always knew Rand might want to enter the family business one day. Part of her even looked forward to it. She wasn't a political neophyte either: up until 2013, she'd been putting her PR skills to use at a Republican communications firm, where she helped elect a number of conservative candidates, including Ted Cruz.

But her experience with Rand's career in politics had been like adopting a baby gorilla: at first, it was a fun little pet that was exciting to have around, and then suddenly, without warning, it was a hulking, uncontrollable beast that had rampaged through their home, and was now hunched, panting, in the middle of their living room. Rand's celebrity and influence had grown with a ferocity and speed that neither of them had planned on—and they were now well ahead of the timeline they'd agreed to when they first got married.

Kelley Ashby met Randy Paul at a backyard oyster roast in Atlanta while he was completing his 1989 surgery internship at the Georgia Baptist Medical Center. While she would later joke to *Vogue*, "I kind of blew him off a little bit because I thought he was about eighteen," the reality was that Randy had grown up quite a bit by the time the two met. His mischief-making college days behind him, he was now working toward a degree at Duke Medical School, intensely focused on his studies, and not smoking pot anymore (or, at least, so he told his just-say-no girlfriend; some of his friends had their doubts). He seemed serious and ambitious. Shortly after he and Kelley wed, she renamed him Rand—a moniker more befitting a well-credentialed surgeon, she thought.

They settled down in Kentucky to be close to Kelley's family—and also because they had just learned that the local eye doctor in the town of Bowling Green had recently died in a freak boating accident. The couple bought an acre and a half of land in a new gated subdivision called Rivergreen, where some of the region's wealthiest families would eventually move and dwarf the Pauls' comparatively modest home with their sprawling mansions and swimming pools. Rand began his ophthalmology career, and together he and Kelley built a relatively quiet, tidy, and happy family life. Dad and kids played basketball in the driveway and fished in the subdivision's large man-made pond. Kelley enforced a healthy diet for her men—dinner often meant small portions of sauceless protein and salad—and when the Paul men splurged, like on an outing one night to an NBA game, all four would split a twenty-piece box of Chicken McNuggets. The lean-framed family kept the temperature in the house high, and Rand stockpiled eight-dollar mock turtlenecks he found on a discount shelf, something that his kids (and, later, the political press) would frequently tease him about. Later, when Jesse Benton was living in the Pauls' basement during the campaign, he found that he was constantly sweating and always hungry—but he was struck by how normal, and relatively peaceful, their lives seemed. Benton, of course, was there to blow all that up.

At the start of their marriage, Rand and Kelley had made a deal that he would wait to run for office until their kids were grown. But when the 2010 Senate race presented him with an opening, Rand asked for her permission to renege, and Kelley agreed—reluctantly.

"It took her a while to come around," said Gayla Warner, a long-time family friend and neighbor, who lived around the corner from the Pauls. When Warner first heard on the radio that Rand was running for Senate, she called Kelley from the car to congratulate her.

"I just heard the news about Rand!" Warner exclaimed. "We want to do a fund-raiser at our house."

Kelley was embarrassed and quickly demurred. "Oh *gosh*," she groaned. "I don't know..."

Privately, Kelley thought of her husband's foray into politics as an exercise in principled agitation—a proud and familiar Paul family tradition that she was willing to indulge, but would rather not get the neighbors involved in.

But even though she was reluctant, the truth was that Kelley had always thought she would make a rather good politician's wife when the time came. And those who knew the couple agreed. Mary Jane Smith, who managed several of Ron Paul's campaigns, would later credit Kelley with saving the younger Paul from repeating his father's career as a batty protest candidate. "Can a wife influence a man? You bet," Smith said. She added that Ron's wife, Carol, "was always the stay-at-home mom. And she would do baking to make some extra money, she taught dancing lessons in their basement...whereas Rand's wife, she does some creative writing and she does a little bit of PR work, and she's a much more sophisticated woman. So obviously that impacts a man's life. I think she is the perfect candidate's wife. She's just classy, classy, classy."

Once her husband's Senate candidacy began to gain traction, however, Kelley would get her first squinty glimpse at the bright hot lights of a high-profile campaign—and the experience would leave her dreading the prospect of living out her adult life as a political spouse.

Less than twenty-four hours after Rand won the 2010 Senate primary in Kentucky, the cavalcade of news vans and satellite trucks that had taken over the Pauls' neighborhood transformed, suddenly, from floats in a victory parade into tanks in an invading army.

A few weeks earlier, Rand had been asked during a little-noticed interview with the editorial board of the Louisville newspaper whether he would have voted for the 1964 Civil Rights Act if he had been in the Senate at the time. He'd responded that while he liked a lot of what was in the law, he thought free markets — not federal legislation — should have been the mechanism to desegregate lunch counters. "I abhor racism," he told the editors. "I think it's a bad business decision to ever exclude anybody from your restaurant. But at the same time, I do believe in private ownership." His new Democratic opponent, Jack Conway, had then gone on MSNBC later that day and pointed to the comments to claim, preposterously, that Rand wanted to repeal the landmark civil rights legislation.

To set the record straight, Rand decided to book an appearance that night on Rachel Maddow's show. When Kelley found out, she told him she had a bad feeling about the interview and urged him at the last minute to cancel.

"It's a setup," she said.

But Rand was undeterred. The media was clamoring for him to explain himself, and he was certain that if he could just give some context to his remarks and fully articulate his position, then this whole ridiculous controversy would fizzle out.

Instead, the interview turned into a disaster, with Maddow asking the candidate the same question over and over again — Do you support the rights of business owners to discriminate? — while Rand tried to educate the host on the philosophical hierarchy of rights and the history of desegregation in Boston's public transit system. The segment, which stretched on for nearly twenty minutes, ended with Rand scolding Maddow for the way she had "dumbed down" the debate and then demanding, "What is the totality of what I'm saying? Am I a bad person? Do I believe in awful things? No!"

He knew as soon as he unclipped the microphone from his lapel at the end of the interview that it hadn't gone perfectly — but he still thought fair-minded viewers would understand where he was coming from. His campaign team was less optimistic. They urged him to take a break from the interviews and stop dumping kerosene on this particular Dumpster fire. He still had an election to win, after all, and he wasn't getting anywhere with all these TV hits. But Rand couldn't help himself. He insisted that he would be able to make his case more effectively with a less partisan interviewer, that people would understand if they just *listened* to him. He was up early the next morning for another round of interviews.

It was Kelley who finally brought him down to earth. She had been getting faux-worried phone calls from nosy neighbors who wanted to express their support for her in this very difficult time—lots of "How ya holdin' up?" and "Is there anything we can do?" It was humiliating. Kelley had worked in public relations, and as far as she was concerned, it didn't take the world's greatest political mind to know that the only acceptable answer to "Would you have voted for the Civil Rights Act?" was "Of course. Next question." After day three of the media pile-on, she told Rand she'd had enough of seeing his stream of consciousness musings on national television. She all but ordered him to cancel his scheduled appearance on *Meet the Press* that Sunday—and he relented. That weekend, he ditched the campaign trail and recharged with a quiet night at home, donning shorts and socks and munching on popcorn as he played board games with his wife and kids.

But the campaign only got worse for Kelley from there. Two months later, on the afternoon of August 6, 2010, Rand was driving across Kentucky with Stafford and Trygve Olson on his way to a campaign event when Jesse Benton called with news. Apparently, a *GQ* writer named Jason Zengerle, who was working on a profile of the candidate, had tracked down someone who knew Rand from the Baylor swim team, and he was seeking comment on a bizarre story she had told him.

Zengerle wasn't revealing the name of his source, but as Benton repeated what the reporter had told him, Rand realized that *GQ* had found his old friend Kristy Ditzler—and that she had told Zengerle about the fateful night of the Aqua Buddha. Zengerle was the first reporter to discover the candidate's participation in his bizarro secret society at Baylor, and to Rand, the reporter's queries might have sounded like the blast of a starting gun. He would spend the next several years trying to outrun kooky episodes like this from his past.

But when Rand got on the phone with his wife to warn her of the coming story, it quickly became apparent to Stafford and Olson that Kelley had been unaware of this particular chapter of her husband's youth. She was sharply demanding answers from Rand, who first offered weakly that he didn't recall the incident, or that he did but he didn't recall the woman, or that *maybe* something like this had happened, but who could say for sure? Mostly, he stuck with his fuzzy-memory defense, which struck one of his travel companions as amusing because memory loss is a side effect of toking.

Rand would later confide to a couple of his closest advisers that Kelley—who was commonly referred to among his mostly male inner circle as "a good Baptist girl"—had known virtually nothing about his Baylor antics and was scandalized by the story.

"This is fucking terrible," the candidate complained later to a campaign confidant. "My wife didn't know about all that."

Back in the car, though, Kelley's emotional reaction over the phone was whipping Rand into a frenzy. The suddenly indignant candidate concluded that the only acceptable response was to sue *GQ* for libel. With his spouse seething on the phone, Rand demanded to be put in touch with a lawyer *at once*.

Stafford and Olson knew that filing suit against a large national magazine would be distracting at best, and disastrous at worst, for his candidacy—but neither of them wanted to overrule Kelley in the midst of a marital dispute. So Olson suggested that they call up Chris LaCivita, the veteran Virginia-based operative who was doing work for the campaign, to ask for his take. They knew that LaCivita had already been notified of the reporter's questions, and his specialty in political crisis management would give them perspective on how to handle this.

Olson dialed and put his cell phone on speaker.

"Dude," LaCivita boomed into the receiver as soon as he picked up. "That story about the chick and the Aqua Buddha is fucking *hilarious*. I love that!"

Olson winced. "You're on speaker here with Rand and Doug."

There was a thick half beat of silence before LaCivita, apparently deciding it was best to ignore what had just happened, adjusted his tone to that of the sober crisis manager.

"Rand, here's what we've gotta do..." he said, before going on to lay out a proposed public relations strategy. (Litigation, he suggested, was not the best move.)

After the election, the story would become lore in Rand World, with aides and advisers cracking up as they recited versions of it over beers and in between meetings. Kelley was not amused.

For all the shrewd machinations that define made-for-TV political couples—the ruthless, plotting Underwoods on *House of Cards;* the loveless, scheming Grants on *Scandal*—the real-life marriages of America's successful politicians tend to be governed by the mundane. They are humans, after all, and their decisions—even the big, potentially history-bending ones, like whether to run for president—are weighed against missed Little League games, and mortgage payments, and kids' college funds.

Most of the time, ambition will triumph over such concerns—but it is often a would-be candidate's spouse who gets final say. In 2011, Indiana governor Mitch Daniels decided to forgo a presidential bid because his wife was mortified at the prospect of reporters exhuming their decades-old divorce and reconciliation and presenting it for public examination. Paul Ryan's wife, Janna, suffered from an acute case of stage fright that made her brief time on the presidential stage in 2012 miserable, and it weighed on her husband's decision about whether to run in 2016. And for Chris Christie's wife, Pat, it took a reassuring phone call from Barbara Bush—who insisted that the White House was, in fact, a lovely place to raise a family—to make her peace with the idea of her husband's presidential bid.

In the case of Ted Cruz and his wife, Heidi, this negotiation was particularly delicate, as the latter was just reaching the pinnacle of her own impressive professional ascent when her husband began talking about running for president. Heidi had long been drawn to public service herself. In fact, when she and her husband both worked in the Bush administration early in their marriage, Ted had floundered while she thrived, earning multiple promotions until she ultimately landed her ideal post, directly reporting to Condoleezza Rice. But after Ted moved back home for his career-making appointment as Texas solicitor general—and they struggled for over a year through the nightmarish logistics of a long-distance marriage—Heidi finally gave up her dream job in the White House to join her husband, and put her Harvard MBA to use in the Houston offices of Goldman Sachs. Frustrated and unfulfilled by the work in finance, she suffered from a brief bout of depression, and on one particularly bad August night in 2005, she left her house and ended up sitting on the grass between an expressway and an on-ramp at around 10 p.m., her face buried in her hands.

Heidi eventually recovered from the depression and went on to become a managing director at Goldman, but her husband's ambitions meant that the 2005 police report from that night—filed after a worried passerby reported a "suspicious person" by the freeway— would almost certainly become public at some point, turning a difficult private moment into public fodder for a presidential campaign, and something that her colleagues could read about online. When the report did ultimately surface, it was in response to a wide-ranging series of public-records requests by my colleagues at BuzzFeed. The report was heavily redacted, making it hard to tell what exactly happened that night, and we were unsure whether such an incident should be covered anyway—but we decided to call a spokesman for Cruz to ask what he knew about it. The reply came back that the Cruzes were resigned to the likelihood that the report would come out in the campaign, and that if we wanted to write about it they had no objections. Besides, for Heidi, a sacrifice far greater than any one story loomed on the horizon: when Ted eventually announced his campaign, she would take an unpaid and indefinite leave from her job at Goldman. It was a political necessity, but for a couple of career-oriented high achievers, it was undoubtedly the subject of many long conversations between the two.

Future wars and world markets hinge on these thoroughly human concerns, which get hashed out over a hundred family dinners and late-night talks in darkened bedrooms. In many ways, they always have.

But in the run-up to 2016, prospective Republican candidates knew they had a special political incentive to make sure their spouses were fully committed to the campaign. The Underwoodian under-tones of the Clintons' relationship would present the GOP with an opportunity for contrast by allowing it to show off its nominee's bright, happy, wholesome marriage. And Bill Clinton's lustful rela-tionship with TV cameras ensured that the role of the Republican candidate's spouse would likely be elevated beyond the expectations of a typical election. Whoever the Republicans nominated to take on Hillary would need a spouse who could perform.

Kelley Paul knew she could do the job—she just wasn't sure she wanted to. The 2010 Aqua Buddha revelation had been a formative experience for her, and it loomed over the couple as they weighed the prospect of a presidential run. Not only had the *GQ* article driven home just how nasty high-level campaign politics could get, but it exposed the fact that there was still a lot she didn't know about her husband's past. Stupid college pranks were forgivable, of course, but how many more stories like this would there be? She couldn't stand the thought of her sons (or herself, for that matter) continuing to learn about Rand's youthful indiscretions on the Internet—especially in the sensationalized, trumped-up tone that typified presidential cam-paign smears.

Even more troubling was the prospect of her kids winding up in the crosshairs of rival campaigns and sociopathic reporters. In 2013, the Pauls' oldest son had been arrested at the Charlotte airport for underage drinking, and his mug shot was splashed across the Web. The incident occurred during a turbulent stretch of adolescence for the nineteen-year-old—one his parents hoped he was now emerging from. This, I would later learn, had been the real reason Kelley had gotten so upset about that *GQ* story: it wasn't pious prudishness but fear that Rand's parental authority would be undermined with his son once the press started chronicling Dad's pot-fueled glory days.

Kelley also fretted about how her son might react to researchers and reporters sniffing around for scandal among his old high school classmates.

Kelley knew that between her husband's college high jinks and her son's rocky teenage years, a presidential campaign was likely to serve up a smorgasbord of family humiliations, and she told Rand she couldn't sign off until she had a clear idea of what exactly might come up. To satisfy this demand, Rand had his political action committee hire researchers to dig into his own background and his family, and prepare an exhaustive menu of past sins that political opponents might seize on.

In the meantime, Rand's team tried its best to keep Kelley away from the media, reasoning that exposing her to the unpleasant pestering of reporters might serve to exacerbate her wariness of a campaign. When I requested an interview with her in October 2014, I was first told that she didn't talk to journalists very often. When I pressed, an aide confessed that they were worried my meeting with her might interfere with Rand's intramarital lobbying efforts. In the end, they relented and allowed me a brief interview with the couple at the senator's Washington office.

Kelley was warm and thoughtful throughout our conversation, showcasing an impressive savvy about politics and a disarming deftness in handling my questions. As our allotted time neared its end, I asked Kelley what hesitations she had about her husband running for president.

Before she could respond, Rand lowered his voice slightly and instructed his wife, "Don't answer. Just tell him you don't have any."

I thought he might have been joking—but if he was, Kelley's face didn't register any amusement.

"I think you can probably guess," she told me. "It's the same hesitations anyone would have. I think that people seem to have this idea that *of course* we know what we're doing. And I don't think they realize how complicated it really is."

She said they needed to have more conversations with immediate and extended family members, and make sure everyone was clear-eyed about how the election process would disrupt their lives.

"You know, politics is a lot different than it was even twenty years ago," she said. "Social media—that's just part of it now. Everyone's got a camera and a recording device on their cell phone, and so you feel like you're constantly sort of being surveilled, I guess...And then bloggers can say just about anything, and you have to psychologically be prepared for that."

At this point Rand chimed in, offering validation for his wife's concerns about the press.

"It used to be there were editors or people who said, 'You really shouldn't take a picture of him eating dinner with food coming out of his mouth, or having a drink of wine,'" the senator said. "You just didn't do that. They gave a little bit of space to people. But now, not only is there no space, but *you* might report it and it might be accurate, and then your editor might place a title on it that makes it a little less accurate, then the next guy places a title on it that makes it less accurate, and within twenty-four hours—or, really, within two hours—people are saying, 'He's eating live babies!'"

This was a commonly aired grievance among the rich and famous, and it had the distinction of being both eminently reasonable and hopelessly unrelatable to the vast majority of Americans, for whom celebrity gossip is a harmless pastime and the online media's hyperbolic aggregation practices are not a day-to-day concern. But it quickly became apparent that Rand was not speaking just then for my benefit, or for the benefit of voters. His audience consisted of one person, and she was sitting next to him.

After completing his media critique, Rand pivoted. "But I think there still is some—" He paused, and then decided to enlist my help in his lobbying efforts. "From your point of view—we'll turn it around—do you think there still is a filter [in the media]?"

I got the impression that whatever answer I gave would become currency in the ongoing pros-and-cons list the Pauls were compiling as they moved toward decision time, so I tried to stay neutral. I said that certain fringe corners of the Web could be unpredictable—my mind instantly flashing back to the Trump-led attack of the fever swamps earlier that year—and that there was no telling how low partisan vigilantes might stoop in the heat of a presidential campaign. But I also argued that, for the most part, mainstream media outlets still seemed to adhere to a set of good-taste standards — including, for example, an agreement that candidates' kids should be off-limits.

"And I think there still is some of that," Rand said, rushing to agree with the second part of my analysis. "I keep trying to reassure Kelley that there aren't that many stories out there about kids."

I glanced at Kelley. She didn't look reassured.

Chapter Nineteen

Midterms

On November 4, 2014, Republicans achieved a sweeping victory in the midterm elections that exceeded even the highest hopes of the most blinkered partisan prognosticators. They reclaimed control of the Senate with an astonishing gain of nine seats. They expanded their control of the House to the largest majority in nearly a century. They triumphed in gubernatorial races and seized state legislatures across the country. Contests that were supposed to be won by Democrats broke late in their favor; races that were supposed to be close turned into GOP blowouts. In one of the party's most decisive electoral statements in decades, Republicans managed to turn an election that had once looked doomed into a spectacular national triumph.

And yet the confetti hadn't even finished falling at the victory parties before Republicans were fighting about it. Rather than provide clarity in the battle over the party's future, the GOP's 2014 coup incited a stampede of stakeholders from every nook and niche of conservatism looking to steal credit and spin the outcome as validation for whatever cause or tribe they represented. After all, the *real* battlefield where the struggle for the party's soul would be won—the 2016 presidential primaries—still loomed ahead, and tonight's election would frame that fight for the next two years.

To the establishmentarians, it was obvious that Republicans had won big by stanching the tide of the Tea Party insurgency and elevating reasonable, reality-based nominees. The GOP's 2014 gains were brought about by "a greater attention to the quality and viability" of the party's candidates, argued one of Karl Rove's top lieutenants in *Politico*. The Republicans may have finally "detoxified themselves" from the radioactive right wing, mused center-right *New York Times* columnist David Brooks. The path forward was "to demonstrate to American voters that our party can effectively govern," pronounced Jeb Bush.

At the same time, the insurgents and ideologues of the conservative movement were pushing an entirely different takeaway in the election's wake. Ted Cruz claimed that his party's 2014 triumph could be directly traced back to the 2013 government shutdown, because it had cast a national spotlight on the failures of Obamacare and rallied conservatives to the polls. It was now "incumbent on [Republicans] to honor our promises and do everything humanly possible to stop Obamacare," Cruz said—including another shutdown if necessary. Donald Trump, meanwhile, used the occasion to suggest that the new Republican Congress should get to work impeaching President Obama. "It would be an absolute embarrassment" for the president, Trump barked on Fox News. "It would go down on his record permanently!" And Ann Coulter urged conservatives to "stay paranoid" even as Republicans took control of Congress, because the party's leadership still couldn't be trusted.

Even in victory, the fractured GOP couldn't coalesce. Each faction remained planted firmly in its own distinct reality—blaming failures on the version of the party it most disliked, attributing successes to the leaders it thought should be in charge, and filtering every development through its own custom-made lens.

There were, however, two things that everyone in the party seemed to agree on when it came to 2014. The first was that the American people had rendered a withering judgment of the president by rejecting his party so decisively. The second was that Republicans were no closer to discovering their winning 2016 coalition than they had been on the night of Mitt Romney's defeat. The electorate that turned out for midterm elections was almost always whiter, older, richer, and more conservative than the voters who participated in presidential races. To triumph in the upcoming national election, Republicans would need a standard-bearer who was capable of unifying the party's warring tribes and coaxing millions of additional voters into the fold.

After two years of fierce ideological clashes, backstage power plays, and nonstop jockeying for position, there were nearly twenty contenders vying for the job — and zero consensus about the party's path to victory.

Of all the Oval Office strivers staking out their positions on election night, none was caught straddling the intraparty divide quite so visibly as Rand Paul. It was just after 10 p.m. when he and his entourage cut through a crowded hotel ballroom in Louisville — power walking past the national press in attendance — on their way to the stage. The U.S. Senate race in Kentucky had just been called for Mitch McConnell, and with Republicans taking control of the Senate, it was all but certain that he would be the next majority leader.

Rand had spent the past week with his arm draped around the senior senator on the campaign trail — and the past year vouching for him with grassroots activists — and now he was being rewarded for his steadfastness with the chance to introduce McConnell on national television. Rand's hope was that the high-profile show of solidarity with a man who was about to become the most powerful Republican in Washington would signal to party elites and high-dollar donors that he had matured — from libertarian mischief-maker (and onetime McConnell nemesis) to serious-minded statesman and 2016 prospect.

Standing at the podium, Rand spoke in a theatrically grand cadence that he reserved for his biggest speeches. "It will be two long years until we get to replace this president," he bellowed. He promised that the new Republican Senate would spend the next two years sending Obama "bill after bill until he wearies of it." And if the president refused to sign them, "then in 2016 the people will rise up and reclaim our heritage, and elect a lover of liberty who will restore the values of our Founding Fathers!"

McConnell came onstage and the two men clasped hands and hoisted their arms in the air in the time-honored pose of two politicians projecting unity, confidence, and imminent victory.

Yet even as the ballroom erupted in clamorous applause and the cameras captured the triumphant scene, there was no escaping the reality of Rand's precarious political position. While he was on TV celebrating the Republicans' big night, his dad (or whichever libertarian hanger-on had taken control of his Twitter account) was launching a caustic online lament of the election's outcome and its consequences.

"Looks like big Republican win tonight. Power shift? Yes. Philosophy shift? No!" read one of the @RonPaul tweets.

"Republican control of the Senate = expanded neocon wars in Syria and Iraq," read another.

Rand's advisers were livid about the tweets, but they knew there was little they could do. Whether or not the senator ultimately succeeded in bridging the rifts that ravaged the GOP, it seemed clearer now than ever that the House of Paul would remain divided as long as he was trying.

Eight days later, more than fifty of Rand's aides and advisers gathered for a two-day closed-door summit at the Liaison hotel, a trendy boutique outfit near Capitol Hill defined by modernist statement furniture and tranquil electronic music eternally fluttering through the lobby. The agenda for the conference was multifaceted, but its purpose was clear: to ensure that Rand hit the ground running the second he made his presidential bid official in a few months.

Every contingent of his 2016 shadow campaign was represented at the gathering: the establishment emissaries, the evangelical ambassadors, the libertarian stalwarts, the minority-outreach experts, and a collection of fund-raisers, lobbyists, and political consultants who had managed to hitch their wagons to the senator's star over the past two years.

There was one notable absence, however: Trygve Olson. As one of the few advisers who had been with Rand since before he was elected to the Senate, Olson had been considered a shoo-in for one of the top spots in his presidential campaign. But when Doug Stafford called to invite him to the Liaison hotel summit, Olson politely declined. He sent an email to Rand apologetically explaining that his family life at the moment wouldn't allow for the long hours and incessant travel of a presidential campaign.

But that was only half the truth. In reality, Olson had become sadly convinced after watching Rand in action over the past two years that he had no chance of capturing his party's nomination. Back in 2013, the principled, gate-crashing libertarian had seemed perfectly positioned for what looked like a sea change in the politics of national security and foreign policy. But then the terrifying rise of ISIS in the summer of 2014 had jolted Republicans back into their neoconservative, combat-ready default mode, and all at once Rand's anti-interventionist vision seemed hopelessly out of step with his party.

Olson still believed in that vision, but in order to make it sing in a national Republican primary—especially given the adverse ideological conditions posed by 2016—Rand would need a much sharper, savvier campaign team than the one he had assembled. Stafford, Olson believed, had only held on to his status as the senator's right hand by validating all of his worst reflexes, and then sidelining any operative who came along proposing a different way of doing things. Olson feared that if he signed on to Rand's campaign, he would have to travel with the candidate nonstop in order to counteract Stafford's unhelpful coddling and intercept his bad ideas. And frankly, it just didn't seem worth missing a year's worth of walks to school with his young daughters to help run a quixotic campaign of agitation.

Reaching these conclusions wasn't easy for Olson. For a while, he had truly believed that Rand was on the brink of ushering in a new era for the Republican Party. But watching him squander that opportunity with a series of self-inflicted wounds and unforced errors had made Olson question whether Rand was temperamentally suited for the presidency. As he later explained to a colleague, "If you can't do that kind of basic political blocking and tackling, how are you going to sit across the table from Vladimir Putin?"

While Rand spent the week after the midterms plotting his presidential campaign at the Liaison, Paul Ryan was in his office on the other side of the Hill, preparing to ascend to one of the most powerful perches in Congress: chairman of the House Ways and Means Committee. Though little known outside the cloistered halls of Capitol Hill, the committee had jurisdiction over all tax legislation and an array of massive federal programs, from social security to welfare to Medicare to unemployment benefits. Whoever wielded the Ways and Means gavel had power over trillions of dollars in the federal budget—and bottomless access to campaign cash from donors angling for influence.

Ryan had eyed the chair ever since he was slinging quesadillas to congressmen as a twenty-three-year-old waiter and wannabe wonk at Capitol Hill's favorite Tex-Mex spot—but now that he finally had it, he found himself eyeing the exits. A relatively young man, in his prime and at the pinnacle of power in Congress, Ryan had endless options before him—but he was openly musing about his imminent retirement, and even setting timelines for himself in public. When a reporter went to Wisconsin to profile him, Ryan said emphatically, "I'm not going to be in Congress ten years from now."

For all his years in Washington, Ryan had never planned to be a lifer, and lately he'd felt the tug of private life. He had young kids at home. The weekly commutes to and from Wisconsin were killing him. And he was eager to get back to the normal Janesville lifestyle his family had been a part of for generations.

But his fading infatuation with Washington also had a lot to do with his recent immersion into the world of the poor. After eighteen months of tutelage from Bob Woodson and his network of grassroots poverty warriors, Ryan had introduced a draft of policy proposals in July designed to confront some of the issues he had witnessed firsthand. The seventy-two-page plan sketched a means of taking the federal money that funded the old welfare programs, which had been foundational to America's social safety net for decades, and channeling it toward more flexible grants that would allow individual states to experiment with their own tailor-made initiatives to help welfare recipients get back into the workforce. He proposed expanding the earned income tax credit for childless adults; reviewing and potentially eradicating regulations that hurt disadvantaged workers, like occupational licensing requirements; and looking for ways to reduce incarceration.

Ryan's proposals were greeted more warmly than he expected, with many ideological foes and longtime skeptics of his motives offering at least qualified praise. "Democrats should welcome Paul Ryan's poverty plan," wrote the left-leaning policy blogger Ezra Klein, who applauded him for "refocusing himself and, perhaps, the Republican Party." Danny Vinik, a writer for the venerable liberal magazine the *New Republic,* ventured that Ryan's tax credit proposal might be "his best idea ever." Of course, the familiar cast of ax-grinding critics in the commentariat served up their usual mockery and derision, but overall, Ryan was heartened by the reception.

Any sense of victory he felt was to be fleeting. Ryan had been up-front about the fact that this was only meant to be the start of the process—he and his aides had drafted proposals, not actual legislation—and it was discouragingly obvious that it would take a herculean effort to actually maneuver any of these ideas through the congressional obstacle course and turn them into law. While well-heeled partisans and professional obstructionists hurled demagogic attacks at one another in committee meetings and on cable TV, how many teenagers would unnecessarily rot in prison? How many addicts would see their employment prospects crumble and their illnesses left untreated? How many struggling moms would be left unable to feed their families, thanks to strict licensing laws that banned them from so much as braiding hair without government approval? Ryan would be the first to admit that he had not always played the most constructive role in the petty, partisan, plodding grind of lawmaking that had suffocated so many good policy ideas in Washington's history—but coming to terms with that only made him more disenchanted with the prospect of staying in Congress.

The high priest of process was losing his faith.

But Ryan wasn't entirely without hope. Two years after setting out, there was no denying that his post-2012 effort to wedge poverty into the Republican Party's national agenda had made serious progress. Potential 2016 standard-bearers from every ideological corner of the GOP were now regularly talking about the plight and problems of the poor, and many were pledging to make those issues cornerstones of their presidential campaigns if they decided to run.

Bobby Jindal was now framing his fight with the Justice Department over Louisiana's school voucher program as a war against "cruel policies that will only perpetuate the cycle of poverty." Rand Paul was traveling to impoverished areas of the country like Detroit to sermonize about the "two separate worlds" where big-government policies allow "the poor to get poorer and the rich to get richer." Marco Rubio had introduced his own set of antipoverty proposals in the Senate, arguing earnestly that "the millions currently trapped in poverty and despair are a tremendous untapped resource," while Chris Christie called for greater national attention to be placed on the working poor, who made up "the backbone of every American community."

Remarkably, complaints about "income inequality" — once widely dismissed by conservatives as a socialist concept — were now being uttered seriously by GOP figures ranging from Ted Cruz to Jeb Bush. Cruz had co-opted a onetime Occupy Wall Street rallying cry and made it Tea Party–friendly by lamenting that in the Obama economy, "the top one percent earn a higher share of our national income than any year since 1928." And Bush would launch his political action committee in January, doing so with a bold declaration that "the income gap is real." In the PAC's mission statement, Bush would write, "While the last eight years have been pretty good ones for top earners, they've been a lost decade for the rest of America. The playing field is no longer fair or level."

Some of these Republicans had been drawn to the issue independently, but throughout the party there was wide acknowledgment that Ryan's crusade had been a driving force behind this new GOP emphasis. After the congressman gave one of his speeches about poverty at the Manhattan Institute, Bush glowingly praised his family-centered approach to lifting the poor without overbearing government programs: "When it comes to the American family, Paul Ryan has it right."

But Ryan was also better acquainted than most with the realities of presidential politics, and knew there could be nothing worse for his agenda than to charge into the crowded, competitive 2016 presidential primaries. Some rivals would no doubt de-emphasize their own poverty talk, figuring Ryan had the market cornered on the issue, while others might even begin blasting away at his proposals in an effort to outflank him on the right. If the goal was to place the issue front and center in the primaries, Ryan decided it would be better to stay on the sidelines, advising everyone in the field and declining to endorse any one contender.

"I didn't want to jeopardize this project and these causes by betting it on a presidential campaign," he would later explain to a reporter. "You know, who knows who's going to win?...I wanted to make sure that this got some distance from being seen as some personal ambitious project for a politician."

In his new position, Ryan knew that his critics would be watching him closely, expecting him to promptly dispose of his poverty agenda now that he wielded such a coveted gavel. And he was committed to proving their doubts wrong. But as Ryan considered the next chapter of his career, he found himself looking back to a meeting a couple of months earlier, held in the towering glass-sheathed building of the National Association of Realtors on Washington's New Jersey Avenue.

In the boardroom that September evening, Woodson later told me, the longtime activist had assembled almost every one of the advocates Ryan had met over the course of his poverty tour, calling it a "family reunion." Looking around the table, Ryan saw pioneering pastors who were coming up with new solutions for homelessness, tireless counselors who spent all their time attending to heroin addicts, and an inspiring band of extra-mile advocates who were pouring their lives into helping actual people each day, instead of dreaming up doomed policy ideas. If his excursions into their churches and halfway houses had convinced him of anything, it was that their day-to-day work was infinitely more meaningful than anything he could accomplish in Washington.

But before the three-hour meeting ended, Woodson and his colleagues sought to remind him that he played a key role in their mission as well. After all, the "Pharaoh-Joseph relationship" that

Woodson liked to talk about couldn't produce miracles without kings in well-appointed boardrooms who were willing to audaciously defy the conventions of power and follow the lead of the righteous visionaries in lower castes.

With great ceremony, Woodson called Ryan to the front of the room and presented him with a mock cover of *Time* magazine that featured a photo of him. As the room dissolved into laughter, Ryan read the cover line: "Paul Ryan Named Ambassador to the Hood."

Chapter Twenty

Shock and Awe

One morning late in 2014, Jeb Bush awoke from his long season of political slumber and decided he was ready to become president now.

For the past year and a half, he had deliberately avoided the frenzied to-and-fro of his party's various intramural skirmishes, enjoying a leisurely respite from the sweaty, wearisome business of politicking. He'd spent the time, instead, reading, and golfing, and tinkering with his special homemade guacamole recipe, and attending various functions in ballrooms where well-dressed Floridians bathed him in affection. Of course, he made certain not to vanish *completely* from the national political stage, stumping for Republican candidates during the midterms and giving the occasional speech to well-heeled donor types. But by and large, he had lain low ever since the unpleasantness of his 2013 book tour, opting to give the young guns in his party a shot at rebuilding the GOP. Just as he'd feared, though, this untested crop of up-and-comers had gone and made an even bigger mess of things—from Marquito's immigration implosion, to Ted Cruz's government shutdown, to Rand Paul's adolescent musings about gutting national security. It was clear to Jeb that none of these neophytes were ready to lead Republicans back to the White House. It was time for a grown-up to step in.

It didn't take much for Jeb to get his operation off the ground once his mind was made up: a quick call to his top lieutenant Sally Bradshaw with the "go" order, a couple of well-placed emails activating his family's expansive political network, and a simple media rollout, designed and executed by the small circle of aides he had kept on his personal payroll just in case.

On December 16, Jeb posted a brief note to his Facebook page, announcing to his followers, "I have decided to actively explore the possibility of running for president of the United States."

The announcement arrived with the force of a monsoon in the middle of a holiday-induced news drought, and the nation's rejoicing political press responded with wall-to-wall coverage. With Jeb now dominating headlines, the rest of the Republican presidential prospects—most of whom were enjoying Christmas vacations when the news broke—were suddenly reduced to flat-footed also-rans, forced to shove aside their eggnog and wrapping paper and scramble to move up their own campaign timelines. Before the year was out, Jeb was topping 2016 polls and attracting a bevy of endorsements from establishment bigwigs. With the flip of a switch, he had transformed himself from a retired elder statesman sipping soda by the pool to the formidable front-runner for the Republican presidential nomination.

Jeb's team was pleased: their sneak attack had gone exactly according to plan. Now it was time to initiate the next stage of the Bush blitzkrieg.

Mitt Romney was taken aback when he read Jeb's December 16 Facebook post. *Gosh,* he thought as he swiped at his iPad screen. *He really is serious about this, after all.* For weeks, Romney had heard rumblings among his former donors that Jeb seemed to be signaling he was serious about the 2016 race—but Romney wasn't sure how much to make of the speculation. The two men weren't pals, per se, but Romney considered Jeb a gentleman, and liked to think they had a mutual respect for each other. They were both sons of the establishment, instilled with a sense of decency and decorum. Surely no well-bred Bush would begin making moves before first seeking out the party's most recent standard-bearer. It was only proper!

Yet here Romney found himself—blindsided by a flippin' Facebook post without so much as a phone call beforehand. *If he had just come and asked me for my blessing, I might have given it to him!* The more he stewed, the more indignant he became, his shock giving way to frustration, and then resentment, and finally defiance. If Jeb thought he was going to sideline him with this little stunt, he was badly mistaken.

Romney's political fortunes had improved dramatically since that fateful November night in 2012. Back then, the defeated candidate had been made to shuffle off the national stage in a kind of disgrace, hauling behind him decades' worth of political baggage that his party was eager to unload. The scapegoating had begun right away, as presidential prospects and party elders alike gave interviews and wrote op-eds trying to saddle Romney with a generation of GOP failures— from the party's historically fraught relationship with people of color, to its off-putting ties with big business and billionaires, to its increasingly self-defeating social agenda. The pile-on had been swift and fierce, a political excommunication meant to restore holiness to the Republican Party.

However unfair the public flogging may have been, Romney did nothing to stop it. He considered it his lot to bear, and he did so with the dutiful, clench-jawed resolve of his pioneer forebears. He reasoned that he had been blessed with a loving family, fantastic wealth, and an altogether wonderful private life. If offering up his public reputation for slaughter would somehow serve his party and country, that was a sacrifice he was willing to make.

But something strange had happened on the way to martyrdom: Americans started to like him again—even *miss* him. The reasons for the Romney renaissance were varied. Part of it was due to the fact that some of his campaign foreign policy rhetoric—including a widely mocked contention that Russia was America's "number one geopolitical foe"—now seemed prescient in the era of Edward Snowden and Russian military incursions. What's more, President Obama's domestic agenda had faltered on almost every front, most notably with the disastrous launch of the government's health-care website, which made Romney's 2012 Obamacare bashing seem prophetic. But something else was changing as well: the legendarily cautious and closed-off Romney felt, for the first time, as though the public was finally getting to know him at a human level.

In January 2014, he had attended the Sundance Film Festival for the splashy premiere of a new documentary titled *Mitt,* which offered a sympathetic portrait of the former candidate and his family. The ad campaign for the movie, which was distributed by Netflix, extended an ambitious challenge to viewers: "Whatever side you're on, see another side." And sure enough, the documentary's portrayal managed to win over pundits and film critics of all partisan persuasions. In the forgiving light of political obsolescence, Romney's gee-golly diction looked sweetly endearing, rather than insufferably anachronistic; his devotion to faith and family seemed authentic and admirable, rather than weird or contrived. It had been just over a year since his defeat, and Romney's public image was, improbably, on its way to full rehabilitation.

He spent 2014 as an in-demand surrogate and fund-raiser, stumping for Republican candidates across the country. He also began to take note of the growing chorus of loyalists who wanted him to run for president a third time. His 2012 finance director, Spencer Zwick—a longtime aide often referred to by family friends as his "sixth son"—was especially insistent, forwarding him encouraging notes from donors and national polls showing that a majority of Americans wished Romney had been elected. Zwick routinely dropped everything to hype Romney's 2016 prospects in the press, once taking time to respond to a reporter's email query on the subject while waiting at the hospital for his wife to give birth. At first, Romney dismissed the lobbying from Zwick and others as a mixture of flattery and delusion. He told interviewers repeatedly that he would not run again, and he waved off news reports to the contrary as nothing but speculation.

But the interviewers kept asking, and the reporters kept speculating, and the chorus kept singing, and—*Goodness gracious!*—if all these folks were really this interested, he couldn't just *ignore* them, could he? His midterm stumping before fired-up Republican audiences made him miss the heat of the campaign and reengaged him in the big policy debates of the day. He continued to believe that his successful business background made him uniquely qualified to address the major challenges facing the United States, and he regretted more than ever that he wasn't in the Oval Office to do it.

Before long, he found himself seriously entertaining the notion of a 2016 run. Quietly, he began huddling with confidants and advisers, weighing his options and talking through how a third campaign might work. He was compelled by an idea floated by Hugh Hewitt — a popular conservative talk radio host and outspoken Romney champion — who argued that Mitt's preeminence in the party might allow him to skip the daily grind of the campaign trail, and lock up the nomination with just a handful of commanding debate performances, high-profile speeches, and well-crafted ads. Romney wasn't convinced it would be *that* easy, but he did believe his status as the party's last nominee should at least buy him the time he needed to deliberate.

But not anymore. Jeb was forcing his hand now, and Romney was not comfortable with being pushed around — especially by someone who hadn't run for office in a decade, and whose pitiful private sector career consisted mainly of handouts from Bush cronies and financial dealings so politically toxic they made his own private equity record look like an afternoon at the soup kitchen. *I mean, good grief:* the guy sat on the board of one of the big banks that took a bailout! "You saw what they did to me with Bain," he told friends. "What do you think they'll do to him over Barclays?"

The more he thought about it, the more decidedly unimpressed he was by Jeb. If this was the best the party had to offer, then Romney felt duty-bound to explore entering the race. After getting approval from his wife, Ann, over Christmas, he fired off his first warning shot on January 9, 2015. At a closed-door meeting in midtown Manhattan, Romney told a group of about thirty former donors not to count him out.

"Everybody in here can go tell your friends that I'm considering a run," he said, adding, "I want to be president."

Jeb knew there was a chance Romney might react to his announcement this way, which was why he and his team had developed a plan to deal with a potential Mitt-ruption. In private, his lieutenants referred to the strategy as "shock and awe"—a military doctrine, employed by Jeb's brother George at the outset of the Iraq War, that aimed to exhaust and discourage the enemy with an early show of overwhelming force. Applied here, the idea was to quickly amass a vast arsenal of high-dollar donors, topflight operatives, and establishment endorsements so intimidating that Romney would conclude he couldn't compete. And along the way, they'd make the process so painful for him that he wouldn't even want to. The goal was to crush Romney's spirit and scare off any other potential challengers who were on the fence.

To carry out this shock-and-awe strategy, Jeb relied on a small team of operatives marshaled by Bradshaw, a tough, Mississippi-born political infighter who had served as Bush's enforcer for two decades. His inner circle also included veteran GOP strategist Mike Murphy and loyal longtime aides Brandi Brown, Josh Venable, and Kristy Campbell.

By the time Romney finally declared his 2016 interest in January, the Bush team's assault was already under way, and he quickly found himself struggling to play catch-up. Romney spent hours every day dialing up former donors and supporters, often to discover that Jeb had gotten there first and extracted ironclad commitments from them.

Whereas Romney's instinct was to approach these early conversations with a friendly, testing-the-waters tone, Jeb's style was blunt and unflinching, directly putting the question to donors—Are you with me, or Mitt? — and then waiting in silence as they squirmed.

Also working the phones on Jeb's behalf was a sprawling network of family friends, fund-raisers, party hacks, senior statesmen, and more than a few former ambassadors whose cushy appointments had come courtesy of either Bush '41 or Bush '43. In their zeal to deliver for the new dynastic heir, these foot soldiers routinely trashed Romney during calls with donors, dubbing him a "loser" and claiming that—contrary to Mitt's own claims—he was planning to build his new campaign around Stuart Stevens and Beth Myers, two of the strategists widely faulted for the failure of his 2012 bid.

Team Jeb's hyperaggressive approach put off some donors, who maintained a personal affection for Romney regardless of whether they supported his 2016 gambit. But many more were impressed by the sharp-elbowed tactics, and signed on with Jeb in hopes that he would take the same fight to Hillary Clinton in the general election.

Meanwhile, Romney was struggling to figure out why his coverage in the press—which, not long ago, had been rife with soft-focus profiles and breathless speculation about his political future—was turning sharply negative all of a sudden. In the *Washington Post,* Dan Balz wrote about "the haste and seemingly haphazard nature" of Romney's trial balloon. In a *Wall Street Journal* column headlined "Don't Do It, Mr. Romney," Peggy Noonan, a former speechwriter for the first President Bush, declared, "This is a moment in history that demands superior political gifts from one who would govern. Mitt Romney does not have them. He never did." And most remarkably, Jennifer Rubin, the conservative *Washington Post* blogger whose shameless Romney shilling throughout 2012 often made her seem like an agent of the campaign, had now inexplicably turned on him. In one bizarrely harsh takedown, Rubin wrote, "The 'rivalry' between Romney and Jeb Bush is like that between San Francisco and Los Angeles. The former is so confident of its own stature that it does not know there is a rivalry. Romney is Los Angeles."

Romney was stung by the ferocity of the media backlash. He had expected some naysayers, sure, but not this kind of virulence. *What in the world?* he kept thinking. *A few weeks ago everybody wanted me to run. What happened?*

Many in Romney's inner circle were convinced they knew the answer. They believed that Murphy—a long-ago Romney adviser who was now working as Jeb's message maven—was behind the anti-Mitt onslaught in the press, using a well-lubricated pipeline of Bush connections to transport hit pieces into influential news outlets. "No one really thinks Peggy Noonan wrote that piece without encouragement from Bush World," grumbled one loyal Romney adviser. "She did it to thank her sponsors."

Romney kept plugging away for three hectic and increasingly miserable weeks—diligently working through his call sheet every day, poring over polling data, and delivering a carefully crafted speech in San Diego designed to test potential themes for a 2016 campaign (more stories about his church service, fewer hymns to the American job creator). On January 22, 2015, he made a last-ditch effort to regain the upper hand when Jeb flew to Utah for a one-on-one meeting at Romney's home in Park City. The appointment had been on the books for months, but recent developments had turned the powwow into a major news event, with reporters and cameramen ambushing Jeb at the Salt Lake City airport and camping out at the perimeter of Romney's property. That afternoon, beneath the soaring cathedral ceilings of his rustic Deer Valley mansion, Romney produced a portfolio of private polling data that one of his former donors had commissioned. Based on thousands of survey respondents across twenty states, the strikingly thorough report revealed widespread support for Romney among Republican primary voters—and serious vulnerabilities for Jeb.

But Bush was undeterred. He was confident the voters would come around eventually—they always did. For now, what mattered was winning the invisible primary, wooing the insiders, and staying the course on his shock-and-awe assault. With his operation flush with fund-raising cash, Jeb began vacuuming up the party's best consultants and operatives with frightening speed and efficiency. The hiring spree created plenty of apparent organizational redundancies, but the point wasn't to effectively staff his future campaign: it was to make sure that other candidates couldn't staff theirs. "Jeb's pitch is one word: juggernaut," said a Republican consultant who was courted by the campaign. "They say, 'We're going to be the Death Star, and you're either on it or you're not.' For guys in my business, a pitch like that is very compelling."

The final blow for Romney came one day late in January, when Republican strategist David Kochel called him to break the news that he was signing on with Jeb. Romney was crushed. A seasoned Iowa-based operative, Kochel had played a senior role in both of his presidential campaigns, and they had logged countless late nights and long bus rides together on the trail. Romney considered Kochel a friend and confidant, and they had kept in close contact since 2012: in recent weeks, Kochel had even participated in conference calls with Mitt and his inner circle, offering up strategy advice and enthusiastically encouraging him to run again. Of course, it was precisely because of his close ties to Romney that Jeb's team had been so determined to poach him. Closing the deal wasn't easy, but in the end, they made him an offer he couldn't refuse: when Jeb officially announced his candidacy, Kochel was promised, he would be named national campaign manager.

Romney's loyalists were enraged when they found out about the defection, ranting to one another about Kochel's unconscionable betrayal and branding him a "Benedict Arnold." But Mitt himself didn't feel angry — just demoralized. The past three weeks had offered a rattling glimpse at how vicious and driven Jeb could be, and Romney now realized it was a fantasy to think he could win the nomination by gliding above the fray: the 2016 primaries were going to be a bloodbath. Already, his sons and their wives — still suffering from a kind of PTSD after their last two tours of duty — were dreading the prospect of a third campaign. Could he really justify dragging his family back into a political war zone now that he knew how savage the fight would be? Then there were the political realities to weigh. Romney's trove of polling data still had him convinced that he would win the nomination if he ran again, but he now worried that he would emerge from the primaries so bruised and bloodied that Clinton would roll right over him in the general election. And frankly, the thought of losing *another* presidential race was almost too much to bear.

Late on the evening of January 29, top Romney supporters across the country received an email inviting them to join Mitt on a conference call the next morning for an "update." The cryptic note was immediately leaked to the press and prompted a twelve-hour frenzy of media speculation, with the general consensus being that Romney was going to declare his intentions to run.

In reality, he was holed up in a Manhattan hotel suite, drafting a statement that explained his decision to bow out, and fending off the inner circle dissenters who were pleading with him to reconsider.

Romney had tried to explain his reasoning to this chorus of confidants, but they were still urging him not to shut the door. They contended that even if he didn't want to launch a formal campaign right now, it would be a mistake to take himself entirely out of the running. They laid out a vivid, detailed scenario in which a fractured Republican Party—divided by a wide field of niche presidential candidates—fails to unite behind a single nominee in 2016, and ends up with a chaotic, historic floor fight at the national convention. Facing a televised descent into disarray, the GOP delegates would naturally turn to Romney—the fully vetted, steady-handed Republican statesman—for salvation.

Your party might still need you, Mitt's loyalists insisted. The *country* might still need you!

All the last-minute lobbying gave Romney pause. Was he certain this was the right choice? Their appeals to his deeply felt sense of duty were compelling. He spent his final hours before the conference call consulting with his family and praying for guidance—and by Friday morning, he had inserted a bit of rhetorical wiggle room into his draft. "I've been asked, and will certainly be asked again, if there are any circumstances whatsoever that might develop that could change my mind," he wrote toward the end of his statement. "That seems unlikely." *Unlikely.* The word managed to appease the die-hards in his orbit, and it served to keep hope alive among some of his most loyal donors. As one of Romney's 2012 fund-raisers would tell me months later, "There are bitter-enders who have read that statement a hundred times, and they think it's going to happen—maybe on the floor of the convention." Some even began to devise the crude outline of a strategy to jump-start a "draft Mitt" movement from the floor, which would involve flipping the delegates in Mormon-heavy states like Utah, Wyoming, and Idaho. In the meantime, the statement gave Romney that rare peace of mind afforded by political flexibility. Yes, he was withdrawing from the race for now—but if, come summer of 2016, his party needed a savior, Mitt Romney would be ready.

On the afternoon of January 30, he got on the conference call—which was now being live-streamed on home pages across the Web—to announce his decision. Reading from his prepared remarks, he thanked the supporters who had stuck with him over the past few weeks and gave them permission to seek out other 2016 candidates if they wished. But he also made a point of steering them away from one particular contender. "I believe that one of our next generation of Republican leaders, one who may not be as well-known as I am today, one who has not yet taken their message across the country, one who is just getting started, may well emerge as being better able to defeat the nominee," he said. Translation: Anybody but Jeb.

Jeb's team didn't mind Mitt's passive-aggressive parting shot. Their shock-and-awe campaign was working: one rival had surrendered, others were cowering in fear, and the entire political world was now buzzing about the ruthless efficiency with which Jeb's lieutenants had disposed of Romney.

But while the political world looked on at the implacability of Jeb's team, his top lieutenants refused to show their hand. When a reporter at *Politico* asked Bradshaw how they had managed to take the entire GOP field by surprise with such an ambitious and sophisticated launch, she replied, "We just do what people who work for Jeb Bush always do, which is to build the plan, execute the plan, and don't talk about it."

When new hires would show up for their first day of work at the Tallahassee offices of Florida governor Jeb Bush, they would find on their desks a bound copy of an 1899 essay titled "A Message to Garcia." Even in its nineteenth-century prose, the 1,500-word pamphlet was a breezy read that could easily be skimmed in the space of a coffee break—but the aides who wanted to thrive were expected to fully internalize its thesis.

In the essay, author Elbert Hubbard relates the story of a U.S. army officer assigned by President William McKinley to deliver an important message to the Cuban rebel general Calixto Garcia, deep in the island's jungles. The exemplary officer takes the order "without asking any idiotic questions," and exhibits none of the "foolish inattention, dowdy indifference, and halfhearted work" that plague so many in the lower ranks. Instead, he dutifully sets off on a boat, disappears into the jungle, and emerges weeks later having executed his mission flawlessly. Praising the officer's quiet diligence, Hubbard writes, "There is a man whose form should be cast in deathless bronze and the statue placed in every college of the land. It is not book learning young men need…but a stiffening of the vertebrae which will cause them to be loyal to a trust, to act promptly, concentrate their energies; do the thing—'Carry a message to Garcia!'"

Inside each pamphlet, the governor's aides would find a handwritten inscription from their new boss: "Be a messenger."

Some of the new staffers no doubt interpreted the gift as little more than a well-intentioned bit of fortune cookie management theory. But the ones who would become the governor's most trusted aides were those who received it as it was intended: a new creed to live by, an invitation to convert. From those baptized into the Bush inner circle, Jeb demanded fierce obedience, a bullet-blocking sense of loyalty, and a monomaniacal drive to get the job done by whatever means necessary. Across Florida, allies and adversaries alike marveled at his Vader-like grip on his troops. "He instills something weird in you," David Johnson, one of Jeb's longtime loyalists, told me. "You really want to please him. It doesn't matter if you're twenty or fifty. You want to make Jeb Bush happy with your work, happy with your competence." And often the fastest way to earn the boss's "Attaboy"s was with sharpened knives and a killer instinct.

Indeed, beneath the glossy exterior of his public profile—that of the compassionate conservative, the happy warrior, the good-natured reformer—Jeb possessed a hard-edged, often ruthless political style that ran through his entire rise and reign in the Sunshine State. "He's been the big bad kid," Chris Smith, a leading Democrat in the Florida house, complained toward the end of Jeb's term. "And he's wielded that power mercilessly."

Jeb had harbored a tendency toward bully tactics ever since he was a prep school giant hulking over pip-squeak classmates at Andover—but he didn't begin to channel that aggression toward politics until after his 1994 gubernatorial campaign. Jeb had viewed the race as a chance to finally take his rightful place in the monarchy—to conquer

Florida and bring it under the Bush clan's banner. He spent the year traveling the state in a campaign bus named Dynasty and solemnly told the *Miami Herald,* "I want to be able to look my father in the eye and say, 'I continued the legacy.'" But on election night—while his screwup brother, George, was celebrating his ascent to the Texas governorship—Jeb found himself sitting on a bed in Miami's downtown Crowne Plaza hotel, smoking his first cigarette in years and wondering what had gone wrong. He was a loser.

He didn't wallow for long. Instead, with the 1998 governor's race now in his sights, Jeb became ferociously, almost single-mindedly driven to win, according to friends who knew him at the time. It was as though experiencing those first, unfamiliar stabs of professional failure — combined with the feeling of letting down his family — had caused him to mutate into a whole new beast, muscles ballooning, clothes tearing, an angry growl roaring from his deepest viscera. He began plotting his comeback with a coterie of devoted allies, who set about systematically clearing the field of potential Republican rivals, wooing the would-be candidates who seemed open to some sort of quid pro quo arrangement and kneecapping the ones who weren't. He had polling commissioned so that he could show it to all potential comers and convince them, in blunt, uncompromising terms, that they had no chance at beating him. He leaned on the mischievous chairman of the Florida GOP—a man who proudly embraced the title "Boss," inspired by corrupt Chicago political operators of yore—to stack the state party with Bush loyalists and steer Republican donors away from other candidates. Jeb's lieutenants, meanwhile, spread rumors, traded favors, and twisted arms—whatever they needed to do to "carry the message." By the time the campaign arrived, they had done away with every single one of Jeb's serious primary opponents.

"We ground them into dirt," one Jeb ally would recall proudly. "It was as though that ninety-eight campaign was marching to liberate Paris."

Once in office, Jeb didn't let up. He had the good fortune of being sworn in at a time when Republicans were in control of both chambers of the legislature, and the state's first-ever term limits for law-makers were about to go into effect—a perfect political storm that would precipitate a massive shift of power from the legislature to the governor's mansion. "Before, members would tell a governor, 'Screw you, you're out in eight years, and I'll be here for twenty,'" said Chris Smith, who served as House Minority Leader during Jeb's governorship. "But now that we have term limits, members think, 'I'm gonna be out of here in a few years. I don't want to have the governor mad at me.'"

Jeb made no secret of when he was mad, meting out retribution to any and all who deigned to cross him. There was the Republican legislator from Miami who pushed back too hard against one of the governor's power plays, only to see money taken away from a children's brain tumor center in his district. Or the Democratic mayor of Tallahassee, who made a public crack about Dubya's country-club upbringing, and then had a pet road project killed as punishment. Or the three GOP senators who refused to toe the party line on a proposed limit to medical malpractice lawsuits, and then discovered that the governor's office was seeking out Republican candidates in their district to challenge them in the next primaries.

"We've had some wars," one of the senators, Mike Bennett, would tell a reporter a couple of years after the episode. "I made Bush so mad that when he ran for reelection, he actually sent my campaign contribution check back to me. But I gotta tell you, I admired that. Who wants to fight a pussy?" Of course, not all of Jeb's victims were so generous in their assessment of his tactics. Tallahassee's mayor at the time, Scott Maddox, viewed the governor's retaliation against him as a temper tantrum thrown by a spoiled son of privilege. "Governor Bush never really had to work hard for anything," he fumed. "If you're always used to being given what you want, you react poorly when you are opposed."

But whatever his motives, the efficacy of Jeb's tactics were indisputable. In his eight years as governor, he pursued an aggressive education agenda that dramatically expanded access to charter schools, he rammed through billions of dollars in tax cuts, and he signed dozens of pro-gun, pro-life, and pro-business bills into law. Jeb's strong-arming made him one of the most productive and powerful governors in state history, a lesson that he—and one of his young constituents—wouldn't forget.

As soon as Romney was knocked out of 2016 contention, the chatter in GOP campaign circles began revolving around a single question: which rival would the Jeb Bush juggernaut direct its firepower at next? The answer quickly became obvious to many of the still-uncommitted donors, consultants, and big wheels in the party once Jeb's lieutenants came knocking. "They're going after Rubio next," said one California bundler who heard from Jeb's team the same day Romney bowed out. "It's like whack-a-mole. They're going to try to take out everyone before the primaries even start."

Chapter Twenty-One

Homeland Security

Marco Rubio was exhausted but wired when he arrived in the Southern California desert on Sunday afternoon. It was January 26, 2015, and he had just come off a forty-eight-hour whirlwind weekend strategizing with his top political donors in Miami Beach when he then hopped a coast-to-coast flight to Palm Springs for the winter meeting of the billionaire Koch brothers' libertarian political operations. The exclusive annual gathering at the Rancho Mirage Ritz-Carlton resort was known for attracting many of the Republican Party's most deep-pocketed contributors—and this year Rubio had been invited to audition for them. He would be participating in a foreign policy forum alongside Rand Paul and Ted Cruz, answering questions from a moderator while the conservative moneymen in the audience sized up the potential 2016 horses.

To the small band of strategists working to get Rubio's presidential campaign off the ground, today's event was being treated like a make-or-break moment. With Jeb Bush now in the picture there was widespread skepticism in political circles about whether a second Florida-based candidate could pull in enough money to fund a 2016 bid. Rubio's two chief advisers, Terry Sullivan and Todd Harris, believed they needed to raise at least $30 million in the first half of the year to show they were serious. If they fell short, no one in the party would see the campaign as credible—donors would scatter, staffers would flee, and the Beltway opinion makers would start prewriting their Rubio obituaries. On the other hand, if they could make a splash with this crowd, it seemed likely that they could gain the momentum they needed to hit their goal.

The stakes were high, and they had taken preparations for the event seriously. Whereas Cruz and Rand had accepted the Kochs' invitation practically on the spot, Rubio had tasked Sullivan with negotiating the terms of the event, and the operative proceeded to spend days peppering the organizers with logistical questions: Will they be standing or sitting? Where will he be on the stage? Who will be the moderator? Will the footage be live-streamed, or posted online later? Does the event violate the RNC's rules?

That last point was an especially sticky one. Just that month, the Republican National Committee had announced a sweeping over-haul of the party's primary debate program. Looking to avoid the free-for-all savagery of the 2012 cycle—during which GOP candidates appeared in nearly two dozen debates to beat one another up on national TV—party officials now said there would be only nine sanctioned debates, and that candidates who took part in unapproved events would be barred. "While I can't always control everyone's mouth," RNC chairman Reince Priebus had said, "I can control how long we have to kill each other."

In truth, the Rubio camp—which believed its candidate's unparalleled skill as a communicator would make him shine onstage—wasn't wild about the party's crackdown. Sullivan, a swaggering, salty-tongued South Carolinian who didn't mince words, had frankly told Priebus it was a bad idea.

"Look, I'm for it until I'm against it," Sullivan told him. "The second my guy needs another debate to stay alive, I'm going to denounce the RNC as backroom power brokers trying to silence the grassroots activists. I'm telling you, there's gonna be a hashtag."

But for now, Rubio wanted to play by the rules, and so they had dragged the Koch organizers into a protracted negotiation with the RNC over how to keep the forum kosher. Sullivan had also pestered a concession out of the organizers to allow him to accompany Rubio into the closed-door event so he could be on hand to assist with the senator's donor schmoozing—something neither Cruz nor Rand had even thought to ask about. By the time Rubio and his entourage finally arrived on Sunday, it was all the Kochs' fed-up organizers could do to refrain from strangling Sullivan and dumping his body in a shallow desert grave.

But if the past few years had taught Rubio and his team anything, it was that even with his natural charisma and uncommon talent as a speaker, the freshman senator could get only so far on the strength of personality alone. In the year and a half since his immigration flame-out, Rubio had retreated from the celebrity-style media coverage that had once thrilled him. He did fewer TV hits, and his press team, led by Alex Conant, routinely turned down pitches from editors who came dangling promises of glossy magazine covers. In the Senate, Rubio channeled his energy and ambition toward policy, drafting serious proposals for welfare reform and boning up on international issues as a member of the Foreign Relations Committee. He began to distinguish himself as one of the party's most energetic and articulate critics of President Obama's Latin American policy, delivering forceful, detailed speeches from the Senate floor with scant notes and railing against the administration for not taking a harder line against communist dictators in Cuba and Venezuela. At a time when Rand was winning headlines and media buzz for his iconoclastic assault on the party's hawks, Rubio fully embedded himself in the GOP's foreign policy establishment, seeking counsel and winning praise from leading neoconservative thinkers and veterans of the Bush and Reagan White Houses.

On a personal level, Rubio was training himself not to agonize over every bothersome bit of trivia that appeared in the press, and he was generally more even-keeled about the political speed bumps he encountered. He developed a mantra of sorts that he repeated every time one of his staffers informed him of a problem. "I'm not worried, man," he would say with the laid-back lilt of a beach bum.

Rubio's advisers, meanwhile, knew it was their job to worry—to scout out the arena and work the refs before sending him into a game. He had always had enough raw skill to outplay everyone on the field; what he'd lacked was a good game plan. Not anymore.

Rubio spent his couple of hours of downtime on Sunday before the event watching a football game in his room, and when the time came, he put on a neatly pressed navy suit and a dark purple tie before descending to the site of the forum. Even after weeks of back-and-forth with the organizers, Sullivan, watching Rubio take his seat, kicked himself for the stuff he had missed. *The lighting on Marco on the end is terrible... Those chairs suck... I should have been able to advance the stage...*

But the worried nitpicking subsided almost as soon as his boss opened his mouth. It was clear right off the bat that Rubio had a greater command of the issues than his two colleagues, holding forth confidently on everything from Iranian nuclear negotiations, to the ISIS terrorist threat, to China. He was, by turns, passionate, funny, and authoritative—righteously railing against President Obama's foreign policy one moment and deftly disarming a loaded question from ABC News journalist Jonathan Karl the next.

At one point, Karl cited a speech delivered at the summit the night before by Wisconsin governor Scott Walker, who had argued that the Republican Party's standard-bearer needed to be a governor with executive experience outside Washington. Rubio had learned of Walker's comment earlier and found it preposterous. He had heard that the Koch organizers had tried to get the governor to join them in this forum, and that his chief handler, Rick Wiley, had pointedly refused, later telling a mutual acquaintance, "I'm not putting my guy onstage. That's bullshit." *Yeah,* Rubio thought. *Because your guy doesn't know anything about foreign policy.*

Responding, indirectly, to Walker's remark, Rubio talked about the importance of having foreign policy experience. "It is important for the next president of the United States to understand the diversity of these challenges, to have a global strategic vision and an understanding of what the U.S.'s role in it is," he said. "Now, does that mean that a governor can't acquire that? Of course they could. But I would also say that taking a trip to some foreign city for two days doesn't make you Henry Kissinger either."

The room erupted in laughter, and Karl again tried pressing him to respond head-on to Walker's comments. Rubio's lips curled into a sly half smile, and he said, "Well, if I was the governor, I'd say the same thing."

As the forum went on, it became almost embarrassingly obvious to Rubio's advisers—those who were watching live in the ballroom and from home on a remote feed—that the event's other two participants had not come to play. Cruz was doing fine, but his shtick seemed a bit tired as he acted out his characteristic drama, at one point issuing a dire warning that Iran might soon launch a nuclear strike in "Tel Aviv, New York, or Los Angeles." Rand's performance, meanwhile, was bizarrely ineffectual, especially given that he was speaking to perhaps the only roomful of Republican megadonors in the country that held sympathies for his libertarian-tinged foreign policy views.

A few days earlier, Cruz and Rubio had been talking about the upcoming event, and both had predicted that Rand would try to use the setting to pick a fight with them.

Sure enough, the Kentucky senator repeatedly tried needling his colleagues with his trademark brand of trolling—but rather than reduce his targets to indignant sputtering, Rand's provocations were continually smacked down by Rubio. When the topic of defense spending came up, Rand tried to accuse his more hawkish rivals of recklessly dumping taxpayer dollars into the Pentagon at the expense of sound fiscal policy.

"I'm not for a blank check," Rand declared, arguing that running up the federal deficit to finance the defense department's lavish spending habits was holding down economic growth.

But Rubio stood firm: "Try *economic growth* while you're under attack."

One Rubio adviser would later joke of Rand, "You almost wanted to pull the fire alarm for the guy."

As soon as the forum ended, Rand slipped off the stage and made a beeline for the exit, while Cruz got a glass of wine and struck up a conversation with a few audience members. Rubio, meanwhile, was mobbed by multimillionaires who lined up to shake his hand, pile on praise, and offer to help him raise money. For the next hour, Sullivan stood just behind his boss, frantically texting names and phone numbers to their finance director up in her hotel room. Even David Koch himself returned multiple times to congratulate Rubio on his impressive showing and crack jokes about how the senator had pushed around poor Karl all night.

The next day, the Republican pollster Frank Luntz conducted a straw poll of the summit's attendees and asked them which of the weekend's guests of honor was most impressive. Rubio won in a landslide.

The senator felt exhilarated, finally on the verge of the comeback he had been impatiently awaiting for the past year and a half. What he didn't yet realize was that Jeb Bush's "messengers" were gunning for him next—and that they had been stockpiling their deadliest ammunition for years.

On December 31, 2009, the campaign manager for Rubio's fledgling U.S. Senate bid wrote a memo ominously warning staff and supporters of an imminent smear campaign that would soon be unleashed on their candidate.

"[A] lot of wild punches. And negative advertising. And mudslinging mail. And anonymous websites. All repeated ad nauseam," he wrote in the staccato state-of-the-race note. "So be forewarned. It's coming. Very, very soon."

Rubio's decision to enter the Senate race earlier that year had been a head-scratcher even for many of his most loyal fans. Florida's moderate Republican governor, Charlie Crist, had already declared his intention to run, and with Crist's high approval ratings and the support of the national party, he was all but guaranteed to glide through the election. Rubio's bid was seen initially as foolhardy, and he had started the race a whopping fifty points behind Crist, with anemic fund-raising and a local press corps that treated him like a joke. But fortunately for Rubio, he was running in an election cycle with broad, built-in themes—an intra-GOP clash between outsiders and insiders, conservatives and centrists—that had the power to turn every race into a national story. Rubio's small band of consultants had savvily seized on this dynamic by pitching their campaign to national conservative media outlets and Tea Party activist groups as a battle for the soul of the party. With the help of a glowing, well-timed *National Review* cover story—and the surge of national media interest that it prompted—Rubio was now galloping toward 2010 with momentum. Fund-raising had taken off, and polls showed the race to be a dead heat.

But many in Rubio's inner circle were nervous. In December, the Crist campaign had taken their first direct shot at their newly ascendant primary rival, claiming that as House Speaker, Rubio had "tucked away" $800,000 in the state budget for new Astroturf on the Miami-Dade fields where he played football. It was a relatively gentle jab as far as campaign combat went, and after a denial from the Rubio camp, the story fizzled. But it was clear now that Crist—and the GOP establishment that he marshaled—was churning its smear machine into gear, as the governor's operatives frantically scavenged the state, from Miami to Tallahassee, in search of dirt on their opponent.

Rubio's team had heard plenty of rumors about their candidate's past—but their shoestring budget hadn't allowed them to undergo the "self-vetting" process that serious campaigns often relied on to sort out fact from fiction. Now, with Crist and co. digging for skeletons, a single question was consuming many in the Rubio campaign's high command: What were they going to find?

Making the situation more precarious was the fact that their candidate seemed to need a fainting couch every time he faced even mild criticism from political rivals or the press. In campaign politics, allegations of pork barrel spending are as common as navy suits and dimpled neckties—but Rubio had been positively wounded when Crist accused him of misusing state funds.

How can they say that? he had mewed to his aides. They can really just *make stuff up* about me?

For all his experience in state politics, Rubio had yet to endure the kind of character assaults that often define high-stakes, high-profile races like the one he was in. "I had never been in political combat like this, and [Crist's] attacks stung me.... It takes a while to get accustomed to [it]," Rubio would later write. As the race continued to intensify, Rubio objected heatedly—and often emotionally—to each and every attack line unleashed by the Crist camp.

When a state senator who was backing the governor referred to Rubio as a "slick package from Miami," he was aghast and ordered his aides to cry foul.

Dog whistle! Anti-Cuban! Racist!

When opponents accused Rubio of steering state funds toward Florida International University in exchange for a faculty job after he left office, he worked himself into a furious tizzy.

Outrageous! Slander!

On the stump, Rubio continued to exude the vigor and optimism of an idealistic ideologue—but inside, the accusations were tearing him up. "Because they were hurting me personally, I was certain these attacks were hurting our campaign," he later recalled in his memoir. "I was sure they would blunt our momentum." But for all the agony they caused Rubio, the attacks were so far doing little to hold down his steadily rising poll numbers.

Then, in March, a bombshell: the *Miami Herald* had gotten hold of statements for the Republican Party of Florida's American Express card that Rubio had used while serving in state leadership, and the paper published a damning front-page exposé detailing his spending habits while in office. The funds were supposed to be reserved for official party business, but the statements featured page after page of expenditures that seemed to shamelessly disregard such rules. They included everything from $10.50 at an AMC movie theater, to $68 at a wine shop near Rubio's house, to $765 at Apple's online store. Rubio's chief of staff had once charged more than $6,000 to cover food and lodging for his boss's family reunion at a plantation resort in Georgia. And Rubio had used the party's Amex to pay for $1,000 in repairs to his family minivan. The single item that got the most attention was a $134 charge to a hair salon, which prompted Crist to go on TV and speculate that Rubio had used the money to pay for an expensive back wax.

Rubio claimed that he had personally reviewed the credit card statements every month when he was Speaker and reimbursed the party for all nonofficial expenses—but his defense did little to quell the coverage of the scandal. With the headlines mounting, he wailed that the press was recklessly hyping an untrue story without giving him a chance to disprove their narrative. Humiliated and depressed, Rubio shrouded himself in a veil of martyrdom. Once again, he was convinced that his candidacy was on the verge of a complete meltdown. *That's it,* he thought. *I'm finished.*

His aides spent the next couple of days playing what Rubio called "whack-a-mole" with the Florida press, scrambling to issue denials, demand retractions, and discredit allegations with whatever scraps of evidence they could round up. After surviving the first forty-eight hours with the candidate's internal tracking numbers still intact, Rubio's senior advisers concluded that the credit card story wouldn't be a deathblow. But they were now more anxious than ever.

Even though the *Herald* was staying mum about how it had obtained the credit card statements, it was obvious to any politico with a pulse that they had been leaked by Jim Greer, the chairman of the Republican Party of Florida and a loyal Crist ally. Such a flagrant violation of decorum—let alone the law—set off alarm bells at Rubio HQ because it signaled that Crist was panicked and playing dirty now. With the corruption charges failing to stick, they knew there was only one arrow left in Crist's quiver: Rubio's widely whispered-about "zipper problem."

Ever since he began to make a name for himself in Tallahassee, Rubio had been trailed by a persistent series of unsubstantiated rumors about his sex life. Jilted mistresses, sordid affairs, secret love children—Rubio's team had heard it all, and the more seasoned strategists among them knew that such tittle-tattle was commonplace in every state capitol. But even as Rubio indignantly denied any suggestion of infidelity, the unconfirmed gossip had proved difficult for him to shake, popping up frequently on local political blogs and via the endless behind-the-scenes speculation of his loose-lipped legislative colleagues.

Some on his team were convinced that it was only a matter of time before Crist persuaded a reporter to write about the rumors. Though Rubio's advisers found the claims to be ludicrous, they had such little regard for their rival that they had no problem believing that he would stoop to the level of gossipmonger. "You just *knew* he was out there floating this bullshit about philandering," one senior Rubio adviser recalled to me. "We were bracing for it."

Greer would later tell me that the Crist campaign thought that it had, in fact, dug up potential evidence of adultery on Rubio's part. He recounted a meeting with the governor's staff in which their campaign opposition researcher briefed them on a trove of Rubio's emails that they had recently obtained. "They had come across an email from a woman who had worked in his office for years, and who had ultimately gone on to a job at Florida International University," Greer said. "The email said something like, 'I can't take this anymore. Why won't you return my phone calls? Why are you doing this to me?'" According to Greer, Crist and his staffers were elated by the discovery, convinced that the email was written by an ex-lover that Rubio was now trying to cast aside. The governor proposed leaking it to the *Miami Herald,* but Greer pumped the brakes.

"I told the campaign manager and the governor one night over at the governor's mansion that it was a mistake," he told me. Greer argued that such an attack would be too nasty, and that they didn't have enough ammo for it anyway: "I said, number one, there's not enough there to know this was a mistress. And from my perspective, I felt, even if it is, I don't think we need to go down this road." He said the conversation ended with an agreement to hold off on any leaks until they further investigated the matter. The email in question never did surface publicly, and a spokesman for Crist later denied Greer's account to me. In 2013 Greer would plead guilty to stealing $125,000 from the state party, earning an eighteen-month prison sentence—and ample reason to doubt his claims.

Nonetheless, the strategists on Rubio's 2010 campaign became convinced that Crist and his cohorts were actively waging a whisper campaign to get the mistress rumors out—not just in Florida, but in DC, too, where they hoped to sow doubts among national party elites and opinion makers. Rubio's team was especially irked by Joe Scarborough, a former Republican congressman from Florida who now co-hosted *Morning Joe,* the MSNBC political chat show that all of official Washington watched from their breakfast nooks and elliptical machines each morning. Scarborough, who remained plugged in to

Tallahassee politics, frequently observed on air that Rubio was relatively un-vetted—and the candidate's aides began to strongly suspect that Crist was spinning the cable host off the record in hopes of pumping gossip into the DC bloodstream.

"Crist would get on the phone late at night with his old buddy Joe Scarborough and feed him all this stuff," one Rubio adviser later told me. "And then Scarborough would go on TV and say, 'I don't know about this Rubio guy. My sources in Florida say there's more coming on him'...It pissed me off." (Scarborough called these suspicions "completely ridiculous," and told me his analysis of the campaign at the time was rooted in conversations with a wide range of Florida politicos. Crist, he said, "was not a source.")

The affair rumors never managed to bubble up into the mainstream press in 2010, and even after Crist left the Republican Party to run as an Independent—turning the race into a three-way showdown—Rubio emerged victorious. On election night, the young senator-elect found himself watching from the edge of the courtyard in Miami's Biltmore Hotel while Jeb Bush stood on a palm-flanked stage singing Rubio's praises in front of an ecstatic crowd of Florida conservatives and scores of reporters.

"Bushes get emotional, so I'm gonna try my hardest..." Jeb said, appearing to choke back tears. "My wife told me, 'Don't cry, don't cry.' But Marco Rubio makes me cry for joy!"

As the euphoria of the win washed over Rubio, he was able for just a moment to stand still and enjoy the feeling. But the serenity would be fleeting. Rubio was headed to Washington now—and the whisper campaign against him was just getting started.

Two years later, when Rubio emerged as the most buzzed-about prospect in the 2012 Republican veepstakes, the attention placed a fresh target on his back, and journalists scrambled to find new angles on the young freshman senator. The *Washington Post* struck first with a report revealing that, contrary to Rubio's claims, his "exile" parents had actually first arrived in the United States before Fidel Castro ever took power in Cuba. A few months later, I reported at BuzzFeed that Rubio had been baptized Mormon as a child, a biographical detail that he had never mentioned before—and one that prompted many pundits to question whether Mitt Romney could conceivably tap a running mate who shared his politically tricky religious background. The new revelations served to rev up the DC rumor mill, and soon the "zipper problem" rumors were resurfacing in the gossip among politicos. Taking note of the chatter, conservative columnist Marc Thiessen wrote, vaguely, that a "malevolent oracle is at work in Washington... seeking to undermine the ascent of a rising GOP star" by "suggesting that Rubio may look good on paper, but he cannot 'pass vet' for the vice presidential nomination." Of course, no one in the staid, starchy DC press corps was willing to explicitly lay out the rumors dogging Rubio—but they gestured toward them all the time with broad suggestions that "another shoe" (a stiletto, perhaps?) was still waiting to drop on the Floridian.

In March 2012, Rubio charged Sullivan with the task of running his PAC, Reclaim America. Practically speaking, the strategist's job was to lay the political groundwork for Rubio's next move, positioning him for either a spot on the 2012 ticket or a future presidential bid of his own. Sullivan knew immediately what his first priority would be: putting an end to the incessant drip-drip of damning intel on Rubio, and figuring out *exactly* what skeletons might still be lodged in his closet.

To do the job, he sought out a Sacramento-based firm named MB Public Affairs, known in campaign circles for its "political vulnerability research" and tight-lipped discretion. Sullivan pulled more than $40,000 out of the PAC's bank account to cover the company's fee, but before setting the researchers loose, Rubio's top aides had a frank talk with the senator. They warned that the process they were about to undertake would be about as invasive and unpleasant as a prostate exam—but just as necessary to his political health. Rubio concurred. Though the senator had taken issue with the way the *Post* handled the story about his parents, the truth was that the paper's findings had genuinely surprised him: he had never heard the full story from his mom and dad. He realized now just how much damage could be wrought by a single, seemingly benign secret—even one that wasn't his own.

The political rectal probe started right away, with the firm's researchers eventually digging through Rubio's messy personal finances and rounding up every piece of paper that had passed through his office in Tallahassee. Field operatives fanned out across the country, descending on the tiny Missouri town where his now-defunct former college once stood, and showing up on distant relatives' doorsteps, from Miami to Las Vegas. Their mission was to dig up any and all dirt that political opponents might try to use against Rubio—especially anything likely to turn up in the vice presidential vetting process. That included quietly dispatching a private investigator to Florida to fully suss the extent of the infidelity rumors.

By now the senator's longest-serving aides had an encyclopedic knowledge of their boss's rumored dalliances, flings, and affairs— and though most of the stories contained all the verisimilitude of *Fifty Shades of Grey* fan fiction, the aides knew that a couple of rumors were particularly persistent in political circles. One dealt with a Tallahassee politico who had supposedly been impregnated by Rubio, and then went on to have an abortion. Reporters in Florida had attempted to run the story down over the years, and none had succeeded. But when Rubio's credit card statements were leaked, they included references to multiple airline tickets purchased on her behalf, and even though she had worked with the then-Speaker on matters that included out-of-state travel together, liberal blogs were buzzing with specula-tion that he had raided GOP coffers to finance an alleged rendezvous with his paramour. Another, even more pervasive rumor on their radar held that Rubio was hiding a secret second family somewhere, and sending regular cash installments to support them (and keep them quiet). The details of this story varied substantially from one telling to another: sometimes the mother was a former Dolphins cheerleader; other times she wasn't. Sometimes there was one kid liv-ing with his mom in New York; other times there were two kids and they lived in Florida. In one version, the entire relationship had taken place before Rubio ever met his wife; in another, the love child was the result of an extramarital affair that he was now desperately trying to keep quiet.

Rubio's operatives found these stories impossible to reconcile with the devoted family man and conscientious careerist they knew and admired. But they also knew that smoke routinely preceded fire in political sex scandals, and they needed to find out for sure if there was a "bimbo eruption" looming on the horizon. Acting on explicit instructions, the research firm investigated the rumors and determined that they lacked concrete evidence, which was enough to give Rubio's advisers peace of mind. But along the way, the firm encountered enough dishy Miami-Dade politicos hocking titillating gossip to fill the entire newsroom of a supermarket tabloid. The firm concluded that, in many cases, the rumors were being fanned by the same South Florida Republicans who claimed to be Rubio's supporters.

And unfortunately for him, many of those Miami gossips would, come 2015, join the cutthroat ranks of the Jeb Bush juggernaut.

Marco Rubio's Rancho Mirage resurgence did not go unnoticed by Jeb's lieutenants. The rave reviews from donors began surfacing from the desert almost immediately, and they confirmed what some in Jeb's circle had already come to believe: Marquito was a threat, and he needed to be neutralized.

Despite the young senator's second tier status in most 2016 polls, they believed there was ample reason to take him seriously. The private polling data that Romney had waved in Jeb's face—rather pathetically, he'd thought at the time—contained evidence that Rubio would be perfectly poised to break out if he chose to run. He still wasn't many voters' *first* choice, but he had the personal favorability ratings of a puppy dog, and he was broadly well liked across the spectrum of primary voters. Plus, his Florida roots, fluent Spanish, and compassionate record on immigration meant that he appealed most directly to the same swath of the electorate that Jeb needed to dominate. The last thing they wanted in 2016 was a younger, handsomer, less white version of Jeb shaking hands and kissing babies on the Bushes' turf.

Rubio, it was decided, needed to go.

For this new mission, Jeb's team adopted a new code name: "Homeland security." Few of Jeb's lieutenants believed they would need to subject Rubio to the same sort of browbeating they had Romney in order to sideline him, and their commander agreed. After all, the kid's entire Florida political network—the fund-raisers, the consultants, the well-placed allies—existed only because of the magnanimity of a certain former governor. All Rubio needed was a gentle reminder of his place in the pecking order, and he would prudently get back in line to wait his turn. And so the word went out to Jeb's army of foot soldiers: Carry the message.

Over the next several weeks, Jeb's messengers rallied his vast matrix of Florida allies in an effort to lock down support in his home state. They set up conference call pep rallies with hundreds of self-proclaimed "alumni" of the Bush gubernatorial administration (including many Rubio supporters) and ginned up excitement about getting the band back together. They moved swiftly to extract endorsements from state lawmakers—wooing them over brown liquor and red meat at the exclusive Governors Club near the capitol, and then encouraging them to make their allegiances publicly known.

When the Republican Party of Florida found itself in need of an interim executive director, Jeb's supporters inside the organization made sure to install David Johnson, a reliable Bush loyalist who was not afraid to use his influential perch to voice his preferences. Speaking with a *New York Times* journalist in Tallahassee to report on how Rubio's entrance into the race could force a Sunshine State showdown, Johnson said bluntly, "I hope that is not going to happen. It's going to cause a lot of problems in the state of Florida."

Meanwhile, Jeb's ever-expanding political operation made a big show of its fund-raising supremacy, particularly in Florida. At an event hosted by his political action committee in Tallahassee, his team branded the donors like cattle, with large red stickers exclaiming "Jeb!"—and then they invited reporters into the formerly private meeting so they could *ooh* and *ahh* and tweet about the impressive herd of millionaires. And with all that cash, Jeb's team began actively buying up every worthwhile Republican consultant in the state—especially those in whom Rubio was showing an interest.

Nine hundred miles away at the Capitol Hill offices of Rubio's Reclaim America PAC, the message came through loud and clear.

Rubio's advisers had hoped to stay off Jeb's radar entirely, quietly raising money and assembling a lean and nimble staff while the juggernaut blasted away at bigger targets and boasted about its gargantuan fund-raising hauls. The loudmouth lieutenants on Jeb's finance team were already bragging to reporters that they had set a $100 million goal for the first quarter of 2015 — an astronomical sum that would shatter any and all fund-raising records if achieved. By contrast, when Rubio had assembled his top donors in Miami Beach at the end of January, his advisers explicitly asked that they resist, for now, any urge to hype their contributions in the media.

"Don't try to steal Jeb's thunder," one Rubio adviser instructed them. "It's like a pendulum. Let them pound their chest and build themselves up, and when they don't hit their goal, it's gonna come crashing back [in] the other direction." In the meantime, they would go about their business without Jeb's interference, and when the fund-raising totals were made public in April, Rubio's haul would far exceed the low expectations.

But it was not to be. The Bush brigade had Florida on full, threat-level-red lockdown, and with the exception of a few loyal backers, Rubio wasn't getting anywhere in his home state. His triumph at the Koch summit had created meaningful buzz in donor circles, but as he hustled around the country in search of money, he knew meeting his goal would be an uphill battle.

Rubio soon found that one of his most effective selling points with donors was his 2013 foray into the immigration debate. While the experience was still a black mark on his transcript as far as conservative activists were concerned, the wealthy contributors who made up the GOP's business wing overwhelmingly supported more lenient immigration laws, for reasons both ideological and financial. In private meetings, Rubio often won donors' praise and admiration by showing off his battle scars from the immigration fight. In public, of course, he continued to stay far away from the issue — but his advisers were increasingly optimistic that conservative voters would eventually absolve him of his legislative transgression. Sullivan had been using his "redneck" friends back home in South Carolina as a sounding board on the issue, and they generally chalked up Rubio's lapse in judgment to good intentions and a sense of ethnic solidarity. As Sullivan put it to his one of his colleagues, "They say, 'Look, immigration was his one problem, and he did it because he was brown, so he gets a pass.'" In the meantime, the Rubio camp was happy to cash the checks.

In March, they bagged their first whale in the fund-raising hunt. Billionaire Miami auto dealer Norman Braman committed to spend as much as $10 million to get Rubio elected president if he ran, a coup that was promptly leaked to the press. "I don't pay any attention to that other distinguished Floridian," Braman told the *Washington Post* when the paper called. "I respect Jeb Bush, but I think we need someone who represents the next generation."

But even as Rubio's team grew increasingly confident that they would surpass their fund-raising goal, they began to notice a curious pattern among the Republican donors who were turning them down. Many of them seemed to like Rubio's ideas and message, but when they explained their doubts about his 2016 prospects, they often used the same vague, coded language: concerns about the wealth of "oppo" that could drag him down, or the "talk coming out of Talla-hassee," or the importance of nominating a "fully vetted" candidate. This, of course, was nothing new for Rubio—he had been trailed by such innuendo in the political class for years. But it seemed oddly top of mind all of a sudden in certain quarters of the GOP money world.

Eventually, word got back to the senator's camp that Jeb's close allies in Florida were working to revive the "zipper problem" meme in a last-ditch effort to freeze Rubio out of the race; they were circulating the rumors anew among donors and politicos and cautioning them to exercise due diligence before signing on with his campaign. From the scraps of intel Rubio's team was getting from donors, it was difficult to tell how widespread or organized the whisper campaign might be, but some on Rubio's staff believed they'd identified at least two of the culprits. The first was Ann Herberger, a Miami-based political fund-raiser now on Jeb's payroll whom Rubio had axed from his Senate campaign for failing to bring in donors. "Marco fired her and now she's bitter," a Rubio strategist told me.

The second culprit they'd identified was Ana Navarro. Few people inspired more acrimony among Rubio's aides these days than the First Lady of the Biltmore, who they regarded as a flighty and spiteful socialite masquerading as a political strategist for TV. They resented how she had allowed reporters to quote her as a "confidante" or "adviser" to Rubio for years, only to bolt to Jeb the second he decided to run for president. They now regularly heard about her dissing Rubio to the important power brokers and politicos who filtered in and out of her boyfriend's hotel, and at least one of the senator's advisers was convinced that she was fanning the infidelity rumors. "That woman couldn't say nice things about her mother," said the adviser. "She's just gonna say acerbic things for the sake of saying them." (Both Herberger and Navarro denied spreading rumors about Rubio.)

Meanwhile, in a series of off-the-record conversations, Jeb's "messengers" tried to convince a number of influential figures in political media that they had the goods on Rubio. Among these was Joe Scarborough, who by now counted himself skeptical whenever somebody told him Rubio still had an explosive career-ending secret lurking in his past. "Everybody who runs against him says he has girlfriends, or financial problems. They throw a lot of shit at the wall," Scarborough told me. "It's the same thing from the Jeb Bush camp. They keep telling me, 'Oh, we've got the thing that's going to take him down.' But nobody's ever produced anything that we all haven't read in the *Tallahassee Democrat*."

To many in Rubio's orbit, the most maddening part of the unkillable zipper meme was not the thousands of dollars they'd already spent trying to debunk it, or even the fact that Jeb's people seemed so dead set against a competitive primary that they'd resorted to shameless gossip-mongering: it was the double standard at work. After all, Jeb had faced his own rumors of adultery in his day. In one of the more enduringly bizarre episodes of his governorship, a reporter had confronted him at a bill-signing ceremony about rumors that he was having an affair with a former model who had worked closely with his administration. Jeb had indignantly, and emotionally, denied the "hurtful" gossip, but the incident gave a *Vanity Fair* writer who profiled him shortly thereafter license to detail the other unsubstantiated Jeb rumors swirling around Tallahassee. And yet no one in the GOP establishment seemed to be wringing their hands over *Jeb's* "zipper problem."

Some of Rubio's advisers came to believe that racial stereotypes were part of what made the speculation so persistent. "He's Cuban and he's from Miami, so of *course* he has mistresses," Sullivan once grumbled sarcastically to a colleague.

Still, most in the Rubio camp had trouble believing that Jeb would personally green-light such a brazen campaign of character assassination against someone who he had, just four years earlier, joyously introduced to the world while choking back tears (or at least pretending to). But one of the privileges of being Prince Jeb was his ability to give an order and then step back in blissful ignorance as a team of duty-bound lieutenants plotted, and strategized, and worked out all the gritty details that entailed "carrying the message."

As for Rubio, he found himself back where he always ended up: restless, and fidgeting, and bouncing on the balls of his feet as he impatiently waited for the bang of the starting gun. Maybe it really was crazy to give up his Senate seat and risk his whole career on an underdog bid against the Jeb Bush juggernaut. But he had only gotten this far on the power of perpetual forward motion. And he wasn't going to stop moving now.

Chapter Twenty-Two

The Crusade

Standing at the center of the vast Louisiana State basketball arena, Bobby Jindal gazed out at the thousands of evangelicals who had gathered for his January 2015 prayer rally, and he began to tell a story he was now an expert at recounting: the dramatic tale of his conversion to Christianity. He paced the stage like a practiced megachurch preacher, pouring his personal journey of faith into the headset mic and brandishing a brown leather Bible above his head for moments of emphasis.

He didn't tell the *whole* story, of course. The late-night exorcism didn't come up, and there was no mention of Opus Dei sparking a controversial wave of Catholic fervor at Brown. But this version of the story was not intended to be footnoted and fact-checked; it was devotional in nature—meant to inspire and motivate and speak to the soul. And Jindal was nailing it.

The Christians in the crowd leapt to their feet repeatedly throughout his sermon, lifting their hands to the heavens and cheering in ecstasy. And when he finished his story, he pleaded with them to pray for America and her president.

"We can't just elect a candidate to fix what ails our country," Jindal told them. "We can't just pass a law and fix what ails our country. We need a spiritual revival to fix what ails our country!"

Back in 2003, Jindal had not yet fully discovered the potent political power of his conversion story. He was thirty-two years old and staring down the first true defeat of his life. His entrance into the Louisiana gubernatorial race earlier that year had been audacious—he could admit that much—and his unlikely surge in the polls, enabling him to emerge as the Republican candidate in the runoff, counted as a remarkable political achievement for someone so young and electorally inexperienced. But Jindal wanted more—he felt *called* to more. He had prayed and pondered and talked it over endlessly with political aides and spiritual advisers, and he felt quite sure he was destined for the governorship. He was having trouble, however, convincing the voters.

More precisely, he was failing to connect with the white, conservative, Christian men—affectionately termed "bubbas"—in Louisiana's rural parishes. These voters had supported a long line of gubernatorial good ol' boys over the course of the Bayou State's political history, and many of them viewed the upcoming November election as a choice between Kathleen Blanco, a well-known lieutenant governor with a record as a conservative Democrat, and, well...the brown-skinned fella.

Jindal had spent years indignantly defending his home state against allegations of racism from the northern Yankee elites with whom he often traveled, insisting that he had never encountered such prejudices while growing up in Baton Rouge. Even now, as pundits speculated about how his ethnicity might hold him back in the election—noting that only twelve years earlier, a former grand wizard of the Ku Klux Klan had captured a majority of the state's white vote—Jindal refused to entertain the notion. Whenever a reporter asked him about how the racial dynamic might sway the race, he insisted, "The voters of Louisiana are going to vote for the best candidate. It doesn't matter whether they are black, white, red, or blue. We are all red, white, and blue. We are all Americans!"

And yet.

Jindal's campaign team always knew his ethnicity might be a problem. And sure enough, the campaign's internal research showed that the bubbas tended to view Jindal as a suspicious, unfamiliar outsider who should be treated with skepticism. No matter how hard Jindal campaigned, nothing—not his glittering academic pedigree, or his record at the helm of the state's higher education system, or his recent post in George W. Bush's cabinet, or his eighteen-point economic plan, or the Southern drawl he had mysteriously picked up in between his last C-SPAN appearance in Washington and his first stump speech in Louisiana—could change that.

Which is why the unexpected phone call Jindal received one morning at his campaign headquarters seemed at least a little bit like divine providence.

"Bobby? It's Todd Hinkie!"

Jindal hadn't spoken to his youth pastor since he walked out of The Chapel on the Campus as a teenager fifteen years earlier. Hinkie had learned of his spiritual protégé's political career when he saw news of the campaign on TV. "How the heck are you running for governor of Louisiana?" he cheerfully demanded.

The two men spent some time on the phone catching up. Hinkie, who now lived in Texas, talked about life as a full-time minister, and Jindal briefly recounted his conversion to Catholicism and his meteoric rise in politics—including a lament that he was having trouble convincing that state's conservative Christian voters that he was one of them. Eventually, they wished each other well, promised to stay in touch, and hung up.

But over the next couple of days, Hinkie couldn't get the campaign off his mind. As the pastor who had introduced Jindal to the Bible, he was better acquainted than anyone with the sincerity of the candidate's faith, and it bothered him that voters seemed to think it was an act. Wondering if there was some way he could help, he called up Timmy Teepell, an old friend from his Baton Rouge days.

Teepell had grown up attending the youth group Hinkie led, and was now working at the Republican National Committee, in Washington. The two had kept in touch over the years, and Hinkie thought Teepell might have some insight into the governor's race. As it turned out, Teepell had actually interviewed to be Jindal's campaign manager. (Though he didn't know the candidate personally, they had many mutual friends. In fact, Teepell's mother had helped organize the church musical that first piqued Jindal's interest in Christianity.) Teepell didn't end up getting the gig on the Jindal campaign, but now his old youth group leader was on the phone asking for his help—and he seemed pretty worked up about getting this guy elected.

"I know his faith is real. I know it. But Bobby told me, according to the polls, [that] the Christians in Louisiana aren't getting it. They don't understand that he's their man," Hinkie testified. "How could I help him?"

Teepell said he'd think and pray on it, and they hung up.

A couple of days later, inspiration struck. Teepell called Hinkie back with an idea: why not turn Jindal's conversion into an Internet chain letter?

"I think you ought to just write the story [of his conversion] down and email it to every Christian you know in Louisiana," Teepell proposed. "Tell them to forward it and say how they know you, like, 'Hey, this is my kid's youth pastor, look what he says about this guy running for governor.' Send." Teepell acknowledged that, in the grand tradition of AOL-era, copy-tweak-and-paste chain emails, "by the time it's forwarded five or six times, it'll be urban myth. But by then you'll have the whole state of Louisiana."

So Hinkie went to work typing up the whole story—from Jindal's visceral reaction to *The Jesus Film* all those years ago, to his insatiable appetite for reading assignments in the Bible, to his climactic teenage conversion. After getting approval from the campaign and sending the story to an English teacher he knew for proofreading, Hinkie blasted it out to his network of Louisiana Christians, and said a quiet prayer that his testimony might have some effect.

The response was overwhelming. The email went viral almost instantaneously, spreading like holy fire across Louisiana, leaping over borders into inboxes in Texas and Mississippi, and setting Bible studies and Rotary Club meetings ablaze with talk of this brave young man who had found the Lord and was now working to become governor.

"My voice mail was completely full. I had emails coming in from everywhere," Hinkie recalled. "I had people coming up to me at church in Texas and saying, 'My mother-in-law in Shreveport got your email,' and 'If I get your stinkin' email one more time...'"

Jindal was seeing results as well. The spread of the Hinkie email corresponded with an eleventh-hour push by the Jindal campaign to get the bubbas on board, and their efforts seemed to be paying off. Internal polling showed conservative Christians and rural voters coming around to Jindal the more they heard about his faith and his pure-right positions on social issues.

"Todd, it worked!" the candidate told Hinkie as the race tightened. "My numbers are shooting up, and it's all because of the Christian voters. They're getting it!" Hinkie was quick to credit Teepell—the operative Jindal had passed up to run his campaign—for the idea.

As the too-close-to-call election came to a conclusion, Jindal was consumed with the confidence of the foreordained. "Bubbas for Bobby" bumper stickers were sprouting up across the state. He had a narrow lead in the polls, and he felt the momentum at his back. Everything was coming together just as he knew it would. Destiny was unfolding.

But then the polls closed—and the final tally proved stubbornly resistant to destiny. Jindal came up just shy of victory, winning 48 percent of the vote, compared with Kathleen Blanco's 52 percent. Watching from a hotel suite as the returns came in, Jindal was crushed—not just because he had lost a tight race, but because he felt God's will had somehow been thwarted.

He would later tell Hinkie that the hardest part of that night wasn't going down to the ballroom full of cameras and conceding the election to Blanco; it was kneeling down with his wife, Supriya, just before his public concession speech and "conceding the election to the Lord."

"I don't get it," Jindal told God in his election night prayer. "I don't understand. But I trust you."

A few days later, when the dust had settled, Jindal headed to the woods for a personal retreat, bringing along a Bible, an empty journal, and a copy of Rick Warren's devotional self-help book *The Purpose Driven Life*. He needed time to process the loss and figure out what God wanted him to do next.

When Jindal returned, he knew exactly what he needed to do. First he called up Teepell and asked him to run his campaign for the U.S. House of Representatives. Next he went to work scheduling appearances at every church in rural Louisiana that would take him. He thought the good Christians in his state might like to hear him give fervent, passionate testimony about how he came to accept Jesus as his personal savior.

A few feet outside the arena where Jindal and his spiritual warriors had gathered for the 2015 rally, protesters were calling the event's sponsors a "hate group" and demanding that the gay-haters leave their school. But within, Jindal had captivated his audience, telling them they were reliving the great rallies of evangelical legend Billy Graham, who used to assemble tens of thousands of believers for events like this one, including at this very school in 1970. Graham's campaign for a widespread spiritual revival in America had preceded a grassroots political movement of Christian conservatives—christened the Moral Majority by Jerry Falwell—that went on to serve as the backbone of the Republican Party for decades.

Times had changed since the days of Graham and Falwell. Even in the decade that had passed since Jindal's first gubernatorial bid, the influence of the religious Right within the GOP had actually declined dramatically. Though the movement remained a potent force in sections of the South and Midwest, its numbers were diminished and its agenda was more unpopular than ever.

And yet as the 2016 race neared, a curious phenomenon began to manifest itself in the Republican presidential field. One after another, candidates emerged to deliver pulpit-pounding sermons about morality, and family values, and preserving America's Christian heritage— and soon there were no fewer than half a dozen conservative contenders preaching directly to the same shrinking choir.

Typically, in a national GOP primary there would be one or two candidates who ran explicitly as religious culture warriors—and they almost never lasted far beyond Iowa. Even at the height of the Moral Majority's influence, the Republican Party had nominated Ronald Reagan—a Hollywood-trained governor who was about as overtly godless as a national politician could get in the eighties. (Reagan admitted in a debate during his reelection bid that he hadn't attended church once during his first term in the White House.)

But the unique dynamics of the 2016 cycle had helped to create a stampede of conservative Christians. With the advance of gay rights—and the insistence of the party's moderate establishment that they evolve with the rest of the country—the denizens of the religious Right had come to feel increasingly estranged, and yearned for a standard-bearer who unapologetically spoke to their issues. Meanwhile, for those candidates looking to carve out a niche in an uncommonly crowded field, the evangelical vote was an obvious choice. They held tremendous sway in the almighty Iowa caucuses, and a dark horse who didn't have millionaires on his speed dial could still have a shot at victory there if he managed to rally the believers.

And so 2015 saw a surge of culture warriors charging into the fray, each with his own slightly altered spin on social conservatism.

There was Rick Santorum, the former Pennsylvania senator who had made his name as a pro-life, antigay crusader and was now trying to reinvent his social conservatism in a way that supported a "pro-family" economic agenda. He wrote a book titled *Blue Collar Conservatives* and toured the country talking about turning the GOP into "the party of the worker."

Ted Cruz, meanwhile, was tailoring his pitch to Christians with his characteristically high-octane theatrics. In the summer of 2014, Houston's first openly gay mayor, Annise Parker, had entangled herself in a battle over antidiscrimination legislation that conservative churches opposed on the grounds that it might coerce them into letting transgender men into women's bathrooms. The pitched legal battle culminated in a wide-ranging set of subpoenas from the mayor's legal team that demanded the pastors turn over the texts of all sermons they had delivered in relation to the dispute—a controversial maneuver that immediately earned the ire of conservative Christians across the country. Cruz saw an opportunity.

The Texas senator dove into the fray, calling the mayor's behavior "shocking and shameful," "un-American," and an "assault against religious liberty." He linked arms with conservative leaders like Glenn Beck, Erick Erickson, and Mike Huckabee, and urged patriots everywhere to ship their Bibles and other religious books to the Houston mayor's office. By the end of October, she had received more than a thousand Bibles, and Cruz was receiving accolades from the religious Right. But the debate over religious freedom laws continued to rage, sharply polarizing Americans and pigeonholing Republicans who endorsed them as conservative culture warriors.

In January 2015, Huckabee left his Fox News show to officially explore a presidential bid of his own. Seven years earlier, in 2008, his campaign had unexpectedly caught fire as conservative Christians rallied to his underdog candidacy with the fervor of the anointed, consumed with the need to save their party and country from the twin evils of Mitt Romney's Mormonism and John McCain's moderation. Ever since then, Huckabee had earned a nice living as a pundit preaching Christian values, and some wondered whether his 2016 waters testing was simply an effort to widen his audience with national buzz. But his rhetoric didn't go over as well with the rest of the country. In one episode, he tried picking a fight with Beyoncé, calling her music "obnoxious and toxic mental poison" and casting her husband, Jay-Z, as a "pimp" who was "exploiting his wife as a sex object." As it turned out, the onetime minister had somewhat overestimated the number of Americans scandalized by the beloved diva's dance moves, and while Huckabee became a laughingstock in the media, many in his own party quietly cringed.

As Rick Perry tried to stoke excitement for a 2016 campaign of his own, the former Texas governor painted his Christian conservatism as part of a general Lone Star State lifestyle he believed would appeal to the party's national base. In the spring of 2014, he traveled to the historic waters of Little Rocky Creek in Washington County, Texas, where Sam Houston, the first president of the Republic of Texas, had been baptized 160 years before. Next to the fields of blooming pink and yellow wildflowers, and surrounded by a small group of friends and family, Perry immersed himself in the waters to renew his baptism. After drying off, he visited the local church and played a hymn on the organ. With his faith revived, he spent much of the next year refining his speeches in Iowa and talking about Christian values.

But the spiritually reborn governor still fumbled when he tried to explain how his religious views on LGBT issues fit in a modern society where the fast-gathering consensus held that gays deserved all the same rights that straight people enjoyed. During a speech in San Francisco, Perry leaned on a common analogy that had once been considered progressive in conservative Christian circles. He said he didn't believe homosexuality was something an individual chose— but that certain sinful proclivities, such as alcoholism, had always been inborn and that God still expected his children to resist such temptations.

The comments drew condemnation and denouncement from all quarters, including from moderates in his own party, and he was forced to begin backpedaling immediately. "I readily admit it," he said. "I stepped right in it."

By the time Bobby Jindal convened his prayer rally in early 2015, his public persona had transformed considerably from that of the uber-bright, wonkish wunderkind who had first appeared on the national stage seven years earlier. Desperate to break out from the GOP's growing pack of presidential contenders—and resigned to the belief that his post-2012 "stupid party" critique was a political dud—Jindal had spent the past two years appealing to the conservative grass roots, as a Christian culture warrior and small-government absolutist. He had taken to saying increasingly inflammatory things that seemed aimed at getting himself booked on TV. He railed against the "radical Left" every time a microphone was within spitting or sputtering distance, and made assertions that sometimes seemed rooted more firmly in right-wing rumor than reality. He repeatedly warned, for example, that Western countries like Great Britain were carving out so-called "no-go zones," where Muslim immigrants enforced orthodox religious laws on all who entered their neighborhoods—a claim strongly refuted by foreign officials and experts.

To those Washington pundits and reporters who had first been introduced to Jindal as the "hall-monitoring, library-inhabiting, science fair–winning class president" described in the *Washington Post* in 2009, Jindal's new act seemed like the worst, most shameless kind of pandering: a Rhodes Scholar reduced to a "dumbed-down" self-parody dying to get conservatives to like him. But among the intellectual compromises Jindal had made on the road to 2016, his full-throated defense of religious freedom wasn't one of them. Though his *Duck Dynasty* foray was often cited by critics accusing him of demagoguery—and, indeed, Jindal had been fully aware of the potential political upsides at the time—he was, at his core, a man of deep faith, whose weird and extraordinary spiritual journey filled him with fervor for the importance of religion's role in America. This would become a central theme of the long-shot presidential campaign Jindal launched later that year. And he took comfort in knowing that even if he never did manage to catch fire in 2016, at least in this one instance—on this one issue—he could say that he truly and fully believed every word he was saying.

Chapter Twenty-Three

Donnybrook in Des Moines

The same weekend Bobby Jindal was rallying believers in Baton Rouge, a crush of conservative activists, political reporters, and presidential wannabes was descending on an antique theater in Des Moines for the Iowa Freedom Summit, a Republican cattle call that had been widely hyped as "the unofficial kickoff of 2016."

Despite Jeb Bush's best efforts to clear the primary field, the summit's sprawling list of scheduled speakers included nearly a dozen likely candidates who were there to audition for the presidency—a sign that the coming primaries were destined to devolve into an out-and-out free-for-all unlike anything the GOP had seen in decades. The party's cast of presidential contenders was shaping up to be the largest in a hundred years, and no single establishment juggernaut— no matter how big, well funded, or ruthless—would be able to pre-empt the chaos. (Jeb, though not yet willing to admit defeat in his shock-and-awe mission, had decided to skip the event.)

With the Republican Party tumbling wildly toward an election year donnybrook of epic proportions, the contenders had converged in Des Moines for twenty-four hours, ready to start the brawl. All they were waiting for now was the first punch to get thrown.

The night before the summit's Saturday morning kickoff, Carly Fiorina arrived at the mezzanine of the downtown Des Moines Marriott for her last in a long series of interviews that day. In the lobby below, off duty reporters were plying off-the-record politicos with liquor and pumping them for campaign gossip. In the suites above, soon-to-be candidates were rehearsing and revising their speeches. And here in a quiet enclave near the elevator bank, Fiorina was perched in a stiff upholstered chair doing everything in her power to dodge my questions about Sarah Palin.

Fiorina had spent the day building ground-level buzz in Iowa as she toured the state giving speeches and interviews that highlighted her status as the sole woman in the GOP's prospective presidential field. It seemed to be resonating: turnout at the events had been better than she expected, and her aides were fielding a steady trickle of phone calls from curious reporters.

And yet it was obvious almost as soon as we sat down that Fiorina had no interest in talking about the most famous mama grizzly in the conservative movement, whom she had gone to bat for in 2008. Every time I mentioned Palin's name, Fiorina shuffled into a little rhetorical tap dance as she tried to remain polite and vaguely upbeat about Sarah from Alaska without inviting comparisons to her.

Asked whether Palin's rise had been a net positive or negative for conservative women, Fiorina said, "It's always good when women play," and then, "Every game is better when everybody gets to play."

Asked whether she still believed that the early criticism of Palin had been motivated by sexism, she said she did, but then quickly changed the subject. "Let me give you a more recent example of this."

The example she gave had to do with Joni Ernst (or, as candidate Fiorina identified her, "the junior senator from the *great state* of Iowa"). Ernst had recently given the Republican response to the 2015 State of the Union, after which the pro-choice women's group EMILY's List put out a statement referring to her as "window dressing" for the GOP.

"This is a soldier, a mother, a sitting U.S. senator, and they're calling her *window dressing?*" said Fiorina indignantly. "Of course they're sexist!"

I mentioned that after Ernst's address, I had seen a number of liberals compare the new senator almost reflexively with Palin, the implicit suggestion being that all Republican women were the same.

"Well, it's more than that," Fiorina responded. "It's, all conservative women must be stupid."

She seemed to realize right away that she had made a mistake because she immediately flashed a taut smile and—in a distinctly non-Palinian show of restraint—stopped talking.

Just after 11 p.m. that same night, a few hours after Fiorina had retired to her room, Sarah Palin herself burst into the Marriott lobby, radiating enough high-wattage celebrity charisma to make her also-notable companions for the evening—Newt and Callista Gingrich, Congressman Steve King, and Citizens United president David Bossie—seem like a bag-carrying entourage. Palin was slated for a prime speaking slot at the summit the next day, and she was toting a binder with her that contained a draft of her planned remarks.

A scrum of buzzed and drunk political reporters crowded around to snap Instagram photos while Palin—all big hair, big glasses, and big personality—soaked up the attention with the practiced nonchalance of an experienced paparazzi fuss object.

Eventually, one of the reporters got around to asking Palin the same question reporters had been asking her for the past seven years: Are you thinking of running for president?

And Palin, with no reason to discontinue the charade, gave the same answer she had been giving for the past seven years: "You can absolutely say I am seriously interested."

At that, she disappeared into an elevator while journalists scrambled to tweet the breaking news and fire off emails to their East Coast editors. By midnight, the "seriously interested" headline was on the *Washington Post*'s home page, and before long it was splashed across the top of the Drudge Report.

Asked the next morning what she thought of the big Palin news, Fiorina shrugged and then offered a bit coldly, "I mean, if she wants to run she should run."

Fiorina's lack of enthusiasm for Palin-mentum wasn't difficult to grok. She was preparing to embark on a presidential campaign premised on the same shrewd brand of "conservative feminism" that

Palin had pioneered. Fiorina knew she had little chance of breaking through as long as Palin was seen as a serious threat to enter the race.

That afternoon, Fiorina strode onstage in the elegantly ornate theater at Des Moines's historic Hoyt Sherman Place to deliver her speech. It was largely made up of the same rhetoric she had been road testing over the past year: she bashed Hillary Clinton, accused Democrats of sexism, and defended pro-life women. As usual, it went over well with the conservative audience—but the full extent of Fiorina's Freedom Summit triumph didn't become clear until shortly after she left the stage and Palin sashayed on to take her place.

The past twelve hours of media tongue wagging over Palin's stated presidential ambitions had heightened the anticipation surrounding her appearance, and she was greeted with wild applause by the 1,200 grassroots Iowans in attendance. Once she started talking, however, the excitement quickly gave way to confusion. Palin rambled and ranted through an extended stream of consciousness tour of personal feuds, petty grievances, and puzzling polemics. If there was something more compelling (or comprehensible) in her notes, she had apparently decided to ignore them. Instead, she exhaustively chronicled minor injustices inflicted upon her by the media, punctuating the stories with jarring outbursts—like "Screw the Left in Hollywood!"—that startled some of the mild-mannered churchgoers who were watching. Even for a political provocateur with a long blooper reel of cringe-inducing shark-jump moments, the performance was bad enough to cause many of Palin's last remaining defenders in the Republican Party to give up and change the channel for good.

By the time Palin exited stage right at around the thirty-five-minute mark, the withering reviews from Republicans were already pouring in. "Bizarro," ruled one conservative columnist. "Barely coherent," said another. Joe Scarborough expressed bafflement at how far she had fallen since her electrifying speech at the 2008 GOP convention, and declared the onstage meltdown a "tragedy." The pile-on was most vividly encapsulated in the conservative magazine of record, *National Review,* where Charles Cooke wrote that Palin's "one-woman variety show" in Des Moines was "the foreordained culmination of a slow and unseemly descent into farce," and that it should "disqualify her from any role in the GOP going forward." The root problem, he argued, was that Palin "isn't really trying to change politics; she's trying to *be* politics."

But to some extent, that had always been true of Palin. What originally made her a Republican superstar was her skill at brandishing her own gender and identity as weapons of culture war; now those same instincts were being cited as cause for excommunication from her party.

While Palin's implosion gave Fiorina the opening she needed in 2016, it also provided her with a cautionary tale. In the coming months, Fiorina would bring conservative audiences to their feet with galvanizing speeches about the Democrats' *real* "war on women." She would righteously call foul on interviewers—from Katie Couric to local radio hosts—who asked if she was really running for vice president. ("Would you ask a *male* candidate that question?") She would stoke outrage on the right by reciting the indignities she suffered as a Republican woman (like being asked on live TV about her menopause). And she would perform with great relish her assigned role as the party's anti-Clinton attack dog, unleashing a regular barrage of barbed one-liners and fiery criticism that male candidates could never get away with. (In one especially pointed instance, she would joke that Bill Clinton's judgment had been "clouded by hormones in the Oval Office.") To the men of the Republican establishment who had coaxed her into the race, all this would be cause for adulation. But, as Palin's downfall had illustrated, that praise could evaporate just as quickly if party elites decided she was "playing the gender card" in a way that they didn't approve of.

By the time Palin and Fiorina were shepherded away from the venue in separate vehicles on Saturday afternoon, the two women had effectively swapped places in the 2016 topography. It wouldn't be the only political tremor to rock Hoyt Sherman Place that weekend.

As Scott Walker stood backstage waiting for his cue, the even-keeled, aw-shucks governor of Wisconsin found himself experiencing an urge he typically felt only during Packers games: an impulse to shed his Midwestern manners and start shouting. During four years in the trenches of nonstop political combat in his state, he had beaten back the enemy three separate times—and now that he was here to tell his war stories, he was feeling uncommonly amped up.

Of course, the conservative activists in the audience were familiar with Walker's heroics in a general way. They had read in the papers about his pitched battle with the public sector unions. They had occasionally seen his smiling mug on Fox. They had heard his voice on talk radio. A few had crossed state lines to serve weekend tours of duty in his defense—knocking on doors, handing out flyers—when he had faced a recall election. But like most conservatives across the country, Iowa Republicans didn't have strong impressions of Walker. When pollsters asked them what they thought of the governor next door as a presidential prospect, more than 40 percent responded with a "don't know enough to answer" shrug.

Walker was determined to change that. The key to making an impression, he believed, was to fill in the broad-strokes picture his audience already had of his war in Wisconsin with the sort of bracing, gritty details that would be difficult to forget. So, when his cue came, the trim forty-seven-year-old governor walked buoyantly out onto the stage, waved at the balcony, and immediately began to recount the "darkest days" of his battle with the savage armies of the Left.

He told of menacing protesters following his elderly mother through a grocery store and hectoring her in the aisles. He quoted from death threats, including one letter addressed to him promising to "gut" his wife "like a deer," and another addressed to his wife vowing that if she didn't stop her husband, he "would be the first Wisconsin governor ever assassinated," and then providing details about where their children went to school. He recounted thousands of demonstrators camping outside his family's suburban home, and people targeting his teenage sons on Facebook.

By the time he finished the brief, searing account, the audience was captivated, and Walker was charged with adrenaline.

"Time and time again, the protesters were trying to intimidate us," he said, his voice rising. "But you know what? All they did was remind me how important it was to stand up for the people of my state. They reminded me to focus on why I ran for governor in the first place."

It wasn't the most sparkling oratory, but it did the trick: the audience erupted in unbridled applause. For the next twenty minutes, Walker energetically touted the "go big and go bold" agenda he had enacted, from passing controversial voter ID laws to defunding Planned Parenthood. What made his story compelling was not the positions themselves, which were generally shared by every speaker at the summit that day, but that he had successfully championed them in a solidly Democratic state and still managed to win three statewide races in a row.

"MSNBC didn't much like our election victory back in June of 2012, and they didn't like it again this last fall," he boasted. "Because you know what? It wasn't just about a victory. It was about showing [that] commonsense could serve in reforms [and] can actually work, and they work in a blue state like Wisconsin."

What the conservatives in Des Moines that day saw in Walker was the possibility that they wouldn't have to choose between electability and ideology in the coming presidential contest. And that promise was enough to propel Walker to the front of the 2016 pack almost immediately after he finished speaking. Within days after the summit, the *Des Moines Register* would release a poll that showed him rocketing from single-digit obscurity to first place, and national polls quickly followed suit. Walker wouldn't officially announce his campaign for another five months, but for all intents and purposes, his bid was launched that day in Des Moines.

As the Saturday summit stretched on, the atmosphere inside Hoyt Sherman Place took on a frenzied, circus-gone-wrong quality, as if a thousand people were trapped inside a Barnum and Bailey tent where the elephants had been set loose.

Inside the theater, the high-octane sound bites being hurled from the stage all seemed to melt together as the interminable marathon of speakers marched past five hours, then six, then seven, and beyond. The lackluster ventilation system made the 150-year-old venue feel stuffy and hot, and the activists in the audience grew increasingly disheveled, punchy, and agitated as they shed sweaters and fidgeted in their seats. In the middle of a lively speech by Rick Perry—whose red-blooded macho-cowboy routine stopped just short of including a lasso and shouts of "Yee-haw!"—a dozen Latino immigration activists stood in unison and began shouting in protest from the balcony. A few overwound audience members charged the demonstrators and got within inches of their faces before guards finally intervened to stop a physical altercation. The whole episode repeated itself again when Chris Christie was speaking. At one point, a bat got into the theater, swooping back and forth from the rafters and adding to the sense that the whole summit was some sort of fever dream.

Those who wanted to escape the delirium taking hold inside the theater wandered out to the cramped halls along the building's perimeter, where Rick Santorum, Mike Huckabee, and a slew of other candidates-in-waiting hocked their books, signed their autographs, and elbowed (in some cases literally) their way through the crowd. The mad hot chaos of the coming Republican primaries was already palpable in Hoyt Sherman Place.

The mood at the scene was personified by the party's most anarchic and unpredictable figure: Donald Trump. The billionaire's aides spent the day walking the halls and passing out postcard-size photos of a young Trump shaking hands with Ronald Reagan. When his turn came to speak, he hunched confidently over the podium and drew loud cheers by musing, "The last thing we need is another Bush." He also said he was "seriously thinking" of running for president in 2016, but it was the dig at Jeb (and the audience's supportive reaction) that made headlines. When it came to Trump, the press knew better than to treat his claims about future political plans as news. After twenty-five years of the same charade, there were few people left anywhere in the political world who believed he was sincere. He was a sideshow to be gawked at, not taken seriously.

By now Trump knew this was how many in the news media and politics viewed him. But with the official start of the 2016 campaign season only months away, he was resolved to prove the jealous losers wrong.

Chapter Twenty-Four

The Promised Land

Lynchburg, Virginia

As Ted Cruz roved the arena stage at the world's largest evangelical Christian university on the morning of March 23, 2015, he implored the ten thousand patriots gathered before him to do something he had been asking of the conservative movement for the past three years: use their imaginations.

"I want to ask each of you to *imagine,*" Cruz intoned. "*Imagine* millions of courageous conservatives all across America, rising up together to say in unison, 'We demand our liberty!'"

The patriots in the audience cheered — and Cruz proceeded to spend the next twenty minutes making their imaginations run wild.

"*Imagine* abolishing the IRS..."

"*Imagine* repealing every word of Common Core..."

"*Imagine* a federal government that works to defend the sanctity of human life," and "uphold the sacrament of marriage," and "defeat radical Islamic terrorism," and "finally, finally, finally secure the borders!"

"*Imagine,*" Cruz said, "millions of people of faith all across America coming out to the polls and voting our values."

More to the point, imagine them voting for Ted Cruz.

"I believe in you," he finally told the patriots. "I believe in the power of millions of courageous conservatives rising up to reignite the promise of America. And that is why today I am announcing that I'm running for president of the United States."

With that, the Tea Party torchbearer from Texas became the first

352

Republican candidate to charge into the presidential field—officially launching the momentous 2016 Republican contest from one of the country's most storied staging grounds in the conservative culture wars.

Liberty University had immediately stood out to Cruz's aides when they were scouting locations for the announcement. It was a short three-and-a-half-hour drive from Washington, which would ensure strong turnout from the political press, and because Cruz would be speaking at a mandatory campus assembly, he was guaranteed an audience of ten thousand God-fearing, right-leaning students who risked academic—and possibly celestial—reprimands if they tried to disrupt the event. (The school's strict rules forbade unapproved demonstrations of any kind, as well as dancing, cursing, kissing, and hugging members of the opposite sex for longer than three seconds.) Drawing a supportive crowd that large was difficult for even the most galvanizing political figures, and it often required weeks of organizing and many thousands of dollars. Here Cruz was being handed the striking, made-for-TV campaign backdrop free of charge and effort.

Most important, though, the setting sent a strong signal to the religious elements of Cruz's right-wing base. Founded in 1971 by conservative Christian icon Jerry Falwell, who proudly nicknamed the school "Bible Boot Camp," Liberty was built on an unabashed mission to train and send forth battalions of born-again foot soldiers in the fight against encroaching secularism and moral perversion in America. Accordingly, many of the students were training for careers in politics, media, law, and the ministry—a campus full of mini-Cruzes. When the candidate's office had asked the university administration if they could hold the event there, the president was so thrilled that he bumped a scheduled visit from Virginia's sitting Democratic governor to clear the calendar.

As with every other stage Cruz had performed on over the years—from the small-town VFWs to the Senate floor—the candidate put on a compelling show at Liberty. He roamed the stage freely, sermonizing without notes or a teleprompter about the need for a religious revival and populist revolution in America. As a crescendo of clamorous applause reached its climax, he planted his feet, stretched out his arms, and opened his palms, letting the adoration wash over him.

To some who had gotten to know Cruz earlier in his career, the onstage display was puzzling. "He was never particularly religious as far as I knew," said one aide who worked closely with him in the Texas solicitor general's office. "I'm not even sure he went to church." To others, it was a masterful performance of a part Cruz had been carefully rehearsing for years. One Republican consultant who had worked on his 2012 Senate campaign told me the arms-out-palms-opened pose was something Cruz had picked up from watching the 1980s televangelist Jimmy Swaggart: it was meant to convey that he was "drawing spiritual energy from the crowd."

Did Cruz actually believe in this divine phenomenon? The question was beside the point. What had always mattered to Cruz was what *they* believed—the bright-eyed evangelical students and the riled-up Tea Party activists, the put-out military veterans and the Breitbart-reading birthers, and all the other patriots who felt alienated by the Washington cartel and ignored by the establishment bosses. Cruz's political power came from capturing their imaginations, convincing them their wildest dreams could come true, and then converting the uncommon fervor that followed into daring, dramatic, destiny-bending action.

Or at least phone numbers for his campaign contact list.

"If you're ready to join a grassroots army across this nation, coming together and standing for liberty," Cruz said at his speech's climactic conclusion, "I'm going to ask you to break a rule here today and to take out your cell phones, and to text the word 'constitution' to the number 33733."

A brief, confused silence fell over the arena, followed by a ripple of nervous laughter.

"Once again," Cruz reiterated. "Text 'constitution' to 33733. God's blessing has been on America from the very beginning of this nation, and I believe God isn't done with America yet."

Louisville, Kentucky

Two weeks later, more than a thousand people filed into a cavernous ballroom at the Galt House convention center in downtown Louisville to see Rand Paul kick off his presidential bid.

And they did get to see that happen, eventually—but not before first being subjected to an hour and a half of watching a determinedly diverse, painstakingly assembled parade of preachers, speakers, students, singers, lobbyists, and libertarians take turns at the podium. Each person stood beneath a large banner unveiling a new all-caps campaign slogan, designed to cater to the libertarian movement with its first line and the mainstream party with its second.

DEFEAT THE WASHINGTON MACHINE
UNLEASH THE AMERICAN DREAM

The program had been carefully planned to highlight Rand's maverick coalition-building efforts over the past couple of years, and each speaker had a story to tell about how the candidate had won him or her over. There was the doctor who had gone on a mission trip with the senator, performing eye surgery on poor children with him in Guatemala. And the college conservative who said she had never seen her liberal classmates respond so enthusiastically to a Republican politician as they did to Rand. And the local black preacher who said he was a lifelong Democrat and former Obama supporter who now considered himself an Independent, proclaiming, "I am telling every Independent it is time to run out here and run with Senator Rand Paul!"

When it finally came time to introduce the candidate himself, Kelley Paul delivered some brief, heartfelt remarks, recalling that when Rand had first approached her about his wish to run for Senate, she responded, "I can't believe you're doing this to me." Onstage, the story had an obligatory happy ending, with Kelley concluding that everything had worked out better than she possibly could have imagined, and that her family was now exhilarated by the prospect of the election. Offstage, though, the public scrutiny inherent in participating in a presidential race would continue to put strain on their family. Just weeks after her husband hit the campaign trail, their oldest son would be cited for driving under the influence. An old mug shot would resurface; another rash of headlines would follow. "That was her worst nightmare, and it happened right away," one family friend would lament to me.

But at this moment, and on this stage, there was a campaign to launch, and a Washington machine to defeat, and a libertarian takeover to execute, and a "New GOP" to build. So Kelley finished her remarks and introduced her husband. Cheers rang out from the floor and music blasted from the speakers as the smiling-and-waving candidate appeared. While Rand basked in the applause, Kelley tried to slink off the stage—but before she could get away, Rand placed two hands on her shoulders and gently twisted her back toward the audience. She stood next to him for a few seconds, doing her best impression of a campaign wife, and the moment the gravitational pull weakened, she broke away and hurried toward the backstage stairs, her smile melting away before she was out of view.

"I have a message!" Rand bellowed from the podium. "A message that is loud and clear and does not mince words. We have come to take our country back!"

As the Kentucky senator went on to deliver the speech he had been waiting to give for much of his adult life, his parents sat in the row of seats behind him on the stage, fully visible to the audience, press, and TV cameras. His mother, Carol, beamed throughout the performance, repeatedly joining the crowd to interrupt her son with supportive soccer mom applause. Ron sat quietly through the entire speech. Not smiling. Not clapping. Not even once—at least not as far as Rand's aides could tell from where they were watching on the floor.

The younger Paul's advisers would have liked the old man to show at least a *little* enthusiasm, but they also believed that the wedge between father and son could help Rand's 2016 chances. If he was going to win over the moderate elements of the Republican establishment, he couldn't have his dad showing up at campaign stops and spouting off about the gold standard, or legalizing heroin, or any of his other politically untenable positions. For the announcement event, Ron had been invited to attend but asked not to speak—and as the campaign got under way in the spring of 2015, there were no plans for the libertarian lion to join his son on the trail at all.

But the Pauls' political estrangement was not to last. In months that followed, Rand's grand vision of a diverse, broad-based coalition of Republican voters fell flat, his candidacy greeted with outright hostility by many in the GOP. (On the day he entered the race, a well-funded neoconservative group launched a million-dollar ad blitz attacking his support for the United States' nuclear negotiations with Iran as "wrong and dangerous.") As his poll numbers sank and the cast of candidates grew, Rand was forced to retreat back to the libertarian niche his father had once occupied—and by the end of the summer, Ron was ready to officially endorse his son for president. In a campaign fund-raising email sent to supporters, the elder Paul wrote, "If you want to know what I really think about my son, Rand, then don't listen to our national media... [they like] to play this little game where they pit us, or certain views, against each other. Don't fall for it. They're trying to manufacture storylines at liberty's expense." A few days later, Rand returned the affection with his own campaign fund-raising email. "Please join me in wishing my dad a very happy birthday," he wrote, linking to a digital card for Ron. "And after you add your name, please chip in a contribution of $20.16 so I can continue to spread the message of Liberty..."

Miami, Florida

When Marco Rubio and his obsessively media-conscious aides set out to plan the senator's presidential announcement, they aimed for exactly the opposite of Rand Paul's long-winded, overly indulgent marathon of videos, speeches, and tributes. As far as Terry Sullivan was concerned, these events shouldn't be about excising family demons or paving the way for the future of some academic philosophical movement. They were television commercials, plain and simple—and ones they didn't have to pay for. So, with Rubio's go-ahead, Sullivan and the rest of the campaign-in-waiting got to work on perfecting the choreography for the kickoff.

Given Rubio's otherworldly gift for oratory, they wanted to get his speech in front of the largest possible number of Republican-primary-voting eyeballs. So, naturally, they called up Fox News. The producers at the network's 6 p.m. newscast, *Special Report with Bret Baier,* said they would be interested in broadcasting the speech live. Sullivan asked how long Fox would be likely to stay on the candidate before cutting away, and the answer came back: thirteen minutes. So Rubio's speechwriters were instructed to keep it to precisely twelve (to leave time for applause).

For the location, they selected Miami's Freedom Tower, the building through which Cuban exiles were first shuffled when they arrived in the States half a century earlier. The symbolism of the setting had the potential to be truly powerful, driving home Rubio's immigrant roots and presenting him as an Obama-like embodiment of the American dream. But his advisers also knew that the power of that message would be sharply undermined if the so-called DREAMer activists who had been harassing Rubio ever since he backed away from the immigration bill in 2013 managed to infiltrate the event and interrupt it. With the stakes—and likely viewership—so high, they needed to ensure that no one got in who didn't belong there. And so a handful of low-level campaign staffers were deputized for a special project. The mission: vet every single one of the thousand or so attendees who had RSVP'd for the event.

In the weeks leading up to Rubio's announcement, his staffers pored over Facebook pages, Instagram accounts, public records, and page upon page of Google searches, looking for hints that some of the attendees might not be on the level. There weren't many hard-and-fast rules, but there was one major red flag the staffers were told to look for: attendees who weren't American citizens. In the end, the vetting mission worked. When the day of the announcement arrived, activists marched around outside the Freedom Tower, chanting, "Undocumented! Unafraid!" But inside the room, the audience of well-dressed politicos, donors, and supporters was unanimously pro-Rubio.

For all the savvy stagecraft and careful choreography, the event was a sincerely personal one for the candidate. Standing inside the Freedom Tower, he couldn't help but think of his parents. His father had died of cancer while Rubio was running for Senate, just eight weeks before the election. The candidate had done his best to be there for his dad in the end, carving out precious days from the campaign calendar to take him to the doctor and sit with him through chemotherapy treatments. But when he died, Rubio had taken only a couple of days off to bury him before returning to the trail. He knew his political success was a tremendous source of pride for his father—an immigrant who had spent his entire life juggling demanding and unexciting jobs so that his kids could have every opportunity possible. Now, thanks to those sacrifices, Rubio was here announcing his candidacy for president of the United States.

The day before Rubio's announcement, Hillary Clinton had officially declared her long-anticipated bid for the Democratic presidential nomination, and many pundits had speculated that she would overshadow the young Florida senator. But Rubio took advantage of the generational contrast with Clinton as he presented himself and his campaign as symbols of America's future. "Now, just *yesterday*, a leader from *yesterday* began a campaign for president by promising to take us back to *yesterday*," Rubio said, in a line that would be played and replayed on TV nonstop for days to come.

He paused for a moment and flashed a slight smirk, before concluding. "Yesterday is over."

Miami, Florida

As the day of his campaign kickoff pep rally approached, Jeb Bush was a man sorely lacking in pep. It had been barely six months since he started actively working toward a presidential bid—far less time than most of his fellow candidates—but already the unpleasantness of the ordeal was wearing on him. Each passing day seemed to bring with it a new indignity to endure: a frivolous photo-op, a pride-swallowing fund-raising call, yet another interminable grip-and-grin in New Hampshire where he spent more time posing for selfies with voters than he did talking about the issues he cared about. Before long, Jeb was privately complaining that his only respite from the mind-numbing monotony of the trail came when some ill-informed voter confronted him with a new Internet-fueled conspiracy theory or false piece of political propaganda that he hadn't heard before. He knew there wasn't really any point in trying to set these people straight—but sometimes he felt like it was the only workout his brain got all day. At least *some* part of this has to be intellectually stimulating, he grumbled to his aides.

As he slogged toward the summer, Jeb found it increasingly difficult to conceal his crankiness and boredom. All year, he had been telling interviewers that his decision about whether to run would ultimately come down to a personal question: "Can I do it joyfully?" But now that he was finally about to enter the race, joylessness seemed to waft off of him wherever he went. His advisers tried to perk up his performance with stylistic tips: smile more, dial back the sarcasm, add some brio to the stump. But it was no use. His problem wasn't a matter of improving aesthetics: Jeb was simply miserable most of the time.

His experience so far as a presumptive candidate had been marked by a vexing series of political setbacks and personal frustrations. Despite the initial success of his team's much-hyped shock-and-awe crusade, he had largely failed to scare off prospective rivals and seize control of the Republican field as planned. Vast swaths of the conservative movement were responding to the threat of a 2016 Bush bid with DEFCON One levels of hysteria, while the right-wing media assailed him daily for his moderate stances on immigration and education with the sort of unbridled ferocity and moral fury they typically reserved for world-historic villains like Osama bin Laden, or Harry Reid. And even as wealthy Bush family loyalists continued to stock Jeb's war chest with six-figure checks, he couldn't seem to consolidate the support of party leaders the way his brother had been able to ahead of his own presidential bid.

In April, after months of underwhelming poll numbers showed Jeb failing to live up to front-runner expectations, the *New York Times* ran an A1 story declaring his campaign "the juggernaut that wasn't."

Jeb had hoped his aggressive backstage maneuvering at the beginning of the year would help him lock down the support of the party establishment early, thus enabling him to run an optimistic, high-toned campaign by the time he officially got in the race. Now, he was glumly resigned to the likelihood that the primaries would be a long-drawn-out, violent affair, and that winning would require systematically and mercilessly mowing down every last opponent standing in his way.

To prepare for this new (and depressing) reality, Jeb ordered a last-minute shake-up of his political organization. A week before his official announcement, it was reported that David Kochel—the perennially cheerful Iowa strategist whom Jeb had poached from Mitt Romney by promising the job of campaign manager—was being shunted off to a "senior adviser" role in favor of a younger, elbow-throwing operative named Danny Diaz. When Jeb explained his decision to reporters, he touted Diaz, who was known for his proficiency in the campaign dark arts of "opposition research" (digging up dirt on opponents) and "rapid response" (churning out attack lines and talking points hour to hour), as a "grinder." This was not the campaign Jeb had dreamed of running.

The candidate's mood was marred by other irritants as well. To get in shape for the race, he had put himself on the trendy Paleo diet, swearing off the Mexican chilaquiles and enchiladas that he so loved in favor of a rigid low-carb regimen designed to replicate Stone Age eating habits. The joy-killing onslaught of unsalted almonds and grilled chicken salad helped him shed forty pounds in six months, but it left him grouchy and constantly complaining about being hungry. "Perpetually starving to death is apparently the source of losing weight," he joked at a Tallahassee fund-raiser, with just a tinge of bitterness.

He was also growing increasingly resentful of the political reporters who kept trying to bait him into bashing his brother. Jeb had expected the press to pester him with questions about George's polarizing presidential record, but from the outset of his 2016 bid he had vowed not to let the media's gotcha games make him betray his deeply felt sense of family loyalty. He was on guard against this temptation every time he convened a press gaggle or sat down for an interview, and he could sometimes feel his body tense up and his words go wobbly when the subject of his brother came up. In May, this fierce fraternal fidelity crash-landed him in a campaign quagmire when Fox News host Megyn Kelly asked him about the Iraq War during an interview. "Knowing what we know now, would you have authorized the invasion?" she inquired.

Jeb responded confidently in the affirmative, and then added feistily, "News flash to the world: if they're trying to find places where there's big space between me and my brother, this might not be one of those."

This seemingly unabashed defense of an unpopular war set off a frenzied round of bipartisan criticism. He tried backpedaling the next day, telling Sean Hannity he had "interpreted the question wrong." But when given a chance to clarify his position, he said he didn't want to engage in a "hypothetical"—a weak demurral that only intensified the outcry from pundits and critics demanding a straight answer. The furor made Jeb seethe with disdain for the media, who he suspected were fanning the flames not because they cared about his philosophy on military intervention, but because they wanted to gin up a juicy sibling feud. He refused to give them the satisfaction. Over four grueling days, he ducked and dodged and dithered on the Iraq question, fumbling through five different non-answers until finally Dubya called up Jeb and told him to knock it off.

"Stop it with this shit," the former president told his little brother. "Say whatever you have to say."

Jeb grudgingly relented, and at a campaign stop in Arizona he brought an end to the imbroglio by testily telling voters that "if we're all supposed to answer hypothetical questions" now, then fine: "I would not have gone into Iraq."

The private phone call between Dubya and Jeb never made the news, but word traveled through the Bush family's network of friends and allies, and those who knew the brothers best weren't surprised. Jeb and George had not been especially close growing up, and they differed dramatically in style and temperament. But they were both the sons of George Herbert Walker and the grandsons of Prescott— members of a family that stood, in their minds, for seriousness and guts and real-deal leadership. The Republican Party was in chaos and its presidential field was being overrun by neophytes, lightweights, and political fame-seekers who were auditioning not for the White House but for radio shows and book deals. Bush 43 didn't give a damn what his little brother said about him on the stump: what mattered was that Jebbie saved the GOP and became Bush 45.

Jeb's deeply held faith in his family and in his own innate presidential character was what gave him the strength to suffer through a campaign process that he found tedious and punishing. But it was also a source of immense consternation. Though the candidate publicly insisted he didn't expect a coronation from his party, friends and confidants who talked to him about the race often came away with the impression that he couldn't believe he wasn't far ahead in the polls.

Jeb spent the final days leading up to his campaign kickoff in Europe — hopscotching across the continent's capitals with an American press corps in tow as he met with high-level foreign dignitaries and gave speeches and interviews that showed off his grasp of international affairs. The trip had been designed with the express purpose of contrasting his confidence and depth of knowledge with the relative unease and inexperience of his Republican rivals. "We wanted to show... that he is ready to be president on day one," his spokesman Tim Miller told me. "There's no learning curve." But while Jeb's maturity and intellect came through over the course of his five-day swing through Europe, so too did his sense of abject dread at the idea of running for president. He tried to stay "joyful" and on message, telling reporters in Berlin, "I'm excited about the prospects of this," but he said it exhibiting roughly the same excitement of a person bracing for gallbladder surgery.

Meanwhile, back in Florida, Jeb's aides were hard at work prepping a campaign launch event they hoped would be so lively and fun and upbeat that it would puncture the cloud of existential gloom that was always hovering around their candidate. The advance team equipped the venue at Miami Dade College with festive flashing lights, and flanked the stage with towering signs displaying the campaign's aggressively cheerful logo: "Jeb!" This iconography dated back to Bush's gubernatorial years, but the punctuation seemed more necessary now than ever. Campaign staffers flooded the room with exclamation points — on stickers, on thunder sticks, on T-shirts and posters; some red, some white, and some upside down in celebration of the Spanish speakers in attendance. ¡Jeb!

The campaign's stagecraft was remarkably effective. By the time the event finally got under way on the afternoon of June 15th with a trim, energetic candidate bounding onto the stage — sporting a light-blue button-down shirt, a broad smile, and no necktie — he looked every bit the happy warrior he claimed to be. He told jokes, said a few lines in Spanish, and made news by setting an ambitious goal for the national economy: nineteen million new jobs and four percent growth. But the line that would make most every lede in the news reports following his speech came when he attempted to allay concerns about his dynastic entitlement.

"I know that there are good people running for president. Quite a few in fact," he said. "And not a one of us deserves the job by right of resume, party, seniority, family, or family narrative. It's nobody's turn. It's everybody's test, and it's wide open — exactly as a contest for president should be."

In truth, the contest had turned out to be more "wide open" than Jeb would have liked. But he and his advisers were confident that any anxiety his party harbored with regard to crowning another Bush would fade once they studied him alongside his opponents. Republican primary voters had a long history of flirtation with firebrands and carnival barkers, but in the end they always nominated a grown-up as their presidential standard-bearer. And when Jeb looked around the GOP these days, he felt there were precious few grown-ups to be found.

New York City

One day later in midtown Manhattan, a golden-haired reality TV star strode across a gold-hued lobby, descended majestically down a gold-framed escalator, and took his place on a stage in front of eight American flags rimmed with gold tassels and affixed to flagpoles with golden bald eagles on top. Above him hung a large banner that spelled out his campaign slogan in uppercase letters and a blunt-force font: "MAKE AMERICA GREAT AGAIN!"

Donald J. Trump had come to the most fabulous of his many world-class eponymous skyscrapers to prove once and for all that the haters in the media, and the losers in the GOP, and the cheap-suit slobs in the DC political class were wrong about him...wrong about *everything*. Yes, The Donald was about to announce his candidacy for the United States presidency — and he was going to do it with all the fanfare money could buy.

Squinting out proudly at the Trump Tower atrium packed with press and the balcony lined with cheering Trump-T-shirt wearers, the billionaire marveled, "That is some group of people! *Thousands!*...It's an honor to have everybody here. This is beyond anybody's expectations. There's been no crowd like this." He proceeded to catalog the logistical shortcomings of recent Republican campaign announcements and mock the candidates' ineptitude. "How are they going to beat ISIS?" he scoffed. "I don't think it's going to happen." But he elected not to mention the legwork that had gone into putting together this particular production.

As it had turned out, assembling a crowd of sign-waving supporters for a Donald Trump campaign rally in Manhattan was a tricky task. A few days before the event, the billionaire's team was reduced to putting out a casting call through a New York–based agency offering fifty bucks to background actors who were willing to wear Trump shirts, carry Trump posters, and cheer Trump on during his big announcement. ("We understand this is not a traditional 'background job,'" the agency noted, "but we believe acting comes in all forms and this is inclusive of that school of thought.")

When the day of the announcement arrived, Trump aides in tailored suits spent the morning on the streets enticing New York City tourists to come take in the spectacle. "Only in New York!" one of The Donald's aides was heard calling out. "Come inside and make some memories." When an older couple showed interest, the aide informed them, "Price of admission is, you have to wear a shirt."

By showtime, Trump's team had succeeded in cobbling together a crowd of a few hundred people. Some of them were actors earning paychecks, others were curious gawkers craning their necks to see a celebrity up close—but all of them were decked out in patriotic Trump swag, or holding up handmade signs that they had been given at the door. Who needed a genuine groundswell of grassroots support when you could buy the Astroturf version that looked just as good on TV?

With the stage set, Trump spent the next hour ad-libbing his way through an irresistibly compelling rant on live television that proved almost impossible to tune out or turn away from. It didn't matter that the rambling remarks had no discernible theme. Virtually every line that tumbled out of his mouth was packed with the potential to become its own miniature media controversy—ricocheting across Twitter, setting off TV news shoutfests, and creating an endless loop of visceral disagreement and emotionally charged debate.

Trump on Islamic terrorists: "They've become rich. I'm in competition with them."

Trump on China "ripping off" the United States in trade negotiations: "It's like, take the New England Patriots and Tom Brady and have them play your high school football team."

Trump on immigration: "When Mexico sends its people they're not sending their best... [they] have lots of problems, and they're bringing those problems to us. They're bringing drugs. They're bringing crime. They're rapists. And some, I assume, are good people."

Eventually, he arrived at the purpose of the day's performance. "Ladies and gentlemen," he proclaimed, grandly extending his arm in a sweeping gesture, "I am officially running for president."

But even after he said the words, Trump's intentions were the subject of widespread skepticism. Reporters punctuated their coverage of the event with caveats about his long history of political publicity stunts. Wishful thinkers in the Republican Party held out hope that this was just another short-lived charade; that he would refuse to file his FEC paperwork or be lured away by a lucrative TV contract. The truth, however, was that Trump had backed himself into a corner. He knew that the sort of attention he craved from the political world would never return unless he made good on his promise to run now.

The Donald considered himself a man out of options—and in the weeks that followed, he behaved as such. Even as his incendiary diatribe about Mexican immigrants drew organized boycotts of his various business enterprises, he refused to back down. ("Somebody's doing the raping!" he reasoned.) The resulting losses were much greater than he could have predicted. NBC dropped him as the host of *Celebrity Apprentice,* and canceled plans to air the Miss USA and Miss Universe pageants that he owned. Macy's announced it would no longer carry his clothing line, and the PGA pulled a major tournament from his Los Angeles golf course. The brand that he had spent

his life building was suddenly being robbed of its most visible plat-
forms. And yet, at the same time, his polls were beginning to sky-
rocket. The combination proved to be darkly liberating for Trump:
his high-wire act had no net, and he had no face-saving way out. He
was going to give his all to this performance, and when he found himself in free fall, he would take as much of the party down with him as
he could.

As Donald Trump's anarchic campaign grew increasingly unpredictable in the final weeks of the summer—with each provocation more
inflammatory than the last, and each stunt more disruptive—the
Republican Party appeared to be in an even worse state of disarray
than on the night of its 2012 implosion. Its national debate had been
hijacked by a reckless joyrider with nothing to lose and no concern
whatsoever for the party's future.

Trump made no secret of his priorities. He repeatedly threatened
that if he wasn't "treated with respect" by the Republican establishment, he would drop out of the primaries and launch a third-party
presidential bid—a move that would likely split the conservative vote
and deliver the 2016 election to the Democrats. And when he faced
partisan pressure to join the rest of the Republican field in promising
to endorse whoever won the nomination, he emphatically refused.
"Why should I give up that leverage?" he demanded. To GOP leaders,
Trump had become like a menacing mobster patting the end of a
baseball bat on his palm as he warned, "Nice little political party you
got here. Be a shame if something happened to it."

His seemingly unstoppable surge in the polls so confounded pundits that it became common to the point of cliché to suggest that the
normal "laws of political gravity" had been suspended for Trump.
Blunders, outrages, flip-flops, and gaffes that would have sent any
other candidate into a tailspin had no effect when they were committed by Trump. During an onstage interview in Iowa, for example, he
cavalierly criticized the military service of Republican senator John
McCain, who had famously spent more than five years in a Vietnamese prison (while Trump used a series of deferments to avoid getting
drafted). "He's not a war hero," Trump said of McCain. "He's not a

war hero. He's a war hero because he was captured. I like people that weren't captured." The insult—which was directed, however unwittingly, not just at the senator but also all prisoners of war—drew instant condemnation from practically every prominent Republican in the country. Marco Rubio called it "offensive," Jeb Bush called it "slanderous," and Rick Perry called on Trump to drop out of the race. Instead, the billionaire refused to apologize and took another shot at McCain, whom he accused, unironically, of spending "too much time on television and not enough time doing his job." When the dust settled, Trump had somehow ticked up several points in the polls.

For months it continued like this for Trump. Explosive allegations about his personal life flared up and then fizzled out. Past sins against conservative orthodoxy were ignored or forgiven by voters. Even Fox News couldn't seem to make a dent in Trump-mania. After Megyn Kelly spent the first Republican presidential debate hammering him with questions about his history of misogynistic statements and political promiscuity, Trump retaliated by suggesting that the host's aggressive performance had been the result of her menstruating. The subsequent wrath from some of the biggest stars in conservative media did nothing to slow him down.

Meanwhile, Trump's talent for showmanship ensured that hardly a half hour passed on cable news all summer without his famous mug and more-famous pompadour filling the nation's TV screens. As the daily Donald show sucked up media oxygen, the rest of the Republican presidential candidates were left desperately gasping for air. Chris Christie, the GOP's *other* brash tough-talker, was relegated to a footnote. Ted Cruz, the Tea Party's most beloved bomb-thrower, vanished from sight. When Ohio governor John Kasich entered the race in July with an optimistic speech touting his two-term record and calling for a return to national unity, the announcement was swiftly crowded out of the news cycle to make room for Trump, after he caustically responded to Lindsey Graham calling him a "jackass" by reading out the senator's personal cell phone number at a campaign rally and urging attendees to "try it."

These provocations were so prolific—and mesmerizing—that *CNN Tonight* host Don Lemon began a regular tongue-in-cheek segment that he called "The Day in Trump." But not everyone in the media was amused. "I swear, he is going to start throwing midgets at Velcro walls to keep us paying attention," one CNN producer griped to me. "It's Donald Trump's reality show, and we're all just living in it."

Several Republican contenders were reduced to wild antics and silly stunts to compete for airtime. Graham, who was running his own long-shot presidential bid, turned his feud with Trump into a viral video that showed him using blenders, knives, and blowtorches to violently destroy his cell phone. Rand Paul sought to remind the electorate of his existence by lighting the federal tax code on fire (literally) and posting the footage online. But compared to The Donald—whose madcap, larger-than-life persona had been honed over decades of disciplined method acting and careful attention to craft—the other candidates' routines seemed forced, or just hopelessly small.

This was especially true in the case of Scott Walker, whose galvanizing breakout speech to Iowa activists in January felt like an eternity ago in those mad, hot, hallucinatory days of summer. As much as he tried, the governor couldn't seem to recapture the same adrenaline-charged excitement he had exhibited onstage in Des Moines. And to many conservatives, his wholesome image as a church-going, football-loving, suburb-dwelling everyman paled in comparison to the visceral escapist fantasy that The Donald's campaign offered. Walker was the guy you wanted to have a beer with. Trump was the guy who bought the brewery, fired and deported the illegal immigrants working there, and then took off in his private helicopter, making an up-yours gesture in Mexico's general direction as he ascended into the sky. By mid-August, Walker was falling fast in the polls, and promising his jittery donors that he was going to "step it up" and start competing harder with Trump.

Theories abounded to explain how a reality TV loudmouth, who just months earlier had been forced to fill out his first campaign event with paid actors, was now managing to cast such a powerful spell over the Republican base. Some chalked up his popularity to a perishable blip of celebrity fascination. Others theorized that the billionaire's lack of reliance on the donor class freed him to jettison the elements of the Republican platform that appealed primarily to the wealthy and focus solely on issues that resonated with middle-class conservatives. (Trump, for his part, modestly explained the phenomenon as the rise of "the silent majority.") But even as he filled football stadiums with tens of thousands of supporters, some of his most hard-core followers still hailed from the right-wing fever swamps—a reality that was illustrated in midsummer when pro-Trump Twitter trolls began attacking his Republican rivals and critics by branding them #cuckservatives. That the term (a portmanteau of "cuckold" and "conservative") originated in a dark "alt right" message board for white supremacists was largely lost on the thousands of Trump fans who used it simply to describe Republicans they believed had sold out the conservative cause—but the buzzword's viral spread during the summer of Trump demonstrated again how much influence a tiny, poisonous fringe could wield when a fractured party lacked a unifying leader.

For all the chaos Donald Trump had wrought, the fact remained that he could flame out at any moment—as most in the GOP still believed was inevitable—and it wouldn't change the reality that after three years of exile and wandering in the wilderness, the Republican Party still had not found its Moses. There was no consensus political figure poised to unite the party by sheer force of will and personality, no single compelling visionary who had captured the imaginations of Republicans from all quarters.

In the wilderness, the traditional taxonomy had crumbled. Old ideologies were renamed, old names were redefined, and countless words had been written in a futile attempt to negotiate a universal vocabulary. Neoconservatives, neoliberals, libertarians, libertarian populists, reform conservatives, compassionate conservatives, right wing, business wing, moderate mainstream, Tea Party extreme—the disagreement over what all these labels meant and stood for had become so fierce as to render them useless.

And while the party had, indeed, spent the past few years divided into a chaotic cluster of competing tribes, the allegiances were still always evolving, battle lines ever shifting, and new fronts presenting themselves every day. From Iran to immigration to drones to race to drugs, provocative questions and unpredictable world events lay buried like land mines in the desert, poised to explode at any given moment—scattering conservatives who would then re-form in new tribes.

In this landscape of constant change, of myriad debates and fickle alliances, of sound bite news, of pundits and polls, of fast rises and faster falls, perhaps only one thing would remain recognizably the same: in the grand tradition of American politics, the fight for the future of the Republican Party, the nomination, and ultimately the presidency itself would be defined by a clash of egos and personalities, as a record class of self-styled prophets fought its way through the commotion, all promising to lead America's conservatives back to the promised land, and then lasting as long as they could.

Acknowledgments

A great number of people made this book possible — so many, in fact, that I won't even attempt a comprehensive list here. I'll be repaying IOUs for years to the many people who worked with me on this project. For now, I'll just recognize a few particularly noteworthy contributions. Thank you, first, to the incredibly talented team at Little, Brown, & Company: my editor John Parsley, who showed endless grace and good judgment throughout the writing and editing process; as well as Malin von Euler-Hogan, Carrie Neill, Nell Beram, and Mike Noon. David Patterson was present — and terrifically helpful — from this project's conception, and no first-time author could ask for a better agent.

Several skilled researchers assisted me with reporting, including Haley Bissegger, Kurt Hanson, Robin Rodgers, and Maegan Vazquez. Kate Havard was especially helpful in tracking down people who knew the subjects in their early lives, as was Maria Santos, whose energetic reporting and essential insights inform much of this book. Jacob Fischler spent about six weeks in the summer of 2015 rigorously fact-checking this book: any errors that may remain are my fault alone. I also benefitted immensely from the reporting and analysis of countless accomplished journalists, including Tim Alberta, Michael Barbaro, Marc Caputo, Marin Cogan, Mark Leibovich, Jonathan Martin, Zeke Miller, Manuel Roig-Franzia, Andrew Sullivan, Dave Weigel, Jason Zengerle, and many others. A full bibliography containing the published works I relied on for this book is available online.

I am indebted to my fantastic colleagues at BuzzFeed: Katherine Miller, who read the manuscript at various stages, provided invaluable notes, and put up with more than one missed deadline from me; Ben Smith, who has been known to refer to nonfiction books as "glorified paywalls" but who nonetheless supported me in this crazy pursuit; John Stanton, Ruby Cramer, Rosie Gray, Andrew Kaczynski, Chris Geidner, Evan McMorris-Santoro, Kyle Blaine, and everyone else on the politics team, who make me smarter just by working within earshot.

Thank you to Rob and Amy Shull for allowing me write much of this book from the spare bedroom in their basement, and for proving to be even better friends than they are landlords. Thank you, also, to my always supportive in-laws, Kevin and Sue Schmidt; and to the cheering section/peanut gallery that comprise my brilliant siblings (and their more brilliant spouses): Kami, Chase, Ashley, Tagg, and Christie. I owe a particularly large debt of gratitude to my parents, David and Carol Coppins. I grew up with the kind of dad who learned how to use Adobe PageMaker just so he could help his fifteen-year-old son redesign his high school newspaper, and the kind of mom who line-edited her kid's (often-not-very-funny) humor column in the local paper — *every week*. Their unfailing encouragement and love are the reason I get to have this fantastically fun career.

The long-suffering spouse is a cliché of authors' acknowledgments sections, but there is no writing around the fact that my incredible, and preternaturally patient, wife, Annie, put up with way too much to let me do this. When I started working on this book our first child, Ellis, had just been born; by the time I finished our second, Alden, was seven months old. The three of them have made me happier than I can possibly express here.

Index

About the Author

McKay Coppins is a senior political writer at BuzzFeed News, where he covers national politics and the Republican Party. Formerly, he was a reporter for *Newsweek*. Coppins was listed as one of the *Forbes* 30 Under 30 in 2012, included on *Politico*'s list of 2012's "breakout reporters," and identified as a rising TV pundit in *Details* magazine. He lives in New York with his wife and two young children.